EUROPEAN COURT PRACTICE

AUSTRALIA AND NEW ZEALAND
The Law Book Company Ltd.
Sydney : Melbourne : Perth

CANADA AND U.S.A.
Oceana Publications Inc.
New York

INDIA
N. M. Tripathi Private Ltd.
Bombay
and
Eastern Law House Private Ltd.
Calcutta
M.P.P. House
Bangalore

ISRAEL
Steimatzky's Agency Ltd.
Jerusalem : Tel Aviv : Haifa

MALAYSIA : SINGAPORE : BRUNEI
Malayan Law Journal (Pte.) Ltd.
Singapore

PAKISTAN
Pakistan Law House
Karachi

EUROPEAN COURT PRACTICE

by

JOHN A. USHER, LL.B

Reader in European Law, University College London
Formerly Legal Secretary at the
European Court of Justice

LONDON
SWEET & MAXWELL
1983

Published in 1983 by
Sweet & Maxwell Limited
of 11, New Fetter Lane, London
Computerset by Promenade Graphics Ltd., Cheltenham
and printed in Scotland

British Library Cataloguing in Publication Data
Usher, John
  European Court Practice.
  1. European Court   2. Courts—European
  Community countries
  I. Title
  341.24'22

ISBN 0–421–26780–1

1,185,799

©
John Usher
1983

PREFACE

The fundamental importance of the part played by the European Court of Justice in the development of the European Communities is amply witnessed by the considerable literature on the role of the Court and the remedies available before it. However, whilst I was a Legal Secretary at the Court, the view was frequently expressed, by colleagues as well as by those appearing before the Court and by other visitors, that there was a need for a practical guide to the procedure before the Court, and the present book is offered as an attempt to fulfil that need. Although the idea was conceived in Luxembourg, its (rather prolonged) gestation took place in the academic environment of the Centre of European Governmental Studies in the University of Edinburgh, but whilst the academic's urge to probe beneath the surface has not always been resisted, the basic aim has remained that of practical utility.

The judicial remedies available before the Court are discussed as such only by way of introduction: the substance of the book is concerned with the conduct of proceedings before the Court. The basic scheme is to deal with the various stages of procedure in chronological order, and in relation to each topic the relevant legislative and administrative provisions are printed together (which was felt to be preferable to paraphrasing them in a narrative text) followed by a commentary on the matters at issue, referring in particular to the relevant judgments and orders of the European Court. These, however, should be read subject to the caveat that whilst the Court departs from its earlier decisions relatively rarely, and in many matters a consistent practice has indeed developed, it is in the last analysis not bound by them. In this context, I should like to express my gratitude to the staff at the Court, who have supplied me with copies of judgments and orders with commendable promptitude, and cheerfully answered such questions as I have raised.

Given the continuing increase in the number of cases heard by the Court, a book such as this runs a risk perhaps even greater than usual of being overtaken by new developments. Although the basic text was completed somewhat earlier, it has been possible to incorporate material available to me in Edinburgh at the end of February 1983. By way of illustration of the developments even in the last few months, on September 11, 1982 President Mertens de Wilmars confirmed his innovation of granting *ex parte* conservatory measures in the *Ford Motors* case (see para. 10–16), and on October 6, 1982 the Court decided for the first time to set up two Chambers of five judges each as well as the usual three Chambers of three judges (see para. 5–05).

Finally, my grateful thanks are due to the forebearance of the publishers, who encouraged me to continue despite supervenient difficulties and the expiry of successive deadlines, to Mrs. Neeltje Brady and Miss Margaret Ainslie, who successively had the unenviable task of

v

deciphering my handwriting, to Mrs. Elizabeth Thompson, who prepared the Tables, and last but not least, to the cheerful tolerance of my family.

Edinburgh,   *J. A. Usher*
March 1983

CONTENTS

TABLE OF CASES

TABLE OF CASES

Numerical

xxiii

263/82R Klöckner-Werke *v.* Commission.
293/82R De Compte *v.* European Parliament.

Other Courts

European Court of Human Rights

United Kingdom

TABLE OF TREATY PROVISIONS

[References in **bold** type indicate where the text of the provision is printed.]

ECSC TREATY

EEC TREATY

EURATOM TREATY

TABLE OF COMMUNITY SECONDARY LEGISLATION

TABLE OF UNITED KINGDOM MATERIALS

Part 1

Introduction

CHAPTER 1

INTRODUCTION

THE EUROPEAN COURT OF JUSTICE AND THE SOURCES OF ITS JURISDICTION AND PROCEDURE

1–01 What is now the Court of Justice of the European Communities was originally set up as the Court of Justice of the European Coal and Steel Community (ECSC) by the 1951 Treaty of Paris, and came into being in December 1952, delivering its first judgment two years later, on December 21, 1954, in Case 1/54 *France* v. *H.A.* [1954 to 1956] E.C.R. 1. When the two Treaties of Rome establishing the Economic Community (EEC) and the Atomic Energy Community (EAEC or "Euratom") were signed in 1957, there was also signed in Rome on the same day a Convention on Certain Institutions common to the European Communities, Articles 3 and 4 of which provide that a single Court should act as the Court of Justice of those two Communities and that it should take over the functions of the Coal and Steel Community Court. This single Court of Justice of the European Communities started to sit in the judicial year beginning in the Autumn of 1958, and delivered its first judgment in February 1959, in Case 17/57 *Gezamenlijke Steenkolenmijnen in Limburg* v. *H.A.* [1959] E.C.R. 1.

The general principles governing the organisation and procedure of the Court are contained in separate Protocols on the Statute of the Court of Justice (hereinafter referred to as the Statutes) annexed to the three basic Treaties, and more detailed rules in these matters are contained in Rules of Procedure adopted by the Court under these Statutes and the Treaties. The original Rules of the Coal and Steel Community Court were adopted in 1953 (J.O. 1953, p. 37), being replaced by the Rules of the Single Court of the three Communites in 1959 (J.O. 348/59), which in turn were replaced after the first Accession by a revised version in 1974 (O.J. 1974, L350/1). These Rules have subsequently been amended, particularly in 1979 in an effort to alleviate the consequences of the increased workload borne by the Court, and a consolidated version, taking account also of modifications consequent upon Greek Accession, was published in 1982 (O.J. 1982, C39/1), albeit for information rather than as a new binding text. Supplementary Rules on certain matters are annexed to the Rules of Procedure, and the Court has also published its Instructions to the Registrar adopted pursuant to article 15 of the Rules of Procedure (O.J. 1974, L350/33, reprinted in O.J. 1982, C39/35). Beyond this legislation, the Court has also made available administrative information, notably the *Notes for the Gui-*

dance of Counsel at Oral Hearings sent to individual counsel (and also published in the 1980 Synopsis of the work of the Court).

1–02   A wide range of jurisdiction is conferred on the Court under the three basic Treaties by provisions which are for the most part parallel in nature but are not identical in terminology, although in some instances there are substantive differences. Hence, under Article 228 of the EEC Treaty, the Court may at the behest of the Council, the Commission or a Member State, give an advisory opinion as to the compatibility of an "envisaged" international agreement with the provisions of the Treaty, a procedure first invoked in Opinion 1/75 [1975] E.C.R. 1355. Under Article 103 of the Euratom Treaty, on the other hand, what is termed a "ruling" may be given by the Court, but only (for reasons which are not at first sight obvious) at the behest of a Member State and in relation to an agreement which a Member State is about to conclude (see Ruling 1/78 [1978] E.C.R. 2151), and no such power exists at all in relation to the ECSC Treaty, no doubt because Article 71 of that Treaty provides that the powers of the Members States' governments in matters of commercial policies are in principle not affected by the Treaty.

Under all three Treaties, it is the Court which has jurisdiction to hear disputes arising under those Treaties between Member States, between Members States and Community institutions, and between the Community institutions themselves, subject to differences in detail. In fact, no action would appear to have been brought by one Member State against another until 1977, when Ireland brought an action against France in relation to French rules governing the import of lamb and mutton, and this was withdrawn before judgment (Case 58/77, O.J. 1978, C76/8). The first case to go to judgment was brought by France in 1978 against the U.K. with regard to U.K. fisheries measures, judgment being given in 1979, in favour of France (Case 141/78 [1979] E.C.R. 2923).

1–03   This relative absence of litigation between Member States may be explained by the fact that Article 89 of the ECSC Treaty requires any other available procedures to be used first, and that Articles 170 of the EEC Treaty and 142 of the Euratom Treaty require the Commission to be informed and to have the opportunity to deliver a reasoned opinion before the matter is brought before the Court. It is the Commission which is basically entrusted with ensuring the application of the Treaties, having a general power under the EEC and Euratom Treaties (Arcticles 169 and 141 respectively) to bring an action against a Member State which it considers to have failed to fulfil a Treaty obligation, under the ECSC Treaty to issue a decision recording such a failure (which would only come before the Court if the Member State chose to challenge it). Hence, in most cases where one Member State has wished to impugn the conduct of another, it has been the Commission which has taken the appropriate steps. It might further be noted that in relation to certain specific sectors the Commission may invoke an expedited form of action against Member States, *e.g.* in relation to state aids under Article 93 of the EEC Treaty, or in relation to nuclear safeguards, under Article 82 of the Euratom Treaty. Member States, on

4

the other hand, are given wide powers to challenge the acts of the Community institutions. Article 173 of the EEC Treaty and Article 146 of the Euratom Treaty enable Member States to have the legality of acts of the Council and Commission, other than recommendations or opinions, reviewed by the Court, on the four specific grounds of lack of competence, infringement of an essential procedural requirement, infringement of the Treaty or of any rule of law relating to its application, and misuse of powers. Article 33 of the ECSC Treaty allows Member States to invoke the same grounds against ECSC decisions or recommendations (which bear no resemblance except in name to recommendations under the EEC and Euratom Treaties, being akin to Directives under those Treaties) of the Commission, which, replacing the former High Authority, is the essential source of secondary legislation under that Treaty. Under Article 38 they may challenge any act of the Council, but only on the grounds of lack of competence or infringement of an essential procedural requirement, and may likewise contest acts of the Assembly, which is not expressly provided for under the EEC or Euratom Treaties, even though under the 1975 Budgetary Treaty it is the Assembly which has the last word with regard to the Community budget; this problem has been brought before the Court in Case 230/81 *Luxembourg* v. *European Parliament* (February 10, 1983), where it was held, following the Opinion of A.G. Mancini, that Article 38 of the ECSC Treaty could be used to challenge acts which were common to all three Treaties, in that case a resolution by the European Parliament determining the location of its sittings.

1–04   Parallel to their power to challenge acts of the Community institutions, the Member States may also attack their failures to act. Under Article 175 of the EEC Treaty and Article 148 of the EAEC Treaty, they may bring an action if either the Council or Commission, in breach of the Treaty, fails to act after having been called upon to do so, and has not "defined its position" within two months of being so called upon. Under the ECSC system (Article 35), only failure to act on the part of the Commission may be disputed, and in form the action is for the annulment of the implied decision of refusal to be inferred from the silence of the Commission on the matter.

Amongst the institutions themselves, the Council has the same power to challenge acts of the Commission, or failures to act on its part, as do the Member States under each of the Treaties. Likewise, the Commission enjoys all the rights of action against the Council enjoyed by the Member States (see, *e.g.* Case 22/70 *Commission* v. *Council* [1971] E.C.R. 263). The Assembly, on the other hand, would appear to enjoy a right of action only under the EEC and Euratom Treaties with regard to failures to act on the part of the Council and Commission, and to be liable to have an action brought against itself only with regard to its acts under the ECSC Treaty and then only by the Commission. It does, however, have the same right to intervene in other proceedings as any other Community institution, as was held in Case 138/79 *Roquette* v. *Council* [1980] E.C.R. 3333, 3357.

Complex as the Court's jurisdiction may be with regard to disputes at the level of the Member States and institutions, it is not at this level that the development of Community law by the Court has occurred, nor is it in this context that most of its workload has arisen.

1–05 A particular feature of the Community legal system is that, quite apart from the special provisions enabling actions before the Court to be brought by staff of the Communities against their employing institutions, the remedies available to Member States and Community institutions against the Council and Commission are also available in principle to individuals, under the EEC and Euratom Treaties, and to individual coal and steel undertakings, under the ECSC Treaty, albeit subject to more restrictive conditions. Likewise, the right to bring actions for damages against the Communities under Article 40 of the ECSC Treaty, Article 215 of the EEC Treaty, or Article 188 of the Euratom Treaty is not restricted to any particular class of litigant. Most important of all, the Treaties recognise that Community law may be at issue in disputes before national courts and enable national courts to refer questions as to the interpretation of Community law and validity of Community secondary legislation to the European Court, under Article 177 of the EEC Treaty and Article 150 of the Euratom Treaty, or to refer questions as to the validity of acts of the Council and Commission under Article 41 of the ECSC Treaty, which gave the Court of Justice exclusive jurisdiction to decide upon the validity of acts of the institutions. The EEC Treaty gives wider powers to refer, yet does not in terms give any exclusive powers. It states that the Court of Justice shall have jurisdiction to give preliminary rulings concerning the interpretation of acts of institutions of the Community. Where such a question is raised before any court or tribunal of a Member State, that court or tribunal may, if it considers that a decision on the question is necessary in order to enable it to give judgment, request the Court of Justice to give a ruling thereon.

This general power to seek the interpretation of Community law anticipates the fact that under the system of the EEC Treaty, although customs policy or agricultural policy, for example, may be subject to directly applicable Community law, the administration of these policies at the national level rests in the hands of the national authorities, so that there may well be disputes between traders and national authorities before national courts relating solely to the application of Community law.

1–06 The general intention behind Article 177 therefore, is to try to achieve some degree of uniform interpretation of provisions of Community law. That is also the reason why protocols to a similar effect have been inserted into later conventions entered into between Member States of the Communities, for example the Convention on Jurisdiction and Enforcement of Civil and Commercial Judgments, in relation to which the Court has had jurisdiction since September 1975.

Whether by coincidence or otherwise, this particular point had been brought to the fore in 1956 in relation to the Geneva Convention on Bills of Exchange, one provision of which deals with the person on whose behalf an "aval" or guarantee is presumed to have been given.

The French text (Article 130 of the Code du Commerce) uses a word which would normally create a rebuttable presumption: "il est réputé donné pour le tireur." However, the French Cour de Cassation, in 1956, in the light of the other language versions, the phraseology of which created an irrebuttable presumption, interpreted the French word *réputé* as creating an irrebuttable presumption (Cass. Comm. January 23, 1956 JCP II 9666). Unfortunately that same year the German Supreme Civil Court interpreted the prima facia irrebuttable presumption in the German text as being rebuttable (Bundesgerichtshof, November 15, 1956 [1962] NJW 745–746). So, a state of complete confusion had been reached in relation to a convention which was supposed to produce a uniform attitude towards bills of exchange. It might be added that in *Ulster Swift* v. *Taunton Meat Haulage* [1977] 3 All E.R. 641, 646, Megaw L.J. noted the existence of 12 different interpretations of Articles 17 and 18 of the Geneva Convention on the Contract for the International Carriage of Goods by Road (CMR).

1–07   The most important consequence of the preliminary rulings procedure has not just been that it affords an avenue for achieving uniform interpretation of Community law within the limits of judicial co-operation, but that it brings before the European Court disputes involving private individuals before national courts. It is from that fact that the European Court has found itself having to decide points arising in such disputes, that it has developed the doctrine that provisions of Community law can have *direct effect*, that is to say, can create rights in favour of private individuals of which they can avail themselves in their national courts without the intermediary of the State or a Community institution, and correlative obligations, a doctrine first enounced in Case 26/62 *Van Gend en Loos* [1963] E.C.R. 1.

CHOICE OF ACTIONS AND THEIR INTERRELATIONSHIP: GENERAL CONSIDERATIONS

1–08   The Rules of Procedure of the Court distinguish between two basic types of substantive action: direct actions, where the action is brought directly before the Court, and references for preliminary rulings, where the action is commenced before a national court. In the case of the EEC Treaty (although it must be confessed that the first direct actions arising in the United Kingdom were mostly concerned with the provisions of the ECSC Treaty) direct actions may, *inter alia*, be brought to challenge acts of Community institutions under Article 173, to challenge failures to act under Article 175, and to obtain damages under Article 178 (relating to Article 215). It must not, however, be thought that Articles 173 and 175 are necessarily the only or most effective ways of challenging the validity or effects of Community acts which an applicant feels may have harmed him. Under Article 173, an individual may only challenge decisions addressed to him or decisions which, although in the form of a Regulation or a decision addressed to another person, are of

7

"direct and individual concern" to him. In fact, very few actions brought by individuals for the annulment of such acts have been held to be admissible (see para. 1–25 *et seq.* below). In particular, the fact that a Regulation may apply only to identifiable persons does not in itself make it of direct and individual concern to them, at least if it applies according to objective rather than subjective criteria, and in Case 101/76 *Koninklijke Scholten-Honig* v. *Commission* [1977] E.C.R. 797 an application by one of the handful of Community manufacturers of isoglucose for the annulment of a Council Regulation reducing and eventually abolishing the production refund on glucose having a high fructose content was held to be inadmissible.

1–09   The Court has, however, developed a general principle that an individual may contest the validity of any general act which underlies a measure which is capable of being challenged by him. Article 184 of the EEC Treaty and Article 156 of the EAEC Treaty provide that a party may, in any proceedings in which a Regulation of the Council or Commission is in issue, invoke the inapplicability of that Regulation, but in Case 92/78 *Simmenthal* v. *Commission* [1979] E.C.R. 777 the Court held that Article 184 of the EEC Treaty extended not only to Regulations as such but also to acts which produce analogous effects, such as a general notice of invitation to tender, and defined the general principle as ensuring that a party has the right to challenge the validity of the acts of the institutions on which the decision at issue is based, if it does not have the right to bring a direct action against those acts.

By way of contrast with these complexities, in the system of references from national courts to the European Court for a preliminary ruling, Article 177 itself places no limitation on the circumstances in which the validity of an act of a Community institution may be raised, provided a national form of action can be found, and so it has been used as a mechanism to challenge the validity of Community acts which an individual could not challenge directly. Hence, it was by virtue of a reference for a preliminary ruling in Case 24/75 *Petroni* v. *ONPTS* [1975] E.C.R. 1149 that the Court considered the validity of article 46(3) of Regulation 1408/71 on social security for migrant workers, which could hardly have been described as being of direct and individual concern to the claimant. The only restrictions imposed by the European Court on the use of this procedure are that the question of validity must be raised by the national court itself, and not by the parties on a reference concerned only with the interpretation of the Community legislation (Case 44/65 *Hessische Knappschaft* v. *Singer* [1965] E.C.R. 965), and that there must be a real dispute between the parties to the national actions (Case 104/79 *Foglia* v. *Novello* [1980] E.C.R. 745). A clear example of the use of Article 177 to overcome the limitations inherent in a direct action under Article 173 is Case 125/77 *Koninklijke Scholten-Honig* v. *Hoofdproduktschap voor Akkerbouwprodukten* [1978] E.C.R. 1991. A direct action brought by KSH under Article 173 for the annulment of a Regulation ultimately abolishing production refunds on isoglucose was held to be inadmissible (Case 101/76, *supra*), but in the Netherlands KSH brought an action to challenge a decision of the Dutch intervention agency taken under the Regulation, and the Dutch court referred a number of questions as to the validity of the Regulations to the European Court, which then found itself having to consider the points it would have had to consider if it had held the direct action to be admissible.

1–10 Indeed in Case 66/76 *CFDT* v. *Council* [1977] E.C.R. 304 where it held an action under the ECSC Treaty by a trade union against an act of the Council to be inadmissible, the Court itself hinted that it would be possible for it to review the validity of the Council act under Article 41 of that Treaty at the instigation of a national court. The CFDT was unable to take advantage of this, however, since its action before the French administrative courts was also held to be inadmissible, as is recorded in the judgment given in its later unsuccessful application to the European Commission of Human Rights [1979] 2 C.M.L.R. 229.

Similarly, although there is no way in which an individual litigant may normally bring an alleged breach of Community law by a Member State directly before the European Court, he may invoke the direct effect, if such there be, of the rule of Community law which the Member State is alleged to have breached, in proceedings before a national court, and that court may refer the matter to the European Court as a question of the interpretation of the rule of Community law; the practical result may well be that the validity of national legislation is put indirectly at issue before the European Court. The Court recognised this possibility of private policing in *Van Gend en Loos* itself ([1963] E.C.R. 1, 13), stating that "the vigilance of individuals to protect their rights amounts to an effective supervision in addition to the supervision entrusted by articles 169 and 170 [of the EEC Treaty] to the diligence of the Commission and of the Member States." One effect of this has been to prevent a settlement of enforcement proceedings brought by the Commission against a Member State from being final, if private interests are involved. In Joined Cases 80 and 81/77 *Ramel* v. *Receveur des Douanes* [1978] E.C.R. 297, French wine importers were able to invoke the direct effect of the relevant provisions of EEC law to challenge before the French courts, and thence on a reference for a preliminary ruling before the European Court, levies imposed by the French authorities on imports of Italian wine in 1975 to 1976, even though the Commission had withdrawn an action it had brought against France under Article 169 alleging that the imposition of such levies was in breach of France's Treaty obligations. Further, in Joined Cases 142 and 143/80 *Italian Finance Administration* v. *Essevi* [1981] E.C.R. 1413 it was recognised that an individual may invoke the direct effects of a Treaty obligation even against conduct of a Member State which the Commission has regarded as permissible in its opinion given under Article 169.

1–11 Returning to direct actions, it has long been recognised that an action for damages can lead to the same result as the annulment of an act having financial implications, but the Court has held, from Case 4/69 *Lutticke* v. *Commission* [1971] E.C.R. 325, that it would be contrary to the autonomy of the action for damages to hold such an action

9

inadmissible simply because the applicant could not have sought the annulment of the act in question. Hence, at first sight the action for damages would appear to be a method of overcoming the difficulties inherent in an action for annulment, although it may not give a second chance to those who could have brought an action for annulment but failed to do so, a problem which is particularly relevant in the context of limitation periods (see paras. 2–14 and 2–27 below).

The development of specific criteria for liability for the harm caused by legislative acts dates back to Case 5/71 *Zuckerfabrik Schoppenstedt* v. *Council* [1971] E.C.R. 975, where the Court held that the Community could not be liable for legislative action involving measures of economic policy "unless a sufficiently flagrant violation of a superior rule of law for the protection of the individual has occurred." After Accession, in Cases 63 to 69/72 *Werhahn* v. *Council and Commission* [1973] E.C.R. 1229 it was argued on behalf of the Community institutions that, having regard to the legal systems of the new Member States, there was no general principle common to the laws of the Member States of liability for legislative acts, but the Court repeated its previous formula, A.G. Roemer stressing in his opinion that the small role played by the European Parliament in Community legislation rendered it necessary to put special stress on the concept of the strengthening by the Court of legal protection within the Community.

1–12 The general principles of Community law would appear to constitute "superior rules of law" in this context, whether derived from the scheme of the Treaties, or from legal concepts accepted in the Member States (see Usher, "The influence of National Concepts on Decisions of the European Court" (1976) 1 E.L. Rev. 359). In Case 74/74 *CNTA* v. *Commission* [1975] E.C.R. 533 it was held that there could be liability for the harm caused by a Regulation, valid in itself, abolishing certain monetary compensatory amounts without providing any transitional provisions and hence, on the particular facts of the case, breaching the principle of the protection of legitimate expectation. A restrictive interpretation of what amounts to a sufficiently "serious" (or flagrant) breach of such a superior rule has, however, been given in Joined Cases 83 and 94/76, 4, 15 and 40/77 *Bayerische HNL and others* v. *Council and Commission* [1978] E.C.R. 1209, where it was stated that individuals may be required to accept "within limits" certain harmful effects on their economic interests as a result of invalid legislative measures, and that, at least in the implementation of the common agricultural policy, the Community should not incur liability unless the institution concerned had manifestly and gravely disregarded the limits on the exercise of its powers.

Such a disregard was held to have occurred in Case 238/78 *Ireks Arkady* v. *Council and Commission* [1979] E.C.R. 2955, 2973, and a group of other cases decided on the same day, where it was found that the legislation in question breached the principle of equality of treatment, which was held to occupy a particular place amongst the rules of Community law intended to protect the interests of the individual, that the breach affected a limited and clearly defined group of commercial operators (shades of "direct and individual concern"?), and, perhaps most important, that the damage caused went beyond the bounds of the economic risks inherent in the activities of the sector concerned. It would appear, however, that these were the first cases in which the Court ordered the payment of damages in actions not brought by Community officials, a factor which may perhaps not encourage the bringing of actions for damages.

MAIN TYPES OF DIRECT ACTION AND THEIR SCOPE

A. ACTIONS FOR ANNULMENT

1. *Nature*

1–13 Under the scheme of the Treaties establishing the European Communities, actions for annulment are available only in relation to challengeable acts issued by Community institutions whose acts are stated to be susceptible to challenge, and they comport in general a control by the Court of the legality of such acts at the time they were issued, as was pointed out by A.G. Warner in his Opinion in Cases 19 and 20/74 *Kali und Salz* v. *Commission* [1975] E.C.R. 499, 526–527, rather than a substitution of the Court's decision for that of the administrative authority. It may indeed be noted that Article 33 of the ECSC Treaty expressly prohibits the Court from examining "the evaluation of the situation, resulting from economic facts or circumstances, in the light of which the [Commission] took its decisions or made its recommendations" unless the Commission is alleged to have misused its powers or to have manifestly failed to have observed the provisions of the Treaty; in this context, it was held in Joined Cases 154/78, etc., *Ferriera Valsabbia* v. *Commission* [1980] E.C.R. 907, 922, that an allegation of misuse of powers should be "supported by appropriate evidence." Even where the act of the administrative authority might appear to be quasi-judicial in character, as where the Commission issues a decision finding a particular undertaking in breach of the EEC competition rules, the Court may only substitute its own decision to the extent that unlimited jurisdiction is expressly conferred upon it (although appeals as such are envisaged under the 1975 Patents Convention). Article 36 of the ECSC Treaty does in fact give the Court unlimited jurisdiction in actions for the annulment of pecuniary sanctions and periodic penalty payments under that Treaty, and Article 144 of the Euratom Treaty provides for unlimited jurisdiction in relation to the granting by the Commission of licences under Article 12 of that Treaty (see para. 2–57 below) and in proceedings against sanctions imposed by the Commission under Article 83 of the Treaty for breach of the safeguards provisions (see para. 2–49 below). However, Article 172 of the EEC Treaty, which is of somewhat greater practical importance, merely enables the Council, in Regulations made under other provisions of the Treaty, to confer on the Court unlimited jurisdiction with regard to the *penalties* provided for in such

11

Regulations. This power was exercised in relation to Commission Decisions on competition cases in Article 17 of Council Regulation 17/62, providing that the Court "shall have unlimited jurisdiction within the meaning of Article 172 of the Treaty to review decisions whereby the Commission had fixed a fine or periodic penalty payment; it may cancel, reduce or increase the fine or periodic penalty payment imposed." The same wording is also used in Article 24 of Council Regulation 1017/68 applying competition rules to transport by rail, road and internal waterway (J.O. 1968, L175/1). Although this might appear to confer a new jurisdiction with regard to the decision itself, the enabling provision of Article 172 refers in terms only to penalties, not to the decision as such, and in practice all that it has meant is that the Court may substitute its own view as to an appropriate penalty for that of the Commission—so far by reducing the fine rather than increasing it. To take a pair of cases where the Commission's decision was annulled on similar grounds, there seems to be little difference between the Court's approach in the *Kali and Salz* case, where no fine was imposed, and in Case 73/74 *Groupement des fabricants de papiers peints de Belgique* v. *Commission* [1975] E.C.R. 1491, where there was a fine.

1–14   With regard to staff cases, although the Court used to exercise a general unlimited jurisdiction as, *e.g.* in Case 32/62 *Alvis* v. *Council* [1963] E.C.R. 49, a new version of article 91 of the Staff Regulations was introduced by Council Regulation 1473/72, restricting unlimited jurisdiction to disputes of a financial character. Emphasis has usually thereafter been placed on the exceptional nature of such jurisdiction, as, *e.g.* in Case 9/75 *Meyer-Burckhardt* v. *Commission* [1975] E.C.R. 1171, 1181. However, in Case 24/79 *Oberthur* v. *Commission* [1980] E.C.R. 1743, the First Chamber extended this concept of unlimited jurisdiction to the award of damages in an action for annulment. Other specific instances of full jurisdiction may be found in Articles 37 and 66(5) of the ECSC Treaty.

No Treaty provision confers upon the Court any general power to make a declaration as to the rights and obligations of parties to proceedings before it. Hence, in Case 44/81 *Germany* v. *Commission* (May 26, 1982) it was held that there was no form of action by which Germany could obtain a declaration that the Commission should pay it a certain sum of money; rather it should seek the annulment of the Commission's refusal to pay. However, the Court did go beyond this in its early decision in Joined Cases 1 and 14/57 *Usines à Tubes de la Sarre* v. *H.A.* [1957 and 1958] E.C.R. 105, 112–113, where, whilst recognising that under Article 33 of the ECSC Treaty it had jurisdiction to annul only decisions and recommendations, the Court declared that an act which purported to be an opinion under Article 54 of that Treaty was in fact "non-existent" since it did not contain a statement of reasons as required under that provision. More recently, in Case 60/81 *IBM* v. *Commission* [1981] E.C.R. 2639, where the Court held that a "statement of objections" issued by the Commission in competition proceedings was not an "act" which could be challenged under Article 173 of the EEC Treaty, it did hint that judicial review might nonetheless be possible in exceptional cases "where the measures concerned lack even the appearance of legality"; this could perhaps be achieved by the method used in *Usines à Tubes de la Sarre*.

2. *Acts Susceptible to Challenge*

1–15 A fundamental distinction between the ECSC Treaty on the one hand, and the EEC and Euratom Treaties on the other, is that whilst the former defines the acts which may be challenged, the latter define the acts which may *not* be challenged. Article 33 of the ECSC Treaty allows decisions and recommendations of the Commission to be challenged (although Article 38 more generally provides for the annulment of "acts" of the Council and Parliament), whereas Article 173 of the EEC Treaty (and Article 146 of Euratom Treaty) allows any act of the Council or Commission other than recommendations or opinions to be challenged. The Staff Regulations on the other hand allow for an action to be brought in relation to an "act adversely affecting" the applicant.

1–16 The Court has in fact taken a broad view of the concept of a "decision" or "recommendation" under Article 33 of the ECSC Treaty, even though specific criteria as to their form are laid down in Decision 22/60 (J.O. 1248/60) of the old High Authority. In Joined Cases 23, 24 and 52/63 *Usines Henricot* v. *H.A.* [1963] E.C.R. 217, 223–224, the Court held that it did not follow that a measure should not be considered a decision merely because it failed to comply with some inessential requirement of form if the fundamental conditions under-lying the concept of a decision were satisfied; those fundamental conditions were stated to be that a decision must appear as "a measure taken by the High Authority, acting as a body, intended to produce legal effects and constituting the culmination of a procedure within the High Authority, whereby the High Authority gives its final ruling in a form from which its nature can be indentified." On this test, it held that letters which did not appear to have been debated and adopted by the High Authority and authenticated by the signature of one of its members, could not be regarded as decisions. On the other hand in Joined Cases 275/80 and 24/81 *Krupp Stahl* v. *Commission* [1981] E.C.R. 2489, working from the hypothesis that the aim of Decision 22/60 is to ensure the use of a form from which the nature of the act may be identified, the Court held that failure to observe its requirements did not invalidate the measure there at issue, since there was no doubt that they were individual decisons applying quotas derived from a general decision which had itself been adopted in accordance with Decision 22/60.

1–17 The Court's interpretation of an "act" under the EEC and Euratom Treaties is in fact remarkably similar. In Case 60/81 *IBM* v. *Commission* [1981] E.C.R. 2639 it was stated that "any measure the legal effects of which are binding on, and capable of affecting the interests of, the applicant by bringing about a distinct change in his legal position is an act or decision which may be the subject of an action under Article 173 [of the EEC Treaty] for a declaration that it is void." It was also

13

emphasised that "the form in which such acts or decisions are cast is, in principle, immaterial as regard the question whether they are open to challenge," and that where the act is adopted by a procedure invoking several stages, it is in principle open to review only if "it is a measure definitively laying down the position of the Commission or the Council on the conclusion of that procedure." Whilst in Joined Cases 8 to 11/66 *Cimenteries* v. *Commission* [1967] E.C.R. 75 the Court found that a Commission notice under article 15(6) of Regulation 17 withdrawing the benefit of exemption from fines from a notified agreement was susceptible to challenge, it did not take the same view in the *IBM* case of the "statement of objections" issued by the Commission at the commencement of the formal proceedings relating to an alleged breach of the EEC competition rules. It was held that although a statement of objections may have the effect of showing the undertaking in question that it is incurring a real risk of being fined by the Commission, it does not, unlike a notice under article 15(6) of Regulation 17, have the effect of depriving the undertaking of the protection hitherto available to it against the application of a fine.

1–18   More generally, it was expressly held in Case 22/70 *Commission* v. *Council* [1971] E.C.R. 263, 277 that the action for annulment is not limited to the acts defined in Article 189 of the EEC Treaty (to which Article 161 of the Euratom Treaty is identical) but is available with regard to all measures adopted by the Council or Commission which are intended to have legal effects; in that case it was held that the definition of a negotiating position by the Council with regard to a proposed international agreement had definite legal effects both on relations between the Community and the Member States and on the relationship between institutions, and was hence susceptible to challenge.

1–19   With regard to actions under the Staff Regulations, it is clear that, as stated in Joined Cases 177/73 and 5/74 *Reinarz* v. *Commission* [1974] E.C.R. 819, 828, "only those acts capable of directly affecting a precise legal position can be regarded as adversely affecting an official"; in the circumstances of that case, where the applicant had just terminated his service, it was held that a letter interpreting the rules governing the payment of a resettlement allowance was such an act. On the other hand, it appears from Joined Cases 28 and 165/80 *Leclerq* v. *Commission* [1981] E.C.R. 2251 that a general policy decision (in that case as to the conclusion of contracts with former officials) is not such an act; neither is a measure which merely affects internal relationships, *i.e.* questions of administration and working organisation within the institution's offices rather than the applicant's position under the Staff Regulations as, *e.g.* in Case 129/75 *Hirschberg* v. *Commission* [1976] E.C.R. 1259, 1270. Where the act does produce legal effects, these must be adverse to the applicant before the act may be challenged; by way of illustration, a promotion decision will not usually adversely affect the official promoted, as was pointed out in Case 188/73 *Grassi* v. *Council* [1974] E.C.R. 1099, 1108. In any event, it was held by the First Chamber in Case 33/80 *Albini* v. *Council* [1981] E.C.R. 2141 that the procedure under the Staff Regulations "may only be directed against the appointing authority" and that the act adversely affecting the official must be an act of that authority. Otherwise, officials of the Communities are left to the same general remedies as other private litigants.

3. *Grounds for Annulment*

1–20   The same four grounds for annulment are recognised under all three Treaties (see para. 1–03 above), although under Article 38 of the ECSC Treaty acts of the Council and of the European Parliament may only be contested on two grounds, lack of competence or infringement of an essential procedural requirement, the remaining two grounds available under the other provisions being misuse of powers and infringement of the Treaty or of any rule of law relating to is application. These grounds may be separately defined, although the definitions may to some extent overlap, and the same fact situation may fall under more than one of them. In particular, since the institutions and their powers derive from the Treaties and legislation made under them, there is a very good chance that any of the other three grounds may also amount to an "infringement of this Treaty or of any rule of law relating to its application," although the converse is not necessarily true. The distinction between "lack of competence" and "misuse of powers" is best explained by keeping to the neologisms employed in the English version of the Treaty rather than by trying to express them in terms of *ultra vires*; "lack of competence" means that the institution did not have the power to do what it purported to do, whereas "misuse of powers" means that it had the power, but used it for wrongful purposes; see Joined Cases 3 and 4/64 *Chambre Syndicale* v. *H.A.* [1965] E.C.R. 441, 454–455. "Infringement of an essential procedural requirement" means exactly what it says, though it might be wondered whether "essential" is not tautologous. However, it appears from judgments under the ECSC Treaty, notably Joined Cases 275/80 and 24/81 *Krupp Stahl* v. *Commission* [1981] E.C.R. 2489, that failure to comply with the formal requirements of Decision 22/60 (see para. 1–16 above) will not necessarily invalidate a decision, at least where the recipient is not misled as to its nature. It could be suggested that what matters in practice is whether the applicant has an interest in raising the point.

1–21   These four grounds for annulment and their potential for overlap can perhaps best be understood in the light of examples of their use in practice. There appears to be no "pure" example of a successful plea of "lack of competence" but in Case 9/56 *Meroni* v. *H.A.* [1957 and 1958] E.C.R. 133, where the Court found itself having to consider the legality of a general decision delegating certain powers with regard to the assessment of a levy on scrap to an agency in Brussels, there is an illustration of what was in fact a lack of competence. After having held that under Article 53 of the ECSC Treaty, in relation to financial arrangements, delegation may only be of precisely defined powers of execution, the Court found that the delegation of powers granted to the agency in question gave to it "a degree of latitude which implies a wide margin of discretion." It continued, however, by saying that this

15

"cannot be considered as compatible with the requirements of the Treaty"; hence, formally, the lack of competence was treated as an infringement of the Treaty.

1–22   An example of an "infringement of an essential procedural requirement" required by a Treaty may be found in Case 138/79 *Roquette* v. *Council* [1980] E.C.R. 3333, where the Council Regulation on agricultural policy was annulled because the Parliament had not been consulted (*i.e.* the Council had not waited to receive its opinion) as required under Article 43(2) of the EEC Treaty. A breach of a requirement not laid down by a Treaty occurred in Case 17/74 *Transocean* v. *Commission* [1974] E.C.R. 1063, which concerned the imposition of a restrictive condition on the grant of an exemption by the Commission to an agreement under Article 85(3) of the EEC Treaty. It transpired that this condition had been imposed without the undertakings concerned having been heard on the point, and although (as interpreted by the Court) no express Community legislation required them to be so heard, the Court found, following the Opinion of A.G. Warner, that there was a general principle "that a person whose interests are perceptibly affected by a decision taken by a public authority must be given the opportunity to make his point of view known" ([1974] E.C.R. 1063, 1080). Under the Court's formulation it was stated that the rule requires that an undertaking be clearly informed in good time of the essence of conditions to which the Commission intends to subject an exemption and it must have the opportunity to submit its observations to the Commission. "This is especially so in the case of conditions which, as in this case, impose considerable obligations having far-reaching effects." Having accepted the existence of this general rule, the Court then said that breach of the rule would be regarded as a breach of an *essential procedural requirement* under Article 173 of the Treaty, and annulled the condition at issue.

As an illustration of an "infringement of the Treaty," Case 24/62 *Germany* v. *Commission* [1963] E.C.R. 63 might be taken, particularly since the formulation used in it has been repeated in a number of cases. The Federal Republic had asked for a tariff quota of 450,000 hectolitres of wine, and the Commission by a Decision of May 11, 1962 had granted a quota of 100,000 litres, stating that on the basis of "the information collected" it took the view that "the production of wines in question is amply sufficient." It was argued on behalf of the Federal Republic that this did not comply with the requirement under Article 190 of the EEC Treaty that the Council and Commission must state reasons for their Decisions. The Court held that Article 190

"seeks to give an opportunity to the parties of defending their rights, to the Court of exercising its supervisory functions, and to Member States and to all interested nationals of ascertaining the circumstances in which the Commission has applied the Treaty. To attain these objectives, it is sufficient for the decision to set out, in a concise but clear and relevant manner, the principal issues of law and of fact upon which it is based and which are necessary in order

16

that the reasoning which has led the Commission to its Decision may be understood."

The Court held that the statement of reasons given did not comply with these criteria—indeed that they contradicted the actual Decision, which allowed a quota, albeit reduced, despite the assertion that production was amply sufficient—and concluded that it did not satisfy the requirement of Article 190. Formally, then it was held to be an infringement of the Treaty, although it is often classified as an infringement of an essential procedural requirement by academic commentators. A similar view was taken with regard to the statement of reasons for a Regulation (albeit on a reference for a preliminary ruling) in Case 158/80 *Rewe Nord* v. *HZA Kiel* [1981] E.C.R. 1805: the recitals there stated that agricultural goods were being imported into the Community free of levy by passengers whose boat had not complied with the basic requirement of calling at a port outside the customs territory of the Community, yet the substantive part of the Regulation expressly authorised such imports, albeit of minimal quantities, rather than prohibiting them.

1–23 However, just as in the *Transocean* case a breach of a general principle of Community law was held, in the circumstances, to be an infringement of an essential procedural requirement, so also it has now been held that breach of such a principle may be regarded as a breach of the Treaty itself. In Case 112/77 *Töpfer* v. *Commission* [1978] E.C.R. 1019 the applicant, who held a large number of licences for the export of white sugar issued before April 26, 1977 in respect of which customs export formalities were effeced after July 15, 1977, brought an action under Article 173 for the annulment of a Commission Regulation which had the effect of reducing the compensation payable in DM to holders of sugar export licences issued before April 26, 1977 with effect from July 15, 1977. The applicant claimed, *inter alia*, that the regulation breached the general principle of the protection of legitimate expectation, one of the general principles of Community law most frequently invoked before the Court. The Court held that a submission based on a breach of that principle was admissible in the context of an application under Article 173, since that principle formed part of the Community legal order, with the result that any failure to comply with it is "an infringement of the Treaty or of any rule of law relating to its application" within the meaning of that provision. The rationale would appear to be that a legal principle, even though derived from national sources, which is accepted as a principle of Community law, is deemed to fall within the system established by the Treaty.

Last, and, in practice, least, is the matter of "misuse of powers." This has been alleged on numerous occasions, but rarely proved. A clear modern example is Case 105/75 *Guiffrida* v. *Council* [1976] E.C.R. 1395. This was an action for annulment of the appointment of a certain Italian official to the post of principal administrator (at Grade A4) in the Council's Directorate General for Regional Policy, following an internal competition which was alleged to have been held for the sole purpose of

17

appointing him to that post. Before his appointment to that post, the official in question had been officially classified in the language service (Grade L/A4), but had in reality, and against the Staff Regulations, been performing administrative tasks for many years. The competition was advertised in February 1975, but even in November 1974 one of the staff unions had criticised the fact that a competition was to be held to enable an official in the language service to transfer to the administrative service without loss of rank, whereas normally in such a situation it was necessary to start in the entry grade of Category "A." The Secretary-General of the Council actually issued a Staff Notice to refute the criticism, stating that "the question of the transfer of an official in Grade L/A4 to Grade A4 as a result of a competition arose out of a desire to mitigate an anomolous situation which has already lasted for some years." During the procedure before the Court, it was admitted that this situation was that of the Italian official in question. In the event, one of the advertised conditions for admission to the competition was that of "having performed category A duties for at least 6 years and held the secretariat for meetings of Council working parties or committees for at least 4 years." This, surprisingly enough, was precisely what the successful candidate had been doing. The Court found that it had not been shown why it was necessary in the interests of the service to lay down such a specific condition, and held that it was clear that the competition had been held "for the sole purpose of remedying the anomalous administrative status of a specific official and of appointing that same official to the post declared vacant. The pursuit of such a specific objective is contrary to the aims of any recruitment procedure, including the internal competition procedure, and this constitutes a misuse of powers" ([1976] E.C.R. 1395, 1403).

1–24   The four grounds for annulment listed in Article 173 all relate to questions of law, but this does not mean that questions of fact are completely excluded. Very often, under the Treaty or secondary Community legislation, particular Community acts may only be issued in certain factual circumstances, and if it can be shown that the relevant Community institution made a material error as to these facts, there will no longer be a legal basis for the resultant act. A very clear example of this came to light in a reference for a preliminary ruling, Case 131/77 *Milac* v. *HZA Saarbrücken* [1978] E.C.R. 1041. The dispute arose in the context of the system of monetary compensatory amounts, which, under the parent Council Regulation, may only be applied to products covered by intervention arrangements under the common organisations of agricultural markets, and to products whose price *depends* on the price of such products. Milac imported into Germany a quantity of powdered whey on which it had to pay monetary compensatory amounts, under the terms of, and at the rate laid down in, the then current Commission implementing regulation. In fact, under the common organisation of the market in milk and milk products, intervention prices are fixed only for butter, skimmed milk powder, and certain cheeses. Milac sought to recover the monetary compensatory amounts it had paid before the Finanzgericht of the Saar, claiming essentially that the price of powered whey was not dependent on the price of any intervention product, and the Finanzgericht referred to the European Court the specific question whether the Commission Regulation was contrary to the present Council Regulation in that the price of powdered whey did not in fact depend on the price of skimmed milk powder.

The Court found that the relevant test was whether the price of the non-intervention product varied perceptibly under the influence of variations in the price of the intervention product. On a comparision of the recorded prices of skimmed milk powder and powdered whey put before it, the Court found not only that there was no correlation between the two prices, but that there was a growing divergence. Hence it was held that the Commisison Regulation was invalid insofar as it fixed monetary compensatory amounts on powdered whey.

4. *Locus Standi*

1–25 Insofar as rights of action are conferred upon them by the substantive Treaty provisons, and with regard to the acts susceptible to challenge under the provisions, no real problems of *locus standi* would appear to arise with regard to actions for annulment brought by Member States, the Council or the Commission (although no right of action is expressly conferred upon any other Community institution). Indeed, in Case 166/78 *Italy* v. *Council* [1979] E.C.R. 2575, 2596, it was held that Italy was not barred from seeking the annulment of a Council Regulation by the fact that its representative at the relevant Council meeting had voted in favour of that Regulation; the implication appears to be that, within its express limits, the right of action conferred upon Member States to seek the annulment of a Community act is unconditional.

At the level of the private litigant, however, problems arise as to who may bring an action, which acts they may challenge, and whether they need to show an interest in the result and in the grounds for annulment which they invoke. Under the ECSC Treaty, private rights of action are conferred only on coal and steel undertakings and associations of such undertakings within the meaning of that Treaty, so that Case 66/76 *CFDT* v. *Council* [1977] E.C.R. 305, an action brought by a trade union, was doomed to failure. The remedies under the Staff Regulations are available to individual officials, former officials, and candidates for a post in disputes relating to their employment, see Joined Cases 81 to 88/74 *Marenco* v. *Commission* [1975] E.C.R. 1247, 1255, but not to staff associations, following Case 175/73 *Union Syndicale* v. *Commission* [1974] E.C.R. 917, 925–926. The action under the EEC and Euratom Treaties are, however, generally available to any "natural or legal person." Disputes as to the scope of this concept appear to have arisen most frequently in the context of intervention in other proceedings (see para. 11–06 below), but it is clear from the *Union Syndicale* case that an unincorporated association such as a trade union may exercise this right of action. Furthermore, in Case 135/81 *Agences de Voyages* v. *Commission* (October 28, 1982) it was held that where the Commission had allowed an *ad hoc* association of travel agencies (taking the form of a "private limited company in the course of formation" under Luxembourg law) to respond to an invitation to tender, that association should be regarded as having the character of a "legal person" under Article 173 of the EEC Treaty.

1–26 With regard to the acts which may be challenged, ECSC coal and steel undertakings may challenge individual decisions or recommendations which concern them without further restriction, but may only challenge general decisions or recommendations which they consider to involve a misuse of powers affecting them. In the silence of the Treaty, the distinction between individual and general decisions and recommendations is a matter of case law. As defined in Case 13/57 *Eisen-und Stahlindustrie* v. *H.A.* [1957 and 1958] E.C.R. 265, 276, a general decision "establishes a legislative principle, imposes abstract conditions for its implementation, and sets out the legal consequences entailed thereby," and according to Case 8/55 *Fédéchar* v. *H.A.* [1954 to 1956] E.C.R. 245, 256, such a decision does not cease to be general simply because its consequences may be individual and varied. Individual decisions, on the other hand, as in Case 18/57 *Nold* v. *H.A.* [1959] E.C.R. 41, 50, relate to the individual conduct of clearly identified undertakings. It was also stated in *Nold* that a decision which is individual with regard to the undertakings to which it is directed cannot at the same time be regarded as a general decision in relation to third parties. It was, however, recognised in *Fédéchar* (at pp. 256–257) that the same instrument (to use a neutral term) could comport both individual and general decisions: in that case, a single letter was held to contain an individual decision with regard to the reduction and withdrawal of equalisation payments from certain collieries, but a general decision insofar as it stated the general criteria under which future equalisation payments would be withdrawn.

If the decision or recommendation is general in nature, it would appear from Case 3/54 *Assider* v. *H.A.* [1954 to 1956] E.C.R. 63, 69, that the application will be admissible if the applicant formally alleges that there has been a misuse of powers affecting it, provided the applicant indicates the reasons for that allegation, although in Joined Cases 154/78, etc., *Ferriera Valsabbia* v. *Commission* [1980] E.C.R. 907, 922, it is stated that such an allegation should be supported by appropriate evidence. However, it was held in Case 13/57 *Eisen-und Stahlindustrie* v. *H.A.* [1957 and 1958] E.C.R. 265, 277, that misuse of powers is the only ground for annulment which may be relied upon in such an action—and no applicant under Article 33 of the ECSC Treaty appears so far to have succeeded in substantiating such an allegation.

1–27 In the context of the Staff Regulations, it has already been noted (see para. 1–19 above) that an act adversely affecting the applicant must be an act having legal effects emanating from the appointing authority.

Under the EEC and Euratom Treaties, the acts which may be challenged by individual litigants may be divided into three categories; decisions addressed to the applicant, decisions addressed to someone else (most usually, addressed to a Member State) which are of direct and individual concern to the applicant, and Regulations which are in reality decisions of direct and individual concern to the applicant. The most obvious example of a decision addressed to a natural or legal person is a decision taken by the Commission in application of the EEC competition rules, the addressee of which is expressly entitled to challenge it. In all other cases, however, it is necessary for the applicant to prove direct and individual concern.

At the level of individual competition decisions, it would appear from Case 27/76 *Metro SB Grossmärkte* v. *Commission* [1977] E.C.R. 1875, 1901 that the Court is prepared to assume such concern on the part of an undertaking which made a formal complaint to the Commission under article 3(2)(b) of Regulation 17 so that if, contrary to the wishes of the complainant, the Commission issues a decision granting exemption or clearance to the agreement or practice in question, the complainant may challenge such a decision even though he is not the addressee. The nearest analogy at the level of decisions addressed to Member States arises in the context of state aids. In Case 730/79 *Philip Morris Holland* v. *Commission* [1980] E.C.R. 2671 it was conceded by the Commission, and must have been accepted by the Court, that where a Commission decision ordered a Member State not to pay state aids to a particular undertaking, that decision was of direct and individual concern to the would-be recipient of the aid. The other actions which have been held to be admissible arising from decisions addressed to Member States have involved applicants distinguished by their legal situation as holders of or applicants for import licences, or as tenderers, and the decision addressed to the Member State has been held to be of direct concern to the applicants insofar as it leaves no discretion to the Member State, and of individual concern insofar as it determines the fate of the individual licence or tender. The examples may be given of Case 62/70 *Bock* v. *Commission* [1971] E.C.R. 897 and Case 29/75 *Kaufhof* v. *Commission* [1976] E.C.R. 431. Both cases were concerned with decisions made by the Commission under Article 115 of the EEC Treaty under which the Commission may authorise Member States to take the necessary protective measures, amongst other things, to avoid deflection of trade. The *Bock* case was concerned with an attempt to import into Germany some Chinese mushrooms which were in free circulation in the Netherlands. The *Kaufhof* case was concerned with attempts to import into Germany some Chinese tinned green beans in pod which were likewise in free circulation in the Netherlands. In each case the applicants had asked for an import licence from the German authorities and in each case the reaction of the German authorities in the particular circumstances existing at the time was to ask the Commission for an authorisation under Article 115 to refuse Community treatment in such goods. In each case the Commission issued such decisions and in each case the decisions were stated to have effect from a date before that on which they were made, these dates being sufficiently far back to cover the date on which the applications for import licences had been made.

1–28   The points of law that are involved in challenging such decisions were dealt with clearly by the Court in the *Bock* case. First there was the problem of whether such a decision can be regarded as being of *direct* concern to the applicant. In each case the Commission authorised Germany not to grant Community treatment to the goods in question, but, of course, the German authorities were in theory left free to decide for themselves whether or not to apply Community treatment. However, particularly in the *Bock* case where the Court dealt in detail with the question, it was stated that the appropriate German authorities had already informed the applicant that they would reject its application as soon as the Commission had granted them the requisite authorisation. They had requested that authorisation with particular reference to applications already before them at that time. It followed therefore that the matter was of direct concern to the applicant. In other words, if the Member State has decided in advance how it is going to exercise its discretion under a Commission decision, then the effect of the Commission decision can be regarded as directly concerning the applicant. With regard to the question of *individual* concern, the decisions were in fact being challenged to the extent to which they covered imports for which applications for import licences were already pending at the date of the decision's entry into force. The Court said, in the *Bock* case, that the number and identity of importers concerned in this way was already fixed and ascertainable before that date, and the defendant, the Commission, was in a position to know that the contested provision in its decision would affect the interests and situation of those importers alone. The factual situation thus created differentiated the latter from all other persons and distinguished them individually just as in the case of the person addessed. In Case 92/78 *Simmenthal* v. *Commission* [1979] E.C.R. 777, the applicant tendered for the purchase of some intervention beef; its tender was forwarded to the Commission by the Italian authorities, and in the light of the various tenders the Commission addressed a decision to Italy fixing the minimum acceptable tender price. Pursuant to this the applicant's tender was rejected—but its application to annul the decision was held to be admissible.

1–29   The applications for the annulment of Regulations which have been held to be admissible have likewise mostly involved the legal consequences attaching to the holding of, or making an application for, particular import or export licences. However, in the case of a Regulation, the problem arises whether proof that it is in fact a decision goes beyond showing direct and individual concern. In Case 100/74 *CAM* v. *Commission* [1975] E.C.R. 1393, 1403, the Court looked only to direct and individual concern in a Regulation which it recognised as being one of a number of provisions having a legislative function; the Regulation at issue prevented holders of advance fixing certificates for the export of cereals obtained before a particular date and not used by a specified later date from taking advantage of an increase in export refunds which would normally have automatically occurred. Thereafter A.G. Warner suggested in his Opinion in the *Japanese ball bearing* cases [1979] E.C.R. 1246 that a Regulation imposing anti-dumping duty could be a decision of direct and individual concern to the exporters concerned, but a Regulation with regard to everyone else. In the light of later judgments, however, he retracted this view in Joined Cases 789 and 790/79 *Calpak* v. *Commission* [1980] E.C.R. 1972, although in Case 307/81 *Alusuisse Italia* v. *Council* (October 6, 1982) the Third Chamber appears to have followed a similar approach in holding that an anti-dumping Regulation was general in nature so far as importers of the product in question were concerned, since the importers, unlike the exporters, were not expressly named. Nevertheless in Case 45/81 *Moksel* v. *Commission* (March 25, 1982) the Third Chamber stated categorically that the same act cannot be both individual and general, reflecting the view under the ECSC Treaty in Case 18/57 *Nold* v. *H.A.* [1959] E.C.R. 41, 50. However, it is submitted that just as under the ECSC Treaty it was recognised in Case 8/55 *Fédéchar* v. *H.A.* [1954 to 1956] E.C.R. 245, 256–257, that the same instrument could contain both general and individual decisions, so also a single instrument made under the EEC or Euratom Treaties may contain certain provisions which constitute Regulations, and others which constitute individual decisions. Support for this view indeed appears in the Court's judgment in the *Japanese ball bearing* cases [1979] E.C.R. 1185 *et seq.* where it examined the provisions of the Regulations at issue separately and applied different tests to determine whether they constituted decisions. Article 3 of the Regulation at issue provided for the collection of amounts secured by way of provisions anti-dumping duty on the products of certain named manufacturers, and was held to constitute a decision relating to named addressees. Articles 1 and 2 of the Regulation suspended the definitive anti-dumping duty unless the named producers violated or evaded certain undertakings they had given, and were held to be of direct and individual concern to the producers which had given these undertakings.

1–30 Since Regulations are by definition of direct application, there is usually little difficulty in showing that they are of direct concern to those caught by their provisions, unless they require or allow for further implemntation in such a way as to allow scope for discretion. Hence in Case 123/77 *UNICME* v. *Council* [1978] E.C.R. 845 it was held that a Regulation limiting imports of Japanese motorbikes into Italy left scope for the Italian authorities to determine the fate of individual applications for import licences, and in Joined Cases 103–109/78 *Beauport* v. *Council* [1979] E.C.R. 17, the Regulation at issue allowed France a discretion to reduce the basic quotas fixed for sugar producers in overseas departments.

Proof of individual concern gives rise to greater problems, and the successful cases may be grouped into two main categories: where individualisation results from facts having legal consequences, and where there is individualisation by specific reference. As already indicated, most of the former catergory involve Regulations affecting holders of, or applicants for, particular import or export licences. In Joined Cases 41–44/70 *International Fruit* v. *Commission* [1971] E.C.R. 411 the Regulation at issue was adopted in the light of individual applications for import licences and determined their fate. In Case 100/74 *CAM* v. *Commission* [1975] E.C.R. 1393 the Regulation at issue altered the normal consequences of holding advance fixing certificates for the holders of a defined category of such certificates (see para. 1–29 above). In Case 88/76 *Société d'exportation des sucres* v. *Commission* [1977] E.C.R. 709 and Case 112/77 *Töpfer* v. *Commission* [1978] E.C.R. 1091, The Regulation at issue altered the normal consequences of holding sugar export licences for the holders of certain defined licences (see para. 1–23 above). By way of contrast, in Case 162/78 *Wagner, Schlüter and Maach* v. *Commission* [1979] E.C.R. 3467, where it might have been thought that the Regulation at issue had the effect of reducing export refunds for the holders of certain sugar export licences, the Court categorised it, in its context, as in reality correcting the relevant monetary compensatory amounts, a matter of general legislation which, according to established case law, traders must usually accept.

A somewhat different kind of factual situation occurred in the *Japanese ball bearing* cases [1979] E.C.R. 1185 *et seq.* at, *e.g.* pp. 1326–1327, where the fact that the applicants had given undertakings to raise their prices was held to make certain provisions of the Regulation, which suspended definitive anit-dumping duty unless those undertakings were violated or avoided these undertakings, of direct and individual concern to the applicants. On the other hand, the exercise of normal trading activity by an identifiable number of persons is not regarded as a distinguishing fact. In Case 101/76 *KSH* v. *Council and Commission* [1977] E.C.R. 797, 808, with regard to a Regulation affecting isoglucose manufacturers (see para. 1–09 above), it was held that an act which "applies to objectively determined situations and produces legal effects with regard to catgegories of persons regarded generally and in the abstract" does not lose its nature as a Regulation simply because it is possible to determine "more or less precisely the number or even the identity of the persons to whom it applies at a given moment." Indeed, otherwise it would not be possible to issue a true Regulation in an economic sector in which there are few operators.

1–31   Individualisation by specific reference was found to have occurred in the *Japanese ball bearing* cases (*supra*) where it was held that the article of the Regulation at issue which provided for the collection of amounts secured by way of anti-dumping duty on the products of certain named manufacturers constituted a decision relating to named addressees. Similarly, in Case 138/79 *Roquette* v. *Council* [1980] E.C.R. 3333, 3356, it was held that the provisions of a Regulation which laid down individual production quotas for named manufacturers of isoglucose constituted measures of direct and individual concern to the undertakings which were the "addressees" of these quotas. On the other hand, a Regulation which sets out the criteria from which individual quotas may be derived, but does not itself implement these criteria, has been held not to be of direct and individual concern to the producers involved, in Joined Cases 789 and 790/79 *Calpak* v. *Commission* [1980] E.C.R. 1961; this is very similar to the distinction under the ECSC Treaty between general and individual decisions noted in Case 8/55 *Fédéchar* v. *H.A.* [1954 to 1956] E.C.R. 245, 256 (see para. 1–26 above), where the withdrawal of equalisation payments from named colleries was held to be an individual decision, but the statement of a criteria under which future equalisation payments would be withdrawn was held to be a general decision.

Of the other problems of *locus standi*, the need to show an interest in the result has most clearly been expressed in staff cases, *e.g.* in Case 15/67 *Bauer* v. *Commission* [1967] E.C.R. 397, 402, it was held that an interest of an abstract character is insufficient to justify the continuation of the proceedings. It would appear, however, that the interest need not be financial, since in Case 7/77 *Von Wüllerstorff* v. *Commission* [1978] E.C.R. 769, 779, where the applicant had subsequently been promoted to a post at the same grade as that offered in a competition to which he had been refused admission by the decision which was at issue, it was said that "the argument that if there are no financial benefits or enhanced official status it is impossible to recognise a substantial interest in performing a certain duty disregards the interest which an official or servant may have in preferring some duties to others." In the context of competition decisions, it was held in Case 77/77 *BP* v. *Commission* [1978] E.C.R. 1513, 1524–1525 that the absence of a fine did not preclude the addressee of a Commission competition decision from having its legality reviewed by the Court; BP in fact argued that they had an interest in obtaining an acknowledgment by the Court of the unfounded nature of the criticism made of them by the Commission. On the other hand, in Case 135/81 *Agences de Voyages* v. *Commission* (October 28, 1982), it was held that a non-profit-making association which did not and could not submit a tender had no interest in seeking the annulment of the decision accepting one of the tenders.

1–32   It further appears that an individual litigant must show an interest not only in the result but also in the grounds put forward for annulment. This was most openly discussed in Case 90/74 *Deboeck* v. *Commission* [1975] E.C.R. 1123, a staff case heard by the First Chamber, where the applicant sought the annulment of an internal competition for the recruitment of secretarial assistants, and one submission of the applicant was that the notice of competition had not been preceded by a notice of vacancy as required by the Staff Regulations. The Court held that she had no interest to raise the point, since she was not eligible for transfer or promotion (the procedures which may precede the holding of a competition) without taking part in a competition, and she had in fact taken part in the competition. This followed an Opinion delivered by Mr. Advocate-General Warner in which he briefly reviewed the situation in the Member States, and was in line with the result of earlier decisions. Examples may also be found in competition proceedings, as in Joined Cases 209 to 215 and 218/78 *Van Landewyck* v. *Commission* [1980] E.C.R. 3125, 3239. It was there claimed that the Commission had wrongly communicated certain confidential information to the complainants, but the Court held that this could not lead to the annulment of the decision unless it could be shown that the decision would have been different in the absence of that irregularity; it was in fact found that the information had not enabled the complainant to put forward any argument likely to affect the substance of the decision.

5. *Pleas of Illegality*

1–33   Perhaps as a consequence of its restrictive attitute to direct challenge by private litigants to general legislation, the Court has developed the plea of illegality as a general principle that an individual who is permitted to challenge an act which is individual in nature may at the same time contest the legality of the general legislation on which the individual act is based and which he is not permitted to challenge directly. Although Article 36 of the ECSC Treaty only envisages that the illegality of the underlying general decision may be invoked where the applicant is seeking the annulment of a decision imposing a pecuniary sanction or periodic penalty payment, this was held in Case 9/56 *Meroni* v. *H.A.* [1957 and 1958] E.C.R. 133 to be merely a specific application of a general principle recognised also in the EEC and Euratom Treaties allowing the applicant to question the legality of the general decisions and recommendation on which any individual decision is based. Article 184 of the EEC Treaty and Article 156 of the Euratom Treaty allow the "inapplicablity" of a Regulation to be invoked in proceeding in which it is at issue, but in Case 92/78 *Simmenthal* v. *Commission* [1979] E.C.R. 777 it was held that the scope of Article 184 of the EEC Treaty should extend to acts of the Community institutions which, even if not in the form of a Regulation, nonetheless produce analogous effects, and hence could not be challenged directly by anyone other than a Community institution or a Member State; in that case, the applicant was able to plead the illegality of general notices of invitation to tender on which the decision at issue was based.

The essential precondition of the plea of illegality is that proceedings in a direct action should already be validly before the Court in which the legality of the general legislation arises: it is not an independent form of direct action, as the Court made clear in Joined Cases 31 and 33/62 *Wöhrmann* v. *Commission* [1962] E.C.R. 501, 507, and neither does it replace the exclusive power of a national court to make a reference for a preliminary ruling where the validity of a Regulation is at issue in national proceedings. This latter point was amplified in Case 44/65 *Hessische Knappschaft* v. *Singer* [1965] E.C.R. 965, 970–971 where it was held that it was not open to the parties to the national proceedings to raise the question of the validity of a Regulation of which the national court had merely sought the interpretation; the Court stated expressly that it could not "entertain within the particular framework or Article 177 a claim based primarily on Article 184."

1–34   Although it now appears that a general plea of illegality is available with regard to any general act on which an individual act at issue before the Court is based, it was formally held in Case 156/77 *Commission* v. *Belgium* [1978] E.C.R. 1881, 1896 that it is not available with regard to an individual decision at issue in other proceedings before the Court, at least where that decision could have been challenged directly, on the basis that the pleas of illegality cannot be used to evade the limitation periods on direct actions. Indeed the logical consequences of *Commission* v. *Belgium* would appear to be that since virtually all binding acts (see para. 1–03 above) may be challenged directly by the Member States (and where appropriate, by the Council or Commission), the plea of illegality is not open to them. Nevertheless, there is a hint in Cases 6 and 11/69 *Commission* v. *France* [1969] E.C.R. 523, 539, that in enforcement proceedings, the Court would be willing to investigate whether legislation the Member State was alleged to have breached lacked "all legal basis in the Community legal system" despite the expiry of the time-limit for direct challenge.

6. *Effects of Annulment*

1–35 The consequential measures which may be ordered are considered in detail in the context of enforcement of the judgments of the Court (see para. 8–15 below). Although express provision with regard to severability is contained only in Article 174 of the EEC Treaty and Article 147 of the Euratom Treaty and there only in relation to Regulations, it is now clear that the Court assumes power to sever the invalid parts of other acts where appropriate rather than annulling the whole measure. Hence, in Case 17/74 *Transocean* v. *Commission* [1974] E.C.R. 1063 (see para. 1–22 above), the Court only annulled the restrictive condition which had been attached to a decision granting exemption to an agreement under Article 85(3) of the EEC Treaty. Further, it would appear that by an extended concept of severability, an act which is annulled need not be treated as void *ab initio*. In Case 4/79 *Providence Champagne* v. *ONIC* [1980] E.C.R. 2823, 2853–2854, where Article 174 of the EEC Treaty was applied by analogy on a reference for a preliminary ruling, the Court ordered that the invalidity of the Regulation there at issue should only be invoked as from the date of its judgment.

B. ACTIONS FOR FAILURE TO ACT

1. *Nature*

1–36 Two distinct types of action for failure to act are recognised in Community law. Under article 35 of the ECSC Treaty (where the remedy is available only against the Commission) and articles 90 and 91 of the Staff Regulations, failure of an institution to respond to an invitation to act within the appropriate time-limit is deemed to be an implied decision of refusal to act which may then be challenged before the Court. The system introduced by Article 175 of the EEC Treaty and Article 148 of the Euratom Treaty, however, allows a challenge to a failure to act as such on the part of the Council or Commission.

A number of important legal consequences flow from these differences. Under the ECSC Treaty, where the action relates to an implied decision of refusal to issue a decision or a recommendation, the only way the Commission may avoid being deemed to have taken such an implied decision is by issuing a binding act capable of being classified as a decision or recommendation within the time-limit laid down in Article

27

35, as was noted in Joined Cases 42 and 49/59 *Snupat* v. *H.A.* [1961] E.C.R. 53, 74. It appears from Joined Cases 7 and 9/54 *Industries Sidérurgiques Luxembourgeoises* v. *H.A.* [1954 to 1956] E.C.R. 175, 193–194 that the implied decision is not affected by a later express refusal to act. On the other hand, it has been held in a number of staff cases, in particular, that a later express decision to the same effect as an implied refusal to act is merely confirmatory, does not in itself adversely affect the applicant, and does not in principle give rise to any new right of action, as in Joined Cases 45 and 49/70 *Bode* v. *Commission* [1971] E.C.R. 465, 475. This is a matter of particular importance in the calculation of limitation periods (see paras. 2–23, 2–24 below).

1–37 Under the EEC and Euratom Treaties, the institution may be sued for failure to act only if it has not "defined its position" within the due time-limit, and it is well established that a "definition of position" may take a form not susceptible to challenge. In Case 48/65 *Lütticke* v. *Commission* [1966] E.C.R. 19 a letter from the Commission to the applicants to the effect that it would not take enforcement proceedings against Germany under Article 169 of the EEC Treaty, (see para. 1–40 below) was held to be a "definition of position" by the Commission, but it was further stated that since under Article 169 the Commission is empowered only to issue an opinion, which is of no binding force, then no measure taken before the issue of the opinion could have any binding force, so that the letter was not an act which could be annulled under Article 173 of the EEC Treaty. Similarly, in Case 125/78 *Gema* v. *Commission* [1979] E.C.R. 3173, where the applicant was a complainant in competition proceedings who wished to see the Commission take a decision under Article 86 of the EEC Treaty with regard to certain practices of Radio Luxembourg, it was held that a letter from the Commission stating that in its view such a decision would not be justified constituted a definition of its position.

Under all three Treaties, the applicant must show in effect that the failure to act constitutes a breach of a Treaty obligation. Under the ECSC Treaty, however, there is the further condition that if the Commission is "empowered" rather than "required" to issue the decision or recommendation, it must be shown that such abstention constitutes a misuse of powers. By analogy with individual actions for the annulment of general decisions under Article 33 of that Treaty, it would therefore appear that an allegation of misuse of powers supported by prima facie evidence must be made in order for the action to be admissible, and that misuse of power must be proved in order for it to succeed (see para. 1–26 above).

2. Locus Standi

1–38 Whilst Article 35 of the ECSC Treaty is silent as to any distinction between the status of the Member States, Council, undertakings, or association of undertakings on whom it confers rights of action, the implied decision to which it gives rise must itself be challenged in the same way as an express decision (see para. 1–26 above), so that it becomes important to know whether the implied decision may be categorised as general or individual, as was pointed out in one of the Court's earliest decisions, in Joined Cases 7 and 9/54 *Industries Sidérurgiques Luxembourgeoises* v. *H.A.* [1954 to 1956] E.C.R. 175, 191–192; this in turn must relate to the nature of the decision or recommendation the Commission was requested to adopt, which in that case was held to be an individual decision. In the result, although an undertaking is not prohibited from challenging a failure to take a general decision under the ECSC Treaty, it must show that the implied decision of refusal constitutes a misuse of powers affecting it, in the terms of Article 33 of the ECSC Treaty, even if that general decision is one which the Commission was required to take in terms of the first paragraph of Article 35.

1–39   The EEC and Euratom Treaties, on the other hand, are more openly restrictive of the rights of action of private litigants; a natural or legal person may only challenge a failure "to address to that person" an act other than a recommendation or an opinion. The logical conclusion that an action may only be brought by a natural or legal person for failure to issue an act which could have been addressed to the applicant, *i.e.* a decision, was drawn by A.G. Gand in his Opinion in Case 48/65 *Lütticke* v. *Commission* [1966] E.C.R. 19, 30, and was applied by the Court in Case 90/78 *Granaria* v. *Council and Commission* [1979] E.C.R. 1081, 1092–1093. There the applicants requested the payment of production refunds on quellmehl, and the Court took the view that the only act by which this could have been done would have been a Regulation authorising the reintroduction of production refunds for quellmehl, which could not be described either in its form or its nature as an act addressed to the applicants. The action was thus inadmissible. This approach was followed by the Second Chamber in Case 246/81 *Bethell* v. *Commission* (June 10, 1982), where the applicant had requested the Commission to undertake an investigation with regard to the fixing of air fares with a view to the possible application of the EEC competition rules; it was held he was asking the Commission not to take a decision in respect of him but to open an inquiry with regard to third parties and to take decisions in respect of them. The applicant was not therefore "the potential addressee of a legal measure which the Commission has a duty to adopt with regard to him," and the application was held to be inadmissible.

C. Enforcement Procedures

1. *Scope of the Commission's Discretion*

1–40   Although all three Treaties allow Member States as well as the Commission to impugn breaches of the Treaties by other Member States, the ECSC provisions require other available procedures to be used first, and the EEC and Euratom provisions require the Commission to be informed and to have the opportunity to deliver a reasoned opinion before the matter is brought before the Court (see para. 1–03 above), so that in practice direct enforcement proceedings are normally brought by the Commission.

There is a fundamental distinction between the Commission's powers under the ECSC Treaty on the one hand the EEC and Euratom Treaties on the other. Under Article 88 of the ECSC Treaty it is for the Commission to issue a decision to the effect that a Member State has failed to fulfil a Treaty obligation, and it is for the Member State to bring the matter before the Court which is granted unlimited jurisdiction in such an action. It would appear also, however, that such a decision, which was categorised as individual in nature in Joined Cases 7 and 9/54 *Industries Sidérurgiques Luxembourgeoises* v. *H.A.* [1954 to 1956] E.C.R. 175, 192, could also be challenged under the general rules of Article 33 of the ECSC Treaty even by a coal or steel undertaking; in that case, it was expressly held that an implied decision of refusal to take such a decision arising under Article 35 of that Treaty could be challenged by an association of steel undertakings. It further appears from this judgment (at p. 190) that the Court took the view that the Commission was under a duty to issue a decision under Article 88 if it considered that a breach of Treaty obligation had occurred, so there was no need to prove under Article 35 that its failure so to do constituted a misuse of powers.

Under the EEC and Euratom Treaties, however, a wide discretion is conferred on the Commission. Article 169 of the EEC Treaty (as also Article 141 of the Euratom Treaty) does not require the Commission to issue a binding decision. Rather, it requires it to issue a reasoned opinion to a defaulting Member State, an act which has no binding effect under Article 189 of that Treaty and which is not susceptible to judicial review under Article 173. The conclusion drawn from this in Case 48/65 *Lütticke* v. *Commission* [1966] E.C.R. 19, was that since the opinion itself could not be challenged, a letter sent to a complainant refusing to issue such an opinion could not be subject to an action for annulment either, although it did constitute a "definition of position" so as to block an action for failure to act under Article 175 of the EEC Treaty. If the Member State does not comply with the opinion, the Commission is then empowered, but not required, to bring the matter before the Court. Hence, the Commission has a discretion which does not appear to be susceptible to direct challenge, although a complainant Member State could bring an action against the defaulting State in its own name once the Commission has issued its opinion, or has failed to do so within three months, under the terms of Article 170, as in Case 141/78 *France* v. *U.K.* [1979] E.C.R. 2923.

1–41   Indirect challenge to the exercise of the Commission's discretion may however, be mounted either by invoking the direct effect (if such there be) of the relevant Community rule before a national court against the defaulting Member State or one of its agencies (see para. 1–10 above), or, it would appear, through an action for damages. In Case 14/78 *Denkavit* v. *Commission* [1978] E.C.R. 2497, 2505 where it was alleged that the Commission had failed to act sufficiently urgently to require the abolition of certain Italian measures, thereby incurring liability to the applicants, the Court was apparently willing to accept that if there was no justification for the Commission's conduct, and this improperly contributed to the maintenance of an obstacle to trade between Member States, then the Commission could incur liability. It was however held that in the circumstances, since the Italian measures related to additives in animal feeding-stuffs, it was reasonable for the Commission to wait to receive the respective reports of a standing committee and of a scientific committee on animal feeding-stuffs.

1–42   The Commission would also appear to enjoy an element of discretion with regard to the use of more specific enforcement procedures insofar as these overlap with the general procedures (see paras. 2–47 to 2–50 below). In practice, the most important of these has been Article 93(2) of the EEC Treaty allowing the Commission to issue a decision requiring the abolition of a state aid which is incompatible with the common market, and to bring the matter directly before the Court if the decision is not complied with in due time. In his Opinion in Case 173/73 *Italy* v. *Commission* [1974] E.C.R. 709, 724, A.G. Warner took the view that the procedure under Article 93(2) was limited to the substantive question whether the aid was compatible with the Treaty, and that proceedings relating to a breach of the rules governing the introduction of new aids, which require their notification to the Commission, should be taken under the general system of Article 169. The Court, however, held the Commission had a choice, and could use Article 93(2) even with regard to procedural breaches.

Since the state aids rules require the Commission to issue a decision rather than an opinion, there is an act which the Member State in question could have challenged, and if the Member State disobeys the decision without challenging it, certain legal consequences may follow. The first is that, as stated in Joined Cases 31/77R and 53/77R *Commission* v. *U.K.* [1977] E.C.R. 921, at least where the breach relates to the introduction of new aid, failure to comply with the decision will in itself be regarded as justifying the imposition of interim measures requiring immediate cessation of the aid in subsequent proceedings brought by the Commission (see para. 10–06 below). The second is that, if the matter is brought before the Court by the Commission, the Member State will not be allowed to plead the illegality of the decision it failed to challenge in time, as was held in Case 156/77 *Commission* v. *Belgium* [1978] E.C.R. 1881, 1896, and hence is not likely to have a defence. This may, however, be subejct to the overriding possibility enounced in the context of general enforcement proceedings in Joined Cases 6 and 11/69 *Commission* v. *France* [1969] E.C.R. 523, 539, that where the Member State is alleged to have breached a provision of secondary legislation (in that case, a decision), the Court would be willing to investigate whether that provision "lacks all legal basis in the Community legal system" despite the expiry of the time-limit for direct challenge.

1–43   With regard to the conduct the Commission may require of a Member State in its opinion or decision, it was accepted in Case 70/72 *Commission* v. *Germany* [1973] E.C.R. 813 that this could be positive to

31

the extent that, in the context of state aids, the Member State could be obliged to require repayment of aid granted in breach of the Treaty, provided this obligation is set out in a sufficiently clear and detailed manner—which was not the case in that action.

A final overall limit in the Commission's discretion is that the Court will not issue a judgment which it regards as serving no useful purpose. Hence, in Joined Cases 24 and 97/80R *Commission* v. *France* [1980] E.C.R. 1319 the Court was not willing to issue an interim order which would have been to the same effect as the binding judgment it had delivered a few months earlier in previous proceedings relating to the same substantive breach of a Treaty obligation.

2. *Concept of Infringement*

1–44 It has long been established that a Member State may be liable for the conduct of public agencies which are legally or constitutionally independent. So, in Case 77/69 *Commission* v. *Belgium* [1970] E.C.R. 237, 243, the Court rejected the defence put forward by the Belgian government that the delay in the elimination of certain discriminatory internal taxation was due to the dissolution of the Belgian Parliament and hence beyond its control. In his Opinion in Case 9/75 *Meyer-Burckhardt* v. *Commission* [1975] E.C.R. 1171, 1187, A.G. Warner was willing to accept that a Member State would be amenable to enforcement proceedings under Article 169 in relation to a persistent failure by its courts, or one of its courts, to comply with the provisions of Article 177 on references for preliminary rulings.

It further appears that a Member State may be held liable for an apparent breach of its Treaty obligations even when it has been corrected in administrative practice. In Case 167/73 *Commission* v. *France* [1974] E.C.R. 359 France was held to be in breach of its obligations by maintaining in its Code du Travail Maritime a provsion requiring a specific proportion of the crew of a merchant ship to be of French nationality, even though as a matter of administration Community nationals were treated as if they were French nationals for this purpose, since it might create uncertainty as to the possibilities open to them in the minds of those concerned. Furthermore, it has been held that a Member State may not rely upon the fact that those concerned may invoke the direct effect of clear and unconditional provisions of a Directive to avoid its express obligation to implement the Directive, in Case 102/79 *Commission* v. *Belgium* [1980] E.C.R. 1473; indeed, although the concept of direct effect is appropriate for the private enforcement of provisions of the Directive against the defaulting Member State, it is a consequence of failure to comply with a Treaty obligation (see Case 148/78 *Ratti* [1979] E.C.R. 1629), and would not appear to be capable of imposing obligations on third parties, in so far as the Directive requires such obligation to be imposed.

Finally, it has frequently been held, as, *e.g.* in Case 39/72 *Commission* v. *Italy* [1973] E.C.R. 101 that belated compliance with its obligations will not prevent a finding that the Member State was in breach of them.

The Court there pointed out that its judgment "may be of substantive interest as establishing the basis of a responsibility that a Member State can incur as a result of its default, as regards other Member States, the Community, or private parties."

D. ACTIONS FOR DAMAGES RELATING TO NON-CONTRACTUAL LIABILITY

1. *General Issues*

1–45 In general, disputes involving contractual liability are only likely to come before the Court by way of arbitration (see para. 1–58 below), the only specific jurisdiction in the matter being conferred in relation to disputes "between the Community and its servants" to use the terminology of Article 179 of the EEC Treaty, and indeed the relationship between most Community officials and their employing institution is statutory rather than contractual, Case 28/74 *Gillet* v. *Commission* [1975] E.C.R. 463, 472–473. However, it would appear that officials other than local staff, who are subject to the jurisdiction of national courts (see para. 2–37 below), are required, where the dispute "originates in the relationship of employment between the person concerned and the institution" to use the procedures under the Staff Regulations to make a claim for damages, as was held in Case 9/75 *Meyer-Burckhardt* v. *Commission* [1975] E.C.R. 1171. This means that a claim for damages, whether the basis be contractual or non-contractual, will normally take the form of an action challenging an express or implied decision of the appointing authority refusing payment of the sum due, *i.e.* an action for annulment or for failure to act, or be ancillary to such an action.

Insofar as a direct action for damages is available to other litigants, and it may be noted (see for example, Joined Cases 9 and 12/60 *Vloeberghs* v. *H.A.* [1961] E.C.R. 197, 214) that none of the Treaties restricts the categories of applicants who may bring an action, it is limited under Article 40 of the ECSC Treaty to reparation for harm caused by a *wrongful* act or omission of the Community or of its servants, whereas Articles 178 and 215 of the EEC Treaty (as also Articles 153 and 188 of the Euratom Treaty) refer to "non-contractual liability" relating to damage *caused* by the Community's institution or servants, which would appear to recognise the possibility of liability without fault. As to the scope of "non-contractual" liability, it was argued by the Commission in Case 46/75 *IBC* v. *Commission* [1976] E.C.R. 65 that quasi-contractual liability was a branch of the law of contract and therefore did not fall within this concept, but A.G. Warner was able to reject this argument in his Opinion by reference to the laws of the Member States (at p. 86). However, in practice a claim based on quasi-contract is unlikely to be made against a Community institution, since the structure of the EEC is such that sums due under Community legislation are generally collected by national authorities, and it is well established (see para. 1–47 below) that claims for restitution must be brought against the national authority which received the payment. The

EEC and Euratom Treaties also refer to liability as being imposed "in accordance with the general principles common to the laws of the Member States," a concept which has never been defined. However, the Court did not regard the Accession in 1973 of new Member States which did not recognise the principle of civil liability for the private harm caused by general legislation as requiring it to change its view that such a concept existed in Community law, despite the urgings of the defendants in Joined Cases 63 to 69/72 *Werhahn* v. *Council and Commission* [1973] E.C.R. 1229, and it could be suggested that the general principle operated by the Court is that which disapproves of the non-liability of the State, as was remarked by A.G. Gand in his Opinion in Case 9/69 *Savag* v. *Leduc* [1969] E.C.R. 329, 340.

2. Jurisdiction

1–46   Given that most Community legislation is administered by the national authorities, the problem arises whether a person claiming to have suffered damage as a result of a Community act should bring an action before his national courts against the national authorities administering that act, or before the European Court against the Community institution which is the author of the act. Although the case law is not always easy to reconcile, certain guidelines have now appeared, although there appears to be a certain overlap with concepts of causation.

Thus, it appears that where a dispute relates to the way in which national authorities have applied Community rules, the action must be brought before the national courts, as in Case 133/79 *Sucrimex* v. *Commission* [1980] E.C.R. 1299, which related to the way in which duplicate export licences should be treated. The Second Chamber stated that the application of the relevant Community provisions was a matter for the national authorities, and that even though the national authorities acted on the basis of a (non-binding) telex from the Commission, "it is not the Commission's disputed telex message but the [national authorities'] decision to ratify it which might be regarded as causing damage to the applicants."

1–47   It is clear that a claim which is in effect for repayment of sums paid to a national authority under Community law, even under a provision of Community law which is the real subject of the dispute, should be brought against the national authority in the national courts. This was first clearly stated in Case 96/71 *Haegeman* v. *Commission* [1972] E.C.R. 1005, where an importer brought an action against the Commission for recovery of charges levied by the Belgian authorities under Commission legislation on imports of Greek wine. It was held that since the collection of "own resources" was basically the responsibility of the national authorities, disputes concerning the levying of such charges should be resolved by the national authorities or before the national courts, subject to the possibility of referring any question as to the interpretation of Community law to the European Court. It might merely be noted that in subsequent cases it has not always proved easy to distinguish between actions for the recovery of agricultural levies, and actions for damages for harm caused by the wrongful acts of Community institutions.

Just as traders seeking to recover sums paid under Community legislation must in principle act against the national authority which collected them, so also a trader seeking payment to himself for sums due under Community legislation must act against the national authority entrusted with making such a payment. The clearest example of this is perhaps Case 99/74 *Grands Moulins des Antilles* v. *Commission* [1975] E.C.R. 1531, where the applicants were claiming export refunds and carry-over payments due under the relevant Community legislation in relation to cereals respectively exported from or stocked in French overseas departments. It was held that their action should be brought against the national authorities, even though their refusal to pay arose because the EAGGF in turn refused to finance such payments in relation to overseas departments, since by Article 227(2) of the Treaty the benefits of the EAGGF do not automatically extend to overseas departments.

It was further held in Case 26/74 *Roquette* v. *Commission* [1976] E.C.R. 677 that if the substantive proceedings fall within the jurisdiction of the national courts, the same is true of ancillary questions such as the payment of interest. Hence, if the national court refuses to order the payment of interest, interest cannot be recovered in an action before the European Court.

1–48   On the other hand, where harm is alleged to have been caused by an act or omission of a Community institution in which national authorities are not involved, no problems arise as to admissibility. The difficult situation is that in which an applicant claims neither restitution nor a fixed sum due under Community legislation, but unliquidated damages for harm caused by an act or omission of a Community institution implemented by the national authorities. Obviously, it is desirable to avoid parallel proceedings before national courts and the European Court and the possible duplication of damages, but the European Court appears to have changed its view twice on the question whether the Community remedy should be regarded as subordinate to the exercise of the national remedy. In Joined Cases 5, 7 and 13 to 24/66 *Kampffmeyer* v. *Commission* [1967] E.C.R. 245, where the applicants told the Court that they had brought parallel actions before the German courts, the Court said:

> "It is necessary to avoid the applicants' being insufficiently or excessively compensated for the same damage by the different assessment of two different courts applying different rules of law. Before determining the damage for which the Community should be held liable, it is necessary for the national court to have the opportunity to give judgment on any liability on the part of the Federal Republic of Germany. This being the case, final judgment cannot be given before the applicants have produced the decision of the national court in this matter."

1–49   However, in Case 43/72 *Merkur* v. *Commission* [1973] E.C.R. 1055, where the applicant sought damages relating to the Commission's failure to fix certain compensatory amounts, and the Commission argued that the action should be brought in Germany in relation to the refusal of the competent customs office to grant the compensatory amounts, the Court held that it had the case before it and within its jurisdiction and "it would not be in keeping with the proper administration of justice and the requirements of procedural efficiency to compel the applicant to have recourse to national remedies." Nevertheless, in Joined Cases 67 to 85/75 *Lesieur Cotelle* v. *Commission* [1976] E.C.R. 391, the Court reverted to a position beyond that which it had stated in *Kampffmeyer* by adjudging the admissibility of the actions in the light of the *availability* or a national remedy which had not been sought. The claims there related to the effect of the Commission's abolition of certain monetary compensatory amounts on advance fixing certificates held by the applicants. It was held that the claims were admissible in so far as they related to certificates issued before the Commission acted, but with regard to certificates issued thereafter, "the applicants were . . . in a position to bring the alleged infringements . . . before the competent national courts." Since it can hardly be for the European Court to determine matters of national law in this context, the distinction may perhaps be explained on the basis of causation; only with regard to the second set of claims could the actions of the national authorities be regarded as having contributed towards the harm suffered by the applicants. It may nonetheless be doubted whether causation is relevant for questions of admissibility.

The matter now appears to have been settled by the Court's decision in Case 126/76 *Dietz* v. *Commission* [1977] E.C.R. 2431. In this case the applicants, who alleged that they had been harmed by the Commission's failure to enact proper transitional measures when monetary compensatory amounts were introduced in trade between Germany and Italy in December 1971, initially brought proceedings before the German courts. Indeed, it would appear that they brought their action before the European Court largely to avoid the availability of such a remedy becoming time-barred under the five-year limitation period laid down by article 43 of the Court's Statute. The Commission expressly claimed in the written procedure that the Court had no jurisdiction to hear the case. In its judgment, the Court reverted to the terms it had used in the *Merkur* decision; the Court had the case before it and within its jurisdiction, and therefore must determine whether the alleged omission was such as to make the Community liable in damages.

1–50   It might be noted that successive Advocates-General have opposed the subordination of the Community remedy to the exercise of the national remedy. In his Opinion in Cases 9 and 11/71 *Compagnie d'approvisionnement* v. *Commission* [1972] E.C.R. 391, 412, A.G. Dutheillet de Lamothe pointed out that there was no justification in the Treaty for the view that an action for damages was in any way a subsidiary type of action, and A.G. Mayras in his Opinion in the *Merkur* case (at p. 1082) stated that to require applicants to exhaust national remedies "starts them on a circular route which must inevitably lead them back to where they started, that is, to this Court." M. Mayras also pointed out, as did A.G. Warner in his Opinions in *Lesieur Cotelle* and in Case 126/76 *Dietz* v. *Commission* [1977] E.C.R. 2431, 2448–2449, the difficulties faced by a national court in a case in which the real question at issue is the validity of the exercise of a Community power by a Community institution, since in assessing damages it may well have to try to determine how the Community institution should have exercised its powers. A solution to this problem had been attempted. In its judgment in Cases 124/76 and 20/77 *Moulins de Pont-à-Mousson and others* v. *ONIC* [1977] E.C.R. 1975 the Court held, on two references for a preliminary ruling, that two Council Regulations were incompatible with the principle of equality insofar as they retained a production refund on certain maize products but no others, and declared, in the judgment given on the references, that the Community institutions should take the necessary steps to remedy the incompatibility. In his Opinion in the *Dietz* case, however, Mr. Warner suggested that in these cases the Court "was unable to rule in such a way as to enable the national Courts to grant any effective remedy."

1–51   What appears to be the definitive position was stated in a group of direct actions for damages arising from the abolition of the same refunds and involving some of the same parties. In Joined Cases 64 and 113/76, etc., *Dumortier* v. *Council* [1979] E.C.R. 3091, 3113, it was expressly recognised that, although the applicants had also brought proceedings before the French courts,

> "the actions pending before the French administrative courts are actions for the annulment of the competent national body's refusal to pay refunds. Those national courts have no jurisdiction to rule on the non-contractual liability of the Commission. Thus, as the subject-matter and the legal basis of the actions brought before the national courts and before the Court of Justice are different, the prinicples applicable to concurrency of proceedings, recognised in the national systems of legal procedure, may not be relied on in order to contest the admissibility of the actions brought before the Court of Justice in this case."

It is now therefore accepted that claims for unliquidated damages relating to harm caused by Community acts or omissions may be brought before the European Court irrespective of concurrent national remedies, and the distinction between such a claim and a claim for a sum due under Community legislation was expressly recognised in Joined Cases 241, 242 and 245 to 250/78 *DGV* v. *Council and Commission* [1979] E.C.R. 3017, 3037. Nevertheless, the application of the principle may still give rise to difficulties, in Case 217/81 *Interagra* v. *Commission* (June 10, 1982), claims which might appear to be for unliquidated damages for the harm caused by the Commission's suspension of advance fixing in relation to exports of butter to the U.S.S.R. were construed by the Third Chamber as relating to the issue of advance fixing certificates by the French authorities, and hence within the jurisdiction of the French national courts.

3. *Causation*

1-52 It will have been noted from the cases on jurisdiction that the Court takes a rather narrow view of causation. In Case 12/79 *Wagner* v. *Commission* [1979] E.C.R. 3657, 3670–3671, the dispute related to the refusal by the German authorities to allow the applicant to cancel a sugar export licence on July 1, 1976. The German authorities thought they were acting on the basis of a Commission Regulation which purported to come into force on July 1, 1976. It transpired, however, that because of a strike, the copy of the *Official Journal* containing the Regulation was only published the next day, and it therefore could only enter into force on that day. The view of the Court was that it was the German authorities which had thus acted unlawfully in the absence of binding Community legislation, and the legality of *their* conduct should be challenged before the national courts.

Moving away from jurisdiction, the applicants in Case 90/78 *Granaria* v. *Council and Commission* [1979] E.C.R. 1081 claimed damages arising from the abolition of production refunds on quellmehl; the Court had previously held that this abolition was unlawful only insofar as quellmehl was used in food for human consumption. It was found that Granaria had not shown that their quellmehl was used for the purpose, and so it had not shown that it had been harmed by the abolition of the refunds. More generally, in Joined Cases 197–200, 243, 245 and 247/80 *Ludingshafener Walzmühle Erling* v. *Council and Commission* [1981] E.C.R. 3211, where the applicants, who were German millers of durum wheat, claimed damages for the harm allegedly caused by fixing the threshold price for durum wheat (from which pasta is usually made) at too high a level in comparison with the price of soft wheat, leaving them open to unfair competition, the Court took the view, *inter alia*, that the real cause of the harm suffered by the applicants was the fact that German legislation did not require pasta to be made from durum wheat, leaving pasta manufacturers with the possibility of substituting a certain amount of soft wheat.

4. *Acts for which Liability may be Incurred*

1-53 With regard to wrongful acts committed by individual Community officials, there appears to be a link between the official's personal immunity, under Article 12 of the Protocol on the Privileges and Immunities of the European Communities, and the vicarious liability of the Community. This was established in two cases arising out of the same incident, when a Euratom engineer used his own car to show two official visitors round certain installations, and was involved in an accident in which one of his passengers was seriously injured. In Case 5/68 *Sayag* v. *Leduc* (*No.* 1) [1968] E.C.R. 395, it was held that the immunity enjoyed by officials under the Protocol "in respect of acts performed by them in their official capacity" only covered acts representing a participation of the official in the performance of the tasks of the institution to which he belongs, and did not extend to driving a motor vehicle unless "this activity cannot be carried out otherwise than under the authority of the Community and by its own servants." With regard to the question of the Community's vicarious liability, it was correlatively held in Case 9/69 *Sayag* v. *Luduc (No. 2)* [1969] E.C.R. 329 that "the Community is only liable for these acts of its servants which, by virtue of an internal and direct relationship, are the necessary extension of the tasks entrusted to the institutions," and such liability did not extend to the official's use of his private car unless the Community would otherwise "have been unable to carry out the tasks entrusted to it." It remains to be seen what view would be taken by the national courts of a Member State with a wider concept of vicarious liability.

1–54   Of greater legal interest is the liability of the Communities for the written word. Although it would appear from Case 133/79 *Sucrimex* v. *Commission* [1980] E.C.R. 1299, 1311, that where a national agency acts in reliance upon non-binding information supplied by a Community institution, it is the act of the national agency which is regarded as giving rise to liability (see para. 1–46 above), nevertheless, where there is no such intervening national act the Community may be liable even with regard to a declaration of intention, where that might reasonably be relied upon by those suffering harm as a result. This was held in Case 169/73 *Continentale France* v. *Council* [1975] E.C.R. 117, where the Council published a Resolution in July 1972 indicating the accession compensatory amounts to be applied in agricultural trade with the new Member States during the transition from national price levels to Community price levels following the 1973 Accessions; the resolution made no mention of article 55(6) of the Act of Accession which restricted the maximum level of these compensatory amounts to the level of import levies charged on imports from third countries, covering the difference between lower world prices and Community prices. In fact, world prices rose to such an extent that the levies fell below the compensatory amounts indicated in the Resolution, and the result the applicant, which had contracted in September 1972 to export cereals to the United Kingdom for delivery between February and June 1973 on the assumption that the compensatory amounts indicated in the Resolution would be paid, suffered a loss in performing its contract. It was held that the Council ought to have included in its Resolution a reservation pointing out the limits imposed by the Act of Accession, and that its failure to do so distorted the task of informing which the Council had assumed and was such as to make it liable. However, on the particular facts, it was also found that the applicant "as a prudent exporter," was fully informed of the conditions of the market, and was not, and could not be, unaware of the true position, and hence could not be regarded as misled by the Council's Resolution.

1–55   With regard to binding normative acts, it has consistently been held since Case 5/71 *Schöppenstedt* v. *Council* [1971] E.C.R. 975 that "where legislative action involving measures of economic policy is concerned, the Community does not incur non-contractual liability for damage suffered by individuals as a consequence of that action . . . unless a sufficiently flagrant violation of a superior rule of law for the protection of the individual has occurred," with the substitution of the word "serious" for "flagrant" in more recent judgments. The general principles of Community law recognised by the Court (see para. 1–12 above) may constitute such "superior rules," but the fact that such a principle has been breached may not in itself be sufficiently "serious," as appears from Joined Cases 83 and 94/76, etc., *Bayerische HNL* v. *Council and Commission* [1978] E.C.R. 1209, 1224–1225. The act there at issue was a Regulation effectively requiring manufacturers of animal feeding-stuffs to purchase intervention skimmed milk powder, which was held to breach both the specific principle of non-discrimination enounced in Article 40(2) of the EEC Treaty and the general principle of proportionality. The Court stated that "individuals may be required . . . to accept within reasonable limits certain harmful effects on their economic interests as a result of a legislative measure without being able to obtain compensation form public funds even if that measure has been declared null and void," and it was held that since the Regulation increased production costs only by a little more than 2 per cent., which was considerably smaller that the variations in the world market prices of similar feeding-stuffs, "the effects of the Regulation on the profit-earning capacity of the undertakings did not ultimately exceed the bounds of the economic risks inherent in the activities of the agricultural sectors concerned." By way of contrast, in Case 238/78 *Ireks-Arkady* v. *Council and Commission* [1979] E.C.R. 2955, 2973, where the Regulation at issue had been held to breach the general principle of equality of treatment in so far as it abolished production refunds on quellmehl whilst retaining them for pre-gelatinised starch, it was found that damage alleged to have been caused "goes beyond the bounds of the economic risks inherent in the activities of the sector concerned," although emphasis was also laid on the fact that a limited number of producers were affected and that the termination of the refunds in question ended an equality of treatment with producers of maize starch which had existed since the beginning of the common organisation of the market in cereals (in 1962). In essence, however, it would appear that a breach of a superior rule will be regarded as sufficiently "serious" if the harm caused goes beyond the Court's assessment of the inherent economic risks of the sector concerned.

1–56   Liability for the harm caused by legislative acts may extend not only to a breach of a superior rule arising from the substance of the act, but also from, *e.g.* the circumstances surrounding its introduction. This was established in Case 74/74 *CNTA* v. *Commission* [1975] E.C.R. 533, where it was held that to abolish certain monetary compensatory amounts without allowing any transitional measures in the absence of overriding considerations of public interest breached the applicant's legitimate expectations; the facts arose at a time when monetary compensatory amounts were calculated in terms of the dollar, and the

Court took the view that "a trader may legitimately expect that for transactions irrevocably undertaken by him . . . no unforseeable alteration will occur which could have the effect of causing him inevitable loss, by re-exposing him to the exchange risk." Whilst it may be that a reasonable trader could regard monetary compensatory amounts based on the values of national currencies in terms of the dollar as covering the exchange risk, it may be doubted whether he could so regard the current monetary compensatory amounts, which cover the difference between a "representative rate" for a national currency determined by the Council and the current value of that currency in terms of a basket of Community currencies.

With regard to liability arising from a failure to act, actions for damages have often related to the harm caused by the legislation the institution has failed to amend, rather than to the failure to amend it, as, *e.g.* in Case 153/73 *Holtz and Willemsen* v. *Council* [1974] E.C.R. 675, 692–693. Where it is alleged that harm arises simply from the failure to act, *e.g.* against a Member State for breach of its Treaty obligations, it would appear that in determining the legality of the institution's conduct, the Court will have regard to the question whether a situation existed in which the institution should have intervened, and whether it acted reasonably, or within the scope of its discretion, in not intervening, as in Case 4/69 *Lütticke* v. *Commission* [1971] E.C.R. 325, 337–338 and Case 14/78 *Denkavit* v. *Commission* [1978] E.C.R. 2497, 2505–2507.

5. *Recoverable Loss*

1–57 In the few cases in which it has become relevant to consider the matter, the Court has taken a narrow view of recoverable loss. In the *CNTA* case [1975] E.C.R. 533, 550 it was held that the protection which could be claimed by the applicant was "that of not suffering loss" rather than that of making the profit which would have accrued to it if the relevant monetary compensatory amounts had not been abolished. However, in later proceedings [1976] E.C.R. 797 it emerged that the applicant had not in fact been exposed to an exchange risk against which it might expect to be protected (see para. 1–56 above), so that it had suffered no recoverable loss. Failure to show loss was indeed treated as sufficient reason to dismiss the application in Case 49/79 *Pool* v. *Council* [1980] E.C.R. 569, 581–582. In Case 238/78 *Ireks-Arkady* v. *Council and Commission* [1979] E.C.R. 2955, 2974, where, following the abolition of production refunds on quellmehl the applicant claimed to have sold at a loss in order to retain its markets, the Court took the view that the loss for which the applicant should be compensated must be calculated as being equivalent to the refunds which would have been paid to it if during the relevant period the use of maize for the manufacturer of quellmehl intended for use in the bakery industry had conferred a right to the same refunds as the use of maize for the manufacture of starch. Since this was one of a group of similar cases involving manufacturers in more than one Member State, and since the relevant period was over three years, this left problems as to the rates at which the refunds, which are calculated in units of account (ECU), should be converted into national currencies. The practical solution adopted in a judgment of May 19, 1982 was to convert the refunds expressed in ECU's into national currencies at the rate prevailing on the date of the judgment on the question of liability.

In this group of cases the Court also considered the question of interest, concluding that it should be payable at a rate of 6 per cent. from the date of the judgment on the question of liability (see, *e.g.* [1979] E.C.R. 2955, p. 2975), on the basis that the obligation to make good the damage was established by that judgment. However, as A.G. Warner poined out in his Opinion in a staff case, Case 115/76 *Leonardini* v. *Commission* [1978] E.C.R. 735, 754, a distinction may be made between the award of interest from a specified date on a sum awarded by way of damages (the power exercised in *Ireks-Arkady et. al.*), and the award of interest as compensation for a wrongful delay. In *Leonardini*, the claim related expressly to the award of interest for the belated payment of a lump sum relating to the applicant's partial permanent invalidity, the amount of which was not itself in dispute. In the circumstances, the First Chamber held that the Commission should pay "default interest" (*i.e.* interest as damages) at the rate of 8 per cent. per annum from September 1, 1968, taken as a "reasonable" date in relation to an accident which occurred in April 1966, until September 30, 1976 when the lump sum was paid, and that it shold pay interest at the rate of 8 per cent. on the amount of "default interest" thus obtained from October 1, 1976 until it was actually paid, so reflecting the distinction made by A.G. Warner.

E. ARBITRATION

1–58 Under all three Treaties, two types of arbitration are provided for, the common factor being an agreement conferring jurisdiction on the European Court. In the numerotation of the EEC Treaty, Article 182 accepts such jurisdiction "in any dispute between Member States which relates to the subject matter of this Treaty" and Article 181 accepts such jurisdiction pursuant to a clause contained in a contract concluded by or on behalf of the Community. It is under this latter provision that the Court may hear contractual disputes involving parties other than Community officials, and two chief problems have been encountered; the first relates to the determination of whether there is a clause conferring jurisdiction on the Court, and the second to the application of the proper law of the contract. The first problem was clearly encountered in Case 23/76 *Pellegrini* v. *Commission* [1976] E.C.R. 1807. Pellegrini had since 1960 had the contract for cleaning the Nuclear Research Centre at Ispra. In 1971 the Commission invited tenders for a three-year contract commencing in 1972 on the basis of a draft agreement it had drawn up. Pellegrini was an unsuccessful tenderer, but, following the withdrawal of the successful tenderer, the Commission asked Pellegrini to continue for two months, subject to the terms and conditions of the draft agreement. This arrangement was confirmed in writing and renewed for periods of one to three months at a time until December 1975, when following a fresh invitation to tender, Pellegrini was informed that a tender from another firm had been accepted. One of the clauses of this draft agreement conferred jurisdiction in disputes relating to the agreement on the Court, and it was held that the exchange of letters between the Commission and Pellegrini read together with the draft agreement to which they referred had the effect of conferring jurisdiction on the Court—a conclusion on which both the parties were in fact agreed. Under the terms of the draft agreement, it was expressed to be governed by Italian law, but the problems of the interpretation and application by the European Court of a national law governing the contact are perhaps more apparent in Case 109/81 *Pace (née Porta)* v. *Commission* (July 1, 1982). The applicant here had been employed as a teacher at the technical school attached to the Ispra Centre from 1963 to 1980, for the first five years without a contract, then under a series of annual contract-letters, and from 1976 on a series of more formal contracts which contained an arbitration clause conferring jurisdiction on the European Court and which were expressed to be governed by Italian law; the Court held that, acting under the jurisdiction conferred by these last contracts, it could take account also of the earlier relationship between the parties. The substantive question raised was entirely a matter of Italian law; the applicant claimed that under that law she should be regarded as having been employed under an indeterminate contract of service, with all the consequences that entailed as to, *e.g.* payment during school holidays, and, most importantly, pension rights. The First Chamber thereupon followed Italian case law to hold that the applicant was an employee rather than an independent contractor, and applied Italian legislation on fixed-term contracts of employment, under which all conracts of employment are deemed to be indeterminate unless they fall within defined exceptions, which were not relevant in this case. It was therefore held that the applicant was entitled to the benefits of an indeterminate contract of service under Italian law, and that the Commission must pay her the equivalent of the Italian pension she would have been entitled to if the Commission had not failed to pay any contributions on her behalf. It was perhaps fortunate that both the President of the First Chamber and the Advocate-General in this case were Italian lawyers.

F. RULINGS AND OPINIONS

1–59 In certain circumstances, the Court is required to advise other institutions or the Member States. Requests for Opinions under Article 95(4) of the ECSC Treaty relate to amendments of that Treaty, and are presented jointly by the Commission and the Special Council, so that there is unlikely to be a dispute before the Court, although the Court may still reject the proposed amendment as in Opinion 1/59 [1959] E.C.R. 259. Requests for Opinions under Article 228 of the EEC Treaty and for Rulings under Article 103 of the Euratom Treaty relate to the compatibility of proposed international agreements with the relevant Community rules. The procedural differences between these provisions are discussed elsewhere (see para. 13–03 below), but it is clear from Opinion 1/75 [1975] E.C.R. 1355, 1360 that the Court's jurisdiction does not depend on the formal designation of the act at issue if it is an "undertaking entered into by entities subject to international law which has binding force." It was also there held that the Court's jurisdiction extends not only to the substance of the proposed agreement but also to the question of competence to enter it, a view applied also in the context of the Euratom Treaty in Ruling 1/78 [1978] E.C.R. 2151, 2167.

Finally, it may be noted that requests for Rulings under Articles 104 and 105 of the Euratom Treaty relate to agreements or contracts concluded by persons or undertakings.

G. ANCILLIARY AND SPECIAL PROCEDURES

1. *Ancillary Procedures*

1–60 A number of ancillary or incidental remedies are available in direct actions before the European Court, notably interim measures, intervention by third parties, third party proceedings, the rectification, interpretation and revision of judgments, the grant of legal aid (which is also expressly available on references for preliminary rulings), and orders on costs. These being essentially procedural matters, each is considered in its own context in the main part of this book.

2. *Special Procedures*

1–61 Under all three Treaties, more specific versions of the general remedies already decribed are envisaged. As an illustration, Article 180 of the EEC Treaty regulates actions for annulment and enforcement proceedings relating the the European Investment Bank, and Articles 21, 38, 81, 82 and 145 of the Euratom Treaty contain special enforcement procedures (for the texts see paras. 2–09 and 2–49 below). On the other hand, there are also special remedies which are *sui generis*, such as the fixing of terms of a licence under Article 12 of the Euratom Treaty, appeals against the Arbitration Committee under Article 18 of that Treaty relating to the grant of licences, and inspection order under Article 81 of the Treaty (though this may also be viewed as a special enforcement procedure). Insofar as these special remedies involve variations from the basic procedure before the Court, they are considered in the relevant context (see paras. 14–03 and 14–05 below).

H. DISCIPLINARY POWERS

1–62 Although the matter will not be considered elsewhere in this book, it may be noted that under Articles 10 and 13 of the 1965 Merger Treaty, the Court has jurisdiction compulsorily to retire a member of the

Commission on application by the Council or Commission, if the member breaches his duty not to engage in any other occupation, or no longer fulfils the conditions required for the performance of his duties, or has been guilty of serious misconduct.

Similarly, under all three Statutes of the Court the Court exercises disciplinary jurisdiction over its own members. Article 6 of the EEC and Euratom Statutes provides that a judge may be deprived of his office or other benefits if, in the unanimous opinion of the other judges and Advocates-General, he "no longer fulfils the requisite conditions or meets the obligations arising from his office," and article 8 applies the same rule to Advocates-General. Articles 7 and 13 of the ECSC Statute contain differences in drafting: with regard to a judge, the decision is to be taken only by the other judges, and in the case of an Advocate-General, the actual decision is to be taken by the Council after the Court has delivered its opinion. Given, however, that Articles 3 and 4 of the Convention on Certain Institutions Common to the European Communities signed at the same time as the EEC and Euratom Treaties provide for a single Court of Justice, there would appear to be scope only for the application of one set of rules in the context of the status of its members, so that the special ECSC rules may perhaps be regarded as redundant.

REFERENCES FOR PRELIMINARY RULINGS

A. Courts and Tribunals

1–63 From the practical point of view, the aim of the system of references for premlinary rulings, at least in the forms set out in the EEC and Euratom Treaties, is to enable a national court before which a question of Community law is at issue to refer the question of its interpretation or validity to the European Court. The essential point, which was emphasised in Case 44/65 *Hessische Knappschaft* v. *Singer* [1965] E.C.R. 965, is that the procedure is available to national courts as such, not to the parties appearing before those courts, so that the parties may not go beyond the scope of the questions referred by the national court. Hence, it is vital to know what constitutes a court or tribunal in this context. The question appears first to have been discussed in Case 61/65 *Vaassen (née Goebbels)* v. *Beambtenfords voor het Mijnbedrijf* [1966] E.C.R. 261, 273, where a reference was made by a "Scheidsgerecht," a Dutch social security arbitration tribunal. It was found that this tribunal was permanently established, and was entrusted with the settlement of disputes relating to a particular social security scheme, and that those covered by the scheme were bound to take disputes between themselves and their insurer to that tribunal. Hence it fell within the scope of Article 177. Similar criteria were applied with regard to private arbitration in Case 102/81 *Nordsee* v. *Nordstern* (March 23, 1982), but here it was found that the parties were under no obligation to go to arbitration and that the public authorities had not entrusted any particular role to the arbitrator in this situation, so that, even though the arbitrator was bound to apply the law and his decision would be binding, he did not constitute a court or tribunal under Article 177. It would further appear that status as a court or tribunal depends not so much on the body making the reference (indeed the arbitrator in *Nordsee* was in fact a judge) as on the function it is performing. In Case 138/80 *Borker* [1980] E.C.R. 1975 where a reference was made by the "Conseil de l'Ordre des Avocates á la Cour de Paris' " the Court declined jurisdiction not because of the nature of that body but because the case before it was not one which it was under a legal duty to try, being a request for a declaration relating to a dispute between a member of the Bar and the courts or tribunals of another Member State, rather than a matter internal to the Paris Bar.

1–64   In the United Kingdom, rules have been made governing references from specified courts: in England, from the Court of Appeal (Civil and Criminal Divisions), High Court, Crown Court and County Court, in Scotland, from the Court of Session, High Court of Justiciary and Sheriff Court, and in Northern Ireland, from the Court of Appeal, Court of Criminal Appeal, High Court and County Court. These rules, however, in no way prejudge the question of which courts and tribunals may make a reference, whether it be the House of Lords, as in Case 34/79 *R.* v. *Henn and Darby* [1979] E.C.R. 3795, the Special Commissioners, as in Case 208/80 *Bruce of Donington* v. *Aspden* [1981] E.C.R. 2205, or a Northern Irish resident magistrate, as in Case 83/78 *Pigs Marketing Board* v. *Redmond* [1978] E.C.R. 2347.

1–65   By way of contrast, the Protocol on the interpretation by the Court of Justice of the Convention of September 27, 1968 on jurisdiction and the enforcement of judgments in civil and commercial matters, as amended by the Convention of Accession of the U.K., Ireland and Denmark, hereinafter referred to as the "1968 Convention," lists by name the court which may make a reference for a preliminary ruling:

Article 2

The following courts may request the Court of Justice to give preliminary rulings on questions of interpretation:
1. — in Belgium; la Cour de Cassation—het Hof van Cassatie and le Conseil d'Etat—de Raad van State,
   — in Denmark: hojesteret,
   — in the Federal Republic of German: die obersten Gerichtshöfe des Bundes,
   — in France: la Cour de Cassation and le Conseil d'Etat,
   — in Ireland: the Supreme Court,
   — in Italy: la Corte Suprema di Cassazione,
   — in Luxembourg: la Cour superieure de Justice when sitting as Cour de Cassation,
   — in the Netherlands: de Hoge Raad,
   — in the United Kingdom: the House of Lords and courts to which application has been made under the second paragraph of Article 37 or under Article 41 of the Convention:
2. the courts of the Contracting States when they are sitting in an appellate capacity;

3. in the cases provided for in Article 37 of the Convention, the courts referred to in that Article.

(Article 37 lists the courts with which an appeal may be lodged against a decision authorising enforcement, and Article 41 lists the courts to which an appeal may be made against a judgment itself given on appeal against a decision refusing an application for enforcement.)

The listed courts are all acting in an appellate capacity, and the policy would appear to be avoid delay in reaching the basic decision as to jurisdiction or enforcement, as is indicated in the Report of the drafting Committee (O.J. 1979, C59 at pp. 67–69). It may, however, be noted that Article 4 of the Protocol (see para. 2–61 below) extends the power to make a reference beyond courts and tribunals to the "competent authority" of a contracting state where there are conflicting interpretations of a relevant provision.

B. Questions Which May be Referred

1–66   There are differences in drafting between the three basic Treaties as to the questions which may be referred to the European Court. Under Article 41 of the ECSC Treaty, only questions as to the validity of acts of the Commission may be referred, whereas under the EEC and Euratom Treaties questions may be referred as to the validity of "acts of the institutions of the Community," a term which would appear to be wide enough to cover acts of the European Parliament, even though its acts are not expressed to be directly susceptible to challenged under those Treaties. The Protocol on the interpretation of the 1968 Convention, on the other hand, makes no provision for questions of validity, being concerned only with Treaties rather than secondary legislation. Whilst the ECSC Treaty makes no provision for questions of mere interpretation, the EEC and Euratom Treaties enable preliminary rulings to be given as to the interpretation of the respective Treaties and for the interpretation of "acts of the institutions of the Community" as well as of "the statutes of bodies established by an act of the Council"; in this last case, however, Article 177 of the EEC Treaty confers jurisdiction "where those statutes so provide" whereas Article 150 of the Euratom Treaty confers jurisdiction "save where these statutes provide otherwise,"a subtle distinction for which the draftsman presumably had reason. The Protocol on the interpretation of 1968 Convention as amended allows more specifically, as might be expected, for the interpretation of that Convention and the Protocol annexed to it, for the interpretation of the interpretation Protocol itself, and for the intereptretation of the Convention on the accession of the U.K., Denmark and Ireland to these instruments.

Whilst the question of the scope of the questions which may be referred will be considered in the context of the admissibility of references for preliminary rulings (see para. 4–95 below), certain basic rules may be indicated here. The question must, on the face of it, relate to a matter of Community law, which was not the case in *e.g.* Case 93/75

47

Alderblum v. *Caisse Nationale d'Assurance Vieillesse* [1975] E.C.R. 2147; provided it does, the Court will be willing to extract from it the aspects which it has jurisdiction to answer, as has been consistently held since Case 6/64 *Costa* v. *ENEL* [1964] E.C.R. 585, but the Court may look behind the reference to ascertain whether the question of Community law is necessary to the settlement of a genuine dispute before the national court, as in Case 104/79 *Foglia* v. *Novello* [1980] E.C.R. 745.

C. NECESSITY TO ORDER A REFERENCE

1–67   The basic precondition to making a reference for a preliminary ruling under the EEC and Euratom Treaties and under the Protocol on the interpretation of the 1968 Convention is that the national court "considers that a decision on the question is necessary to enable it to give judgment." The view of the European Court has in principle been that the assessment of such necessity is a matter for the national court, even where the question (at least on a point of interpretation, see para. 4–100 below) has already been answered in another case, as in Joined Cases 28, 29 and 30/62 *Da Costa* v. *Nederlandse Belastingadministratie* [1963] E.C.R. 31. General guidelines were, however, mentioned in Joined Cases 36 and 71/80 *Irish Creamery Milk Supplies* v. *Ireland* [1981] E.C.R. 735, 748, where it was suggested that it "might be convenient" in certain circumstances for the facts to be established and for questions of purely national law to be settled before a reference is made to the European Court, "so as to enable the latter to take cognizance of all the features of fact and of law which may be relevant." However, it was emphasised that this was not intended to restrict the discretion of the national court "which is . . . in the best position to appreciate at what stage in the proceedings it requires a preliminary ruling"; the reference in that case was in fact made by the Irish court on an interlocutory motion on the basis that it involved a pure question of Community law to be determined independently of the facts which were in dispute. In his Opinion, A.G. Warner also pointed out ([1981] E.C.R. at p. 789) that cases do arise where the national court cannot be sure what the relevant issues of fact are until it has received a preliminary ruling on the relevant rules of Community law. Indeed, in Case 43/71 *Politi* v. *Italy* [1971] E.C.R. 1039, 1047–1048, the Court was expressly willing to accept a reference made in *ex parte* proceedings without the defendant having been heard, a view it had already impliedly taken and has subsequently maintained.

1–68   On the whole, this approach has been accepted by courts in the United Kingdom. However, as Graham J. pointed out in *Löwenbräu* v. *Grunhalle* [1974] 1 C.M.L.R. 1, 10, there is a double aspect to necessity: that the resolution of the question of Community law should be necessary to enable judgment to be given, and that the national court should feel it necessary to seek the assistance of the European Court to resolve that question. The former aspect has given rise to little difficulty; indeed, in *EMI* v. *CBS* [1975] 1 C.M.L.R. 285, 297, he himself did in fact in interlocutory proceedings refer a series of questions to the European Court the answers to which he thought would be "necessary" to enable him to give final judgment even though they were not necessary to enable him to give a decision in the interlocutory proceedings, and in fact he issued an injunction to preserve the status quo whilst the matter was before the European Court; also in making the order for reference in *Polydor* v. *Harlequin Record Shops* [1980] 2 C.M.L.R. 413, 428, Ormrod L.J. stated that he would regard the word "necessary" as meaning "reasonably necessary" in ordinary English, and not "unavoidable."

1–69 The latter aspect has, however, given rise to greater differences of opinion. In his famous judgment in *Bulmer* v. *Bollinger* [1974] 2 C.M.L.R. 97, Lord Denning M.R. accepted, *inter alia,* the "acte clair" theory, stating that if the English court considers a point reasonably clear and free from doubt, "there is no need to interpret the Treaty but only to apply it," and effectively suggesting that an English court should decide a point of Community law for itself unless it is difficult and important. However, on two occasions on which the English Court of Appeal has interpreted Community law for itself, it has incurred the disapproval of the House of Lords. In *Schorsch Meier* v. *Hennin* [1975] 1 All E.R. 152, the civil division of the Court of Appeal, including Lord Denning, without applying the usual criteria to determine whether a provision produces direct effects, and despite the opposite view of the Judge at first instance, held that Article 106 of the EEC Treaty, which appears in the section of the Treaty entitled "Balance of Payments" and related to the liberalisation of payments, overruled the principle of English law that judgment could only be given in sterling, and hence that a German creditor could receive payment of a debt calculated in deutschmarks in German currency rather than in devalued pounds. However, in a disapproving comment on that decision in the later House of Lords case of *Miliangos* v. *Frank* [1975] 3 All E.R. 801, 810–811, which however involved a non-Community currency, it was stated in strong terms by Lord Wilberforce, with whom Lords Simon and Cross concurred, that "any other court in which such issues may arise would be well advised to refer them to the European Court for clarification." The second case was *R.* v. *Henn and Darby* [1978] 3 All E.R. 1190, 1195, where the Criminal Division of the Court of Appeal held that a question as to the interpretation of restrictions on imports justified on grounds of public morality or public policy within the meaning of Article 36 of the EEC Treaty was "too clear to be argued." On further appeal to the House of Lords, however, the point was referred to the European Court for a preliminary ruling as Case 34/79 *R.* v. *Henn and Darby* [1979] E.C.R. 3795.

1–70 The current approach of the House of Lords is perhaps best illustrated by the speech of Lord Diplock in *Garland* v. *BREL* [1982] 2 C.M.L.R. 174, 179, explaining why a reference was made in that case: "There was not . . . so considerable and consistent a line of case law of the European Court . . . as would make the answer too obvious and inevitable to be capable of giving rise to what could properly be regarded as 'a question' within the meaning of Article 177." The presumption would therefore appear to be that a reference should be made in the absence of a decision of the European Court on the point, always assuming, as was noted by Pennycuick V.-C. in ordering a reference in *Van Duyn* v. *Home Office* [1974] 1 C.M.L.R. 347, 357, that the point is arguable.

D. The Obligation to Refer

1–71   Under the EEC and Euratom Treaties, if a relevant question is raised before a court or tribunal "against whose decisions there is no judicial remedy under national law," that court or tribunal "shall" bring the matter before the European Court, and the Protocol on the interpretation of the 1968 Convention imposes the same obligation on the courts named in Article 2(1) of that Protocol (see para. 1–65 above). The European Court itself has had little occasion to consider these provisions, although it was suggested by A.G. Warner in his Opinion in Case 9/75 *Meyer-Burckhardt* v. *Commission* [1975] E.C.R. at 1187 that failure to comply with them was amenable to enforcement proceedings by the Commission under, in that case, Article 169 of the EEC Treaty. However in Case 107/76 *Hoffman-LaRoche* v. *Centrafarm* [1977] E.C.R. 957, the Court held that a national court from which there is no appeal in interlocutory proceedings is not *bound* to refer a question— although it *may* do so if it desires—if the point at issue can be reconsidered, with the consequent possiblity of a reference, in the substantive proceedings.

Further guidance has now been given by the Court in Case 283/81 *CILFIT* v. *Italian Ministry of Health* (October 6, 1982) on a reference from the Italian supreme civil court. There it was pointed out that the mere fact that a party contends that there is a question of the interpretation of Community law does not in itself mean that a court against whose decisions there is no judicial remedy is obliged to order a reference; such a court retains the discretion to decide whether a decision on the question is necessary to enable it to give judgment. Thus, there would be no obligation to order a reference where the question has already been dealt with by the European Court. Perhaps of greater importance, however, is that the Court recognised that "the correct application of Community law may be so obvious as to leave no reasonable doubt as to the manner in which the question raised is to be resolved." It nevertheless emphasised that the national court must be convinced that the matter is equally obvious to the courts of the other Member States and to the Court of Justice, bearing in mind that Community legislation is drafted in several equally authentic languages, that Community law uses its own terminology, that legal concepts do not necessarily have the same meaning in Community law and in the laws of the Member States, and that provisions of Community law should be interpreted in their context and in the light of the objectives of Community law and of the state of its evolution at the relevant time. It might respectfully be suggested that the court most easily able to apply those criteria is the European Court itself, and that the national court would probably find it more convenient to order a reference.

1–72   In the United Kingdom, it is clear that the House of Lords is bound by this obligation, as is the Scottish High Court of Justiciary in criminal matters. Less obvious is the situation where there is no appeal as such from a lower court, or appeal is subject to leave. In the former case, it was held by a National Insurance Commissioner in *Re a Holiday in Italy* [1975] 1 C.M.L.R. 184, 188 (decided before a right of appeal against decisions of the re-named Social Security Commissioner was introduced by section 14 of the Social Security Act 1980), that since his decision could be set aside by an order of *certiorari* he did not constitute a tribunal against whose decision there is no judicial remedy, even though an application for *certiorari* required the leave of the High Court. The problem of a right of appeal being subject to leave has arisen particularly with regard to the English Court of Appeal. Although Lord Denning M.R. suggested in *Bulmer* v. *Bollinger* [1974] 2 All E.R. 1226, 1233 that only the House of Lords was obliged to make a reference, it was expressly stated by Buckley L.J. in *Hagen* v. *Moretti* [1980] 3 C.M.L.R. 253, 255 that the Court of Appeal also fell within the scope of the obligation to make a reference if leave to appeal against its decision was refused; this presumably would mean that the Court of Appeal might be obliged to order a reference after having given its substantive judgement.

The effects of an appeal against a decision of a lower court ordering a reference for a preliminary ruling are discussed in the context of the written procedure in references for preliminary rulings (see para. 4–103 below).

E. Availability of Direct Actions

1–73   As has already been observed, the system of references for preliminary rulings has enabled individual litigants, through their national courts, to bring before the European Court questions as to the validity of Community legislation which they could not have challenged directly, as in Case 24/75 *Petroni* .v. *ONPTS* [1975] E.C.R. 1149, or to bypass the institutional enforcement procedures, as in Joined Cases 80 and 81/77 *Ramel* v. *Receveur des Douanes* [1978] E.C.R. 927. The problem remains, however, whether the Court may consider on a reference for a preliminary ruling the validity of an act which the parties to the national proceedings could have challenged directly. This particular fact situation was raised directly in Case 218/82 *Hamburg University* v. *HZA Hamburg-Kehrwieder* (commencement of proceedings, O.J. 1982 C230/3), but Case 59/77 *De Bloos* v. *Bouyer* [1977] E.C.R. 2359 was not very far removed from it. It arose from a dispute between the parties to an exclusive dealing contract which had been notified and which the Commission had stated in a letter in 1969 to be capable of benefiting from exemption by categories under Regulation 67/67 (J.O. 849/67). One of the parties to the domestic action, which was commenced in 1973, wished to invoke the invalidity of the agreement and of the

Commission's assessment of it, and the Belgian court asked, *inter alia*, whether a Community act which is being challenged by a party who is out of time for bringing proceedings under Article 173, can be called in question before a national court under Article 177. The Court avoided answering that question by holding that in any event the agreement was an "old" one to which, on the established case law, the national court must give effect. However, in Case 156/77 *Commission* v. *Belgium* [1978] E.C.R. 1881 albeit in the context of a discussion as to whether a Member State can invoke the "plea of illegality" under Article 184 to contest the validity of a decision it could have challenged under Article 173, the Court has expressly recognised that the validity of a Community act can always be queried under Article 177 even if the time-limit for challenging it under Article 173 has expired, the justification being that Article 177 is available in relation to any Community act, and was intended for the sole benefit of national *courts* (presumably: rather than individual parties). In his Opinion in *De Bloos* [1977] E.C.R. 2359, 2376–2377, however, A.G. Mayras suggested that the validity of the letter could not be considered under Article 177, for two reasons. The second, which would not be relevant if a genuine decision were at issue, was that the letter was a mere internal instruction; the first was that to assess its validity would amount to assessing the compatibility of a specific contract with Article 85 or Regulation 67/67, *i.e.* applying Community law to a particular case, whereas in M. Mayras' view that could only be done within the framework of proceedings for annulment under Article 173 or where it devolves upon the national court to apply Community law to a specific case. It is however submitted that if Article 177 is at the service of the national courts, the Court must answer any questions they put which fall within its scope (see para. 4–94 below).

1–74   Finally, it is now clear from the second *Brasserie de Haecht* case [1973] E.C.R. 7, and from Case 127/73 *BRT* v. *SABAM* [1974] E.C.R. 51, that a reference for a preliminary ruling may be made by a national court in proceedings arising from an agreement or practice with regard to which procedures have been commenced before the Commission under Regulation 17/62 (J.O. 204/62) implementing the EEC competition Rules. This is on the basis that the provision of Regulation 17/62 conferring jursidiction on the Commission cannot prevent interested individuals from invoking the direct effect of the relevant Treaty rules before their national courts (see [1974] E.C.R. 51, 63, paras. 17 and 20) and cannot fetter the discretion of these courts to refer a request for a preliminary ruling to the European Court. It is however subject to an exception explained on grounds of legal certainty and to considerations of practicality; on grounds of legal certainty, it is held that "old" agreements (*i.e.* those entered into before the entry into force of Regulation 17/62 or the Accession of a new Member State, where they relate to new Member States) may not be declared void by a national court, at least where they have been duly notified to the Commission, until the Commission has taken a decision on them or has indicated that it does not contemplate taking a decision on them. This last point appears from case 99/79 *Lancôme* v. *Etos* [1980] E.C.R. 2511, 2535, where a senior Commission official had sent the undertaking concerned a letter indicating that in the Commission's opinion there was no need to take further action in respect of the 'old' contract in question, and it was held that the national court must therefore proceed to judgment, taking the letter into account as a non-binding factor. On grounds of practicality, it appears from the *Brasserie de Haecht* and *BRT* v. *SABAM* cases that the national court should consider whether there is cause to suspend the proceedings to await the outcome of the procedure before the Commission, but that it should continue to judgment if it decides either that the agreement or behaviour in dispute is clearly not capable of having any appreciable effect on competition or on trade between Member States, or that there is no doubt that the agreement or behaviour is incompatible with Article 85 or Article 86 of the EEC Treaty. In so far as this could nonetheless lead to differences of approach between the European Court on a reference, and the Commission under Regulation 17/62, it may be recalled that in Case 19/77 *Miller* v. *Commission* [1978] E.C.R. 131, 161, A.G. Warner suggested, albeit in a somewhat different context, that the Commission's competition decisions are not law-creating.

appear, more than 80,000 Euros. In *Enrail* (No. 1) EC R 2515, 2519
where a legal Commission official had seen the unfair advantage required
and that indication that in the Commission's opinion there is no need to
take further action to regulate the said antitrust situation, and it was
held that the antitrust court may therefore proceed to judgment taking
the latter into account as a non-binding factor. On grounds of
practicality, it appears from the Enrail case *Enrail* and *BRT* v
SABAM case that the antitrust court should consider, whether there is
one, to suspend the proceedings to await the outcome of the proceedings
before the Commission, but that it should undertake its judgment if it
decides either that the agreement or behaviour in dispute is clearly not
capable of having an appreciable effect on competition or on trade
between Member States, or that there is no doubt that the agreement or
behaviour is incompatible with Article 85, or Article 86 of the EEC
Treaty. In so far as this could nonetheless lead to differences of
approach between the European Court on a reference, and the
Commission under Regulation 17/62, it may be hoped that in *Case*
16/72 *Wilhelm v Commission* [1974] ECR ..., [Article 9] of Wilmot
suggested, that in a somewhat different context, that the Commission's
and competition decisions are not law creating.

Part II

Procedure

CHAPTER 2

LIMITATION PERIODS

DIRECT ACTIONS

A. GENERAL PRINCIPLES

EEC Statute of the Court
Article 42

2–01   Periods of grace based on considerations of distance shall be determined by the rules of procedure.

No right shall be prejudiced in consequence of the expiry of a time limited if the party concerned proves the existence of unforseeable circumstances or of force majeure.

(Article 43 of the Euratom Statute and the second and third paragraphs of article 39 of the ECSC Statute are in identical terms.)

Rules of Procedure
Article 37

3. All pleadings shall bear a date. In the reckoning of time limits for taking steps in proceedings, the only relevant date shall be that of lodgment at the Registry.

Article 80

1. In the reckoning of any period of time prescribed by the ECSC, EEC or Euratom Treaties, the Statutes of the Court or these rules for the taking of any procedural step, the day of the event from which the period is to run shall be excluded.

Time shall continue to run during vacations.

2. If the period would otherwise end on a Sunday or on an official holiday it shall be extended until the end of the first following working day.

A list of official holidays drawn up by the Court shall be published in the *Official Journal of the European Communities*.

Article 81

2–02   2. The extension, on account of distance, of prescribed time limits shall be provided for in a decision of the Court which shall be published in the *Official Journal of the European Communities*.

ANNEX I

DECISION ON OFFICIAL HOLIDAYS

THE COURT OF JUSTICE OF THE EUROPEAN COMMUNITIES

Having regard to Article 80(2) of the Rules of Procedure requiring the Court to draw up a list of official holidays.

HAS DECIDED AS FOLLOWS:

Article 1

For the purposes of Article 80(2) of the Rules of Procedure the following shall be official holidays:

New Year's Day;
Easter Monday;
1 May;
Ascension Day;
Whit Monday;
23 June;
24 June, where 23 June is a Sunday
15 August;
1 November;
25 December;
26 December.

The official holidays referred to in the first paragraph hereof shall be those observed at the place where the Court of Justice has its seat.

Article 2

Article 80(2) of the Rules of Procedure shall apply only to the official holidays mentioned in Article 1 of this Decision.

Article 3

This Decision, which shall constitute Annex 1 to the Rules of Procedure, shall enter into force on the same day as those rules.

It shall be published in the *Official Journal of the European Communities*.

ANNEX II

DECISION ON EXTENSION OF TIME LIMITS ON ACCOUNT OF DISTANCE

THE COURT OF JUSTICE OF THE EUROPEAN COMMUNITIES

Having regard to Article 81(2) of the Rules of Procedure relating to the extension of procedural time limits on account of distance.

HAS DECIDED AS FOLLOWS:

Article 1

In order to take account of distance, procedural time limits for all parties save those habitually resident in the Grand Duchy of Luxembourg shall be extended as follows
—for the Kingdom of Belgium: two days,
—for the Federal Republic of Germany, the European territory of the French Republic and the European territory of the Kingdom of the Netherlands: six days,
—for the European territory of the Kingdom of Denmark, for the Hellenic Republic, for Ireland, for the Italian Republic and for the United Kingdom: 10 days,
—for other European countries and territories: two weeks,
—for other countries, departments and territories: one month.

Article 2

This Decision, which shall constitute Annex II to the Rules of Procedure, shall enter into force on the same day as those rules.

It shall be published in the *Official Journal of the European Communities*.

2–03 Although the length, commencement and even existence of limitation periods vary according to the provisions under which an action is brought, it is clear from article 37(3) of the Rules of Procedure that it is the date of lodgment of the application which determines whether or not an action has been brought in time. Thus when in Joined Cases 36 to 38, 40 and 41/58 *Simet* v. *H.A.* [1959] E.C.R. 157, 165, it was argued that the date of posting should be taken into consideration, the Court held such a claim to be "in contradiction with" the wording of the Rules of Procedure, pointing out that it would nullify any justification for the extensions on account of distance provided for in article 81(2) and Annex II of the Rules. If an application lodged after the expiry of the relevant time-limit, this, as was formally held in Joined Cases 220 and 221/78 *ALA and ALFER* v. *Commission* [1979] E.C.R. l693, 1698, is a matter which is not capable of being rectified. Indeed, it has long been held that the observance of time-limits is a matter of public policy which may be examined by the Court of its own motion: in Joined Cases 32 and 33/58 *SNUPAT* v. *H.A.* [1959] E.C.R. 127, 138, the Court examined whether the time-limits relating to a failure to act under Article 35 of the ECSC Treaty had been observed, even though the defendant did not raise any objections to the admissibility of the action, and in fact found that the action was admissible. Similarly, in Case 4/67 *Muller (née Collignan)* v. *Commission* [1967] E.C.R. 365, 372, the First Chamber stated that, although the Commission was reluctant to take the point, "the periods for instituting proceedings are mandatory in nature and are not subject to the discretion of the parties or of the Court" and held the application to be out of time; also in Case 33/72 *Grunnella* v. *Commission* [1973] E.C.R. 475, 480, where a claim that the application was out of time was made only at the hearing, the

Second Chamber held that since time-limits are a matter of public interest, it was for the Court to examine whether they had been observed even of its own motion (see above para. 4–69).

2–04   Against this background of a strict enforcement of time-limits, three possibilities for their extension are provided in the Statutes and Rules of Procedure. With regard to the basic calculation, article 80 of the Rules, after providing that time starts to run the day after the relevant event (which had been treated as a generally accepted rule in *SNUPAT* [1959] E.C.R. at 138), provides that if the period would otherwise end on a Sunday or an official holiday, it shall be extended to the end of the first following working day; it may be noted that the list of official holidays contained in Annex I to the Rules was amended in 1981 following Greek Accession to make it clear that the Easter Monday, Ascension Day and Whit Monday there referred to are those celebrated in Luxembourg. Secondly, article 81(2) of the Rules implementing the first sentence of article 42 of the Statute allows for extensions on account of distance from Luxembourg. As was pointed out in Joined Cases 36 to 38, 40 and 41/58 *Simet* v. *H.A.* [1959] E.C.R. 157, 165, these extensions are the correlative of the fact that account is taken only of the date of lodgment and not of the date of posting in determining whether an action has been brought in time, and in effect they provide a flat-rate compensation for postal delays. Annex II to the Rules, which lists these extensions, does not expressly state the relevant connecting factor between the country and the party, except that it excludes those "habitually resident" in Luxembourg. Nevertheless, it appears from Case 28/65 *Fonzi* v. *Commission* [1966] E.C.R. 477, that what is relevant is current residence during the proceedings: there the applicant, a Euratom official who had been employed at the research centre at Ispra, in Italy, and who was challenging a decision to second him to Brussels, was held to be entitled only to the two-day extension appropriate to Belgium since he was actually working in Brussels at the relevant time. It was also held to be irrelevant that he was represented by an Italian advocate with chambers in Milan; the First Chamber stated that what was to be considered was "the habitual place of residence of the parties, not of their lawyers"—a view which might well discourage the employment of lawyers from more distant Member States.

2–05   The third possibility for extension is the most general: article 42 of the EEC Statute and its equivalents in the other Statutes allow a party to prove the existence of "unforeseeable circumstances" or of "force majeure." As was noted in Case 158/73 *Kampffmeyer* v. *Einfuhr-und Vorratsstelle Getreide* [1974] E.C.R. 101, 110, "the concept of force majeure differs in content in different areas of the law and in its various spheres of application' and its precise meaning "has to be decided by reference to the legal context in which it is intended to operate." In the context of limitation periods the concept has rarely in fact been expressly invoked. An example of "unforeseeable circumstances' is to be found in Joined Cases 25 and 26/65 *Simet* v. *H.A.* [1967] E.C.R. 33, 42, where it was held that the fact that the applications did not reach the court until four days after their arrival in Luxembourg was an enforceable circumstance so far as the applicants were concerned. In fact, what had happened there was that the applications had been sent by parcel post from Italy and had arrived at Luxembourg railway station on April 30, 1965, the last day of the limitation period in Case 25/65 and the day after its expiry in Case 26/65; as appears from the Opinion of A.G. Gand, under the local postal regulations, it was for the Court's services to collect the postal packets from the customs office at the station, which as a matter of theory could have been done that day, but was in fact only done on May 4, notification of their arrival having been received on May 3. In effect, it might be said that this case is authority for the proposition that documents are deemed to be lodged from the moment they become available to the Court's services, rather than from their actual receipt by the Court; even on this interpretation, however, Case 26/65 was held to be out of time, since the application in that case was not available for collection until a day after the expiry of the limitation period. *A fortiore,* an application is treated as lodged when it is received by the Court's services, even if it is only entered in the register at a later date, as is shown in the analogous situation of the lodging of an internal complaint under the Staff Regulations (see below para. 2–36) in Case 195/80 *Michel* v. *Parliament* [1981] E.C.R. 2861. There the applicant was able to adduce proof from the Luxembourg post office that the registered letter containing his complaint was received by the Parliament's mail department on June 3, 1980, the last day of the relevant time-limit, even though it was only recorded as received by the Parliament on June 4, 1980. The fundamental point which may, however, be drawn from these cases is the vital importance of lodging an application either by registered post or by personal delivery.

2–06   Although the "force majeure" provisions of the Statutes have rarely been invoked, the Court seems to be willing to allow time-limits to be postponed or otherwise overcome on equitable grounds, in particular where the applicant has been misled or put under a misapprehension with regard to his true legal position. The question whether the applicant has been under a misapprehension or misled has itself however usually been at issue. In Case 23/69 *Ficker* v. *Commission* [1970] E.C.R. 547, 559, an application for compensation under the Staff Regulations was prima facie out of time with regard to the decision to which it related; however, the decision in question was taken in response to a request submitted by the applicant on the basis of incorrect information supplied by the Commission as to the date at which she would become entitled to receive a pension. It was therefore held by the First Chamber that "the period for bringing an action against the said decision can only begin to run from the time it became evident that the request . . . , which was the basis for the adoption of the decision in question, was made under the influence of an error occasioned by a wrongful act or omission on the part of the Commission"; it was further said that since this could only be determined by examining the substance of the case, the application could not be dismissed as being out of time. In the result, the

Commission was ordered to pay compensation on the ground that it had failed to rectify the incorrect information it had supplied within a reasonable time. The applicant was less fortunate in Case 102/75 *Petersen* v.*Commission* [1976] E.C.R. 1777. There again, the application was prima facie out of time with regard to the basic decision at issue relating to the applicant's grade as an official; it was argued that he only discovered the criteria for grading officials recruited from the then new Member States a year later, and that time should begin to run only from when he was in a position to discover his mistake. After reviewing the laws of the Member States, A.G. Warner concluded (at p. 1801) that it was enough for the applicant to show that he could not with reasonable diligence have discovered the relevant criteria before a date three months before he submitted a formal complaint under the Staff Regulations (three months being the time-limit for the lodging of a formal complaint under article 90(2) of the Staff Regulations—see below para. 2–36). However, the First Chamber took the view that consideration of the criteria used by the Commission must be joined to that of the substance of the case—which meant that the case was heard—but concluded that the criteria constituted purely internal measures which could not confer rights or expectations of any kind on those concerned and hence could not be called in aid by the applicant, with the result that the application was dismissed. Nevertheless, in Case 25/68 *Schertzer* v. *Parliament* [1977] 1729, 1740–1741, the results of a misapprehension were dealt with separately, in the context of an internal complaint under the Staff Regulations. There, the applicant lodged a complaint, in time, with the President of the European Parliament, whereas it should have been lodged with the chairman of the political group by which he was employed. By the time the President replied pointing out this fact, it was too late to lodge a complaint with the chairman of the group; however, the Second Chamber held that in view of the difficulty he experienced in identifying the authority competent to receive his complaint, the wrongly addressed complaint "may be regarded as having preserved the applicant's right of action." Whilst an analogous situation is unlikely to arise other than in a staff case, it might be noted that since the range of defendants in a direct action before the European Court is limited, an applicant in any doubt as to the appropriate defendant would be well advised to bring a timeous action against all the possible defendants, at the risk of having the application declared inadmissible against certain of them, as in Case 100/74 *CAM* v. *Commission* [1975] E.C.R. 1393, 1396, where the application was originally brought against the Council as well as the Commission, rather than relying on the Court's accepting a claim that he had difficulty in identifying the appropriate defendant.

2–07   One particular problem of misapprehension on the part of the applicant which has frequently been encountered in staff cases arises from the fact that whilst the Staff Regulations have since 1972 been drafted so as to require an internal complaint to be lodged before an action may be brought before the Court, the Court itself has consistently held that certain types of dispute may and should be brought directly before it. An example is with regard to the decision of selection boards, where, from Case 44/71 *Marcato* v. *Commission* [1972] E.C.R. 472, 433, it has been held that a complaint to the appointing authority against a decision adopted by a selection board is pointless since the appointing authority is not competent to annul or amend the decisions of such a board. The applicant there had voluntarily (the facts having arisen before the 1972 amendments to the Staff Regulations) used the internal complaints procedure, but the First Chamber held that the action must be treated as having been brought against the decision of the selection board, and the time-limit for actions against this decision "must be considered not to have expired." Following the 1972 amendments, the Court maintained the view that actions against selection board decisions should be brought directly before it in the judgement of the First Chamber in Case 31/75 *Costacurta* v. *Commission* [1975] E.C.R. 1563, 1570; the applicant there had again followed the internal complaints procedure, so that his action against the selection board decision was prima facie out of time, but the First Chamber held that "it would be contrary to the rules of fairness' to hold it against the applicant for having followed the procedure clearly laid down in the amended Staff Regulations. A similar view has been taken by the Second Chamber, in Case 117/78 *Orlandi* v. *Commission* [1979] E.C.R. 1613, 1620, where it was said that "such an error as to the inapplicability of [the internal complaints procedure] to the present case is excusable having regard to the present wording of the provisions in question and, in the absence of any imperative reasons to the contrary, it cannot result in the applicant's being time-barred," and in Case 34/80 *Authié* v. *Commission* [1981] E.C.R. 665, 676, where it was pointed out that insofar as the ineffectiveness of an internal complaint against a selection board decision was "not formally acknowledged either by a provision of a regulation or by an express warning in the decisions themselves, it seems inequitable to deprive a person of his right of redress where he has made his [internal] complaint before the expiry of the period for taking legal action following the actual decision."

2–08   Whilst these decisions have been given in the context of the specific rules governing staff cases, they nontheless indicate a willingness on the part of the Court to temper the strict time-limits with considerations of equity and fairness, having regard to the situation of the applicant. Indeed in Joined Cases 532, 534, 567, 600, 618 and 660/79 *Amesz and Others* v. *Commission* (December 15, 1982), it was held by the First Chamber that where the applicants were aware that negotiations were going on with regard to their complaint, it was legitimate to await their outcome before commencing formal proceedings. In so far as limitation periods may be altered, it was held in Case 34/59 *Elz* v. *H.A.* [1960] E.C.R. 101, 105–106, in the context of the repeal of the 1957 Rules of Procedure relating to staff cases (J.O. 110/57) by the 1959 Rules of Procedure, that the entry into force of the new Rules of Procedure affected neither the rights of action accrued before that date, nor the extinguishment of rights during the time the former rules were in force.

B. ACTIONS FOR ANNULMENT

EEC Treaty
Article 173

2–09   The Court of Justice shall review the legality of acts of the Council and the Commission other than recommendations or opinions. It shall for this purpose have jurisdiction in actions brought by a Member State, the Council or the Commission on grounds of lack of competence, infringement of an essential procedural requirement, infringement of this Treaty or of any rule of law relating to its application, or misuse of powers.

Any natural or legal person may, under the same conditions, institute proceedings against a decision addressed to that person or against a decision which, although in the form of a regulation or a decision addressed to another person, is of direct and individual concern to the former.

The proceedings provided for in this Article shall be instituted within two months of the publication of the measure, or of its notification to the plaintiff, or, in the absence thereof, of the day on which it came to the knowledge of the latter, as the case may be.

(Article 146 of the Euratom Treaty is in identical terms.)

Article 180

The Court of Justice shall, within the limits hereinafter laid down, have jurisdiction in disputes concerning:
    (a) . . . . . .
    (b) measures adopted by the Board of Governors of the Bank. In this connexion, any Member State, the Commission or the Board of Directors of the Bank may institute proceedings under the conditions laid down in Article 173,
    (c) measures adopted by the Board of Directors of the Bank. Proceedings against such measures may be instituted only by Member States or by the Commission, under the conditions laid down in Article 173 and solely on the grounds of non-complience with the procedure provided for in Article 21(2), (5), (6) and (7) of the Statute of the Bank.

(This provision relates to the European Investment Bank; the relevant paragraphs of article 21 of its Statute relate to the obtaining of opinions with regard to applications for loans or guarantees.)

ECSC Treaty
Article 33

2–10   The Court shall have jurisdiction in actions brought by a Member State or by the Council to have decisions or recommendations of the High Authority declared void on grounds of lack of competence, infringement of an essential procedural requirement, infringement of this Treaty or of any rule of law relating to its application, or misuse of powers. The Court may not, however, examine the evaluation of the situation, resulting from economic facts or circumstances, in the light of which the High Authority took its decisions or made its recommendations, save where the High Authority is alleged to have misused its powers or to have manifestly failed to observe the provisions of this Treaty or any rule of law relating to its application.

Undertakings or the associations referred to in Article 48 may, under the same conditions, institute proceedings against decisions or recommendations concerning them which are individiual in character or against general decisions or recommendations which they consider to involve a misuse of powers affecting them.

The proceedings provided for in the first two paragraphs of this Article shall be instituted within one month of the notification or publication, as the case may be, of the decision or recommendation.

(Article 33 is also expressly referred to in article 63(2), with regard to actions by purchasers against restrictions on dealings imposed by the Commission, and in article 66(5), with regard to decisions declaring a concentration unlawful.)

Article 38

The Court may, on application by a Member State or the High Authority, declare an act of the Assembly or of the Council to be void.

Application shall be made within one month of the publication of the act of the Assembly or the notification of the act of the Council to the Member States or to the High Authority.

The only grounds for such an application shall be lack of competence or infringement of an essential procedural requirement.

Article 88

If the High Authority considers that a State has failed to fulfil an obligation under this Treaty, it shall record this failure in a reasoned decision after giving the State concerned the opportunity to submit its comments. It shall set the State a time limit for the fulfilment of its obligations.

The state may institute proceedings before the Court within two months of notification of the decision; the Court shall have unlimited jurisdiction in such cases.

ECSC Statute of the Court

Article 39

2–11   The proceedings provided for in Articles 36 and 37 of this Treaty must be instituted within the time limit of one month provided for in the last paragraph of Article 33.

(Article 36 of the ECSC Treaty concerns actions challenging penalties imposed by the Commission, and article 37 concerns actions challenging decisions relating to "fundamental and persistent disturbances" in the economy of a Member State.)

Rules of Procedure

Article 81

1. The period of time allowed for commencing proceedings against a measure adopted by an institution shall run from the day following the receipt by the person concerned of notification of the measure or, where the measure is published, from the 15th day after publication thereof in the *Official Journal of the European Communities*.

65

1. *The Basic Time-Limits*

2–12 The limitation periods for action for annulment are characterised by their brevity, in principle two months under the EEC and Euratom Treaties, and one month under the ECSC Treaty, the exception being that actions under Article 88 of the ECSC Treaty, which is in reality an enforcement provision (see para. 2–46 below), are subject to a two-month limitation period. As was pointed out by A.G. Gend in Joined Cases 25 and 26/65 *Simet* v. *H. A.* [1967] E.C.R. 33, 48, since these periods are expressed in months they may vary slightly according to the number of days in the various months of the year, and they are not fixed periods of 30 days; that this was also the view of the Court may be deduced from the fact that it agreed with his calculation of the relevant period, which included a 31-day month.

In the light of these short basic periods, the rule enounced in article 81(1) of the Rules of Procedure, which can be traced back to article 85(1) of the 1953 Rules of Procedure, that where a measure is published in the *Official Journal*, time runs from the fifteenth day after such publication, is of considerable practical importance, adding in effect 25 or 50 per cent. to the respective basic periods. Just as the extensions on account of distance, in article 81(2), add a flat-rate element to allow for postal delays, so also the extension in article 81(1) would appear to be a method of allowing for delays in the delivery of the *Official Journal* and the diffusion of its contents to those concerned, since, as was held in Case 99/78 *Decker* v. *HZA Landau* [1979] E.C.R. 101, 110, a measure is regarded as published on the date at which the relevant copy of the *Official Journal* is avilable at the Office of Official Publications, and not on the dates on which it becomes available in the various Member States. An illustration of the use of this extension can be found in Case 101/76 *KSH* v. *Council and Commission* [1977] E.C.R. 797, 801, 803 and 805, where the Council would appear not to have allowed for it when claiming that the application was out of time.

2–13 Where the measure at issue is notified to the applicant, a term usually appropriate to measures which are individual in nature (see para. 2–16 below), article 81(1) of the Rules provides that time runs from the day following receipt of the notification. Indeed, in Joined Cases 32 and 33/58 *SNUPAT* v. *H.A.* [1959] E.C.R. 127, 138, the Court suggested that there is a "generally accepted rule" that time-limits are calculated exclusive of the day of the measure which sets time running.

The purpose of these short limitation periods was said in Case 3/59 *Germany* v. *H.A.* [1960] E.C.R. 53, 61 to be that they fulfil "a generally recognised need, namely the need to prevent the legality of administrative decisions from being called in question indefinitely, and this means that there is a prohibition on re-opening a question after the limitation period has expired." In that particular case it was held that a Member State which was the addressee of an individual decision under the ECSC Treaty could not, once the time-limit for challenging the decision under Article 33 of that Treaty had expired, contest its validity in proceedings under Article 88 of the Treaty for the annulment of a Commission decision holding that State in breach of its Treaty obligations in failing to comply with the original decision; nor could it plead the illegality of the decision under article 36 (see above para. 1–33), since it was individual in nature. A similar view was taken under the EEC Treaty in Case 156/77 *Commission* v. *Belgium* [1978] E.C.R. 1881, where, in the context of an action brought under Article 93(2) of the EEC Treaty (see below para. 2–47) in relation to Belgium's failure to comply with a Commission decision relating to the payment of certain aids for Belgian railways, it was held that "it is impossible for a Member State which has allowed the strict time-limit laid down in . . . art. 173 to expire without contesting by the means available under that article the legality of the Commission decision addressed to it, to be able to call in question that decision by means of art. 184," which provides for the plea of illegality under the EEC Treaty. The aim of the time-limit was said to be to safeguard legal certainty. The same view was taken of an attempt to plead the illegality of an individual ECSC decision addressed to an undertaking after the expiry of the time-limit laid down by article 33 in Case 21/64 *Dalmas e Figli* v. *H.A.* [1965] E.C.R. 175, 187. It may however be noted that there is a hint by the First Chamber in Case 34/65 *Mosthaf* v. *Commission* [1966] E.C.R. 521, 531 that decisions of Community authorities, the time-limit for the annulment of which has expired, may nonetheless be called in question if "there are new and serious reasons for doing so," which would appear to relate to the possibility of extending time-limits on general grounds of fairness (see para. 2–06 above).

2–14   Despite this basic policy that Community acts should only be susceptible to direct challenge for a very short period, there do exist possibilities of circumvention. Although it has been made clear in the above cases that the plea of illegality may not be used by the addressee of an individual decision against that decision, and it would appear from *Commission* v. *Belgium* and Case 92/78 *Simmenthal* v. *Commission* [1979] E.C.R. 777 that it may not be used by any party against an act that party could have challenged directly, that plea enables an individual litigant when challenging an individual act to contest also the legality of the underlying general legislation "notwithstanding the expiry of the period laid down in the third paragraph of article 163," to quote the terms of Article 184 of the EEC Treaty. It may further be observed that it has consistently been held since Case 5/71 *Schöppenstedt* v. *Council* [1971] E.C.R. 975 that an action for damages for non-contractual liability arising from the harm caused by a legislative act of a Community institution, for which the normal limitation period is five years (see para. 2–28 below), may be brought even though an action for the annulment of the act would be inadmissible; on the other hand, at least in staff cases, this is not the rule where the harm is caused by an act the applicant could have challenged directly, as recently reaffirmed in Case 106/80 *Fournier* v. *Commission* [1981] E.C.R. 2759.

2–15   The most general and important circumvention, however, is the fact that under all three Treaties the Court may pronounce upon the validity of acts of the Community institutions on a reference for a preliminary ruling from a national court, even where a direct action by one of the parties to the national proceedings has expressly been held inadmissable, as in Case 125/77 *KSH* v. *Hoofdproduktschap voor Akkerbouwprodukten* [1978] E.C.R. 1991. In *Commission* v. *Belgium* [1978] E.C.R. 1881, 1897, the Court openly recognised that, in the context of the EEC Treaty, "the validity of a Community measure may be called in question by means of the procedure for obtaining a preliminary ruling referred to in Article 177 of the Treaty, in spite of the expiry of the period laid down in the third paragraph of article 173," but maintained that since the Article 177 procedure corresponded solely to the requirements of the national courts, the possibility of its use could not justify a derogation from the principle of the time-barring of applications under Article 173. However, insofar as such time-barring has been justified on grounds of legal certainty, it may be noted that in the context of a declaration of invalidity under Article 177, the Court in its judgment in Case 4/79 *Providence Agricole de la Champagne* v. *ONIC* [1980] E.C.R. 2823, 2853, invoked considerations of legal certainty to apply by analogy Article 173 of the EEC Treaty enabling it to state which of the effects of a regulation which has been annulled shall be considered as definitive; on that basis it held that the invalidity of the Regulations at issue could not be invoked to challenge charges levied or payments made before the date of its judgment. It may be submitted that in the light of this safeguard, the justification for the short limitation periods for direct actions for annulment seems less convincing.

2. *Notification, Publication and Knowledge*

2–16   Whilst the ECSC Treaty provisions refer only to actions being brought within the requisite period from the notification or publication of the act at issue, under the EEC and Euratom provisions, time runs from notification or publication or, "in the absence thereof," from the day on which the act came to the knowledge of the applicant. This has led A.G. Capotorti to suggest in his Opinion in Case 730/79 *Philip Morris* v. *Commission* [1980] E.C.R. 2671, 2695 that where the act has been published, "the date of acquisition of knowledge is of no relevance"; conversely, A.G. Gend took the view in Case 69/69 *Alcan* v. *Commission* [1970] E.C.R. 385, 397, that where an act was neither published nor notified, time did not run until the applicants "in fact knew" of the act, irrespective of the manner in which they were informed.

2–17   Under the scheme of the Treaties, notification is generally required of acts which are individual in nature. Article 15 of the ECSC Treaty provides that "where decisions and recommendations are individual in character, they shall become binding upon being notified to the party concerned," and Article 191 of the EEC Treaty provides that "directives and decisions shall be notified to those to whom they are addressed and shall take effect upon such notification," although Article 38 of the ECSC Treaty also assumes "notification" of acts of the Council to Member States or to the Commission. Publication, on the other hand, is envisaged for general acts, Article 15 of the ECSC Treaty providing that decisions and recommendations which are not individual in character "shall take effect by the mere fact of publication," and Article 191 of the EEC Treaty requiring regulations to be published in the *Official Journal*, although again Article 38 of the ECSC Treaty assumes "publication" of acts of the European Parliament. The neatness of these distinctions is however, somewhat blurred by the facts that in practice EEC and Euratom decisions and directives are usually published, that measures are in fact taken for which neither notification nor publication is envisaged, and that applicants may have obtained independent knowledge of acts which are published. Case 730/79 *Philip Morris* v. *Commission* [1980] E.C.R. 2671 involved the first and third of these factors: a decision addressed to the Netherlands government was communicated to the applicant on August 9, 1979 and was published in the *Official Journal* on August 25, 1979; as has already been observed, A.G. Capotorti was of the opinion that since the decision had been published, the date of acquisition of knowledge was of no relevance (at p. 2695), but the Court did not need to decide the point since the action was in time whichever of these dates was relevant. However, in its judgment in Case 76/79 *Könecke* v. *Commission* [1980] E.C.R. 665, 667 where it was also alleged that the applicant had advance knowledge of a decision which was later published, the Court did consider whether the communication in question did contain any details "which would have permitted the applicant to identify the decision taken and to ascertain its precise context in such a way as to enable it to exercise its right to institute proceedings." Having found that the communication did not contain any such details, the Court thus held that time began to run from publication in the *Official Journal*. Despite the attractions of A.G. Capotorti's view, it may be that an applicant who does acquire actual knowledge of the substance of a decision not addressed to him would be well advised to bring the action within the relevant period from that date, rather than waiting to see whether it is published. The converse problem has also been encountered, where the question has been whether publication constitutes notice of a measure which does not require to be published. In Joined Cases 31 and 33/62 *Wöhrmann* v. *Commission* [1962] E.C.R. 501, 511, A.G. Roemer took the view that where the decisions addressed to the German Government had been published in the *Official Journal*, time ran from such publication, although the Court itself seemed (at p. 508) to be prepared to consider whether the applicants had acquired knowledge of the decisions, and to impute knowledge to the applicants from the fact of the publication of implementing measures in the national "Bundesgesetzblatt"; in any event, the actions were out of time. In his Opinion in Joined Cases 10 and 18/68 *Eridania* v. *Commission* [1969] E.C.R. 459, 486, A.G. Roemer did however point out that publication in the *Official Journal* of the fact that certain individual decisions had been taken, rather than of the decisions themselves, did not necessarily start time running, stating that the applicant must be put in a position to judge whether it really has an interest in commencing legal proceedings, and "for that, it is

69

certainly necessary to know the complete terms of the decisions"; he did nevertheless suggest that such publication imposed on them the duty "to make the effort to obtain knowledge in good time of the terms of these measures."

2–18   With regard to acts whose notification or publication is not foreseen in the Treaties, it may be noted that in Case 22/70 *Commission* v. *Council* [1971] E.C.R. 263, 266 the Commission brought its action for the annulment of a negotiating position agreed by the Council just within two months from the actual adoption of that position.

So far as the mechanism of notification is concerned, it was stated in Case 6/72 *Continental Can* v. *Commission* [1973] E.C.R. 215, 241 that a decision is notified within the meaning of the Treaty "if it reaches the addressee and puts the latter in a position to take cognizance of it." In that case it was held that a notification sent through the post to an American undertaking rather than through diplomatic channels complied with this test if it actually reached that undetraking. If the notification is not sent by registered post, however, the addressee may be given the benefit of the doubt as to the date it was received. Hence in Joined Cases 32 and 33/58 *SNUPAT* v. *H.A.* [1959] E.C.R. 127, 136, where a letter was dated May 12, 1958, and the action would only be within the time-limit if that letter was received by the applicant on or after May 26, 1958, it was held that although it was unlikely that a letter would have taken so long to get from Brussels to a town in France, it was not absolutely impossible, and since it had not been sent by registered post "the applicant must be accorded the benefit of the doubt." The matter was put in more precise terms in Case 108/79 *Belfiore* v. *Commission* [1980] E.C.R. 1769, 1781, where the Third Chamber clearly held that the onus of providing notification and the date thereof lies with the institution whose act is at issue; there, the letter at issue was dated February 12, 1979, and since the Commission had failed to register it or have it accompanied by a form of acknowledgement of receipt, the applicant was given the benefit of the doubt with regard to his claim not to have received it until April 5, 1979. The same view was taken in Case 195/80 *Michel* v. *Parliament* [1981] E.C.R. 2861 with regard to the applicant's claim not to have received an unregistered letter dated February 21, 1980 until March 3, 1980; it was stated that "the addressee of an unregistered letter is not required to show the reasons for any delay in its delivery." Extrinsic evidence may be admissible to show the date by which the applicant may be taken to have acquired knowledge of the act at issue. In Case 135/81 *Agences de Voyages* v. *Commission* (October 28, 1982), it was held that a letter from a Luxembourg government civil servant to the Commission showed that the applicants were aware of the decision in question by the date that letter was written.

2–19   Under article 3 of Regulation 1/58 of the Council (O.J. 385/58) "documents which an institution of the Community sends to a Member State or to a person subject to the jurisdiction of a Member State shall be drafted in the language of such State." Where the addressee is established or resident outside the Community, it was held in the

Continental Can case ([1973] E.C.R. at p. 241) that the choice of the language of the decision had to be based on what relations existed within the Community between the applicants and one state or another of the Community. One of the American applicants (and addressees of the decision) in that case had opened an office in Brussels and set out its written observations in the administrative procedure in French, and the Commission could therefore choose French as the official language of the decision.

2–20 The dividing line between notification and the acquisition of knowledge becomes somewhat blurred where communication is alleged to occur in a document which is not specifically devoted to notification of the act at issue. In particular, there are some staff cases in which a salary slip has been held to be notification of a decision to the applicant. In Joined Cases 15 to 33, etc./73 *Schots-Kortner and others* v. *Council, Commission and Parliament* [1974] E.C.R. 177, 189 some of the applicants claimed that decisions withdrawing or refusing expatriation allowance under the Staff Regulations had not been notified to them, but the Second Chamber stated that they could have realised the allowance had been withdrawn or refused simply by reading their salary statements, and the sending of the monthly salary statement had the effect of starting the time for bringing an action running, where it clearly showed the decision taken. However, it would appear to have been conceded by the applicants that they did have knowledge of the decisions resulting in the withdrawal or refusal of the expatriation allowance from a date outside the limitation period. The view that, in the context of a claim for an allowance, the sending of the monthly salary slip has the effect of starting the time running where it clearly shows the decision taken, was repeated *simpliciter* in Case 1/76 *Wack* v. *Commission* [1976] E.C.R. 1017, 1023. However, a different view has emerged in the judgment of the First Chamber in Case 185/80 *Garganese* v. *Commission* [1981] E.C.R. 1785, which again concerned a claim relating to the expatriation allowance, where it was said that the absence from the monthly salary slip of a statement regarding the allowance could not be assimilated to a decision under the Staff Regulations capable of causing time to start to run (particularly since there was evidence that the Commission's internal services did not think a decision had been taken on the matter), so that time only began to run from the date of the Commissions's final reply to a complaint from the applicant about the allowance. This view was applied more generally by the Second Chamber in Case 145/80 *Mascetti* v. *Commission* [1981] E.C.R. 1975 in a dispute over grading: the Commission argued that submission of a second contract of employment to the applicant for signature, following her objections to her first contract, constituted notification of a final decision on the part of the administration, but the Second Chamber held that the applicant was entitled to treat a later letter from the Commission "which was the first to give any reasons," as the administration's formal decision against which an internal complaint ought to be lodged.The Second Chamber similarly held in Case 806/79 *Gerin* v. *Commission* [1980] E.C.R. 3515, 3524, that an unsigned

71

printed form bearing a handwritten message to the effect that the applicant's son was not regarded as a dependent child, without any statement of reasons, could not be regarded as "an express manifestation of an administration intention which creates legal effects," so that time began to run from the later notification of a reasoned decision of the appointing authority. It is submitted that the decision in *Garganese, Mascetti* and *Gerin* accord with the view of the Court in Case 76/79 *Könecke* v. *Commission* [1980] E.C.R. 665, 677, reflecting the Opinion of A.G. Roemer in Joined Cases 10 and 18/68 *Eridania* v. *Commission* [1969] E.C.R. 459, 488 that, for time to start running, the applicant should be put in a position to identify the decision taken and to ascertain its content in such a way as to be able to exercise the right to institute proceedings.

2–21   Be that as it may, the problem remains of the steps to be taken on becoming aware of an apparent decision or apparent evidence of a decision. In Case 148/79 *Korter* v. *Council* [1981] E.C.R. 615, the applicant commenced proceedings following receipt of a communication which the Council later claimed to be "purely informative"; it was eventually held that he had not shown the existence of an act susceptible to challenge, but the Council was ordered to pay the costs, especially because of the "legal ambiguity" which it maintained (see also para. 17–12 below). Going beyond this, in Joined Cases 161 and 162/80 *Carbognani* v. *Commission* [1981] E.C.R. 543, 560, proceedings were commenced against letters dated December 17, 1979 which, in the view of the Second Chamber, the applicants could not be blamed for having considered to be decisions taken by the appointing authority, whereas in fact such decisions were not adopted until July 31, 1980. It was recognised that if the applicants had failed to challenge the 1979 letters they would, given that the letters appeared to contain final decisions, have risked becoming time-barred; the solution adopted was to state that since the purport of the letters and of the ultimate decision was identical, "the two acts may be considered as a single decision for the purpose of challenging them in court." It remains to be seen whether this approach will be followed more generally.

2–22   Turning to the mechanism of publication, the matter was considered in some detail in a pair of cases decided the same day, one of which is Case 99/78 *Decker* v. *HZA Landau* [1979] E.C.R. 101, 109–110. Two fundamental principles were regarded as at issue. The first is that a measure should not be applicable to those concerned before they have the opportunity to make themselves acquainted with it; the obvious implication in the context is that publication in the *Offical Journal* provides this opportunity, and hence constitutes notice. The second is that the date on which an act is regarded as published should not vary from Member State to Member State. From this, the Court laid down that in principle the date of publication is the date appearing on the relevant issue of the *Official Journal*, but that if evidence is produced that it was not available at that date, then account should be taken of the date at which it was in fact available at the seat of the Office for Official Publications; in that particular case it was found that an issue dated

March 9, 1973 was not in fact available until March 12, 1973. It is in the light of this single date of publication, based on availability at the Office for Official Publications, that the importance of the 15-day extension provided for in article 81(1) of the Rules of Procedure may be seen (see para. 2–11 above).

With regard to the acts whose publication is required under the Treaties, *i.e.* EEC and Euratom Regulations, and general decisions and recommendations under the ECSC Treaty, it was pointed out in Case 185/73 *HZA Bielefeld* v. *König* [1974] E.C.R. 607, 617 that they could only be applied and take effect on publication; it would therefore seem that A.G. Capotorti's view in the *Philip Morris* case ([1980] E.C.R. at p. 2695) that advance knowledge is irrelevant in this context, since the advance knowledge could not be of a binding act susceptible to challenge.

3. *Confirmatory Acts*

2–23   The question whether the measure at issue in an action for annulment is in fact susceptible to challenge is of particular interest where it is alleged that it merely confirms an earlier measure which was not challenged in time. There is a consistent line of case law to the effect that a purely confirmatory act cannot start a fresh period to run and that time runs from the original binding act, whether that was an express decision as in, *e.g.* Joined Cases 50–51, 53 to 54 and 57/64 *Loebisch* v. *Council* [1965] E.C.R. 825, 831, and Case 103/79 *Moat* v. *Commission* [1980] E.C.R. 2579, 2592, or an implied decision of refusal under the ECSC Treaty or the Staff Regulations, as in, *e.g.* Case 24/69 *Nebe* v. *Commission* [1970] E.C.R. 145, 151 and Joined Cases 33 and 35/79 *Kühner* v. *Commission* [1980] E.C.R. 1677, 1693–1694. There has, however, been some change with regard to the concept of confirmation. In Case 1/76 *Wack* v. *Commission* [1976] E.C.R. 1017, 1023, it was held that a Commission decision in 1975 refusing to award the applicant an expatriation allowance merely confirmed a decision taken when she joined the service of the Commission in 1972 which was notified in her first salary statement (see para. 2–20 above), so that an action against the 1975 decision was time-barred. However, in Case 185/80 *Garganese* v. *Commission* [1981] E.C.R. 1785, where it was argued that a decision taken in June 1980 refusing such an allowance was merely confirmatory of an implied decision notified in a salary slip received in October 1979, it was found that the 1980 decision in no way referred to a previous express or implied decision, and it was therefore sufficient in itself to start time runnng; however, it was also there held that the absence of any mention of the allowance in the salary slip could not be assimilated to a decision so as to cause time to start to run, so that there was no earlier measure to confirm.

2–24   Apart from a proviso to article 91(3) of the Staff Regulations, allowing time to run afresh where an express decision is taken confirming an earlier implied decision within the time-limit for challenging the implied decision (see para. 2–36 below), it has long been accepted that a confirmatory act may start time running if it contains some new element of fact or law. In Joined Cases 42 and 49/59 *SNUPAT* v. *H.A.* [1961] E.C.R. 53, 75, the Court stated that although in general a measure which merely confirms a previous measure cannot afford those concerned the opportunity of reopening the question of the legality of the measure which is confirmed, this does not apply "if there is a new fact of such a character as to alter the essential circumstances and conditions which governed the adoption of the first measure," and appeared to accept that a judgment could be such a new fact (at p.76). It would also appear that an act which repeals and replaces an earlier measure on the same matter will not be regarded as merely confirmatory, even with regard to provisions re-enacted from the earlier measure. In his Opinion in Case 2/57 *Hauts Fourneaux de Chasse* v. *H.A.* [1957 and 1958] E.C.R. 199, 234, A.G. Lagrange suggested that where such a consolidating measure was complete in itself, an action would not be barred on the grounds that certain provisions could have been challenged in their earlier form; the Court simply held that time ran afresh for the new decision "notwithstanding the existence of an earlier decision on the same subject." It would appear to follow from this that the concept of the confirmatory act is only of relevance where the original measure (or implied measure) continues to produce its effects.

C. Actions for Failure to Act

EEC Treaty

Article 175

2–25   Should the Council or the Commission, in infringement of this Treaty, fail to act, the Member States and the other institutions of the Community may bring an action before the Court of Justice to have the infringement established.

The action shall be admissible only if the institution concerned has first been called upon to act. If, within two months of being so called upon, the institution concerned has not defined its position, the action may be brought within a further period of two months.

Any natural or legal person may, under the conditions laid down in the preceding paragraphs, complain to the Court of Justice that an institution of the Community has failed to address to that person any act other than a recommendation or an opinion.

(Article 148 of the Euratom Treaty is in identical terms.)

ECSC Treaty

Article 35

Wherever the High Authority is required by this Treaty, or by rules laid down for the implementation thereof, to take a decision or make a recommendation and fails to fulful this obligation, it shall be for States, the Council, undertakings or associations, as the case may be, to raise the matter with the High Authority.

The same shall apply if the High Authority, where empowered by this Treaty, or by rules laid down for the implementation thereof, to take a decision or make a recommendation, abstains from doing so and such abstention constitutes a misuse of powers.

If at the end of two months the High Authority has not taken any decision or made any recommendation, proceedings may be instituted before the Court within one month against the implied decision of refusal which is to be inferred from the silence of the High Authority on the matter.

2–26   Despite the formal distinction that whilst the action under the EEC and Euratom Treaties relates to a failure to act, the action under the ECSC Treaty (like that under the Staff Regulations—see para. 2–36 below) is for the annulment of an implied decision of refusal to act, the pattern of time–limits is very similar under all the Treaties, falling into three phases. The first requires a request to be made to the institution, the second is a period of two months (under all the Treaties) at the expiry of which the institution is deemed to have acted, or to have refused to act, and third is a period of two months under the EEC and Euratom Treaties, and one month under the ECSC Treaty, following that failure to act, during which the action may be brought.

So far as the first phase is concerned, no time-limit is laid down in the Treaties during which the request for action may be made, as was noted in Case 59/70 *Netherlands* v. *Commission* [1971] E.C.R. 639, 652–653. The Court there deduced from the fact that the institution is given only two months in which to act and the complainant is given only one or two months thereafter to bring an action that "the exercise of the right to raise the matter with the Commission may not be delayed indefinitely." It was found that the Netherlands Government was aware of the matter on which it reqested action to be taken some 18 months before it submitted a formal request to the Commission under Article 35 of the ECSC Treaty, and it was held that to wait so long "cannot be regarded as reasonable." There appears, however, to be no positive authority as to what constitutes a "reasonable" period, but if the criteria are to be derived from the specific periods laid down in the Treaty provisions, it may well only be a couple of months. It may also be of some relevance that the complaint in the *Netherlands* case related to a specific act on the part of another Member State in granting low-interest loans to its steel industry, it may be wondered how far a time-limit is appropriate where the complaint relates to a continuing existing situation.

2–27   With regard to the second phase, it was held in Joined Cases 32 and 33/58 *SNUPAT* v. *H.A.* [1959] E.C.R. 127, 138 that the two month period within which the institution must act begins to run the day after the request is received by that institution, following what was described as a "generally accepted rule" which excludes the day of the measure which sets time running from the calculation. The periods for bringing an action thereafter are similar to those for bringing an action for annulment (see above para. 2–10). There are, however, certain matters specific to the fact that under the ECSC Treaty (and the Staff Regulations) there is an implied decision of refusal to act: in particular, a later express decision to the same effect will be treated as merely confirmatory, so that time begins to run from the original implied decision as in, *e.g.* Case 24/69 *Nebe* v. *Commission* [1970] E.C.R. 145, 151. Conversely, the implied decision may be treated as merely confirmatory of an earlier express decision, as in Case 10/67 *Moulijn* v. *Commission* [1969] E.C.R. 147, 149; this, however, would appear to be an illustration of the general principle that an action for failure to act may not be used to by-pass the time-limit on an action of the annulment of the earlier act, *i.e.* it is not possible to ask the institution to rescind or amend its earlier act, and then bring an action for failure to act in relation to that request, since such an action would effectively seek the annulment of the earlier act. The principle was enounced in the ESC context in Joined Cases 21 to 26/61 *Meroni* v. *H. A.* [1962] E.C.R. 73, 78, and applied under the EEC Treaty in Joined Cases 10 and 18/68 *Eridania* v. *Commission* [1969] E.C.R. 459, 483.

Finally, it might be observed that it has consistently been recognised since Case 4/69 *Lütticke* v. *Commission* [1971] E.C.R. 325, 336 that an action for damages may lead to a result similar to that of an action for failure to act, even after such an action has been brought and failed (see Case 48/65 *Lütticke* v. *Commission* [1966] E.C.R. 19).

D. ACTIONS FOR DAMAGES

EEC Treaty

Article 178

2–28   The Court of Justice shall have jurisdiction in disputes relating to compensation for damage provided for in the second paragraph of Article 215.

(Article 151 of the Euratom Treaty is in parallel terms.)

Article 215

The contractual liability of the Community shall be governed by the law applicable to the contract in question.

In the case of non-contractual liability, the Community shall, in accordance with the general principles common the laws of the Member States, make good any damage caused by its institutions or by its servants in the performance of their duties.

The personal liability of its servants towards the Community shall be governed by the provisions laid down in their Staff Regulations or in the Conditions of Employment applicable to them.

(Article 188 of the Euratom Treaty is in identical terms.)

EEC Statute of the Court

Article 43

Proceedings against the Community in matters arising from non-contractual liability shall be barred after a period of five years from the occurence of the event giving rise thereto. The period of limitation shall be interrupted if proceedings are instituted before the Court or if prior to such proceedings an application is made by the aggrieved party to the relevant institution of the Community. In the latter event the proceedings must be instituted within the period of two months provided for in Article 173 the provisions of the second paragraph of Article 175 shall apply where appropriate.

(Article 44 of the Euratom Statute is in parallel terms.)

ECSC Treaty

Article 34

2–29   If the Court declares a decision or recommendation void, it shall refer the matter back to the High Authority. The High Authority shall take the necessary steps to comply with the judgment. . . .

If the High Authority fails to take within a reasonable time the necessary steps to comply with the judgment, proceedings for damages may be instibued before the Court.

Article 40

Without prejudice to the first paragraph of Article 34, the Court shall have jurisdiction to order pecuniary reparation from the Community, on application by the injured party, to make good any injury caused in carrying out this Treaty by a wrongful act or omission on the part of the Community in the performance of its functions.

The Court shall also have jurisdiction to order the Community to make good any injury caused by a personal wrong by a servant of the Community in the performance of his duties. The personal liability of its servants towards the Community shall be governed by the provisions laid down in their Staff Regulations or the Conditions of Employment applicable to them.

All other disputes between the Community and persons other than servants to which the provisions of this Treaty or the rules laid down for implementation thereof do not apply shall be brought before national courts or tribunals.

ECSC Statute of the Court

Article 40

Proceedings provided for in the first two paragraphs of Article 40 of this Treaty shall be barred after a period of five years from the occurrence of the event giving rise thereto. The period of limitation shall be interrupted if proceedings are instituted before the Court or if prior to such proceedings an application is made by the aggrieved party to the relevant institution of the Community. In the latter event the proceedings must be instituted within the time limit of one month provided for in the last paragraph of Article 33; the provisions of the last paragraph of Article 35 shall apply where appropriate.

1. Contractual Liability

2–30   It would appear that questions of contractual liability are likely to come before the European Court only by virtue of an arbitration clause (see para. 2–51 below) or under the Conditions of Employment of Other Servants of the European Communities (laid down, like the Staff Regulations, in Council Regulation 259/68, as amended). Although officials as such of the Community are regarded as employed on a statutory rather than a contractual basis, Case 28/74 *Gillet* v. *Commission* [1975] E.C.R. 463, 472–473, temporary staff, auxiliary staff, local staff and special advisers are engaged under contract. Although disputes involving local staff fall within the jurisdiction of national courts, articles 46, 73 and 83 of the Conditions of Employment apply the provisions of the Staff Regulations relating to actions before the Court by analogy to disputes between temporary staff, auxiliary staff and special advisers and their respective employing institutions, so that the European Court has jurisdiction but subject to the time-limits laid down in the Staff Regulations (see below para. 2–36). Given this limited jurisdiction, it is hardly surprising that there is no specific Treaty provision laying down a Community law limitation period for an application to the European Court for damages for breach of contract. This was noted by the First Chamber in a staff case the facts of which arose before the enactment of the Staff Regulations, Case 25/60 *De Bruyn* v. *Parliament* [1962] E.C.R. 21, 27–28. In the absence of any Treaty provision, the Court considered whether the applicant's delay in bringing the matter before the court should be interpreted as a waiver of the right of action. The applicant had in fact originally brought her action before a Luxembourg employment court, which declined jurisdiction, and there was a delay of about a year between the judgment of the Luxumbourg court and the lodging of the application before the European Court; it was held that this was not evidence of a waiver. Whilst the particular facts are unlikely to recur under current legislation, it is submitted that the general test to be applied in the absence of specific limitation periods is whether the applicant's conduct constitutes a waiver of his right of action.

2. *Non-contractual Liability*

2–31   With the exception of Article 34 of the ECSC Treaty, the basic period of limitation laid down for actions for damages arising from non-contractual liability is five years. Article 34 of the ECSC Treaty, on the other hand, creates an action for damages following the failure of the Commission to comply with the terms of a judgment annulling a decision or recommendation, and the original action will therefore have been commenced within the time-limit of one month laid down in Article 33 of that Treaty; there appears to be no authority as to whether the "reasonable time" within which the Commission must act is to be determined in the light of the time-limit for actions for annulment, or the time-limit for actions for damages, or as a question of fact in each case.

2–32   The basic five-year period laid down by the three Statutes with regard to actions for non-contractual liability is stated to be "interrupted" if "proceedings are instituted before the Court or if prior to such proceedings an application is made by the aggrieved party to the relevant institution of the Community" in which event "the proceedings" must be instituted within the time-limits laid down for actions for annulment or actions for failure to act, respectively. This is hardly the clearest of drafting, and its interpretation has given rise to differences of opinion, largely on the question of which "proceedings" are which, *i.e.* whether, in terms of the EEC Treaty, it is the Article 173/175 proceedings for annulment (or failure to act) or the Article 178 proceedings for damages which must be brought within two months. However, in Joined Cases 5,7 and 13 to 24/66 *Kampffmeyer* v. *Commission* [1966] E.C.R. 245, 259–260, the Court held:

> "The defendant itself admits, however, that the reference to Articles 173 and 175 can only apply to the possibility of interruption of the period of limitation of five years laid down in the first sentence of the said Article 43. It follows from the actual wording of the second and third sentences of that provision that it is not intended to shorten the period of limitation of five years, but that it is intended to protect those concerned by preventing certain periods from being taken into account in the calculation of the said period. Consequently the aim of the third sentence of Article 43 is merely to postone the expiration of the period of five years when proceedings instituted or a prior application made within this period start time to run in respect of the periods provided for in Articles 173 or 175. As the events which gave rise to the present applications occurred . . . less than five years from the lodging of the said applications, they are therefore admissible."

This was followed by the Second Chamber in Case 11/72 *Giordano* v. *Commission* [1973] E.C.R. 417, 424–425 where it is said that: "in no case can the application of these provisions have the effect of cutting down the five year period of limitation laid down by the first sentence of Article 43 of the Statutes." However, a dictum to the contrary by the First Chamber may be found in its judgment in Case 9/75 *Meyer-Burckhardt* v. *Commission* [1975] E.C.R. 1171, 1183, where the point was neither argued nor at issue. The Commission had accepted that a limitation period of five years applied if the action in question could be brought under Articles 178/215. However, the real point at issue in *Meyer–Burckhardt* was whether an action for damages brought by an official against the institution by which he is or was employed is subject to the time-limits laid down in the Staff Regulations or to the general time-limits for actions for damages. It was held that such a dispute is governed by the rules of the Staff Regulations (see para. 2–36 below) "where it originates in the relationship of employment between the person concerned and the institution," thus effectively reversing the suggestion in Case 79/71 *Heinemann* v. *Commission* [1972] E.C.R. 579, 589, that an action for damages is not subject to the time-limits laid down in the Staff Regulations. On this point, the decision in *Meyer-Burckhardt* was expressly followed in Case 48/76 *Reinarz* v. *Commission and Council* [1977] E.C.R. 291, 298 and Case 543/79 *Birke* v. *Commission and Council* [1981] E.C.R. 2669.

2–33   With regard to the calculation of the general five-year period, a particular problem arises where the liability is alleged to be incurred as the result of the enactment of legislation: is the "event giving rise" to liability the enactment or the later sustaining of damage as a result? The matter was considered by the Court in Joined Cases 256, 257, 265 and 267/80 and 5/81 *Birra Würher and others* v. *Council and Commission*

[1982] E.C.R. 85, where it was argued by the defendants that the period of limitation must commence from the date of publication of the Regulations at issue. In his Opinion, A.G. Capotorti took the view that the period should run from the entry into force of the Regulations, but that where the harm was on a continuing basis, a claim could be made for the five years preceding the action. The Court, however, held that the limitation period could not begin "before all the requirements governing an obligation to provide compensation for damage are satisfied and in particular before the damage to be made good has materialized" and that where liability derived from a legislative measure the period of limitation could not begin before the injurious effects of that measure had been produced; in these cases, where the Regulations at issue abolished certain production refunds, the injurious effects were said to be produced when the applicants completed the transactions which would have entitled them to the refunds. It therefore concluded that the commencement of the period of limitation cannot be the date of the entry into force of the measures or their date of publication.

2–34   This may be contrasted with the decisions in Joined Cases 56 to 60/74 *Kampffmeyer* v. *Commission and Council* [1976] E.C.R. 711, 741 and in Case 44/76 *Milch- Fett- und Eier-Konter* v. *Council and Commission* [1977] E.C.R. 393, 407, which were invoked by the defendants in *Birra Wührer.* In these cases, it was held that the Court may be asked "to declare the Community liable for imminent damage forseeable with sufficient certainty even if the damage cannot yet be precisely assessed"; in particular in the former cases, the applications were brought in July 1974 in relation to harm which it was alleged would occur in the 1974–1975 marketing year beginning in August 1974, but it was held that the applicants were justified in bringing an action for damages "as soon as the Community rules in question were published and before they were put into effect." It would therefore appear that an action for damages may be brought before the *commencement* of the limitation period as defined in *Birra Wührer.*

2–35   As has been noted in the context of actions for annulment and actions for failure to act (see paras. 2–09 and 2–25 above), a claim for damages may be made after the expiry of the limitation periods for those actions, even though the practical result of the action for damages may be very similar to that of the action for annulment or action for failure to act, a view reaffirmed in Joined Cases 197 to 200, 243, 245 and 247/80 *Walzmühle Erling* v. *Council and Commission* [1981] E.C.R. 3211. None of these cases appear, however, to have involved an act or failure to act which the applicant for damages could clearly have challenged. There is, on the other hand, a line of staff cases, from Case 59/65 *Schreckenberg* v. *Commission* [1966] E.C.R. 543, 550 and Case 4/67 *Muller (née Collignon)* v. *Commission* [1967] E.C.R. 365, 373 to Case 799/79 *Bruckner* v. *Commission and Council* [1981] E.C.R. 2697 and Case 106/80 *Fournier* v. *Commission* [1981] E.C.R. 2795 to the effect that officials may not make use of actions for damages in order to endeavour to redress the pecuniary consequences of individual decisions which they have not contested in time. Although there does not appear to be any non-staff case in which the question has arisen of the admissibility of a claim for damages relating to the harm caused by an act which the applicant clearly could have challenged, or a similar failure to act, it may be suggested that the principle enounced in the staff cases is of general application: an action for damages may not circumvent the limitation period governing a remedy the applicant could and should have used.

E. STAFF CASES

Staff Regulations

Article 90

2–36   1. Any person to whom these Staff Regulations apply may submit to the appointing authority, a request that it take a decision relating to him. The authority shall notify the person concerned of its reasoned decision within four months from the date on which the request was made. If at the end of that period no reply to the request has been received, this shall be deemed to constitute an implied decision rejecting it, against which a complaint may be lodged in accordance with the following paragraph.

2. Any person to whom these Staff Regulations apply may submit to the appointing authority a complaint against an act adversely affecting him, either where the said authority has taken a decision or where it has failed to adopt a measure prescribed by the Staff Regulations. The complaint must be lodged within three months. The period shall start to run:

—on the date of publication of the act if it is a measure of a general nature:

—on the date of notification of the decision to the person concerned, but in no case later than the date on which the latter received such notification, if the measure affects a specified person; if, however, an act affecting a specified person also adversely affects another person, the period shall start to run in respect of that other person on the date on which he receives notification thereof but in no case later than the date of publication;

—on the date of expiry of the period prescribed for reply where the complaint concerns an implied decision rejecting a request as provided in paragraph 1.

The authority shall notify the person concerned of its reasoned decision within four months from the date on which the complaint was lodged. If at the end of that period no reply to the complaint has been received, this shall be deemed to constitute an implied decision rejecting it, against which an appeal may be lodged under Article 91.

3. A request or complaint by an official shall be submitted through his immediate superior, except where it concerns that person, in which case it may be submitted direct to the authority next above.

Article 91

1. The Court of Justice of the European Communities shall have jurisdiction in any dispute between the Communities and any person to whom these Staff Regulations apply regarding the legality of an act adversely affecting such person within the meaning of Article 90(2). In disputes of a financial character the Court of Justice shall have unlimited jurisdiction.

2. An appeal to the Court of Justice of the European Communities shall lie only if:

—the appointing authority has previously had a complaint submitted to it pursuant to Article 90(2) within the period prescribed therein, and

—the complaint has been rejected by express decisions or by implied decision

3. Appeals under paragraph 2 shall be filed within three months. The period shall begin:

—on the date of notification of the decision taken in response to the complaint;

—on the date of expiry of the period prescribed for the reply where the appeal is against an implied decision rejecting a complaint submitted pursuant to Article 90(2); nevertheless, where a complaint is rejected by express decision after being rejected by implied decision but before the period for lodging an appeal has expired, the period for lodging the appeal shall start to run afresh.

4. By way of derogation from paragraph 2, the person concerned may, after submitting a complaint to the appointing authority pursuant to Article 90(2), immediately file an appeal with the Court of Justice, provided that such appeal is accompanied by an application either for a stay of execution of the contested act or for the adoption of interim measures. The proceedings in the principal action before the Court of Justice shall then be suspended until such time as an express or implied decision rejecting the complaint is taken.

5. Appeals under this Article shall be investigated and heard as provided in the Rules of Procedure of the Court of Justice of the European Communities.

Conditions of Employment of Other servants

Article 46 (Temporary Staff)

2–37   Title VII of the Staff Regulations, concerning appeals, shall apply by analogy.

Article 73 (Auxiliary Staff)

Title VII of the Staff Regulations, concerning appeals, shall apply by analogy.

Article 81 (Local Staff)

Any dispute between the institution and member of the local staff shall be submitted to the competent court in accordance with the laws in force in the place where the servant performs his duties.

Article 83 (Special Advisors)

Article 11, the first paragraph of Article 12, Article 14, the first paragraph of Article 16, Articles 17, 19 and 22, the first and second paragraphs of Article 23 and the second paragraph of Article 25 of the Staff Regulations, concerning the rights and obligations of officials, and Articles 90 and 91 of the Staff Regulations, concerning appeals, shall apply by analogy.

Rules on Sickness Insurance for Officials of the European Communities

Article 16

Appeals

1. Any person to whom these Rules apply shall be entitled to resort to the appeal procedure provided for in Articles 90 and 91 of the Staff Regulations.

2. Before taking a decision regarding a complaint submitted under Article 90(2) of the Staff Regulations, the appointing authority shall consult the Management Committee.

The Management Committee may instruct its chairman to make further investigations. Where the point at issue is of a medical nature, the Management

Committee may seek expert medical advice before giving its Opinion. The cost of the expert opinion shall be borne by the Scheme.

The Management Committee shall give its Opinion within two months of the request being received. The Opinion shall be transmitted simultaneously to the appointing authority and to the person concerned.

Should the Management Committee fail to deliver an Opinion within the period prescribed above, the appointing authority may take its decision.

Rules on the Insurance of Officials of the European Communities against the risk of accident and of occupational disease

Article 28

2–38   Decisions taken under these Rules may be the subject of a complaint under Article 90 of the Staff Regulations by the official or those entitled under him to the appointing authority of the institution to which the official belongs and of an appeal by the same persons to the Court of Justice of the European Communities under the conditions laid down in the Treaties establishing the Communities and in Article 91 of the Staff Regulations.

European Investment Bank Staff Regulations

Article 41

Disputes, of any nature, between the Bank and individual members of staff, shall be brought before the Court of Justice of the European Communities.

In addition to proceedings being instituted before the Court of Justice, an amicable settlement shall be sought before the Bank's Conciliation Board in respect of disputes other than such as arise from application of the disciplinary measures provided for under Article 38.

The Conciliation Board shall consist of three members. When the Board is obliged to meet, one of its members shall be nominated by the President of the Bank, another by the official concerned, both nominations being made within one week of one party so requesting the other. The third member, who shall be the Chairman of the Board, shall be nominated by the first two nominees within one week of their being nominated. He need not be a member of the Bank. If, within one week following their nomination, the first two members are unable to agree on the nomination of the Chairman, such nomination shall be undertaken by the President of the Court of Justice of the European Communities.

The conciliation procedure shall be deemed to have failed if:

(1) the President of the Court of Justice has not nominated the Chairman referred to in the foregoing paragraph within four weeks of communication of the President of the Bank's petition to this effect;

(2) the Conciliation Board does not reach a settlement acceptable to both sides within two weeks of its formation.

2–39   Although the European Investment Bank has its own conciliation procedure, which was applied in Case 110/75 *Mills* v. *European Investment Bank* [1976] E.C.R. 955, disputes between officials (including temporary staff, auxiliary staff and special advisers) of the Communities and their employing institutions are in general subject to the procedures and time-limits laid down in Articles 90 and 91 of the Staff Regulations. In principle, these provisions require an internal remedy to be sought before the matter may be brought before the

Court, and allow slightly longer limitation periods than the corresponding general provisions relating to actions for annulment and failure to act. An official wishing to challenge an act adversely affecting him must submit an internal complaint within three months, and the appointing authority has four months within which to reply, at the end of which it is deemed to have taken an implied decision rejecting the complaint. If the complaint is rejected expressly within that period or by implication at the end of it, then the official may bring an action before the Court within a further three months. An official may also request his appointing authority to take a decision concerning him, and if that authority does not notify the official of its decision within four months, it is deemed to have taken an implied decision rejecting that request. Such an implied decision or an earlier express rejection or unfavourable decision may then be challenged as an act adversely affecting the official, in the manner outlined above; one practical consequence of this is that an action for failure to act under the Staff Regulations involves two implied decisions of refusal to act.

2–40   In principle, the general considerations concerning limitation periods already outlined apply both to the internal procedure and the action before the Court, but certain specific points may be noted. Article 90(2) of the Staff Regulation is clearly drafted on the basis not only that publication of a general act constitutes notice, but also that publication of an act affecting a specified person (*i.e.* an individual act) may constitute notice to any other person adversely affected thereby (*cf.* para. 2–16 above). Another peculiarity is that, whilst (or perhaps because) most of the leading cases on the principle that a purely confirmatory act cannot start a fresh period to run, and that time runs from the original binding act, are staff cases, *e.g.* Case 24/69 *Nebe* v. *Commission* [1970] E.C.R. 145, 151 (see para. 2–23 above), it is expressly provided in article 91(3) of the Staff Regulations that where a complaint which has already been rejected by implied decision is later rejected by express decision within the time-limit for challenging the implied decision before the Court, the period for bringing the action before the Court "shall start to run afresh." This was generously interpreted in Case 5/76 *Jänsch* v. *Commission* [1976] E.C.R. 1027, 1034, where the express decision was taken within the limitation period for challenging the implied decision, but not notified until after its expiry. The Second Chamber there held that the date of adoption of the express decision was relevant for determining whether the complaint was rejected within the limitation period, but that the new limitation period only commenced to run from the date of notification of the express decision, *i.e.* after the expiry of the original period.

2–41   Despite the wording of articles 90 and 91 of the Staff Regulations, the Court has held that there is no need to use the internal procedure where the appointing authority has no power to change the decision at issue, *e.g.* where it is a decision of a selection board whether to admit a candidate to a competition, as in Case 7/77 *Von Wüllerstorff* v. *Commission* [1978] E.C.R. 769, 778–779, or where an official wishes to challenge his periodic report, as in Joined Cases 6 and 97/79 *Grassi* v.

Council [1980] E.C.R. 2141, 2157–2158. However, since officials may take the provisions of the Staff Regulations at their face value, it has been held, expressly on grounds of fairness (see para. 2–07), that an official who uses the internal procedure in such circumstances will not be held to be out of time, following Case 31/75 *Costacurta* v. *Commission* [1975] E.C.R. 1563, 1570. There is also an express exception in article 91(4) of the Staff Regulations, which allows an official to bring an action before the Court immediately after submitting his complaint to the appointing authority if the application in this action is accompanied by a request for interim measures. Effectively, this is merely a device to allow interim measures to be requested (see para. 10–13), since the proceedings in the main action are suspended until an express or implied decision is taken on the complaint, and it was said by the President of the First Chamber in Case 75/72R *Perinciolo* v. *Council* [1972] E.C.R. 1201, 1203 that the admissibility of the main action must not be prejudged.

2–42   Whilst articles 90 and 91 of the Staff Regulations may seem at first sight to be concerned essentially with actions for annulment or for failure to act, it has been consistently held since Case 9/75 *Meyer Burckhardt* v. *Commission* [1975] E.C.R. 1171, 1182, that a claim for damages originating in the relationship of employment between the applicant official and the defendant institution should be brought under this procedure. In Case 131/81 *Berti* v. *Commission* (October 7, 1982), the First Chamber held that material harm arising during children's holidays arranged by the employing institution could fall within the employment relationship, but that the "moral" (*i.e.* non-material) harm suffered by the official's child did not. It would appear that damages may be claimed either in the action following the rejection of the internal complaint as, *e.g.* in Joined Cases 10 and 47/72 *Di Rollo* v. *Commission* [1973] E.C.R. 763 or by way of a request under article 90(1) that the appointing authority takes a decision (to pay damages) relating to the applicant. In the latter case there is, of course, no express time-limit on the making of the original request; there is, however, as has been noted, a line of authority from Case 59/65 *Schreckenberg* v. *Commission* [1966] E.C.R. 543, 550 and Case 4/67 *Muller (née Collignon)* v. *Commission* [1967] E.C.R. 365, 373, to Case 106/80 *Fournier* v. *Commission* [1981] E.C.R. 2759 to the effect that officials may not make use of a claim for damages in order to endeavour to redress the pecuniary consequences of individual decisions which they have not contested in time or which they have unsuccessfully contested. It would therefore appear that a claim for damages may only be considered in isolation if it does not arise from a challengeable decision.

2–43   The provisions of the Staff Regulations do not, however, mean that an official may never use the more general remedies: the procedure there laid down is only relevant to claims involving the appointing authority in the institution by which the applicant is, has been or hopes to be employed. Hence, in Case 64/80 *Guiffrida* v. *Council* [1981] E.C.R. 693, the applicant officials brought an action under Article 173 of the EEC Treaty for the annulment of a Council Regulation amending the Staff Regulations with regard to salaries and remuneration—and failed since they could not show the Regulation was of direct and individual concern to them; indeed, in Case 33/80 *Albini* v. *Council* [1981] E.C.R. 2141 it was expressly held by the First Chamber that under the provision of the Staff Regulations, the complaint, and therefore the application to the Court, "may only be directed against the appointing authority" and the act adversely affecting the official "must be an act of that authority," and the application was held to be out of time under Article 173 of the EEC Treaty, even though it was within the time-limits of the Staff Regulations, since the acts at issue were Council Regulations.

F. ENFORCEMENT PROCEEDINGS

1. *General Provisions*

EEC Treaty
Article 169

2–44   If the Commission considers that a Member State has failed to fulfil an obligation under this Treaty, it shall deliver a reasoned opinion on the matter after giving the State concerned the opportunity to submit its observations.

If the State concerned does not comply with the opinion within the period laid down by the Commission, the latter may bring the matter before the Court of Justice.

Article 170

A Member State which considers that another Member State has failed to fulfil an obligation under this Treaty may bring the matter before the Court of Justice.

Before a Member State brings an action against another Member State for an alleged infringement of an obligation under this Treaty, it shall bring the matter before the Commission.

The Commission shall deliver a reasoned opinion after each of the States concerned has been given the opportunity to submit its own case and its observations on the other party's case both orally and in writing.

If the Commission has not delivered an opinion within three months of the date on which the matter was brought before it, the absence of such opinion shall not prevent the matter from being brought before the Court of Justice.

(Articles 141 and 142 of the Euratom Treaty are in identical terms.)

ECSC Treaty
Article 88

2–45   If the High Authority considers that a State has failed to fulfil an obligation under this Treaty, it shall record this failure in a reasoned decision after giving the State concerned the opportunity to submit its comments. It shall set the State a time limit for the fulfilment of its obligation.

The State may institute proceedings before the Court within two months of notification of the decision; the Court shall have unlimited jurisdiction in such cases.

If the State has not fulfilled its obligation by the time limit set by the High Authority, or if it brings an action which is dismissed, the High Authority may, with the assent of the Council acting by a two-thirds majority:

(a) suspend the payment of any sums which it may be liable to pay to the State in question under this Treaty;

(b) take measures, or authorize the other Member States to take measures, by way of derogation from the provisions of Article 4, in order to correct the effects of the infringement of the obligation.

Proceedings may be instituted before the Court against decisions taken under subparagraphs (a) and (b) within two months of their notification; the Court shall have unlimited jurisdiction in such cases.

If these measures prove ineffective, the High Authority shall bring the matter before the Council.

Article 89

Any dispute between Member States concerning the application of this Treaty which cannot be settled by another procedure provided for in this Treaty may be submitted to the Court on application by one of the States which are parties to the dispute.

2–46 The enforcement procedure under Article 88 of the ECSC Treaty comes before the Court as an action for the annulment of a Commission decision, subject to a two-month time-limit rather than the one-month limit more usual under that Treaty (see para. 2–10 above). On the other hand, the procedures under Articles 169 and 170 of the EEC Treaty and Article 89 of the ECSC Treaty come before the Court at the instigation of the complainant, be it the Commission or another Member State, and no express time-limits are laid down (except with regard to the issue of a reasoned opinion by the Commission under Article 170 of the EEC Treaty). The matter was however expressly considered by the Court in the context of the Euratom Treaty in Case 7/71 *Commission* v. *France* [1971] E.C.R. 1003, 1016, where, with reference to enforcement proceedings brought by the Commission, it was said that "the action for a declaration that a State has failed to fulfil an obligation . . . does not have to be brought within a predetermined period, since, by reason of its nature and its purpose, this procedure involves a power on the part of the Commission to consider the most appropriate means and time-limits for the purposes of putting an end to any contraventions of the Treaty," adding that the fact that the Commission only commenced its action after a lengthy period of time cannot have the effect of regularising a continuing contravention. The implication appears to be that as a matter of policy enforcement proceedings cannot be time-barred.

Under Article 170 of the EEC Treaty, although a Member State may bring an action before the Court if the Commission has not issued an opinion within three months, it would appear that the complainant may await a longer period until the opinion is actually sent, and indeed wait to see if the opinion is complied with, as in Case 141/78 *France* v. *U.K.* [1979] E.C.R. 2923, 2927–2928.

2. *State Aids*

EEC Treaty

Article 93

2–47   2. If, after giving notice to the parties concerned to submit their comments, the Commission finds that aid granted by a State or through State resources is not compatible with the common market having regard to Article 92, or that such aid is being misused, it shall decide that the State concerned shall abolish or alter such aid within a period of time to be determined by the Commission.

If the State concerned does not comply with this decision within the prescribed time, the Commission or any other interested State may, in derogation from the provisions of Articles 169 and 170, refer the matter to the Court of Justice direct.

The enforcement of the EEC state aids rules may be brought before the European Court either in an action brought by the Member State for the annulment of the Commission decision, which is subject to the normal two-month time-limit under that Treaty (see para. 2–09), or in an action brought by the Commission or another Member State in relation to the addressee State's failure to comply with the decision, for which no limitation period is laid down. Although it was held in Case 120/73 *Lorenz* v. *Germany* [1973] E.C.R. 1471 that the Commission, on being notified of a new or amended aid, should take a decision within a "reasonable period," which was taken to be two months, it would appear that considerations similar to those noted in the context of general enforcement proceedings militate against the time-barring of actions relating to the Member State's failure to comply with the decision. It is clear from Case 156/77 *Commission* v. *Belgium* [1978] E.C.R. 1881 that the Commission may bring enforcement proceedings long after the expiry of the period during which the Member State could have sought the annulment of the decision, and indeed (at p. 1897) that a Member State which has failed to challenge the decision in time may not contest its validity in the subsequent enforcement proceedings.

3. *Serious Internal Disturbances, Serious International Tension, etc.*

EEC Treaty

Article 225

2–48   If measures taken in the circumstances referred to in Articles 223 and 224 have the effect of distorting the conditions of competition in the common market, the Commission shall, together with the State concerned, examine how these measures can be adjusted to the rules laid down in this Treaty.

By way of derogation from the procedure laid down in Articles 169 and 170, the Commission or any Member State may bring the matter directly before the Court of Justice if it considers that another Member State is making improper use of the powers provided for in Articles 223 and 224. The Court of Justice shall give its ruling *in camera*.

Articles 223 and 224 are concerned respectively with measures taken by Member States in the essential interest of its security, or in the event of, *inter alia*, serious internal disturbances or serious international tension. No limitation period is provided for the use of the enforcement procedure under the second paragraph of Article 225, which does not appear to have been used in practice, but presumably the same policy considerations are relevant as with other enforcement procedures.

4. *Euratom Special Provisions*

Euratom Treaty

Article 21

2–49   If the proprietor does not propose that the matter be referred to the Arbitration Committee, the Commission may call upon the Member State concerned or its appropriate authorities to grant the licence or cause it to be granted.

If, having, heard the proprietor's case, the Member State, or its appropriate authorities, considers that the conditions of Article 17 have not been complied with, it shall notify the Commission of its refusal to grant the licence or to cause it to be granted.

If it refuses to grant the licence or to cause it to be granted, or if, within four months of the date of the request, no information is forthcoming with regard to the granting of the licence, the Commission shall have two months in which to bring the matter before the Court of Justice.

The proprietor must be heard in the proceedings before the Court of Justice.

If the judgment of the Court of Justice establishes that the conditions of Article 17 have been complied with, the Member State concerned, or its appropriate authorities, shall take such measures as enforcement of that judgment may require.

Article 38

The Commission shall make recommendations to the Member States with regard to the level of radioactivity in the air, water and soil.

In cases of urgency, the Commission shall issue a directive requiring the Member State concerned to take, within a period laid down by the Commission, all necessary measures to prevent infringement of the basic standards and to ensure compliance with regulations.

Should the State in question fail to comply with the Commission directive within the period laid down, the Commission or any Member State concerned may forthwith, by way of derogation from Articles 141 and 142 bring the matter before the Court of Justice.

Article 81

(3) If the carrying out of an inspection is opposed, the Commission shall apply to the President of the Court of Justice for an order to ensure that the inspection be carried out compulsorily. The President of the Court of Justice shall give a decision within three days.

(4) If there is danger in delay, the Commission may itself issue written order, in the form of a decision, to proceed with the inspection. This order shall be submitted without delay to the President of the Court of Justice for subsequent approval.

Article 82

Inspectors shall be recruited by the Commission.

They shall be responsible for obtaining and verifying the records referred to in Article 79. They shall report any infringement to the Commission.

The Commission may issue a directive calling upon the Member State concerned to take, by a time limit set by the Commission, all measures necessary to bring such infringement to an end; it shall inform the Council thereof.

If the Member State does not comply with the Commission directive by the time limit set, the Commission or any Member State concerned may, in derogation from Articles 141 and 142, refer the matter to the Court of Justice direct.

Article 145

If the Commission considers that a person or undertaking has committed an infringement of this Treaty to which the provisions of Article 83 do not apply, it shall call upon the Member State having jurisdiction over that person or undertaking to cause sanctions to be imposed in respect of the infringement in accordance with its national law.

If the State concerned does not comply with such a request within the period laid down by the Commission, the latter may bring an action before the Court of Justice to have the infringement of which the person or undertaking is accused established.

2–50   Although Article 145 of the Euratom Treaty, concerning infringement other than of the safeguards provisions, is unusual in that it allows an infringement by an individual or undertaking to be established directly before the Court, it is drafted in a manner similar to the general enforcement provisions, and would appear to be subject to similar considerations with regard to the absence of limitation period. Articles 38 and 82, although enabling the Commission to issue a directive rather than a decision, are otherwise similar in structure to Article 93(2) of the EEC Treaty relating to state aids (see para. 2–47 above). Article 81(3), on the other hand, since it requires the President of the Court to give a decision within three days, would seem to be simply a similar time scale within which the Commission must make its application. Finally, Article 21, which is concerned with the grant of a licence, and therefore may affect private property rights, gives the Commission only two months from the national authorities' refusal or failure to grant the licence or cause it to be granted in which to bring the matter before the Court.

G. Other Forms of Direct Action

1. *Arbitration*

EEC Treaty

Article 181

2–51   The Court of Justice shall have jurisdiction to give judgement pursuant to any arbitration clause contained in a contract concluded by or on behalf of the Community, whether that contract be governed by public or private law.

Article 182

The Court of Justice shall have jurisdiction in any dispute between Member States which relates to the subject matter of this Treaty if the dispute is submitted to it under a special agreement between the parties.

(Articles 153 and 154 of the Euratom Treaty are in identical terms as are also Articles 42 and 89 (second paragraph) of the ECSC Treaty.)

The Treaties in effect envisage two different types of arbitration, arbitration arising out of a contract and arbitration in the context of a dispute between Member States, although other conventions or agreements have gone further: *e.g.* Article 25(2) of the 1963 Association Agreement between the EEC and Turkey (O.J. 1973, C113/2) enabled disputes with Turkey to be submitted to the Court. In neither case is there any express limitation period. It would, however, be possible for a contractural arbitration clause expressly to include one, although none appears to have been included in the draft agreement at issue in Case 23/76 *Pellegrini* v. *Commission* [1976] E.C.R. 1807; otherwise, the matter could appear to be subject to the proper law of the contract. Where there is an arbitration clause, it was held in Case 109/81 *Pace (née Porta)* v. *Commission* (July 1, 1982) that the admissibility of the proceedings under the arbitration clause is not affected by the fact that an attempt was erroneously made to bring the matter before the Court under another head of jurisdiction, in that case the Staff Regulations. With regard to disputes between Member States, the Treaty provisions also envisage an agreement which presumably could deal with the matter expressly; otherwise it might be suggested that enforcement procedures provide the nearest analogy (see para. 2–44 above).

2. Requests for Opinions and Rulings

EEC Treaty

Article 228

2–52 1. Where this Treaty provides for the conclusion of agreements between the Community and one or more States or an international organization, such agreements shall be negotiated by the Commission. Subject to the powers vested in the Commission in this field, such agreements shall be concluded by the Council, after consulting the Assembly where required by this Treaty.

The Council, the Commission or a Member State may obtain beforehand the opinion of the Court of Justice as to whether an agreement envisaged is compatible with the provisions of this Treaty. Where the opinion of the Court of Justice is adverse, the agreement may enter into force only in accordance with Article 236.

Euratom Treaty

Article 103

2–53 Member States shall communicate to the Commission draft agreements or contracts with a third State, an international organization or a national of a third

State to the extent that such agreements or contracts concern matters within the purview of this Treaty.

If a draft agreement or contract contains clauses which impede the application of this Treaty, the Commission shall, within one month of receipt of such communication, make its comments known to the State concerned.

The State shall not conclude the proposed agreement or contract until it has satisfied the objections of the Commission or complied with a ruling by the Court of Justice, adjudicating urgently upon an application from the State, on the compatibility of the proposed clauses with the provisions of this Treaty. An application may be made to the Court of Justice at any time after the State has received the comments of the Commission.

Article 104

No person or undertaking concluding or renewing an agreement or contract with a third State, an international organization or national of a third State after the entry into force of this Treaty may invoke that agreement or contract in order to evade the obligations imposed by this Treaty.

Each Member State shall take such measures as it considers necessary in order to communicate to the Commission, at the request of the latter, all information relating to agreements or contracts concluded after the entry into force of this Treaty, within the purview thereof, by a person or undertaking with a third State, an international organization or a national of a third State. The Commission may require such communication only for the purpose of verifying that such agreements or contracts do not contain clauses impeding the implementation of this Treaty.

On application by the Commission, the Court of Justice shall give a ruling on the compatibility of such agreements or contracts with the provisions of this Treaty.

Article 105

The provisions of this Treaty shall not be invoked so as to prevent the implementation of agreements or contracts concluded before its entry into force by a Member State, a person or an undertaking with a third State, an international organization or a national of a third State where such agreements or contracts have been communicated to the Commission not later than thirty days after the entry into force of this Treaty.

Agreements or contracts concluded between the signature and the entry into force of this Treaty by a person or an undertaking with a third State, an international organization or a national of a third State shall not, however, be invoked as grounds for failure to implement this Treaty if, in the opinion of the Court of Justice, ruling on an application from the Commission, one of the decisive reasons on the part of either of the parties in concluding the agreement or contract was an intention to evade the provisions of this Treaty.

ECSC Treaty

Article 95

2–54   In all cases not provided for in this Treaty where it becomes apparent that a decision or recommendation of the High Authority is necessary to attain, within the common market in coal and steel and in accordance with Article 5, one of the objectives of the Community set out in Articles 2, 3 and 4, the decision may be taken or the recommendation made with the unanimous assent of the Council and after the Consultative Committee has been consulted.

Any decision so taken or recommendation so made shall determine what penalties, if any, may be imposed.

If, after the end of the transitional period provided in the Convention on the Transitional Provisions, unforeseen difficulties emerging in the light of experience in the application of this Treaty, or fundamental economic or technical changes directly affecting the common market in coal and steel, make it necessary to adapt the rules for the High Authority's exercise of its powers, appropriate amendments may be made; they must not, however, conflict with the provisions of Articles 2, 3 and 4 or interfere with the relationship between the powers of the High Authority and those of the other institutions of the Community.

These amendments shall be proposed jointly by the High Authority and the Council, acting by a nine-tenths majority of its members, and shall be submitted to the Court for its opinion. In considering them, the Court shall have full power to assess all points of fact and of law. If as a result of such consideration it finds the proposals compatible with the provisions of the preceding paragraph, they shall be forwarded to the Assembly and shall enter into force if approved by a majority of three quarters of the votes cast and two thirds of the members of the Assembly.

2–55 None of the provisions governing requests for opinions or rulings specify a time-limit. Nonetheless, Article 103 of the Euratom Treaty requires the Commission to make its comments known within one month of receiving communication of a draft agreement or contract, and also requires the Court to give its ruling "urgently," but allows the Member State to make its application "at any time." In fact in Ruling 1/78 [1978] E.C.R. 2151, the Commission informed the Belgian Government of its comments on April 28, 1978, and the Belgian Government referred the matter to the Court on June 7, 1978.

2–56 In relation to Opinions under Article 228 of the EEC Treaty, it was expressly held in Opinion 1/75 [1975] E.C.R. 1355, 1360–1361, that since it provided for a non-contentious procedure, no time-limit was laid down, so that the fact that discussions on the agreement at issue were at an end could not "constitute a valid argument on which to base a finding that the request for an opinion is out of time." On the other hand, in Opinion 1/78 [1979] E.C.R. 2871, 2908, where it was argued by the Council that the negotiations on the agreement in question were still not at an advanced stage, so that there was no "agreement envisaged," the Court held that, at least where the question of powers to negotiate the agreement is to be determined, it was in the interest of all the States concerned that such a question should be clarified "as soon as any particular negotiations are commenced."

The requests for Opinions under the ECSC Treaty, which are presented by the Commission and Council jointly (see para. 13–02 below) are perhaps the supreme example of a non-contentious procedure, for which in the Court's view a time-limit is inappropriate. However, in practice such requests have been presented within the range of two days (Opinion 1/61 [1961] E.C.R. 243) to about a month (Opinion 1/59 [1959] E.C.R. 259, Opinion 1/60 [1960] E.C.R. 39).

93

3. *Special Euratom Procedures*

Euratom Treaty

Article 12

2–57   Member States, persons or undertakings shall have the right, on application to the Commission, to obtain non-exclusive licences under patents, provisionally protected patent rights, utility models or patent applications owned by the Community, where they are able to make effective use of the inventions covered thereby.

Under the same conditions, the Commission shall grant sub-licences under patents, provisionally protected patent rights, utility models or patent applications, where the Community holds contractual licences conferring power to do so.

The Commission shall grant such licences or sub-licences on terms to be agreed with the licensees and shall furnish all the information required for their use. These terms shall relate in particular to suitable remuneration and, where appropriate, to the right of the licensee to grant sub-licences to third parties and to the obligation to treat the information as a trade secret.

Failing agreement on the terms referred to in the third paragraph, the licensees may bring the matter before the Court of Justice so that appropriate terms may be fixed.

Article 18

An Arbitration Committee is hereby established for the purposes provided for in this Section. The Council shall appoint the members and lay down the rulse of procedure of this Committee, acting on a proposal from the Court of Justice.

An appeal, having suspensory effect, may be brought by the parties before the Court of Justice against a decision of the Arbitration Committee within one month of notification thereof. The Court of Justice shall confine its examination to the formal validity of the decision and to the interpretation of the provisions of this Treaty by the Arbitration Committee.

The final decisions of the Arbitration Committee shall have the force of *res judicata* between the parties concerned. They shall be enforceable as provided in Article 164.

2–58   Article 18 specifies that appeals against decisions of the Arbitration Committee, relating to the grant of non-exclusive licences in the absence of amicable agreement, must be brought within one month of their notification. In the context of disputes as to the grant of licences by the Commission, Article 12 does not specify any time-limit within which the matter must be brought before the Court, but nevertheless assumes continuing negotiations.

H. EXCEPTIONAL AND ANCILLARY FORMS OF PROCEDURE

2–59   The time-limits, limitation periods, or other considerations of time relevant to applications for interim measures (see para. 10–01), applications to intervene (see para. 11–01), third party proceedings (see para. 12–01), applications for the rectification, interpretation and revision of judgments (see paras. 8–22 and 8–25), applications for legal aid (see para. 16–01) and requests for an order on costs (see para. 17–05) are considered in the context of the relevant procedures.

REFERENCES FOR PRELIMINARY RULINGS

EEC Treaty

Article 177

2–60   The Court of Justice shall have jurisdiction to give preliminary rulings concerning:
  (a) the interpretation of the Treaty;
  (b) the validity and interpretation of acts of the institutions of the Community;
  (c) the interpretation of the statutes of bodies established by an act of the Council, where those statutes so provide.
  Where such a question is raised before any court or tribunal of a Member State, that court or tribunal may, if it considers that a decision on the question is necessary to enable it to give judgment, request the Court of Justice to give a ruling thereon.
  Where any such question is raised in a case pending before a court or tribunal of a Member State, against whose decisions there is no judicial remedy under national law, that court or tribunal shall bring the matter before the Court of Justice.
  (Article 150 of the Euratom Treaty is in identical terms, except that in paragraph (c) the words "where these statutes so provide" are replaced by the words "save where these statutes provide otherwise.")

ECSC Treaty

Article 41

  The Court shall have sole jurisdiction to give preliminary rulings on the validity of acts of the High Authority and of the Council where such validity is in issue in proceedings brought before a national court or tribunal.

Protocol concerning the interpretation by the Court of Justice of the Convention of 27 September 1968 on jurisdiction and the enforcement of civil and commercial judgments

Article 3

2–61   1. Where a question of interpretation of the Convention or of one of the other instruments referred to in Article 1 is raised in a case pending before one of the courts listed in Article 2(1), that court shall, if it considers that a decision on the question is necessary to enable it to give judgment, request the Court of Justice to give a ruling thereon.
  2. Where such a question is raised before any court referred to in Article 2(2) or (3), that court may, under the conditions laid down in paragraph 1, request the Court of Justice to give a ruling thereon.
  (Effectively, only appellate courts may make a reference under this convention.)

95

Article 4

The competent authority of a Contracting State may request the Court of Justice to give a ruling on a question of interpretation of the Convention or of one of the other instruments referred to in Article 1 if judgements given by courts of that State conflict with the interpretation given either by the Court of Justice or in a judgment of one of the courts of another Contracting State referred to in Article 2(1) or (2). The provisions of this paragraph shall apply only to judgments which have become *res judicata*.

2. The interpretation given by the Court of Justice in response to such a request shall not affect the judgments which gave rise to the request for interpretation.

3. The Procurators-General of the Courts of Cassation of the Contracting States, or any other authority designated by a Contracting State, shall be entitled to request the Court of Justice for a ruling on interpretation in accordance with paragraph 1.

4. The Registrar of the Court of Justice shall give notice of the request to the Contracting States, to the Commission and to the Council of the European Communities; they shall then be entitled within two months of the notification to submit statements of case or written observations to the Court.

5. No fees shall be levied or any costs or expenses awarded in respect of the proceedings provided for in this Article.

2–62   None of the provisions in force governing references for preliminary rulings contain any specific time-limits relating to the reference as such, a feature shared also by Article 2 of the Protocol on the interpretation by the Court of Justice of the Convention of February 29, 1968 on the mutual recognition of companies and bodies corporate and by Article 73 of the Convention of December 15, 1975 for the European Patent for the Common Market. As between the European Court and the national court, the proceedings are classified as non-contentious, as was stated, *e.g.* in Case 62/72 *Bollman* v. *HZA Hamburg-Waltershof* [1973] E.C.R. 269, 275; hence, on the view expressed in Opinion 1/75 [1975] E.C.R. at 1360–1361 a time-limit is inappropriate. In Case 208/80 *Bruce of Donington* v. *Aspden* [1981] E.C.R. 2205 the fact that nearly a year elapsed between making the order for reference and its notification to the Court did not occasion any comment.

So far as the substantive proceedings before the national court are concerned, even if the whole basis of the proceedings is an alleged breach of Community law, they will, "in the absence of any relevant Community rules" remain subject to the national limitation periods appropriate to the form of action invoked, provided such period is "reasonable" and does not make it "impossible in practice to exercise rights which the national courts have a duty to protect," as was held in Case 33/76 *Rewe* v. *Landwirtschaftskammer Saarland* [1976] E.C.R. 1989, 1998, and Case 45/76 *Comet* v. *Produktschap voor Siergewarren* [1976] E.C.R. 2043, 2053 where national time-limits of respectively one month and 30 days were at issue.

2–63   There is not in fact a total absence of Community rules governing claims by or against national authorities. In the area of customs legislation, articles 2, 3, 5 and 10 of Regulation 1430/79 on the repayment or remission of import or export duties (O.J. 1979, L175/1), article 2 of its implementing Regulation 1575/80 (O.J. 1980, L161/13) and article 2 of Regulation 1697/79 on the post-clearance recovery of import duties or export duties (O.J. 1979, L197/1), set out specific time-limits during which relevant claims or actions must be brought. In the context of the Convention on Jurisdiction and the Enforcement of Judgments, Article 36 of that Convention specifies that an appeal against an order for the enforcement of a judgement must be brought within one month of its service on the party against whom enforcement is sought. In the absence of such rules, however, national time-limits are applicable to the national proceedings.

2–64 As has been noted in the context of action for annulment, it is possible for a national court to refer the question of the validity of a Community act to the Court even after a direct action for the annulment of that act had been held inadmissible, as in Case 125/77 *KSH* v. *Hoofdproduktschap voor Akkerbouw-produkten* [1978] E.C.R. 1991, where the validity of a Regulation was considered as a reference after a direct action to challenge it failed in Case 101/76 *KSH* v. *Council and Commission* [1977] E.C.R. 797. More specifically, it was recognised in Case 156/77 *Commission* v. *Belgium* [1978] E.C.R. 1881, 1897 that the validity of a Community measure may be called in question by means of a reference for a preliminary ruling despite the expiry of the time-limit for a direct action for annulment under Article 173 of the EEC Treaty. This was explained on the basis that the system of references "is laid down in respect of *all* measures adopted by the institution" as opposed, presumably, to the limited range of measures susceptible to direct challenge, and that "it corresponds solely to the requirements of the national courts" rather than, it may be supposed, the needs of an individual applicant. On the view that references for preliminary rulings serve the needs of national courts as such, it may be wondered whether the Court will be prepared to ignore the fact that the measure at issue could in fact clearly have been challenged by one of the parties to the national proceedings, and that the party in question failed to make such a challenge within the relevant time-limit. This would ensure the point taken by A.G. Mayras in his Opinion in Case 59/77 *De Bloos* v. *Bouyer* [1977] E.C.R. 2359, 2376–2377, that to assess the validity of an individual competition decision under Article 177 would amount to applying Community law to a specific case, which he said the European Court could only do within the framework of proceedings for annulment under article 173; such a decision is a measure adopted by an institution, and if the national court feels it necessary, it may refer a suitably abstract question as to the validity or interpretation of that decision.

CHAPTER 3

LANGUAGE OF THE CASE

CHOICE OF LANGUAGE

Rules of Procedure

Article 29

3–01 1. The language of a case shall be Danish, Dutch, English, French, German, Greek, Irish or Italian.'

2. The language of a case shall be chosen by the applicant, except that:

(a) where the application is made against a Member State or a natural or legal person having the nationality of a Member State, the language of the case shall be the official language of that State; where that State has more than one official language, the applicant may choose between them;

(b) at the joint request of the parties the Court may authorise another of the languages mentioned in paragraph 1 of this Article to be used as the language of the case for all or part of the proceedings;

(c) at the request of one of the parties, and after the opposite party and the Advocate-General have been heard, the Court, may, by way of derogation from sub paragraphs (a) and (b), authorise another of the languages mentioned in paragraph 1 of this Article to be used as the language of this case for all or part of the proceedings; such a request may not be submitted by an institution of the European Communities.

Where Article 103 of these rules applies, the language of the case shall be the language of the national court or tribunal which refers the matter to the Court.

3. The language of the case shall in particular be used not only in parties' written statements and oral addresses to the Court and in supporting documents but also in the minutes and decisions of the Court.

Supporting documents expressed in any other language must be accompanied by a translation into the language of the case.

In the case of long documents translations may be confined to extracts. However, the Court or Chamber may of its own motion or at the request of a party, at any time call for a complete or fuller translation.

Notwithstanding the foregoing provisions, a Member State shall be entitled to use its official language when intervening in a case before the Court or when taking part in any reference of a kind mentioned in Article 103. This provision shall apply both to written statements and to oral addresses. The Registrar shall cause any such statement or address to be translated into the language of the case.

Article 31

Texts of documents drawn up of the language of the case or in any language authorized pursuant to Article 29 of these rules shall be authentic.

Instructions to the Registrar

Article 4

3–02 2. Unless otherwise expressly authorised by the President or the Court, the Registrar shall decline to accept or, as the case may be, shall without delay return by registered post any pleading or other document not provided for in the Rules of Procedure or not worded in the language of the case.

It is expressly recognised in Article 217 of the EEC Treaty and Article 190 of the Euratom Treaty, and repeated in Council Regulation 1 of April 15, 1958 determining the languages to be used by the EEC (J.O. 385/58), that the Court of Justice may lay down in its Rules of Procedure the languages to be used in proceedings before it. Such a faculty had indeed already been exercised in article 27(1) of the 1953 Rules of Procedure adopted under the ECSC Treaty (J.O. 1953, p. 37).

The result, in the current Rules of Procedure, is that Irish is added to the languages used in the other institutions for the purposes of proceedings before the Court. In practice, the Court has shown itself even more liberal than its Rules of Procedure. These were only amended to enable Danish, English or Irish to be used in December 1974, and to allow Greek to be used from July 1981, but from Accession onwards the Court has been willing to allow a language of a new Member State to be the language of a case. Hence, in 1973, English was used in the applications for interim measures in Joined Cases 6 and 7/73R *Commercial Solvents* v. *Commission* [1973] E.C.R. 357 and in Joined Cases 160 and 161/73R *Miles Druce* v. *Commission* [1973] E.C.R. 1049.

3–03 In principle, in direct actions, it is for the applicant to choose the language of the case, except where the defendant is a Member State or a natural or legal person having the nationality of a Member State. Although the latter situation is not impossible, *e.g.* in an action brought before the Court pursuant to an arbitration clause in a contract under Article 181 of the EEC Treaty, the exception is usually only relevant in actions brought against Member States. The applicant in such actions will normally be the Commission or another Member State (see paras. 1–02, 2–44 above); the well-known exception, Case 6/60 *Humblet* v. *Belgium* [1960] E.C.R. 559, arose under the interpretation provision of the now defunct Protocol on the Privileges and Immunities of the Coal and Steel Community. It was made clear in Case 1/82 *D.* v. *Luxembourg* (October 27, 1982) that following the repeal of that provision, similar proceedings should be brought before a national court, which would be able to avail itself of the general interpretation procedure under Article 177 of the EEC Treaty. Hence the privilege granted to Member States is not likely to inconvenience private litigants.

On the other hand, the 1979 amendments to the Rules of Procedure have added a new provision to article 29(3) recognising that a Member State may use its own language if it intervenes in an action between other parties. This erects into a right what could already have been claimed as a concession under Article 29(2)(c). In any event, the Court had already held, in its order of February 18, 1960 in Case 30/59 *Steenkolenmijnen in Limburg* v. *H.A.* [1961] E.C.R. 1 at p.48, that a

99

would-be intervener is only bound by the language of the case once his application to intervene has been accepted, and hence that he may draw up his application in another language.

3–04 Insofar as the applicant has a choice of language, this is not limited either by the applicant's nationality or by that of his counsel, although presumably most counsel prefer to use their own language. By way of example, in Case 17/74 *Transocean Marine Paint Association* v. *Commission* [1974] E.C.R. 1063, an association with offices in the Netherlands employed Dutch counsel to conduct the case in English, and in Case 113/77 *NTN Toyo* v. *Council* [1979] E.C.R. 1185, a Japanese company employed German counsel to conduct the case in English. What these cases may reflect is the realisation that if a "majority" language such as French or English is used, it is likely that few, if any, of the judges will have to rely on translation or interpretation.

In references for preliminary rulings, on the other hand, there is no choice of language for the parties; they are limited to the language of the court making the reference. Here also the Court has gone beyond a literal reading of its Rules of Procedure; the first reference from a United Kingdom court, in Case 41/74 *Van Duyn* v. *Home Office* [1974] E.C.R. 1337, was heard in English even though it came before the Court before the Rules were amended to recognise English as a language of procedure. As in the case of interventions in direct actions, a Member State putting in observations in a reference is entitled to use its own language by virtue of the 1979 amendments, which give legislative effect to what was already the normal practice.

3–05 Once the language of the case has been settled, the parties must abide by it unless an express derogation is sought; the Registrar is in principle instructed not to admit any document which is not in the language of the case. However, if the Court does admit, or itself requests the production of, such a document, it can take account of its contents, provided it is in an official language, without its being translated into the language of the case. This appears from the judgment in Case 1/60 *FERAM* v. *H.A.* [1960] E.C.R. 165, in connection with documents, not in the language of the case, of which the Court itself had requested the production. It was there held that there is an irrebuttable presumption that the Court is cognisant of its official languages; it was further stated that the provisions on the language of the case could not be regarded as a matter of "ordre public." The result was that although the party affected could have requested a translation of the documents in question, the fact that it had not done so did not prevent the Court taking account of them.

TRANSLATION AND INTERPRETATION

Rules of Procedure

Article 22

3–06 The Court shall set up a translating service staffed by experts with adequate legal training and a thorough knowledge of several official languages of the Court.

Article 29

3. (See para. 3–01 above).

4. Where a witness or expert states that he is unable adequately to express himself in one of the languages referred to in paragraph 1 of this Article, the Court or Chamber may authorise him to give his evidence in another language. The Registrar shall arrange for translation into the language of the case.

5. The President of the Court and the Presidents of Chambers in conducting oral proceedings, the Judge Rapporteur both in his preliminary report and in his report at the hearing, Judges and Advocates-General in putting questions and Advocates-General in delivering their opinions may use a language referred to in paragraph 1 of this Article other than the language of the case. The Registrar shall arrange for translation into the language of the case.

Article 30

1. The Registrar shall, at the request of any Judge of the Advocate-General or of a party, arrange for anything said or written in the course of the proceedings before the Court or a Chamber to be translated into the languages he chooses from those referred to in Article 29(1).

2. Publications of the Court shall be issued in the languages referred to in Article 1 of Council Regulation No. 1.

Article 37

3–07   1. . . . (relates to pleadings in direct actions.)

2. Institutions shall in addition produce, within time limits laid down by the Court, translations of all pleadings into the other languages provided for by Article 1 of Council Regulation No. 1.

Article 72

. . . . . .

(b) where copying or translation work is carried out at the request of a party, the cost shall, in so far as the Registrar considers it excessive, be paid for by that party on the scale of charges referred to in Article 16(5) of these rules.

Article 104

1. The decisions of national courts or tribunals referred to in Article 103 of these rules shall be communicated to the Member States in the original version, accompanied by a translation into the official language of the State to which they are addressed.

Instructions to the Registrar

Article 20

3–08   Registry charges shall be as follows:

(a) . . . . . .

(b) for a translation made pursuant to Article 72(b) of the Rules of Procedure: Lfrs 500 a page;

No page shall contain more than 40 lines.

This scale applies to the first copy; the charge for further copies shall be Lfrs 50 for each page or part of a page.

The charges referred to in this Article shall as from 1 January 1975 be increased by 10 per cent. each time the cost-of-living index published by the Government of the Grand Duchy of Luxembourg is increased by 10 per cent.

Article 24

There shall be published in the languages referred to in Article 1 of Council Regulation No. 1 "Reports of Cases before the Court" which shall, subject to a decision to the contrary, contain the judgments of the Court together with the submissions of the Advocates-General and the opinions given and the interim orders made in the course of the calendar year.

3–09   A clear distinction is made between translation into the language of the case, and translation from the language of the case into another official language. Under article 29(3) of the Rules of Procedure, it is the parties' responsibility to ensure that material put in by them in another language is accompanied by a translation into the language of the case, subject to the possibility of translating only extracts in the case of long documents. The Court's services are responsible for translation into the language of the case only in the three exceptional cases envisaged in article 29(3), article 29(4) and article 29(5), none of which concern material put in by the original parties. article 29(3) relates to the translation of material but in by a Member State intervening in a direct action or submitting observations in a reference for a preliminary ruling and making use of its own language. Article 29(4) is concerned with the translation of evidence given by witnesses and experts; it may be noted that such witnesses and experts are called by the Court, not by the parties themselves (see para. 6–07 below). Article 29(5) provides for the translation of what is said or written by the Members of the Court, who obviously cannot be expected to have full command of all the languages listed in article 29(1). By way of example, it is the usual practice for an Advocate-General to deliver his Opinion in his native language rather than the language of the case, unless that language is one which he knows well and the Opinion is brief, as in Case 68/74 *Alaimo* v. *Préfet du Rhône* [1975] E.C.R. 109, 115, the first of a number of cases in which A.G. Warner delivered an unreserved Opinion in French rather than in English. Furthermore, the 1953 Rules of Procedure expressly empowered the Court to choose the language in which the judgment would be drafted, in article 27(2), and provided for its translation into the language of the case. This provision has disappeared, but the reality remains that the judges must initially draft the judgment in a language which they can all understand. In the case of the Full Court, this has usually meant that the judgment is drafted in French and then translated into the language of the case.

3–10   Primary responsibility for translation from the language of the case into the other recognised languages rests with the Court's services, under article 30 of the Rules of Procedure. The practical importance of this provision is to enable the Members of the Court to be able to follow a case in a language which they understand; a request for translation is unlikely to be made by a party to the action except perhaps where the language of the case or part of it has been determined under article 29(2)(c). Where, however, such a request is made, the party making it may be required to pay the charge set out in article 20(b) of the Instructions to the Registrar insofar as the cost of translation is, in the terms of article 72 of the Rules of Procedure, considered "exessive," a point on which there appears to by no authority. With regard to the requests which could be made by the Members of the Court, in order to avoid the development of a situation whereby every statement and document in every case has to be translated into every language, a convention has developed whereby material will automatically be translated into French if the language of the case is not French, but the Judges and Advocates-General will not usually request a translation into another language unless there is a special reason, *e.g.* a question of technical vocabulary. In effect, French has so far been the internal working language of the Court. The pressure on the Court's own translation service in this context is alleviated to some degree by an agreement with the other Community institutions that, in litigation in which they are involved in which the language of the case is not French, they will provide their own translations of written material submitted by them. In direct actions, this in turn represents something of a reduction of their obligation under article 37(2) of the Rules of Procedure to produce translations of their pleadings into all the languages except Irish.

3–11   On the other hand, although it is unusual, there would appear to be nothing to prevent a private litigant submitting his or its own translation of its own pleadings, provided the original is lodged in the language of the case. By way of example, in Case 77/77 *BP* v. *Commission* [1978] E.C.R. 1513, where the language of the case was Dutch, BP also lodged its own English versions of certain documents.

However, in the case of references for preliminary rulings, the revised article 104(1) of the Rules of Procedure requires the Court's services to provide a translation of the order for reference into the language of each Member State when it is notified to the Member States under article 20 of the EEC Statute of the Court. The Court's services are also effectively required to produce translations of judgments, orders, and opinions of Advocates-General for publication, but only, under article 30(2) of the Rules of Procedure and article 24 of the Instructions to the Registrar, in the languages laid down by Council Regulation No. 1 of April 15, 1958 (J.O. 385/58) as amended by the Act of Accession, which does not include Irish. If this is taken literally, it would appear to mean that the Court is under no obligation to publish the Irish version of a judgment given in a case heard in Irish—though no doubt the necessary arrangements would be made if such a situation arose.

3–12   The term "translation" is used in articles 29 and 30 of the Rules of Procedure in the context of both written and oral procedure. However, the translating service set up by the Court under article 22 of the Rules of Procedure, which consists of lawyers with linguistic ability rather than the other way round, is concerned solely with the translation of the written word. Translation of the spoken word is referred to as "interpretation," and the Court did not begin to employ its own interpretation service until 1981. As appears from the Report of the House of Lords Select Committee on the European Communities on the European Court (Session 1979–1980, 23rd Report, para. 46, and

Minutes of Evidence, p. 75, para. 265), the Court had previously been refused the finance necessary to employ such a service, and had to "borrow" interpreters from the European Parliament who were not necessarily legally qualified. Given the generality of the term "translation" as used in the Rules of Procedure, it may perhaps be doubted whether such a situation complied with the requirements of article 22 of those Rules. The practical consequence has been to enhance even further the importance of the written procedure, as opposed to the oral procedure, particularly where the litigants wish to use a minority language.

CHAPTER 4

WRITTEN PROCEDURE

THE ROLE OF THE REGISTRY

EEC Statute of the Court of Justice

Article 18

4–01 The procedure before the Court shall consist of two parts: written and oral.

The written procedure shall consist of the communication to the parties and to the institutions of the Community whose decisions are in dispute, of applications, statements of case, defences and observations, and of replies, if any, as well as of all papers and documents in support or of certified copies of them.

Communications shall be made by the Registrar in the order and within the time laid down in the rules of procedure.

(Article 18 of the Euratom Statute and article 21 of the ECSC Statute are in identical terms.)

Article 20

In the cases governed by Article 177 of this Treaty the decision of the Court or tribunal of a Member State which suspends its proceedings and refers a case to the Court shall be notified by the Registrar of the Court to the parties, to the Member States and to the Commission, and also to the Council if the act the validity or interpretation of which is in dispute originates from the Council.

(Article 21 of the Euratom Statute uses parallel terms; corresponding provisions for cases governed by Article 41 of the ECSC Treaty are contained in the first sub-paragraph of article 103(3) of the Rules of Procedure).

Rules of Procedure

Article 16

4–02 1. There shall be kept in the Registry, under the control of the Registrar, a register initialed by the President, in which all pleadings and supporting documents shall be consecutively entered in the order in which they are lodged.

2. When a document has been registered, the Registrar shall make a note to that effect on the original and, if a party so requests, on any copy submitted for the purpose.

3. Entries in the register and the notes provided for in the preceding paragraph shall constitute official records.

4. Rules for keeping the register shall be prescribed by the Instructions to the Registrar referred to in Article 15 of these rules.

5. Interested persons may consult the register at the Registry and may obtain copies or extracts on payment of a charge on a scale to be fixed by the Court acting on a proposal from the Registrar.

The parties to a case may on payment of the appropriate charge also obtain copies of pleadings and authenticated copies of judgments and orders.

6. Notice shall be given in the *Official Journal of the European Communities* of the date of registration of an application originating proceedings the names and permanent residences of the parties, the subject-matter of the dispute, the claims made in the application and a summary of the contentions and of the main arguments adduced in support.

7. Where the Council or the Commission is not a party to a case, the Court shall forward to it copies of the application and of the defence, without the annexes thereto, to enable it to assess whether the inapplicability of one of its acts is being invoked under the third paragraph of Article 36 of the ECSC Treaty, Article 184 of the EEC Treaty or Article 156 of the Euratom Treaty.

Article 17

1. The Registrar shall be responsible, under the authority of the President, for the acceptance, transmission and custody of documents and for effecting such service as is provided for by these rules.

Article 79

1. Where these rules require that a document be served on a person, the Registrar shall ensure that service is effected at that persons's address for service either by the dispatch of a copy of the document by registered post with a form for acknowledgement of receipt or by personal delivery of the copy against a receipt.

The Registrar shall prepare and certify the copies of documents to be served, save where the parties themselves supply the copies in accordance with Article 37(1) of these rules.

2. The official record of dispatch together with the acknowledgment or the receipt shall be annexed to the original of the document.

Instructions to the Registrar

Article 1

4–03 1. The Registry shall be open to the public from Monday to Friday from 10 a.m. to 12 noon and from 3 p.m. to 6 p.m. except on the official holidays listed in Annex 1 to the Rules of Procedure.

Outside the opening hours of the Registry procedural documents may be validly lodged with the janitor, who shall record the date and time of such lodging.

2. In any event the Registry shall at every public hearing held by the Court or a Chamber be open to the public half an hour before the hearing begins.

Article 2

The Registrar shall be responsible for maintaining the files of pending cases and for keeping them fully up to date.

Article 3

2. The Registrar shall ensure that where the ECSC, EEC or Euratom Treaty, the ECSC, EEC or Euratom Statute, the Rules of Procedure or any other act giving powers to the Court of Justice provide for a document to be served, a notice to be given or a communication to be made the steps are carried out in accordance with the Rules of Procedure; the documents, notices and communications shall be sent by registered post, accompanied by a note signed by

106

the Registrar giving the number of the case and the registration number of the document, together with a brief indication as to its nature. A copy of the note shall be appended to the original document.

3. The parties shall be served with the pleadings and other documents relating to the proceedings.

Where a document is very bulky and only one specimen of it is lodged at the Registry, the Registrar shall, after consulting the Judge-Rapporteur, inform the parties by registered letter that the document may be inspected by them at the Registry.

4. Where in the submission in the application originating proceedings it is contended that an act of a Community institution not being a party to the action is illegal, the Registrar shall transmit a copy of the application to the institution in accordance with the second paragraph of Article 18 of the Statutes of the Court of Justice of the EEC and the Euratom and the second paragraph of Article 21 of the Statute of the Court of Justice of the ECSC.

The Registrar shall not transmit other written pleadings to the institution unless the institution has been allowed to intervene in accordance with Article 93(4) of the Rules of Procedure.

Article 4

1. A party who has lodged a procedural document at the Registry shall, if he so requests, be given a receipt.

Article 11

The Registrar shall be responsible for keeping up to date the Register of cases brought before the Court.

Article 12

When an application originating proceedings is registered, the case shall be given a serial number followed by a mention of the year and a statement of either the name of the applicant or the subject matter of the application. Cases shall be referred to by their serial numbers.

An application for the adoption of interim measures shall be given the same serial number as the principal action, followed by the letter "R."

Article 13

The pages of the Register shall be numbered in advance.

At regular intervals the President and the Registrar shall check the Register and initial it in the margin against the last entry.

Article 14

4-04   The procedural documents in cases brought before the Court, including documents lodged by the parties and documents served by the Registrar, shall be entered in the Register.

An annex which has not been lodged at the same time as the procedural document to which it relates shall be separately registered.

Article 15

1. Entries in the Register shall be made chronologically in the order in which the documents to be registered are lodged; they shall be numbered consecutively.

2. Procedural documents shall be registered as soon as they are lodged at the Registry.

Documents drawn up the Court shall be registered on the day of issue.

3. The entry in the Register shall contain the information necessary for identifying the document and in particular:
—the date of registration
—the reference to the case,
—the date of the document.

The entry shall be made in the language of the case; numbers shall be written in figures and usual abbreviations shall be permitted.

4. Where a correction is made in the Register a note to that effect, initialed by the Registrar, shall be made in the margin.

Article 16

The registration number of every document drawn up by the Court shall be noted on its first page.

A note of the registration, worded as follows, shall be stamped on the original of every document lodged by the parties.

"Registered at the Court of Justice under No. . . . Luxembourg, ... day of . . . 19 . . . "

This note shall be signed by the Registrar.

Article 20

Registry charges shall be as follows;
(a) for an authenticated copy of a judgment or order, a certified copy of a procedural document or set of minutes, an extract from the Court Register, a certified copy of the Court Register or a certified copy made pursuant to Article 72(b) of the Rules of Procedure: Lfrs 60 a page;
(b) . . .

No page shall contain more than 40 lines.

This scale applies to the first copy; the charge for further copies shall be Lfrs 50 for each page or part of a page.

The charges referred to in this Article shall as from 1 January 1975 be increased by 10 per cent. each time the cost-of-living index published by the Government of the Grand Duchy of Luxembourg is increased by 10 per cent.

Article 25

4–05 The Registrar shall cause the following to be published in the *Official Journal of the European Communities*:
(a) notices of applications originating proceedings, as referred to in Article 16(6) of the Rules of Procedure;
(b) notices of the removal of cases from the Register;

4–06 The Registry has a pivotal role in the written procedure before the Court. Its work can be divided into three distinct elements, each of fundamental practical importance: the maintenance of the case-files and register of cases, the service of documents, and making public the fact that the action has commenced.

A. REGISTER AND FILES

4–07 As pleadings and other documents are received in the Registry, the details listed in article 15(3) of the Instructions to the Registrar are entered in the Register, and the document is only entered in the file of the case to which it relates once a note of its registration has been stamped on it under article 16 of those Instructions. Although article 12 of the Instructions uses terminology apposite only to direct actions, wherever a document is registered which has the effect of commencing proceedings before the Court, be it an application or an order for reference, the case is given a serial number. These numbers being allocated consecutively throughout each calendar year, so that Case 1/80 is the first case in which the application or order for reference was registered in 1980. In practice this number is followed not only by the name of the applicant, a term appropriate only to a direct action, but by the names of the parties to a direct action or of the parties to the relevant action in which a reference for a preliminary ruling was made, set out in adversary form where appropriate, and sometimes where it might not seem wholly appropriate as in Case 110/76 *Pretore of Cento* v. *A person or persons unknown* [1977] E.C.R. 851 which in fact was a reference in criminal investigation proceedings before the Pretore of Cento. Despite the statement in article 12 of the Instructions that cases shall be referred to by their serial numbers, the practice is to refer to them by their names as well, a point confirmed in paragraph 6 of the Notes for the Guidance of Counsel at Oral Hearings (see para. 7–25 below) which requests Counsel to cite cases by the names of the parties as well as the numbers.

4–08   Once a number has been allocated to a case, that same number, with the addition of a suitable suffix will be used in any ancillary proceedings. Article 12 of the Instructions expressly mentions that an application for the adoption of interim measures will be given the same serial number followed by the letter "R," and in fact "RR" has been used in the case of an application for the suspension of the operation of a contested act until the Court's decision on a further application for its suspension until judgment was given in the main action, *e.g.* Case 71/74 R and RR *Frubo* v. *Commission* [1974] E.C.R. 1031. A similar system, however, is also used in the case of an application for revision of a judgment, *e.g.* Case 56/75 rev. *Elz* v. *Commission* [1977] E.C.R. 1617, in the case of an application for the interpretation of a judgment, *e.g.* Joined Cases 41, 43 and 44/73—Interpretation: *SA Générale Sucrière* v. *Commission* [1977] E.C.R. 445, in third party proceedings, *e.g.* Joined Cases 42 and 49/59—Third Party Proceedings: *Breedband* v. *Aciéries du Temple* [1962] E.C.R. 145, in an application to intervene in an application for interim measures, *e.g.* Case 113/77R—Int. *NTN Toyo* v. *Council* [1977] E.C.R. 1721, and even in instances where it was held that the order sought was of a type the Court had no jurisdiction to give, *e.g.* Case 4/73—Enforcement: *Nold* v. *Ruhrkohle A.G.* [1977] E.C.R. 1. In Case 567/79A *Flamm* v. *Commission* and Case 618/79A *Knoeppel* v. *Commission* (July 1, 1982) the suffix "A" was added to the original serial number when additional applications submitted by the same applicant were treated as new applications. The practical advantage of this system is that any documents in the ancillary proceedings will be filed together with the documents in the main proceedings, thus facilitating any cross-reference.

Whilst, under article 16(5) of the Rules, the register may be consulted by "interested persons," a term which has not given rise to any pronouncement on the part of the Court, and the Registry itself is open to the public at the times stated in article 1 of the Instructions to the Registrar, the actual files relating to each case and the pleadings and other documents which they contain are treated as confidential and available only to those taking part in the proceedings, the members of the Court, and officials of the Court who need to translate or consult the relevant documents. This is underlined by article 3(4) of the Instructions to the Registrar which, although it should be amended to take account of the fact that article 16(7) of the Rules, which was introduced in 1979, requires the defence as well as the application to be forwarded to the Council and/or Commission in cases in which one or both is not a party, expressly forbids the transmission of other pleadings even to a Community institution unless it has been permitted to intervene in the case. Hence, although an interested outsider can find out from the register which pleadings and other documents have been submitted in a particular case, he will not be permitted to inspect them.

B. SERVICE OF DOCUMENTS

4–09 In the written procedure before the Court, by virtue of article 18 of the Statute, and articles 17 and 79 of the Rules of Procedure, the service or communication of documents is the responsibility of the Registrar. As will be seen (see para. 4–28 below), all that an applicant in a direct action or a national court making an order for reference need do is to ensure that the application or the reference reaches the Court's Registry. Article 79 of the Rules refers to service at a persons' "address for service" a term really only appropriate to direct actions, and even here a defendant's address for service will only be known after the defence has been lodged. However, since the defendant in most direct actions is a Community institution, or, very much less frequently, a Member State, the Registry has so far encountered little difficulty in discovering the address of the defendant for the purpose of serving the initial application.

Greater problems may arise with regard to the communication of a national court's order for reference to the parties under article 20 of the Statute, particularly where the form of the national judgment does not make it immediately apparent who the real parties are, as in an English application for judicial review. By way of example, in Case 41/77 *R*. v. *National Insurance Commissioner ex p. Warry* [1977] E.C.R. 2085, the Registry officials had to consult English-trained lawyers on the Court's staff to find out that the National Insurance Commissioner was not a real defendant, and that the real dispute was between a local insurance officer named Warry and a claimant named Kelly, and it required active investigation by the Registry to discover that Kelly was a resident in Germany and to find his address so as to be able to notify the reference to him. It is, however, well established that the expression "parties" in article 20 of the Statute means the parties to the action pending before the national court, a point reaffirmed in Case 62/72 *Bollmann* v. *HZA Hamburg-Waltershof* [1973] E.C.R. 269, 275.

4–10 It may be observed that the Member States, Commission, and Council where its acts are involved, are put in a privileged position with regard to the notificaton of references for preliminary rulings. This can be defended on the grounds that the Community acts in question will almost always have emanated from the Commission or Council, and that a reference for the interpretation of Community law can often disguise a challenge to national rules, as in the very first reference from a U.K. court, Case 41/74 *van Duyn* v. *Home Office* [1974] E.C.R. 1337, where the question whether a provision in an EEC Directive could produce direct effects was raised so as to enable that provision to be used, unsuccessfully in the event, to challenge the then U.K. policy prohibiting the entry of aliens to take up employment with the church of scientology.

4–11 A similar privileged position has now been created in favour of the Council and Commission in direct actions, by virtue of the new Article 16(7) introduced into the Rules of Procedure by the 1979 amendments. This requires copies of the application and defence to be forwarded to the Council and Commission as appropriate in any case to which one or other of them is not a party. This is expressed to be to enable them to see if one of their acts is being indirectly challenged by virtue of a plea of illegality. Although the Member States are not mentioned expressly, since the Council consists of representatives of the Member States, it would appear to be not wholly unlikely that the relevant information will also percolate to the Member States who will then be better equipped to know whether to intervene. It had indeed previously been a complaint of the U.K. Treasury Solicitor's office, in evidence to the House of Lords Select Committee on the European Communities (Session 1979–80, 23rd Report, Minutes of Evidence pp. 61–62, para. 178) that they could not be certain that a case might affect national interests until they got the papers, but that they could not get the papers unless they intervened in the case—a clear illustration, incidentally, of the confidentiality of the files. It was, however, also hinted in this evidence that the amendments to the Rules of Procedure then proposed (and now in force) did take account of this problem.

C. PUBLICITY

4–12 Although the pleadings and other documents in the file of each case may not be available to the public, a limited amount of the information they contain is required to be published in the *Official Journal*, and under article 25 of the Instructions to the Registrar, such publication is the responsibility of the Registrar. In direct actions, the scope of the information to be published has been broadened by the amendments made to article 16(6) of the Rules of Procedure in 1979. It now permits that, in addition to a formal note of the names of the parties, the subject-matter of the dispute and the claims of the applicant (*i.e.* the remedies sought), there would also be published "a summary of the

111

contentions and of the main arguments adduced in support" of the application. This could be regarded as the positive aspect of the new time-limits for intervention introduced by the 1979 amendments to article 93(1) of the Rules of Procedure (see para. 11–15 below). This time-limit runs from the publication of the notice under article 16(6), and the expanded form of notice should make it easier for outsiders to determine whether the case is one in which they should apply to intervene.

On the other hand, although publicity may be useful to would-be interveners, it is not always welcome to the parties themselves. It would appear, however, that the express terms of article 16(6) of the Rules of Procedure cannot be avoided. The example could be given of the undertaking which, having complained to the Commission about an alleged abuse of a dominant position by another undertaking, commenced proceedings against the Commission in relation to its supposed failure to act on the complaint, only to withdraw the action when it discovered there was no way it could prevent its name appearing in the *Official Journal*, since it did not wish the second undertaking to become aware that it had complained. Even in instances where the Court refers to the applicant by an initial in its published judgment, *e.g.* in staff cases involving the medical characteristics of an official, such as Case 152/77 *B.* v. *Commission* [1979] E.C.R. 2819 (an example taken because the applicant's name is in any event indirectly referred to in the Advocate-General's Opinion), the name of the applicant can be found simply by looking up the original notice of commencement of proceedings in the "C" series of the *Official Journal*. However, although not expressly alluded to in the judgments, a practice does seem to have developed recently of not publishing the name of a party whose personal characteristics are at issue in the proceedings. Thus the commencement of proceedings in Case 1/82 *D.* v. *Luxembourg* (October 27, 1982), which was in any event held inadmissible on other grounds, was published as "*X* v. *Luxembourg*" (O.J. 1982 C20/4), presumably because it involved an expulsion order against one of the applicants, and the commencement of proceedings in Case 257/81 *K.* v. *Council* (January 12, 1983), which involved a question of occupational disease, was published under that name (O.J. 1981 C259/5).

4–13   Although article 16(6) is in terms apt only to cover direct actions, notice is also given in the *Official Journal* of the registration of references for preliminary rulings. The information published usually consists of the name of the court making the reference, the names of the parties, and the question or questions referred. No change in the information published with regard to references for preliminary rulings has occurred as a result of the 1979 amendments. Indeed, the suggested rationale of increased information with regard to direct actions is not evident in preliminary rulings, because the Court has consistently held that intervention is not permissible in such references. It has so held on the ground that article 20 of the EEC Statute, which allows the parties to the main action, the Member States, the Commission and, where appropriate, the Council, to submit observations to the Court (see para.

4–111) is exhaustive, as in its order of June 3, 1964 in Case 6/64 *Costa* v. *ENEL* [1964] E.C.R. at p. 614 and in the judgment in Case 19/68 *De Cicco* v. *LVA Schwaben* [1968] E.C.R. 473, 479. More fundamentally, it could be argued that since it is clear, as Case 62/72 *Bollmann* v. *HZA Hamburg-Waltershof* shows, that a reference is merely a step in an action already before a national court, it is not for the European Court to let new parties join in.

In the result, the publication of information about references for preliminary rulings would appear to be little more that a simple matter of information.

DIRECT ACTIONS

A. REPRESENTATION OF THE PARTIES

EEC Statute of the Court

Article 17

4–14   The States and the institutions of the Community shall be represented before the Court by an agent appointed for each case; the agent may be assisted by an adviser or by a lawyer entitled to practise before a court of a Member State.

Other parties must be represented by a lawyer entitled to practise before a court of a Member State.

Such agents, advisers and lawyers shall, when they appear before the Court, enjoy the rights and immunities necessary to the independent exercise of their duties, under conditions laid down in the rules of procedure.

As regards such advisers and lawyers who appear before it, the Court shall have the powers normally accorded to courts of law, under conditions laid down in the rules of procedure.

University teachers being nationals of a Member State whose law accords them a right of audience shall have the same rights before the Court as are accorded by this Article to lawyers entitled to practise before a court of a Member State.

(Article 17 of the Euratom Statute is in identical terms, as is article 20 of the ECSC Statute, except that the phrase "undertakings and all other natural or legal persons" appears instead of "other parties" at the beginning of the second paragraph.)

Rules of Procedure

Article 37

1. The original of every pleading shall be signed by the party's agent or lawyer.

Article 38

. . . . . .

3. The lawyer acting for a party must lodge at the Registry a certificate that he is entitled to practise before a Court of a Member State.

. . . . . .

5. An application made by a legal person governed by private law shall be accompanied by:

(a) . . . . . .

(b) proof that the authority granted to the applicant's lawyer has been properly conferred on him by someone authorised for the purpose.

Article 76

1. (Relates to applications for legal aid.)

2. If the application is made prior to proceedings which the applicant wishes to commence, it shall briefly state the subject of such proceedings. The application need not be made through a lawyer.

1. *Who May Act?*

4–15 The litigant in person is unknown in direct actions before the European Court. A distinction is, however, made between Community institutions and Member States on the one hand, and private litigants on the other. The institutions and Member States must be represented by an agent, who need not necessarily be a practising lawyer, and he in turn may be assisted by an adviser or lawyer. The Council and Commission normally appoint one of their legal advisers to act as agent, and he may be assisted by another member of the legal service of the relevant institution and/or a private lawyer. It is not, however, impossible for the agent for one institution to be assisted by a member of the legal service of another institution: in the application for interim measures in Case 113/77R *NTN Toyo* v. *Council* [1977] E.C.R. 1721, a legal adviser of the Council was assisted by a member of the Commission's legal service. Insofar as the institutions do employ private lawyers, their choice tends to be influenced by, *inter alia*, the linguistic and geographic aspects of the particular case. So, in Case 30/78 *Distillers* v. *Commission* [1980] E.C.R. 2229, the Commission's legal adviser was assisted by two Scottish advocates (although, ironically, the Distillers Co. employed a Belgian "avocat"). As far as the other institutions are concerned, the European Parliament used normally to appoint its Secretary-General as agent, assisted by private lawyers, although it has recently appointed the Director-General of administration, personnel and finance as its agent, *e.g.* in Case 142/79 *Fronti* v. *Parliament* [1980] E.C.R. 1617, the European Investment Bank has been represented by the Director of its Directorate for Legal Affairs, the Court of Auditors by its Secretary, and the European Court itself by its Registrar, or more recently by its Director of Administration as in Case 2/80 *Dautzenberg* v. *ECJ* [1980] E.C.R. 3107.

Different Member States adopt different practices with regard to their choice of agent, but the tendency of the United Kingdom is to appoint an Assistant Treasury Solicitor.

4–16 Private litigants, on the other hand, must be represented by a "lawyer entitled to practise before a court of a Member State." This phrase represents an adaptation rather than a simple translation of the equivalent passages in the original language versions of the Statute,

114

which themselves are not identical, *e.g.* "avocat inscrit á un bureau de l'un des Etates membres" and "Anwalt . . . der in einem Mitgliedstaat zugelassen ist." The terms used in the English version are apt to cover both sides of the divided profession in the three United Kingdom jurisdictions and in Ireland, since solicitors have to a greater or a lesser degree a right of audience in those jurisdictions. This indeed was recognised in the working agreement drawn up by representatives of the Bar Council and the English (and Welsh) Law Society in 1971, to the effect that

> "In the European Court at Luxembourg both barristers and solicitors should for the purpose of the protocol have the same rights as a French 'avocat' but solicitors would by practice rule be prohibited.
> (1) (Refers to references for preliminary rulings.)
> (2) In any other case in which a solicitor is acting for a party which is the United Kingdom Government or a corporation incorporated in the U.K. or a natural person ordinarily resident in the U.K. and in which a barrister is instructed to appear, from taking part in the oral presentation or from undertaking, except in conjunction with the barrister, the written presentation. A solicitor is under no obligation to instruct a barrister in this class of case but he may not instruct an outside solicitor. If he requires another English lawyer, it must be a barrister."

4–17 No such practice rule was in fact made, and on June 19, 1981 the Council of the Law Society agreed that the 1971 agreement should be rescinded so far as it restricted the rights of audience of solicitors. There had, however, previously been little evidence of any desire to breach the agreement; indeed, only in 1980 can an example be found of a United Kingdom solicitor acting alone on behalf of a client, in Case 175/80 *Tither* v. *Commission* [1981] E.C.R. 2345, although there was an example of an Irish solicitor conducting a direct action in Case 110/77 *Mulcahy* v. *Commission* [1978] E.C.R. 1287. There have been examples, on the other hand, of a barrister alone representing an applicant, in Case 130/75 *Prais* v. *Commission* [1976] E.C.R. 1589, although there the applicant was herself a solicitor, and in Case 167/80 *Curtis* v. *Parliament and Commission* [1981] E.C.R. 1499.

It might finally be noted in this context that no agreement between the branches of the profession was entered into in Scotland or Northern Ireland.

2. Status as a Lawyer

4–18 The question of who is a lawyer entitled to practise before a court of a Member State is ultimately a matter of national law, as also is the question of the legal effect of any restriction placed on his ability to practise. In Case 18/57 *Nold* v. *HA* [1959] E.C.R. 41, the application was signed by a "Rechtsanwalt" who was found to have been suspended from practice; however, the Court also found that under the relevant legislation of the Land of Hesse, a suspension from practice does not affect the legality of the acts undertaken by the advocate concerned, and concluded that the application was formally valid.

This perhaps discloses a chink in the requirement in article 38(3) of the Rules that the lawyer should produce a certificate, which had been introduced in article 4 of the 1954 Additional Rules of Procedure (J.O. 1954, p. 302). In many Member States, the certificate will be a contemporaneous document signed by the senior judge of the local court to which the lawyer is attached; on the other hand, United Kingdom solicitors would normally produce a current practising certificate issued by the relevant Law Society. Nevertheless, it must not be forgotten that the certificate is required to be of "entitlement to practise" only in the English version; in French for example it is required only to state that the "avocat" in question "est inscrit á un Barreau." A degree of uniformity has been introduced on the initiative of the CCBE (Consultative Committee of the Bars and Law Societies of the European Community). Following the issue of Council Directive 77/249/EEC of March 22, 1977 (O.J. 1977, L.78/17) intended to "facilitate the effective exercise by lawyers of freedom to provide services," under article 7 of which competent authority of the host Member State may request the person providing the services to establish his qualifications as a lawyer, the CCBE agreed the form of a lawyer's Professional Identity Card to be issued through the constituent bars and law societies: It may, however, be noted that there is no fixed period of validity for the card—it merely describes the holder's status on the date of issue, and in practice the European Court will only accept such a card if it has been issued or validated within the previous 12 months.

3. *Authority to Act*

4–19 In principle, authority to act is a matter between the litigant and his agent or lawyer. However, under article 38(5) applications made by companies must be accompanied by proof that such authority has been properly granted to the lawyer signing the application. This rule does not apply to actions brought by natural persons: in Case 14/64 *Gualco (née Barge)* v. *H.A.* [1965] E.C.R. 51 where a lawyer had, apparently by a clerical error, intially produced an authority to act in earlier proceedings with the result that the High Authority claimed he had no authority to act when the application was lodged, the Court held that "the lawyer acting for a party is required only to establish his professional status as a lawyer and is not required to produce a duly executed authority to act in the lodging of an application, subject to proof if challenged that he is so authorised." The requirement of proof at the time of the application in the case of companies (and other legal persons governed by private law) would appear in reality to relate to the question of authority within the company to appoint the lawyer rather that to the lawyer's own authority to act.

4. *Enforcement of the Obligation*

4–20 The obligation to be represented by an agent or lawyer is encountered from the very beginning of the written procedure in direct actions: article 37(1) of the Rules of Procedure quite simply requires the original of every pleading to be signed by the party's agent or lawyer. Even an applicant who seeks legal aid is not excused this obligation, since under article 76(2) of the Rules it is only the application for legal aid, rather than the application commencing proceedings, which need not be made through a lawyer. Given the very short limitation period for commencing most direct actions, and in the absence of any authority as to whether an application for legal aid can be treated as "unforseeable circumstances" or "force majeure" under article 42 of the EEC Statute so as to allow the time limits to be circumvented, in practice applicants for legal aid would appear to instruct a lawyer to lodge an application commencing proceedings and immediately submit an application for legal aid, which will be granted only when the necessary information as to the applicant's circumstances has been obtained. As an example, in Case 121/76 *Moli* v. *Commission* [1977] E.C.R. 1971, the application commencing proceedings was lodged on December 20, 1976, and legal aid was granted by an order of April 28, 1977.

The question whether an application which has not been signed by a lawyer is inadmissible or can be rectified was before the Court, but not decided, in Joined Cases 220 and 221/78 *A.L.A. and A.L.F.E.R.* v. *Commission* [1979] E.C.R. 1693. There, the applicants lodged on July 20, 1978 applications for the annulment of an ECSC Decision notified to them on June 5, 1978. The applications were returned by the Registry since they were not signed by a lawyer, and applications which were signed by a lawyer, and were thus registered, were received at the Court on October 20, 1978. The Court found that there was no need to consider whether the later applications could be considered as rectifications of the original applications, since in any event the initial applications were received outside the time limit of one month (plus extensions on account of distance) for challenging ECSC Decisions.

5. *Right and Obligations of Agents and Lawyers*

4–21 This is dealt with in the context of the oral procedure (see para. 7–10 below).

B. PLEADINGS

I. *GENERAL PROVISIONS*

Rules of Procedure

Article 37

4–22 1. The original of every pleading must be signed by the party's agent or lawyer.

The original, accompanied by all annexes referred to therein, shall be lodged together with five copies for the Court and a copy for every other party to the proceedings. Copies shall be certified by the party lodging them.

3. All pleadings shall bear a date. In the reckoning of time limits for taking steps in proceedings, the only relevant date shall be that of lodgment at the Registry.

4. To every pleading there shall be annexed a file containing the documents relied on in support of it, together with a schedule listing them.

5. Where in view of the length of a document only extracts from it are annexed to the pleading, the whole document or a full copy of it shall be lodged at the Registry.

Instructions to the Registrar

Article 14

4–23   An annex which has not been lodged at the same time as the procedural document to which it relates shall be separately registered.

There are certain requirements common to all the written pleadings in direct actions:

(a) Signature

4–24   The need for every pleading to be signed by the party's agent or lawyer has been considered in the context of representation of the parties (see para. 4–16 above). However, given that representation by an agent or a lawyer, as the case may be, is required by the Statute, it may be of interest to note that article 33(1) of the original 1953 Rules of Procedure allowed the pleadings to be signed by the parties themselves.

(b) Annexes

4–25   It is now clearly laid down in the second paragraph of article 37(1), as amended in 1979, that all annexes referred to in each pleading should be lodged with the original of that pleading. It could be suggested that this was already required by article 37(4) providing that a file of the documents relied on in support should be annexed to every pleading, but in practice it had become not uncommon for parties to state in the pleadings that certain annexes would follow later, a practice which might appear to be allowed in article 14 of the Instructions to the Registrar. The disadvantage of this practice was that late lodging of an annex could prejudice the efforts of the other party to comply with procedural time limits if he wished to take account of the information in the annex, or at least put the onus on that other party to ask for an extension of time. The result of the amendment would appear to be to force a party who finds that he cannot produce an annex in time to ask for an extension of time for the lodging of the pleading itself, where such an extension is possible, *e.g.* under articles 40(2) and 41(2) of the Rules of Procedure (see paras. 4–59, 4–65 below). In any event, each pleading must be accompanied by a schedule of the annexes, under Article 37(4).

There appears to be no authority on the question of what length of document justifies mere extracts being annexed to the pleading, but it might be suggested, that what really matters is how much of the document is relevant to the pleading rather than its physical bulk. Experience seems to show that parties tend to err on the side of putting in the whole document, leaving the selection of what is relevant to those who have to read it.

(c) Copies

4–26 From 1953 to 1979, each party was required to produce two copies of every pleading for the Court, plus a copy for every other party to the proceedings. The present version of article 37(1) requires five copies to be produced for the Court. The significance of this figure is not immediately apparent, since the Court will in fact have to run off copies for all the members of the Court and their legal secretaries, for translators and for research staff, a total which will be nearer 10 times five.

The copies which each party is required to produce must be certified by "the party" lodging them, a phrase which can be traced back to article 33(2) of the 1953 Rules of Procedure which allowed parties to sign the pleadings, but in reality it is always the agent or lawyer who certifies the copies.

(d) Dates

4–27 The requirement that each pleading be dated appears to be purely formal. Article 37(3) of the Rules makes it clear that in the context of procedural time-limits, the only date that is taken into account is that of lodgment at the Registry. This was strictly applied by the Court in Joined Cases 36 to 38, 40 and 41/58 *Simet* v. *H.A.* [1959] E.C.R. 157, where two of the applicants, whose applications were received at the Registry four days after the expiry of the relevant time-limit, argued unsuccessfully that the date of posting should be taken into consideration; the Court there simply stated that the applicant's claim was in contradiction with the wording of the Rules of Procedure.

II. *APPLICATIONS*

EEC Statute of the Court of Justice

Article 19

4–28 A case shall be brought before the Court by a written application addressed to the Registrar. The application shall contain the applicant's name and permanent address and the description of the signatory, the name of the party against whom the application is made, the subject matter of the dispute, the submissions and a brief statement of the grounds on which the application is based.

The application shall be accompanied, where appropriate, by the measure the annulment of which is sought or, in the circumstances referred to in Article 175 of this Treaty, by documentary evidence of the date on which an institution was, in accordance with that Article, requested to act. If the documents are not submitted with the application, the Registrar shall ask the party concerned to produce them within a reasonable period but in that event the rights of the party shall not lapse even if such documents are produced after the time limit for bringing proceedings.

(Article 19 of the Euratom Statute is identical, except that it refers to Article 148 of the Euratom Treaty rather than Article 175 of the EEC Treaty; article 22 of the ECSC Statute contains minor differences in terminology appropriate to the forms of action under the ECSC Treaty; in particular, in the second paragraph, it refers to "the decision" rather than "the measure" of which the annulment is sought, and the phrase "in the circumstances referred to in Article 175 of this Treaty" is replaced by "in the case of proceedings against an implied decision.")

Rules of Procedure

Article 38

4–29   1. An application of the kind referred to in Article 22 of the ECSC Statute and Articles 19 of the EEC and Euratom Statues shall state:
(a) the name and permanent residence of the applicant:
(b) the name of the party against whom the application is made;
(c) the subject matter of the dispute and the grounds on which the application is based;
(d) the form of order sought by the applicant;
(e) the nature of any evidence founded upon by him.
2. For the purpose of the proceedings, the application shall state an address for service in the place where the Court has its seat. It shall also give the name of a person who is authorized and has expressed willingness to accept service.
3. The lawyer acting for a party must lodge at the Registry a certificate that he is entitled to practise before a Court of a Member State.
4. The application shall be accompanied, where appropriate, by the documents specified in the second paragraph of Article 22 of the ECSC Statute and in the second paragraph of Articles 19 of the EEC and Euratom Statutes.
5. An application made by a legal person governed by private law shall be accompanied by:
(a) the instrument or instruments constituting and regulating that legal person;
(b) proof that the authority granted to the applicant's lawyer has been properly conferred on him by someone authorized for the purpose.
6. An application submitted under Articles 42 and 89 of the ECSC Treaty, Articles 181 and 182 of the EEC Treaty and Articles 153 and 154 of the Euratom Treaty shall be accompanied by a copy of the arbitration clause contained in the contract governed by private or public law entered into by the Communities or on their behalf, or, as the case may be, by a copy of the special agreement concluded between the Member States concerned.
7. If an application does not comply with the requirements set out in paragraphs 2 to 6 of this Article, the Registrar shall prescribe a reasonable period within which the applicant is to comply with them whether by putting the application itself in order or by producing any of the above-mentioned documents. If the applicant fails to put the application in order or to produce the required documents within the time prescribed, the Court shall, after hearing the Advocate-General, decide whether to reject the application on the ground of want of form.

Article 39

The application shall be served on the defendant. In a case where article 38(7) applies, service shall be effected as soon as the application has been put in order or the Court has declared it admissible notwithstanding the failure to observe the formal requirements set out in that Article.

Article 69

1. . . . . . .

4–30   2. The unsuccessful party shall be ordered to pay the costs if they have been asked for in the successful party's pleading.

Article 92

1. Where it is clear that the Court has no jurisdiction to take cognizance of an application lodged with it in pursuance of Article 38(1), the Court may be reasoned order declare the application inadmissible. Such a decision may be adopted even before the application has been served on the party against whom it is made.

Instructions to the Registrar

Article 5

1.The Registrar shall, after consulting the President and the Judge Rapporteur,take all measures necessary for implementing Article 38(7) of the Rules of Procedure.

He shall prescribe the period mentioned in that Article and shall communicate it to to the person concerned by registered letter with a form for acknowledgement of receipt.

If the person concerned does not comply with the directions of the Registrar,the latter shall refer the matter to the President of the Court.

(a) Form of the application

4–31   Writs, summonses and other formal documents concerning proceedings are unknown in direct actions before the European Court. All that is required is that a written application should be addressed to the Registrar, and no specific rules are laid down with regard to its physical presentation; there is, for example, no requirement that it should be printed and bound—the normal practice, however, is for applications to be typed. On the other hand, this does not mean that there are no formal requirements with which an application must comply: apart from the requirements common to all pleadings, every application should at least contain the information listed in article 38(1) and (2) of the Rules of Procedure, and should be accompanied, where appropriate, by the documents listed in article 38(3) to (6). There is early authority to the effect that the Court may examine compliance with these formal requirements of its own motion; in Joined Cases 19 and 21/60 and 2 and 3/61 *Fives Lille Cail* v. *H.A.* [1961] E.C.R. 281, the Court found that it was not clear whether the defendant wished to challenge the applications in two of the cases from the viewpoint of procedural requirements, but held that "nevertheless, the Court must of its own motion consider this question since the provisions governing the form of applications affect not only the interests of the parties but also the right of the Court to exercise its powers of judicial review." It may be noted, however, that the Court was there concerned with the adequacy of the statement of grounds for the application, a matter which could be regarded as going to its jurisdiction, and that with regard to the requirements set out in article 38(2) to (6), the Registrar may give the applicant the opportunity to effect any necessary rectification under article 38(7).

Apart from the relevant names and addresses, Article 19 of the Statute and Article 38 of the Rules, despite apparent differences in terminology, require an application to contain four important items of information: the subject-matter of the dispute, the grounds for the application, the form of order sought (which corresponds to the "submissions" mentioned in the English version of article 12 of the Statute), and the evidence which the applicant wishes to lead.

(b) Names and address

4–32   Apart from the obvious need to name the applicant and the defendant, the application must, under article 38(2) of the Rules, state an addess for service in the place where the Court has its seat, *i.e.* Luxembourg, and name a person authorised and willing to accept service. This can be seen as a correlative of the Registry's obligation to effect service of procedural documents (see para. 4–09 above); in reality, after service of the initial application, the obligation in direct actions is merely to effect service on the parties' local agents. In most cases where the applicant or his lawyer are not actually resident in Luxembourg, a Luxembourg *avocat* will be asked to accept service, and his office will be used as the address for service. There is, however, no obligation to use a local lawyer, and instances can be found of United Kingdom based applicants who have made use of private addresses in Luxembourg, *e.g.* Case 130/75 *Prais* v. *Commission* [1976] E.C.R. 1589, and Case 49/79 *Pool* v. *Council* [1980] E.C.R. 569; indeed, in the latter case, the address for service was in Strassen, which is outside the Luxembourg city boundary, and this raises the interesting question whether the place where the Court has its seat is the city of Luxembourg, or extends into the Grand-Duchy. Nevertheless, in most cases, the lawyer advising a private applicant is likely to want to preserve a professional relationship with the local agent.

The same rule applies, of course, to institutional litigants: of the Community institutions with offices in Luxembourg, the Commission normally chooses the office of one of its legal advisers based in Luxembourg, the Parliament, at least in staff cases, chooses the office of the Luxembourg *avocat* assisting its agent, and the Investment Bank has done likewise. On the other hand, the Council usually chooses the office of the Director of the Legal Service of the European Investment Bank as its address for service. The Court itself, as a litigant in staff cases, has not always chosen an address for service, *e.g.* Case 15/60 *Simon* v. *ECJ* [1961] E.C.R. 115. When it has been represented in such cases by its Registrar as agent, it would perhaps be taking legal fiction too far to require him to serve documents on himself. When, however, it was represented by its Director of Administration in Case 2/80 *Dautzenberg* v. *ECJ* [1980] E.C.R. 3107, it did choose the office of the Luxembourg *avocat* assisting him as its address for service. The Member State normally chooses an address for service at their embassies in Luxembourg, and Luxembourg itself uses its Ministry of Foreign Affairs as the relevant address, *e.g.* in Joined Cases 2 and 3/62 *Commission* v. *Luxembourg and Belgium* [1962] E.C.R. 425.

(c) Subject-matter of the dispute

1–33   The requirement that the application must state the subject-matter of the dispute means essentially that the applicant must set set out the facts underlying his action, and, more specifically in direct actions, that he must identify the Community acts or failures to act which he wishes to challenge or which he claims to have harmed him. The precise facts must be set out, and a reference to supposed general knowledge will not suffice. In Joined Cases 46 and 47/59 *Meroni* v. *H.A.* [1962] E.C.R. 411, the applications related to the alleged liability of the High Authority for its failure to avoid the situation in which fraudulent certificates relating to ferrous scrap were issued by a Dutch official ('the van der Grift affair'), and to its liability for "all other acts of fraud subsequently discovered." These latter acts were not initially specified, nor was it indicated what was supposed to constitute a wrongful act or omission on the part of the High Authority's services or which irregularities had caused the applicant's injury. The Court found that the defendant had a right "to be obliged to reply only to facts explicitly defined and to refute only clear and precise allegations," and that to allow arguments made with such a lack of precision "would deprive the defendant to a considerable extent of its opportunities . . . to submit its defence with full knowledge of the facts." In the event, the Court held that the application must be interpreted as referring only to the "van der Grift affair." An illustration of failure to indicate the contested Community acts with sufficient precision can be found in Case 30/68 *Lacroix* v. *Commission* [1970] E.C.R. 301. There the applicant sought, *inter alia*, the annulment of "all decisions to appoint or assign officials which affect the applicant adversely owing to the Commission's failure to observe [certain provisions of the Staff Regulations." The Court found that the subject matter of this part of the application was not indicated with sufficient precision to enable it to be examined profitably, and that in any event there was a breach of the requirement in the second paragraph of article 19 of the Statute that the measures of which the annulment is sought should be annexed to the application. It was held that the applicant had left the Court the task of finding out which of the measures described were really the subject of the application and that "in order to protect the rights of the defence and of third parties concerned such imprecise requests must be regarded as inadmissible."

1–34   On the other hand, the precision required is not absolute; what is required is that the defendant should be able to understand the subject-matter of the dispute from the description of it in the application. In Joined Cases 25 and 26/65 *Simet and Feram* v. *H.A.* [1967] E.C.R. 33, the application was expressly directed against a decision imposing the obligation to pay a contribution to the ferrous scrap equalisation scheme, but the defendant claimed that the argument in reality related to another decision of the same date fixing the basis of the applicant's assessment to contribution, and that this discrepancy rendered the application inadmissible. The Court found that the decision cited in the application referred expressly in its recitals to the other decision, that for practical purposes the two decisions constituted

123

a single whole, and held that the application must be regarded as directed also against the other decision, so far as was necessary, justifying this holding on the ground that "the High Authority was under no misapprehension on this point and its rights of defence were in no way prejudiced."

4–35　That a single application can be made to challenge more than one Community act was settled in the very first judgment to be delivered by the European Court, in Case 1/54 *France* v. *H.A.* [1954 to 1956] E.C.R. 1, where three decisions were challenged in a single action. Similarly a single application can relate the two different fact situations, provided there is a legal connection between them: in Joined Cases 7 and 9/54 *Industries Siderurgiques Luxembourgeoises* v. *H.A.* [1954 to 1956] E.C.R. 175, a single application was lodged with regard to the High Authority's implied refusal to terminate the activities of the Luxembourg "Office Commercial du Ravitaillement" and to abolish the "Caisse de Compensation" attached to that "Office," and it was held that the two claims in the application were "obviously related" and hence that the single application was admissible. Conversely, a single act may be challenged in one application by multiple applicants, as was decided in Case 13/57 *Eisen-und Stahlindustrie* v. *H.A.* [1958] E.C.R. 265 where five different applicants sought to challenge a single decision; it was held that since they all contested the decision on the same points and relied on the same submissions, a joint application might properly be submitted. It might be suggested that such a procedure is preferable to the apparently more common practice whereby applicants, even represented by the same lawyers, commence separate but parallel actions on the same subject-matter as, *e.g.* in Cases 36 to 82/78 of Joined Cases 32/78 and 36 to 82/78 *BMW* v. *Commission* [1979] E.C.R. 2435, where Belgian BMW dealers represented by the same counsel challenged a Commission decision imposing fines on them. Quite apart from the amount of paper involved, the effect of starting separate actions is to add a further, albeit minor, stage to the proceedings, in that if the actions are to be joined for procedural purposes, the Court will have to make a formal order to that effect. However, it would appear from the argument in the *Eisen-und Stahlindustrie* Case (at p. 270) that in some national legal systems, joint applications are not permitted, and it could be that counsel in cases before the European Court tend to retain their national habits.

4–36　Where parallel but separate applications are brought, it would appear not to be sufficient simply to refer to the application in one of the other cases with regard to the statement of its subject-matter. This was decided in relation to the statement of grounds for the application in Case 9/55 *Charbonnages de Beeringen* v. *H.A.* [1954 to 1956] E.C.R. 311, where the application referred to a statement in the application in Case 8/55 *Fédéchar* v. *H.A.* [1954 to 1956] E.C.R. 245 for the grounds for one of the heads of claim. The Court held that, particularly since there was no request in the application for the cases to be joined, this was not sufficient and the claim was inadmissible; *a fortiori*, the same rule could be expected to apply with regard to the statement of the subject-matter of the dispute. Where, however, the application in a particular case itself adequately states its subject-matter, there is no objection to adding a supplementary reference to the application in another case, as in Case 4/69 *Lütticke* v. *Commission* [1971] E.C.R. 325. There it was found that the application gave all the details necessary to establish with certainty the subject-matter of the dispute, and that the reference, in addition, to other proceedings brought before the Court did not affect the admissibility of the action.

(d) Grounds on which the application is based

4–37   The statement of the grounds for the application sets the legal basis for the application. As interpreted by the Court, the fundamental requirement is that there should be a clear indication of the legal principles involved and how they relate to the facts of the case, rather than a precise citation of the relevant Treaty rules or other provisions of Community legislation. In Cases 3 to 7/57 of Joined Cases 7/56 and 3 to 7/57 *Algera* v. *Common Assembly* [1957 to 1958] E.C.R. 39, applications were lodged which claimed the payment of damages without including any precise provision on which they were based; in particular, no mention was made of Article 40 of the ECSC Treaty governing liability for a wrongful act or omission on the part of the Community. Nonetheless, the Court held that although Article 40 was not expressly pleaded by the applicants, the nature of the facts stated by them in their applications and the form of order they sought justified its application, and there was no need to cite the Articles on which they relied. It might, however, be noted that this was a staff case decided before the modern rules on actions by officials of the Communities against the institutions were enacted in the Staff Regulations, and that a similar dispute now would be held to be governed by articles 90 and 91 of the Staff Regulations, as was decided in Case 9/75 *Meyer-Burckhardt* v. *Commission* [1975] E.C.R. 1171. Another example of this approach is to be found in Joined Cases 2 and 10/63 *San Michele* v. *H.A.* [1963] E.C.R. 327, where the applicants sought a reduction of the fines imposed on them and remission of the periodic penalty payments imposed on them by the contested decisions, but did not expressly mention Article 36 of the ECSC Treaty, giving the Court unlimited jurisdiction in appeals against pecuniary sanctions and periodic penalty payments. The Court simply held that "any appeal against pecuniary sanctions imposed by the High Authority is by its very nature based on Article 36 of the Treaty, and there is no need to invoke that Article expressly."

An application may indeed even be admissible where the wrong provision of Community law is cited, provided it remains clear what is the real ground for the action. An example of this can be found in Case 12/68 *X* v. *Audit Board* [1969] E.C.R. 109, where the applicant complained that the Audit Board took the decision at issue without having previously heard him "as required by article 87 of the Staff Regulations." The defendant claimed that the application was inadmissible, since the relevant provision was in fact the last paragraph of article 7 of Annex IX to the Staff Regulations, but the Court held that a mistake made by the applicant in designating the relevant provision could not lead to the inadmissibility of that head of complaint.

4–38   Where an applicant correctly cites a provision which itself sets out specific grounds on which the Court may, for example, annul a Community act, it would again appear that there is no need to refer to these grounds by name, provided it can be discovered which grounds are being invoked. Case 4/73 *Nold* v. *Commission* [1974] E.C.R. 491 was commenced by an application requesting the annulment of a decision under Article 33 of the ECSC Treaty, but without specifying by name any of the grounds set out in that Article. The Court looked, however, at the substance of the case, concluded that "the applicant's written and oral arguments invoke in substance the grounds of infringement of an essential procedural requirement and infringement of the Treaty or of any rule of law relating to its application" and considered the application on that basis. As the Court suggested in Case 11/63 *Lemmerz Werke* v. *H.A.* [1965] E.C.R. at p. 696, what is required is that the application should make it possible to identify the complaints which the applicant intends to raise and the essence of the arguments invoked in support of them.

Whilst it is accepted that the statement of grounds for the application need not conform to the phraseology or the lists in the relevant Treaty provisions, and may be expressed in terms of their substance rather than of their legal classification (to borrow the terms used by the Court in Joined Cases 19 and 21/60 and 2 and 3/61 *Fives Lille Cail* v. *H.A.* [1961] E.C.R. 281, 295), it is not sufficient just to state the grounds in the abstract; the grounds must be set out in relation to the facts. This emerges from the *Fives Lille Cail* case itself, where the applicants accused the High Authority of "excès de pouvoir," a term which the Court found capable of embracing all the grounds for annulment listed in Article 33 of the ECSC Treaty, without specifying what amounted to an "excès de pouvoir," and more specifically accused it of breaching a rule of law relating to the application of the Treaty, without identifying the rule of law in question. Hence the Court found that the grounds had not been established in relation to the facts.

4–39   Further, it should be noted that it is not only in relation to the main claim in the application that supporting grounds must be adduced; it has now been made clear that they are also required with regard to ancillary matters, such as a plea of illegality. In Joined Cases 26 and 86/79 *Forges Thy-Marcinelle* v. *Commission* [1980] E.C.R. 1083 the applicants sought the annulment of an individual decision imposing a fine on them for selling certain types of steel at a price lower than that fixed by a general decision, Decision 962/77/ECSC of May 4, 1977 (O.J. 1977, L. 114/1), incidentally raising the question of the legality of that general decision. In Case 26/79 the legality of the general decision was challenged for "various reasons" which were not specified, and it was held that this was not a sufficient statement of grounds. At first sight, this is difficult to reconcile with the early decision in in Case 14/59 *Fonderies de Pont-à-Mousson* v. *H.A.* [1959] E.C.R. 215. There, the applicant

challenged an individual decision refusing exemption from the equalisation levy, on the grounds, *inter alia*, that it was discriminatory. The
Court, however, found that discrimination could only be claimed to
arise from the parent general decision, Decision 2/57 (J.O. 62/57), not
from the individual decision, and, although the applicant had not
invoked the illegality of the general decision, the Court decided to
consider the legality of the general decision of its own notion, on the
basis that it was inappropriate to allow doubt to persist on the matter.
By definition, if the Court is to consider questions of legality of its own
motion (which does not however, appear to be the modern practice), it
is difficult to see the relevance of the applicant being required to state
grounds for a plea of illegality; nevertheless, what actually happened in
the *Pont-à-Mousson* case was that the Court considered the legality of
the general decision in the light of the grounds invoked for the
annulment of the individual decision, *i.e.* the allegation of discrimination. Returning to the *Forges Thy-Marcinelle* case, although the
application in Case 26/79 did not adequately state the grounds for the
plea of illegality, the application in Case 86/79 invoked an alleged
breach of the principles of non-discrimination and proportionality, thus
complying with the requirements of article 38(1) of the Rules. Since the
two cases had been joined, it was held that the admissibility of the plea
of illegality in the second application could compensate for the
inadmissibility of the plea in the first application, with the result that
points taken in both cases might be considered. This can be contrasted
with the early view expressed in Case 9/55 *Charbonnages de Beeringen*
v. *H.A.* [1954 to 1956] E.C.R. 311 that where there is no application for
the cases to be joined, a general reference to a statement made in
another case is not sufficient compliance with the requirement to state
the grounds for the claim.

(e) Form of order sought ("submissions")

4-40   The meaning of the phrase "the form of order sought" is fairly
self-evident to an English-language reader. What is not so immediately
apparent is that the term "submissions" in the English version of article
19 of the Statute, and perhaps even more unfortunately in article 93 of
the Rules of Procedure with regard to interventions (see para. 11–08
below), is a translation of exactly the same word—"conclusions" in
French. The phrase "form of order sought," which is accurate if
cumbersome, was introduced in the English version of the 1974 Rules of
Procedure; the English translation of article 38(1)(d) of the 1959 Rules
of Procedure (O.J. Sp. Ed. 1959/62 Supplement) itself used the term
"submissions." The confusion is worse confounded by the fact that from
the middle of 1974 onwards (and in the pre-Accession reports translated
since then), the English-language European Court Reports have used
the word "conclusions" to describe the statement of the form of order
sought, which they had initially termed "submissions," and have used
"submissions" to describe the arguments put forward by the parties.
     As was stated in Joined Cases 46 and 47/59 *Meroni* v. *H.A.* [1962]
E.C.R. 411, the applicant must present his "conclusions" in an

unequivocal manner, otherwise the Court risks either giving judgment *ultra petita* or failing to give judgment on one of the heads of the "conclusions." Provided, however, that the form of order sought is stated in a clear and accurate manner, it was recognised in Case 14/63 *Clabecq* v. *H.A* [1963] E.C.R. 357 that it can be set out briefly. The essential aim is to make it clear, both to the Court and to the defendant, what the applicant is seeking.

4–41   Just as it was held that a single application can deal with more than one subject, if the subjects are related, it was also recognised in Joined Cases 7 and 9/54 *Industries Sidérurgiques Luxembourgeoises* v. *H.A.* [1954 to 1956] E.C.R. 175 that the same application may contain more than one "conclusion." It has also been admitted, at least since the judgment in Joined Cases 7/56 and 3 to 7/57 *Algera* v. *Assembly* [1957 and 1958] E.C.R. 39, that alternative forms of order may be sought; in that case the alternatives were different methods of assessment of damages, but it has since become quite usual, particularly but not exclusively in staff cases, to lodge a single application seeking the annulment of a Community act and damages for the harm caused thereby either in addition or as an alternative; indeed, at one stage the case law of the Court indicated that damages could be claimed for the harm caused by a Community act only where that act had been annulled, see Case 25/62 *Plaumann* v. *Commission* [1962] E.C.R. 95, a view eventually reversed in Case 5/71 *Shöppenstedt* v. *Council* [1971] E.C.R. 975.

It is not only the main claims which should be specifically mentioned in the application. Any ancillary measures requested should also be stated, and in particular an application should be made for the costs. This is not mentioned in article 38 of the Rules, but article 69(2) provides that the unsuccessful party will be ordered to pay the costs "if they have been asked for in the unsuccessful party's pleading." Although the French text uses the phrase "s'il est conclu en ce sens," it does not appear to be absolutely essential that the request for costs should be included in the application itself. There are indeed instances where costs have been successfully requested at a later stage in the proceedings, *e.g.* Case 121/76 *Moli* v. *Commission* [1977] E.C.R. 1971, 1974, where the request was made in the reply. However, the safest way of ensuring that the question is not forgotten is to deal with it at the earliest possible moment, and follow the usual practice in direct actions before the European Court by inserting a request for costs in every application commencing proceedings before that Court. In Case 138/79 *Roquette* v. *Council* [1980] E.C.R. 3333 on the other hand, the Court refused to award costs to a successful applicant who had failed to ask for them.

4–42   Although the principle is well established that the statement of the form of order sought should be clear and accurate, and despite the absence of any formal machinery for the amendment of pleadings (see para. 4–67 below), the Court has, particularly in actions for damages, accepted "conclusions" which have required amplification later in the proceedings. In Joined Cases 27 and 39/59 *Campolongo* v. *H.A.* [1960]

E.C.R. 391, a reference in the application to "the allowances on termination of service, with all the legal consequences" in the context of a claim for the annulment of a decision relating to such allowances was held to amount to a request for an examination of all the pecuniary consequences of the applicant's resignation, allowing him to put in a list of seven claims for specific sums in his reply. Similarly, in Cases 25/62 *Plaumann* v. *Commission* [1963] E.C.R. 95, a request in the application for a declaration that the defendant was obliged to compensate the applicant for damage which might result from the contested decision was held to be sufficient to permit the applicant to specify and set a value on the damage later in the proceedings. In Joined Cases 29, 31, 36, 39 to 47, 50 and 51/63 *Usines de la Providence* v. *H.A.* [1965] E.C.R. 911, the applicants claimed damages without producing the figures on which they based their calculations; it was held that this did not render the applications inadmissible, and in particular that the defendant had not been put at a disadvantage since it had been able to discuss the figures produced by the applicants later in the procedure.

4–43   With this may be contrasted the view of the Second Chamber in Case 3/66 *Alfieri* v. *Parliament* [1966] E.C.R. 437, where a claim in the application for payment of specific sums for both material and non-material damage was held to be inadmissible "since the orginating application contains no indication how these amounts have been assessed"—even though it may be submitted that the statement of the form of order sought in the application was considerably clearer that it had been in, *e.g. Campolongo* or *Plaumann.* Similarly, in Case 5/71 *Schöppenstedt* v. *Council* [1971] E.C.R. 975, an alternative general claim for compensation, no more vague, it might be suggested, than the alternative claim which was held admissible in *Algera*, was held to be inadmissible, on the ground that "a claim for any unspecified form of damages is not sufficiently concrete and must therefore be regarded as inadmissible."

More recently, on the other hand, there appears to have been a return to a more open attitude in Joined Cases 56 to 60/74 *Kampffmeyer* v. *Commission and Council* [1976] E.C.R. 711. Faced with an application, lodged before the beginning of the 1974–1975 cereal marketing year, claiming that the Community was liable to compensate the applicant for harm suffered by them as a result of the Regulations governing prices and aids for durum wheat during that year, the Court said that Article 215 of the EEC Treaty did not prevent the Court from being asked to declare the Community liable for imminent damage forseeable with sufficient certainty "even if the damage cannot be precisely assessed."

4–44   Nonetheless, prudence would suggest that a claim for damages in an application should be drafted as specifically as possible, at least where the harm can already be ascertained.

In effect, the statement of the form of order sought fixes the limit of the proceedings, and in principle the European Court will not go beyond what is asked of it by the applicant. In Case 37/71 *Jamet* v. *Commission* [1972] E.C.R. 483, the "conclusion" in the application requested the partial annulment of a decision. The Court, however,

129

found that the parts whose annulment was requested were inseparable from the decision as a whole, so that in their absence it could no longer produce legal effect; on the other hand, the Court held that it would act *ultra petita* if it annulled the whole decision. In the result, it held that that particular "conclusion" was inadmissible. Nevertheless, quite apart from the power of the Court under article 92 of the Rules to consider the question of its own jurisdiction (see para. 4–67 below), there are instances where the Court has given judgment, or stated that it had power to give judgment, in a form not requested by the parties, particularly in the exercise of its "full jurisdiction." In Case 8/56 *Alma* v. *H.A.* [1957 and 1958] E.C.R. 95, the application sought the annulment of a decision imposing a fine upon the applicants; the Court noted that it had unlimited jurisdiction in the matter under Article 36 of the ECSC Treaty, since the application related to a pecuniary sanction, and hence that it was empowered not only to annul but also to amend the decision at issue, concluding that even in the absence of any formal "conclusion" to that effect, it was authorised to reduce the amount of an exessive fine. The Court did, however, expressly consider whether it would be acting *ultra petita*, and took the view that reduction of the fine would amount to a partial acceptance of the application rather than going beyond it.

4–45   The Court went slightly further in Case 44/59 *Fiddelaar* v. *Commission* [1960] E.C.R. 535. There a claim for damages had been held to be inadmissible since it had not been included either expressly or by implication in the "conclusions" set out in the application, the main aim of which was to seek the annulment of the applicant's dismissal from the Commission's language service. At the time, the Staff Regulations had not been enacted, and the Court took the view that it had unlimited jurisdiction in staff disputes under Article 179 of the EEC Treaty; on this basis, it held that it had, even in the absence of valid "conclusions," the power "not only to annul but also, if need be, of its own motion to order the defendant to pay compensation." A similar approach has been followed recently by the First Chamber in Case 24/79 *Oberthur* v. *Commission* [1980] E.C.R. 1743, another staff case in which the applicant sought the annulment of a series of promotions. The First Chamber thought that it would be excessive to annul some 40 promotions for the sake of the irregularities which had been shown to have occurred, but held that, since it was a case in which it had unlimited jurisdiction, it could, repeating the terms of *Fiddelaar*, not only annul but also of its own motion order the payment of compensation. The problem with this judgment is that it is expressly provided in Article 91(1) of the current Staff Regulations only that the Court shall have unlimited jurisdiction "in disputes of a financial character," and it might be suggested that the dispute in *Oberthur* only took on a financial character after the supposed unlimited jurisidiction had been exercised.

4–46   The example might finally be given of a case where the Court has acted of its own motion on policy grounds rather than in the exercise of unlimited jurisdiction. In Case 14/59 *Fonderies de Pont-á-Mousson* v. *H.A.* [1959] E.C.R. 215, in which the applicants challenged an

130

individual decision, the Court, despite the lack of any "conclusions" to that effect, considered the legality of the underlying general decision, on the ground that "it appears to be inappropriate to allow doubts as to [its] legality . . . to persist." This may be contrasted, as has already been mentioned, with the view in Joined Cases 26/79 and 86/79 *Forges Thy-Marcinelle* v. *Commission* [1980] E.C.R. 1083 that a plea of illegality made *expressly* must be supported by adequate grounds. Admittedly, the grounds on which the Court considered the legality of the general decision in *Pont-á-Mousson* were those invoked against the individual decision, but it could be suggested that as its workload has increased, the Court has come to take the line that the legality of a Community act is less a question of policy and more a question to be raised by the parties; it is instructive to compare the attitude taken with regard to references for preliminary rulings in Case 44/65 *Hessische Knappschaft* v. *Singer* [1965] E.C.R. 965 that the validity of a Community act cannot be considered on a reference unless it is raised by the national court itself.

In conclusion, it may be suggested that the statement of the form of order sought should expressly list all the heads of claim.

(f) Evidence

4–47 The scope of the requirement that the applicant should state in the application "the nature of any evidence founded upon by him" is perhaps best expressed in the French version of article 38(1)(e) of the Rules, which refers to "offres de preuve": the applicant should state what he intends to prove and how he intends to prove it. It is here perhaps that the conflict between accusatorial and inquisitorial techniques most clearly emerges; in principle it is the Court itself which directs the "preparatory inquiries" (see para. 6–07 below) which are concerned with establishing the facts of the case, but the onus still rests with each party to prove, or make available proof of, each allegation that he makes. This emerges from Joined Cases 42 and 49/59 *SNUPAT* v. *H.A.* [1961] E.C.R. 53, with regard to an allegation made by an intervener, but the principle applies equally to an applicant; adapting it to the situation of an applicant, what the Court said was that "it is not acceptable to rely on the Court to take the initiative in obtaining for itself by measures of inquiry information intended to prove the cogency of the argumement relied upon by the [applicant], which itself possesses that information." The real question here was one of confidentiality, on which nowadays a different view might be taken under the amended article 93(4) of the Rules, (see para. 6–48 below), but essentially the intervener relied upon a contract which it had not produced and of which it had not indicated the terms; the Court held that since it was the intervener itself which was relying on the contract, it was not prepared to order its production, and it concluded that the intervener had not adduced proof of its allegation.

Although it is obviously advisable to indicate the nature of any evidence relied upon at the earliest stage, it is expressly provided in article 42(1) of the Rules, that further evidence can be indicated in the reply, provided reasons are given for the delay, and in this respect the statement of the nature of the evidence relied upon is treated somewhat more generously than the other information required to be contained in the application.

(g) Accompanying documents

4–48   Apart from the annexes which must accompany every pleading as required under article 37 of the Rules, article 19 of the Statute and article 38 of the Statute require certain specific documents to be produced with the application.

Lawyer's certificate

This has been considered in the context of the requirement of legal representation (see para. 4–18 above). It is clear from Case 14/64 *Gualco (née Barge)* v. *Commission* [1965] E.C.R. 51 that the aim is that the lawyer should establish his professional status, and that he is not required to show any authority to act in the lodging of the application, unless challenged, except where he is appearing for a "legal person governed by private law," where the provisions of article 38(5) of the Rules apply.

Measure at issue, or proof of failure to act

In actions for annulment, the measure at issue must accompany the application. Usually, and particularly where the act has been published, this should give rise to little difficulty, except in the case of a decision addressed to another individual; in any event, article 19 of the Statute allows it to be produced wthin a "reasonable" time, even after the expiry of the limitation period for lodging the application. It would appear from Case 30/68 *Lacroix* v. *Commission* [1970] E.C.R. 301 that it is, however, too late to do so during the oral procedure. The applicant had there not only failed to annex the measures at issue to the application, but had only given a general indication as to their nature; he gave more precise details during the oral procedure, but the Court held "as this event took place in the last stage of the proceedings, it cannot rectify the omissions."

In the case of an alleged failure to act on the part of a Community institution, the documentary evidence of the date on which the institution was requested to act is of vital importance, for the very existence of a failure to act, in the terminology of the EEC and Euratom Treaties, or of an implied refusal to act, in the terminology of the ECSC Treaty and of the Staff Regulations, depends upon the lapse of a defined period of time. The limitation period for bringing the action in turn runs from the date upon which the institution can be deemed to have failed to act or to have refused to act. Again, the documentary evidence may be produced within a "reasonable" time, but whether it is produced before or after the time-limit for bringing proceedings may depend upon its own nature.

It was early settled in Joined Cases 7 and 9/54 *Industries Sidérurgiques Luxembourgeoises* v. *H.A.* [1954 to 1956] E.C.R. 175, that a copy of a letter sent to the relevant institution requesting it to act may constitute documentary evidence of the date on which the institution was requested to act.

Documents to be produced by legal persons

4–49   Additional documents must be filed with an application lodged on behalf of a "legal person governed by private law." This definition raises two major problems of legal theory—although it does not appear to have given rise to any difficulties in practice; the problems relate to the concept of a legal person, and to the distinction between public and private law. If the requirements related to legal persons in the strict sense, then similar types of business enterprise in different Member States, or even in different parts of the same Member State would be treated differently: to take the most obvious example, an English partnership does not have legal personality and would be exempt from article 38(5), unlike its French equivalent or indeed a Scottish partnership. It may be submitted, however, that the obvious purpose of article 38 is to regulate applications which are *not* lodged on behalf of a *natural* person, rather than to apply a strict test of legal personality, and that article 38 should be complied with by any undertaking, association or other entity empowered, under the national law to which it is subject, to bring an action in a name other than that of the natural persons who may be its members—which would include an English partnership, by virtue of R.S.C. Ord. 81. This view would also accord with the fact that Articles 33 and 35 of the ECSC Treaty expressly confer rights of action upon "associations of undertakings" regardless of whether they are incorporated, and that an action brought by a group of trade unions, Case 72/74 *Union Syndicale* v. *Council* [1975] E.C.R. 401, was not held to be inadmissible on the grounds of their lack of legal personality, despite being brought under Article 173 of the EEC Treaty, which refers to "natural or legal persons." Further, in the context of the right to intervene under article 37 of the EEC Statute, the term "person" was held to cover "bodies not having legal personality . . . if they display the characteristics which are at the foundation of such personality, in particular, the ability, however circumscribed, to undertake autonomous action and to assume liability" in the Order of December 11, 1973 allowing the Italian consumers' union (Unione Nazionale Consumatori), which under Italian law did not have legal personality, to intervene in the *Sugar Cases* [1973] E.C.R. 1465. It is clear from the reference in the Order to the "Statute" of the union that it had produced the documents which would have been required of an applicant under article 38(5) of the Rules.

4–50   The distinction between public law and private law is described by David ("Major Legal Systems" p. 63) as characteristic of the Romano-Germanic family of legal systems, although the extent of its recognition may differ between the three legal systems of the United Kingdom. French writers (*e.g.* Carbonnier, "Droit Civil I"; Goldman "Droit commercial européen") seem to agree that a company formed under the general law by private persons is a legal person governed by private law,

133

and that a nationalised coporation established under separate legislation is a legal person governed by public law, but they have coined the phrase "société d'économie mixte" to describe an apparently ordinary trading company in which all the shares are in fact held by the state or one of its emanations—of which there is no shortage of examples in the United Kingdom. The view of Goldman is that in their relations with outsiders, such companies remain subject to ordinary commercial law, and for all practical purposes it would appear that those acting on behalf of any "person" (in the extended sense) which is not, on the fact of it, an emanation of the state, should comply with the requirements of article 38(5).

4–51   The first of these requirements is the production of the "instruments" or instruments constituting and regulating that legal person." At first sight, it might be wondered from the English version whether production of the certificate of incorporation of a registered company would be sufficient compliance, although it could hardly be said to "regulate" the legal person, but the French text refers expressly and only to the production of the "statutes," which are the equivalent of the memorandum and articles of association of a registered company, even though in France, at least since 1966, commercial companies derive their legal status from the fact of registration (Law No. 66–537 of July 24, 1966, article 5). In practice these "persons" of a type subject to registration produce both proof of registration and their constitutive documents. This requirement should not give rise to much difficulty, except for certain non-Community companies: in the *Japanese ball bearing* cases [1979] E.C.R. 1185 *et seq.*, the Japanese applicants had to produce translations at least of extracts from the documents equivalent to their memorandum and articles of association into the languages of the cases.

The production of these documents should in fact enable the Registrar to check, if he felt it necessary, that the second requirement of article 38(5) has, on the face of it, been complied with. This second requirement is proof that authority has been properly conferred on the applicant's lawyer, which is a question of national law, as is shown by Case 18/57 *Nold* v. *H.A.* [1959] E.C.R. 41, although that case was decided before the introduction of the present requirement into the Rules of Procedure. The application there was lodged on behalf of a German limited partnership, which was technically in liquidation because it no longer had a partner with unlimited liability, and the lawyers lodging the application had been authorised to act by a certain Erich Nold, who was not in fact a partner at the time, although the partners made a written declaration that they had given him a power of attorney to that effect. The defendant claimed both that partners in a limited partnership in liquidation were not entitled to authorise anyone to bring an action in the name of the firm and that no power of attorney could be valid unless it was in writing. The Court, however, following its German Advocate-General (A.G. Roemer), held that as a matter of German law, partners in a partnership in liquidation could authorise actions to be brought insofar as was necessary for the purposes of the liquidation, and that, also as a matter of German law, there was no need for the power of attorney to be in writing: hence, to that extent, the action was admissible. Presumably the later written declaration of the partners would now be sufficient compliance with the requirement of article 38(5) of the Rules.

In this context, use may perhaps be made by United Kingdom litigants of the decision of the House of Lords on a Scottish appeal in *Ward* v. *Samyang* [1975] 2 All E.R. 424 to the effect that the bringing of an action on behalf of a company by persons who were not at the time authorised to act (which is not inconceivable in the circumstances of the short limitation periods for actions for annulment) may later be ratified by a properly constituted organ of the company (in that case, the liquidator).

Arbitration clause, etc.

4–52   In general, the production of the arbitration clause or special agreement required under article 38(6) where jurisdiction arises from such a clause or agreement should be straightforward; the difficulties arise where the dispute is as to the existence of the contract containing the arbitration clause, or arises under a contract separate from, but allegedly related to, such a contract. Case 23/76 *Pellegrini* v. *Commission* [1976] E.C.R. 1807 illustrates the latter situation. Pellegrini tendered unsuccessfully for a cleaning contract on the basis of a "draft agreement" which contained an arbitration clause, but the unsuccessful tenderer withdrew, and so the Commission asked Pellegrini to carry out the cleaning, under a succession of short-term contracts subject to the terms and conditions of the "draft agreement," for a period of some four years until, following a fresh invitation to tender, another tender was accepted. Pellegrini lodged an application before the European Court claiming damages for breach of contract, and it was held to be sufficient compliance with article 38(6) of the Rules for Pellegrini to produce the "draft agreement" *and* the later correspondence referring expressly to it.

(h) Rectification

4–53   As well as the specific provision of article 19 of the Statute enabling the Registrar to allow a reasonable period for the production of measures of which the annulment is sought and for the production of proof of the date on which an institution was requestd to act, article 38(7) of the Rules contains a general provision to the same effect, enabling a reasonable period to be allowed for the production of any of the formal accompanying documents (but *not* for annexes relating to the substance of the case, which under article 37(1) of the Rules, must accompany the pleading to which they relate). Since article 38(7) refers back to article 38(2), it also allows a period to be prescribed for compliance with the requirement to state an address for service; however, no provision is made for the rectification of the other contents of the application, listed in article 38(1) of the Rules.

Article 38(7) expressly provides that it is the Court which decides whether failure to comply with the Registrar's requirements renders the application inadmissible; conversely, it may be suggested that a request for rectification and subsequent acceptance of a document by the Registrar will not necessarily bind the Court, although the clearest example of this did not in reality involve the exercise by the Registrar of his powers under article 38(7). In Joined Cases 220 and 221/78 *ALA and ALFER* v. *Commission* [1979] E.C.R. 1693, the initial applications were not signed by a lawyer; this is not a matter covered by articles 38(2) to (6), but the applications were returned by the Registry, with a letter stating that this was so that the applicants might "comply with the provisions of articles 37 and 38 of the Rules of Procedure." In the opinion of A.G. Capotorti, the applicants must have taken this to be an exercise of the powers under Article 38(7), although in his view it could not be, and two months later lodged similar applications signed by a lawyer which were registered at the Court. However, as the Court pointed out, even the original applications were out of time, and hence inadmissible, quite apart from the fact that they were not signed by a lawyer, and so there was no possibility, despite the letter from the Registry, that they could be made to comply with the provisions of the Rules of Procedure.

(i) Service

4–54 Service of the application is the responsibility of the Registry (see para. 4–09 above). However, under article 92(1) of the Rules, the application may be declared inadmissible where it is clear that the Court has no jurisdiction to take cognisance of the application, even before it has been served on the defendant. This occurred in Case 46/81 *Benvenuto* [1981] E.C.R. 809 where the application sought a declaration that certain Italian legislation was void.

III. *DEFENCE (AND JUDGMENT BY DEFAULT)*

A. DEFENCE

Rules of Procedure

Article 40

4–55 1. Within one month after service on him of the application, the defendant shall lodge a defence stating:
  (a) the name and permanent residence of the defendant.
  (b) the points of fact and law relied on;
  (c) the form of order sought;
  (d) the nature of any evidence founded upon by him.
The provisions of Article 38(2) to (5) of these rules shall apply in a corresponding manner to the defence.
  2. The time limit laid down in paragraph 1 of this article may be extended by the President on a reasoned application by the defendant.

4–56 The requirements as to the contents of the defence, and as to the documents which must accompany it, correspond very closely to those governing applications. The defendant must state not only his or its own name and address but also, by virtue of the reference to article 38(2) of the Rules, an address for service in Luxembourg—although, of course, the Registry will have been required to serve the application before this was known (see para. 4–09). Like the applicant, the defendant must state the form of order sought by him, which will usually be to the effect that the application should be dismissed (as being inadmissible or unfounded or both) and that the applicant should be ordered to pay the costs, bearing in mind the requirement of article 69(2) of the Rules that the costs must be asked for (see para. 4–41 above). No express reference is made to the possibility of a counterclaim, although presumably it would fall within the definition of "the form of order sought," and as will be seen, it is difficult otherwise to explain the reference to article 38(4) in the last paragraph of article 40(1). However, in Cases 31/77 R and 53/77 R *Commission* v. *United Kingdom* [1977] E.C.R. 921, where the United Kingdom was accused in Case 31/77 of failure to comply with a Commission decision requiring the termination of an aid to pig producers, it lodged simultaneously a defence in Case 31/77 and a separate application, Case 53/77, for the annulment of the commission decision, rather than making a counterclaim. At first sight, for the defendant to raise a plea of illegality under Article 184 of the EEC Treaty might seem remarkably akin to a counterclaim, but this is likely to be relevant only in an action brought by the Commission against a Member State for breach of its obligations, or in the context of state aids, and it would appear from Case 156/77 *Commission* v. *Belgium* [1978] E.C.R. 1881 that it is not open to a Member State to plead the illegality of an act which it could have challenged directly under Article 173 of the EEC Treaty once the time-limit under that provision has expired; it should, however, be borne in mind that in that case, Belgium sought to plead the illegality of a Commission decision of which it was the addressee, an act which in any event does not fall within the scope of Article 184. It remains to be seen whether a genuine counterclaim would be admissible in, *e.g.* a contractual dispute coming before the Court by virtue of an arbitration clause.

4–57   Also like the applicant, the defendant must state the nature of the evidence founded upon by him, but unlike him he is not formally required to state the subject-matter of the dispute or the "grounds" of the defence. Rather, the defendant is merely required to state "the points of fact and law relied on." In practice these will usually serve the same function as the statement of the subject-matter of the dispute, and the grounds for the application, and be set out in a similar way, but the vaguer requirements for the defence can no doubt be explained on the basis that the onus is not on the defendant to identify the dispute or to lay a legal basis on which the Court can act; he may simply content himself with attacking what is set out in the application.

In the matter of accompanying documents, the rules governing the application apply also to the defence with regard to the production of the lawyer's certificate of entitlement to practise and with regard to the production of the instrument constituting a defendant who is a "legal

137

person" (see para. 4–49 above) and to the production of proof that authority has been properly conferred on the lawyer acting for such a defendant. By virtue of the reference to article 38(4), the defendant is also supposed to produce measures of which the annulment is sought, or evidence of the date on which the institution was requested to act in the case of an alleged failure to act; this requirement would appear only to be relevant in the event of a defendant in an action brought by the Council or the Commission making a counterclaim with regard to the act or failure to act of the applicant.

4–58 On the other hand, the defendant is obviously not required to produce a copy of an arbitration clause or special agreement giving the Court jurisdiction under article 38(6) of the Rules, though he may well wish to dispute such a clause or agreement produced by the applicant. Less obviously, there is no express reference to the possibility of rectification of the defence to the limited degree permitted in the case of the application under article 38(7) (see para. 4–53 above). However, since the defence is specifically required to comply with the provisions of article 38(2) to (5), and since it is with regard to those provisions and article 38(6) that the Registrar is authorised to allow rectification of the application, it may be suggested that the same opportunity should be offered to the defendant; indeed it would appear that such is the practice of the Registry.

4–59 There is, however, an advantage which is offered to the defendant with regard to procedural time-limits. The Court has no discretion to extend the limitation periods (including extensions on account of distance) for lodging the application, except in the rare case where the applicant can show the existence of unforeseeable circumstances or of a *force majeure* under article 42 of the Statute, but the President is expressly authorised by article 40(2) of the Rules to extend the time-limit for lodging the defence if a reasoned application is made by the defendant. In practice, this application should be made *before* the time-limit has expired so as to avoid any risk of an application for judgment by default or any need to prove *force majeure* or unforeseeable circumstances, but an honest statement that it is a complicated case or that the defendant's adviser is over-worked appears to be acceptable at that stage as a reasoned application. Such extension as is likely to be given reflects the fact that the basic time-limit is only one month, so that in a really difficult case it may be necessary to ask for successive extensions.

B. Judgment by Default

EEC Statute of the Court of Justice

Article 38

4–60 Where the defending party, after having been duly summoned, fails to file written submissions in defence, judgment shall be given against that party by default. An objection may be lodged against the judgment within one month of it being notified. The objection shall not have the effect of staying enforcement of the judgment by default unless the Court decides otherwise.

(Article 39 of the Euratom Statute is identical, but article 35 of the ECSC Statute only allows for judgment by default "in proceedings in which the Court has unlimited jurisdiction," the most important consequence of which is that judgment by default is not available in actions for the annulment of decisions which do not impose penalties.)

Rules of Procedure

Article 94

1. If a defendant on whom an application originating proceedings has been duly served fails to lodge a defence to the application in the proper form within the time prescribed, the applicant may apply for judgment by default.

The application shall be served on the defendant. The President shall fix a date for the opening of the oral procedure.

2. Before giving judgment by default the Court shall, after hearing the Advocate-General, consider whether the originating application is admissible, whether the appropriate formalities have been complied with, and whether the applicant's submissions appear well founded. The Court may order a preparatory inquiry.

3. A judgment by default shall be enforceable. The Court may, however, grant a stay of execution until the Court has given its decision on any application under paragraph 4 to set aside the judgment, or it may make execution subject to the provision of security of an amount and nature to be fixed in the light of the circumstances; this security shall be released if no such application is made or if the application fails.

4. Application may be made to set aside a judgment by default.

The application to set aside the judgment must be made within one month from the date of service of the judgment and must be lodged in the form prescribed by Articles 37 and 38 of these rules.

5. After the application has been served, the President shall prescribe a period within which the other party may submit his written observations.

The proceedings shall be conducted in accordance with Articles 44 *et seq.* of these rules.

6. The Court shall decide by way of a judgment which may not be set aside. The original of this judgment shall be annexed to the original of the judgment by default. A note of the judgment on the application to set aside shall be made in the margin of the original of the judgment by default.

4–61   Although a complex set of rules governing judgments by default has been laid down, they do not appear so far to have been used, and it could be suggested that it is highly unlikely that they ever will be used, for the very simple reason that the defendant in the vast majority of direct actions brought before the European Court is a Community institution, and the only other possible defendants, except in cases arising under arbitration clauses or in what might generically be termed disciplinary proceedings, are Member States. It may be expected that their legal services would not let the time limit for lodging the defence pass without at least requesting an extension.

Article 94(1) of the Rules is perhaps drafted in more general terms than is justified having regard to the limitations set in article 35 of the ECSC Statute; nevertheless, it may be observed that article 72(1) of the 1953 Rules, introducing the original procedure for judgment by default, was expressed to apply independently of the hypothesis postulated in article 35 of the ECSC Statute, and purported to make the procedure available for failure to submit any of the pleadings in time and indeed even for failure to appear at the hearing. The present article 94(1) clearly only applies where the defence is not lodged in time, and the essential feature of the system it lays down is that judgment by default is not automatic; it must be requested by a separate application which must itself be served on the defendant.

In any event, the Court must consider whether the original application is admissible and whether the information it contains supports the order which is sought ("submissions" in article 94(2) appears, from the other language versions, to be used in the sense of "conclusions").

4-62 Even when judgment has been granted by default, the defendant may still apply, within one month plus available extensions, to have this judgment set aside. His application to this end must in effect comply with the requirements laid down for applications commencing proceedings, although it does not commence a complete new written stage, since the procedure envisaged in article 94(5) omits the possibility of lodging a reply and rejoinder. The judgment given on the application to set aside the judgment by default is not itself susceptible of being set aside.

IV. *REPLY AND REJOINDER*

Rules of Procedure

Article 41

4-63 1. The application originating the proceedings and the defence may be supplemented by a reply from the applicant and by a rejoinder from the defendant.

2. The President shall fix the time limits within which these pleadings are to be lodged.

Article 42

1. In reply or rejoinder a party may indicate further evidence. The party must, however, give reasons for the delay indicating it.

Article 82

Any time limit prescribed pursuant to these rules may be extended by whoever prescribed it.

4-64 The application and the defence are the only compulsory parts of the written procedure in direct actions. Whether or not a reply and a rejoinder are lodged is a matter of choice for the parties, although in the vast majority of cases they are in fact put in, and some lawyers regard it as a matter worthy of comment if they are not. There are no formal indications as to the content of the reply and rejoinder, except that article 42(1) expressly allows further evidence (in the sense of *offres de preuve*) to be indicated. This in itself perhaps typifies the usual function of the reply and rejoinder, which is essentially to expand or refine the material already contained in the application and the defence. Given that article 42(2) of the Rules, as will be seen (at para. 4–67 below), in principle prohibits the raising of new issues, the only novel aspect is likely to be that the reply may specifically answer points taken in the defence and that the rejoinder may raise counter arguments to those answers; it might even be suggested that is the only useful purpose the reply and rejoinder serve. Indeed, one way in which the applicant can, if he so wishes, hasten the disposal of his case is to indicate, once the defence has been served on him, that he does not wish to lodge a reply; this will also have the effect of depriving the defendant of the opportunity to lodge a rejoinder. This tactic has on occasions been used by the Commission in actions against Member States, *e.g.* in Case 231/78 *Commission* v. *U.K.* [1979] E.C.R. 1447, although there the effect was disturbed by the fact that France intervened in support of the United Kingdom. Even where the applicant lodges a reply, the defendant retains complete liberty not to put in a rejoinder if he or it so wishes; as an example, France refrained from lodging a rejoinder in Case 232/78 *Commission* v. *France* [1979] E.C.R. 2729.

4–65 The time-limits for lodging the reply and rejoinder are fixed by the President, or the judge acting as President, and under the general provision in article 82 of the Rules he may extend these limits. As in the case of requests for the extension of the period for lodging the defence (see para. 4–59 above), the extension should in practice be requested before the expiry of the original time-limit; although orders relating to the extension of time-limits are not usually published, it would appear that the view is taken in the Court that a time-limit can only be extended whilst it still exists, in the absence of unforeseen circumstances, and indeed article 72(1) of the 1953 Rules of Procedure allowed for judgment by default at the request of either party if the other did not produce any one of his pleadings within the time set.

V. *AMENDMENT OF PLEADINGS AND NOVEL POINTS*

Rules of Procedure
Article 42

4–66 2. No fresh issue may be raised in the course of proceeding unless it is based on matters of law or of fact which come to light in the course of the written procedure.

If in the course of the written procedure one of the parties raises a fresh issue which is so based, the President may, even after the expiry of the normal procedural time limits, acting on a report of the Judge Rapporteur and after hearing the Advocate-General, allow the other party time to answer on that issue.

The decision on the admissibility of the issue shall be reserved for the final judgment.

Article 92

2. The Court may at any time of its own motion consider whether there exists

any absolute bar to proceeding with a case, and shall give its decision in accordance with article 91(3) and (4) of these rules.

4–67   No provision is made in the procedure before the European Court for the amendment of the pleadings. Rather, there is a prohibition on the raising of any fresh "issue" unless it is based on matters of law or fact which come to light in the course of the written procedure, although it might be noted that the French text uses the word "moyens," of which the English equivalent elsewhere, as in article 38(1) of the Rules prescribing the ccontents of the Application, is "grounds." This in itself is perhaps an indication that the prohibition might not be so absolute as at first sight appears. On the other hand, article 92(2) of the Rules effectively allows the Court itself to take points as to its jurisdiction at any time, a power which has influenced its attitude as to new points on jurisdiction and admissibility in general taken by the parties. Hence new points relating to jurisdiction can be considered separately from the other fresh issues.

(a) Jurisdiction

4–68   An example of the Court taking a somewhat technical point as to jurisdiction of its own motion can be found in Joined Cases 27 and 30/64 *Fonzi* v. *Commission* [1965] E.C.R. 481. This was a staff case in which the applicant sought, *inter alia*, the annulment of what was alleged to be a decision to transfer or second him; the defendant, the Commission, contested the admissibility of other heads of claim on the ground that they were out of time, but did not expressly challenge the admissibility for this particular claim. However, the Court noted that under the Staff Regulations it had jurisdiction to review the legality of measures with regard to officials only if they are "adversely affected" by such measures, and proceeded to consider of its own motion the admissibility of the claim. To this end, it looked at the wording of the measure in question, coming to the conclusion that it did not amount to a secondment or transfer, that a transfer was in fact effected by a later decision with which the action was not concerned, and that the measure should be regarded as an internal matter which could not "adversely affect" the applicant within the meaning of the Staff Regulations. Hence it held that the claim was inadmissible.

The fact that it could take such points of its own motion has meant that the Court has been prepared to consider challenges to its jurisdiction raised by the parties at a very late stage in the proceedings. In Joined Cases 67 to 85/75 *Lesieur Cotelle* v. *Commission* [1976] E.C.R. 391, the admissibility of the applications was contested by counsel for the Commission only towards the end of the hearing. The applicants claimed that the challenge was out of time, but the Court asserted that "that argument is irrelevant because the admissibility of the proceedings must be examined by the Court of its own motion" and went on to hold, contrary to the Opinion of A.G. Warner, that the applications were in part admissible and in part inadmissible. It might, however, be suggested that the results of accepting a plea of inadmissibility without the benefit of full argument were not wholly satisfactory in that case: the Court there appeared to lay down a test that actions for unliquidated damages could only be brought before it insofar as the applicant could not be expected to have brought an action before his national courts, a view which was reversed after the benefit of full argument in Case 126/76 *Dietz* v. *Commission* [1977] E.C.R. 2431, where the applicants expressly mentioned that they had brought parallel proceedings before the German courts.

4–69 The acceptance (or raising by the Court of its own motion) of new points on jurisdiction is less controversial with regard to objectively ascertainable matters such as the expiry of time-limits, as in Case 33/72 *Gunnella* v. *Commission* [1973] E.C.R. 475. In this staff case, the Commission raised the point that the application had been lodged out of time at the hearing, and the Court stated that this was a matter which it should examine of its own motion, on the ground, however, that the observance of time-limits was a matter of public interest; no mention was made of article 92 of the Rules of Procedure as such. It was found that the application had indeed been lodged too late, not so much by mathematical calculation as because the application purported to challenge an alleged decision contained in a letter dated March 9, 1972, which the Court found was merely confirmatory of a decision which had already been taken in October 1965 which was the act the applicant should have challenged; obviously the application in that case was literally years too late to do this (see para. 2–36 above).

A similar fact situation has underlain cases where the Court has held that it may consider of its own motion the question whether an action is inadmissible by reason of the doctrine of *lis pendens*. In Joined Cases 45 and 49/70 *Bode* v. *Commission* [1971] E.C.R. 465, the Court found that the application in Case 49/50 sought the annulment of a decision which merely confirmed the implied decision which was the subject of Case 45/70; it thus held that Case 49/70 was inadmissible because the matter was *lis peendens*, stating that it was a point which it must raise of its own motion (though in fact the admissibility of Case 49/70 had been challenged by the Commission from the outset). Exactly the same power was claimed in Joined Cases 58 and 75/72 *Perinciolo* v. *Council* [1973] E.C.R. 511, where Case 75/72 was held to be inadmissible in that it sought the annulment of an act which was merely confirmatory of the acts which were being challenged in Case 58/72, the matter thus being *lis pendens*.

4–70 It would appear that the Court regards itself as able to consider of its own motion not only issues which relate to the admissibility of the substantive action but also issues which relate to the admissibility of certain ancillary or incidental claims. This was established with regard to the plea of illegality in Joined Cases 154, 205 and 206, 226 to 228, 263 and 264/78 31, 39, 83 and 85/79 *Ferriera Valsabbia and others* v. *Commission* [1980] E.C.R. 907, a series of actions seeking the annulment of individual decisions imposing fines on them for breach of General Decision 962/77/ECSC fixing minimum prices for certain concrete reinforcement bars (O.J. 1977, L114/1). Under article 36 of the

ECSC Treaty, applicants contesting fines imposed on them may plead the illegality of the general decision they are alleged to have breached, and all the applicants made use of this possibility. However, article 36 of the ECSC Treaty only allows the legality of the general decision to be contested under the same conditions it could have been challenged directly under the first paragraph of article 33 of the Treaty, under which the Court is precluded from examining the evaluation of the situation resulting from economic facts or circumstances in the light of which the Commission took its decision, unless the Commission is alleged to have misused its powers. The Commission eventually took the point that the plea of illegality would entail an evaluation by the Court of the situation resulting from economic facts or circumstances, but, although it had claimed that the plea of illegality in four of the cases was inadmissible on the grounds, the point was not mentioned in its written "conclusions." Nonetheless, the Court held that "even where that argument has not been formally pleaded, the Court may raise it of its own motion as it concerns the Court's *jurisdiction*" (emphasis added). It remains to be seen how far this broad concept of "jurisdiction" will extend.

4–71   By way of contrast, there is an example of the Court's having refused to consider a late plea of inadmissibility. This was in Joined Cases 54 and 60/76 *Loheac and others* v. *Council and Commission* [1977] E.C.R. 645. In its rejoinder, the Council put forward the general contention that the Court should declare the applications inadmissible, and the Court dismissed it on two grounds, in the first place because it was not accompanied by any reasoning or arguments, and secondly because it was out of time having regard to articles 40 and 42 of the Rules of Procedure. If it was the first point which was decisive, then all that *Loheac* means is that even points as to jurisdiction must be sufficiently precise to enable the Court to give judgement on them; on the other hand, the second ground appears to be the first hint which the Court has given that even points as to its jurisdiction should be raised at a sufficiently early stage to be fully argued—but the weight of the case law so far is in the opposite direction.

(b) Other issues

4–72   It has already been mentioned that although the English version of article 42(2) of the Rules of Procedure prohibits the raising of what are rather vaguely termed fresh "issues," the French version prohibits the raising of fresh "moyens," a term rendered into English more specifically as "ground" in the description of the contents of the application. Indeed, most of the case law on raising fresh issues, other than points relating to jurisdiction, has arisen in the context of attempts either to change the "grounds" of the application or the defence or to change the statement of the form of order sought by the applicant or the defendant.

Grounds

4–73   Even using the other language versions to interpret "issues" narrowly, it is clear that in principle no new grounds can be raised unless they are based on matters which came to light in the course of the procedure, although there may be room for debate as to what is a "ground." In Joined Cases 19 and 21/60 and 2 to 13/61 *Fives Lille Cail* v. *H.A.* [1961] E.C.R. 281, the applicants sought the annulment of decisions ordering them to repay sums wrongly paid to them under the ferrous scrap equalisation scheme, and, *inter alia*, they alleged that the decisions were "contrary to the rules of law relating to the application of the ECSC Treaty" (*cf.* Article 33 of that Treaty), but without indicating the rules of law which were alleged to have been infringed. In their reply, the applicants specified the rules of law in question as being "the general principle governing the legality of the invocation of administrative measures." This the Court regarded as being an entirely new "ground" for annulment, which was referred to neither directly, nor by implication, in the application, and which could not be regarded as a more detailed statement of the ground set out in the application. A more recent example is Case 12/79 *Wagner* v. *Commission* [1979] E.C.R. 3657. This was an action claiming damages from the Commission for the harm caused to the applicant by the refusal of a German intervention agency, acting on the basis of Commission Regulation 1579/76 (O.J. 1976, L172/59), to allow the applicants to cancel an export licence for sugar on July 1, 1976. It had been held in an earlier case that, although that Regulation stated that it entered into force on July 1, 1976, since it had only been published on July 2, 1976, because of a strike in the Official Publications Office, it could only be applied from that date. The applicants alleged that the Commission was liable for the consequences of the Regulation having been applied to them on July 1, 1976, putting forward two grounds, that the Commission was responsible for the functioning of the Official Publications Offices and that it failed to inform the German agency of the postponed entry into force of the Regulation. In their reply, the applicants put forward the further ground that in any event the Commission's Regulation was unlawful. The Court held that this was a fresh issue within the meaning of article 42(2) of the Rules of Procedure, and had been put forward too late. Conversely, in Case 11/81 *Dürbeck* v. *Commission* (April 1, 1982) where the applicants originally sought damages on the grounds that the introduction of certain safeguard measures by the Commission breached the principle of legitimate expectation, it was held to be a fresh issue for the applicants to claim that this principle was breached by the failure of the Commission to inform it that certain importations could still be carried out under the safeguard measures.

4–74   The rigour of this rule has, however, been relaxed in two ways. The first, which would appear only to have been used in some early judgments, is that the Court may take account of a late point if it considers that public policy so requires; the second, which has been more commonly used, is to distinguish between the "grounds" put forward in support of the order sought and the "arguments" supporting the grounds. Both these approaches, and an application of the basic rule, appear in one of the first judgments delivered by the Court, in Case 2/54 *Italy* v. *H.A.* [1954 to 1956] E.C.R. 37. Here, with regard to

ECSC Decisions of which it sought the annulment, Italy raised three new points in its reply. One was that the Decisions contained an insufficient statement of reasons, which the Court treated as new ground raised out of time, thus applying the basic rule. The second new point was a claim that the ECSC Consultative Committee had not been consulted as required by the Treaty; the Court held that it should consider this of its own motion since "if it were well-founded the Court should be justified in annulling the decision of its own motion." By way of contrast, it said with regard to the alleged insufficiency of the statement of reasons that "public policy" did not require the Court to consider the matter of its own motion. Whether or not such a distinction can be satisfactorily explained, it appears from the subsequent case law that the Court has only tended to consider new grounds of its own motion where they have related to its jurisdiction or questions of admissibility except that in Case 108/81 *Amylum* v. *Council* (September 30, 1982), where the late "ground" related to the competence of the Council to enact the measure at issue, the Second Chamber took the view that it should explain why it rejected the substance of the point, even though it held it to be inadmissible. The remaining new point taken in *Italy* v. *H.A.* was that the system introduced by the contested Decisions allowed undertakings to conceal discriminatory transactions for a certain period, which was held to be a new "argument," supporting the ground already put forward for the annulment of the Decisions that they infringed the Treaty, rather than a new ground in itself, and hence admissible.

4–75   It might be wondered why the alleged insufficiency of the statement of reasons or the supposed failure to consult the Consultative Committee could not also be regarded as arguments in support of the claim of infringement of the Treaty, but the Court laid down no criteria for distinguishing between a ground for the application and arguments in support of these grounds other than a simple assertion as to the status of the particular point. Some elucidation was, however, given in Case 2/57 *Hauts Fourneaux de Chasse* v. *H.A.* [1957 and 1958] E.C.R. 199, where the applicant sought the annulment of a Commission decision on the ground of misuse of powers, and put forward a number of new points in support of that contention in the reply. The Court held that the applicant had not introduced new grounds but "merely developed those made in its application by invoking a number of arguments some of which were adduced for the first time in the Reply." Also in Case 19/58 *Germany* v. *H.A.* [1960] E.C.R. 225, where the applicant had, *inter alia*, alleged that a decision constituted a "misuse of powers in so far as there has been a departure from the legitimate objectives of the Treaty," and then in its reply stated that the High Authority "should have applied Article 67 of the [ECSC] Treaty instead of the second paragraph of Article 10 of the Convention [on Transitional Provisions]," the Court held that since the ground of misuse of powers had already been raised, this second argument could legitimately appear for the first time in the reply. What both these cases in fact seem to involve is an amplification in the reply of the grounds as stated in the application, bearing in mind,

146

as was noted in the context of the application (see para. 4–37 above), that those grounds must be set out in relation to stated facts and not in the abstract.

4–76   It could also be suggested that such a test would also allow for the new points which the applicants took in Case 30/78 *Distillers* v. *Commission* [1980] E.C.R. 2229. In its application for the annulment of a decison taken under Article 85 of the EEC Treaty with regard to its conditions of sale and price terms, Distillers had alleged that there was an infringement of essential procedural requirements in that the consultation with the Advisory Committee on Restrictive Practices and Dominant Positions was defective, and in an addendum to its reply, lodged after the rejoinder, it further alleged that the documents put before that Committe did not include an expert's economic appraisal of Distillers' pricing system put forward on its behalf, but that they did include a full copy of the original complaint against Distillers which it had not seen and certain of the contents of which it would have challenged. These two points could be regarded as simply an amplification of the ground for annulment set out in the application; Distillers argued, however, that they were based on matters which came to light in the course of the written procedure, in this case in the rejoinder and in the complainant's application to intervene. A.G. Warner was prepared to accede to this view, but the Court did not find it necessary to pronounce upon the admissibility of the new issues. The rationale of the prohibition on raising new grounds has been considered in a number of recent Opinions of Advocates-General. In Case 46/75 *IBC* v. *Commission* [1976] E.C.R. 65, where counsel for the applicant raised the quesion of the retroactivity of the Commission Regulations at issue at the hearing, A.G. Warner, taking the view that the point was not implicit in the grounds raised in the application, justified the prohibition on the basis that "the raising of a fresh ground at the Hearing may catch the defendant unprepared to deal with it." This approach was developed by A.G. Capotorti in Case 112/78 *Kobor* v. *Commission* [1979] E.C.R. 1573. There the applicant sought the annulment of a selection board decision refusing to allow her to take part in tests relating to a competition for the creation of a reserve of administrative assistants. In her application, she alleged that this was the result of an erroneous assessment of her practical experience, but in her reply she took the further point that the statement of reasons on which the decision was based was insufficient. A.G. Capotorti remarked that although the provisions of article 42(2) of the Rules of Procedure might not seem to allow for any derogations, its specific function was to avoid one party being denied the opportunity to reply to the new point during the written procedure, concluding that "the important point is to establish whether the party against whom the new complaint has been raised has been handicapped in resisting it as a result of the other party's conduct of the procedure." In this case the defendant, the Commission, had in fact mentioned the point itself, and indeed expressly stated that it did not wish to challenge the admissibility of the new ground, and the Court (Second Chamber)) gave judgment in favour of the applicant, on

147

the ground that the decision was insufficiently reasoned, without discussing whether the point was admissible. The views of A.G. Warner and A.G. Caportorti were expressly adopted by A.G. Mayras in Case 24/79 *Oberthür* v. *Commission* [1980] E.C.R. 1743, where in her reply the applicant put forward new grounds which alleged a breach of article 25 of the Staff Regulations, breaches of articles 45 and 24 thereof having been put forward as the grounds for the action in the application. A.G. Mayras stated that the Commission had in fact been able to make observations both in writing and at the hearing on the new issues, and concluded that they were admissible. The Court, however, did not find it necessary to pronounce upon the point.

4–77   There appears to be a difference of approach between the judgments of the Court, mostly in relatively early cases, which deal expressly with the matter and the opinions in recent cases of the Advocates-General. The approach of the Court is more formal: leaving aside the vexed question of pubic policy, new points would appear to be admissible insofar as they are arguments in support of grounds already put forward or within their general scope. The approach of the Advocates-General, apart, it must be said, from the assertion by A.G. Reischl in Joined Cases 209 to 215 and 218/78 *Van Landewyck* v. *Commission* [1980] E.C.R. 3125, 3302 that "particularly important issues may be raised by the Court of its own motion," is more functional: a new point is admissible if the fact that it was taken late does not deprive the other party of the chance to comment upon it fully. This is perhaps reflected in the judgment of the Court in Case 139/79 *Maizena* v. *Council* [1980] E.C.R. 3393, 3423–3424, where the applicant put forward a point at the hearing arising from information revealed in the rejoinder; although it did not find it necessary to decide the point, the Court stated that it had been taken so late that it did not have enough information before it to decide the point.

Form of order sought

4–78   If the prohibition on the raising of fresh issues in article 42(2) of the Rules is taken as being a prohibition on raising fresh grounds for the action, then there is no express prohibition on changing the statement of the form of order sought (hereinafter referred to as "conclusions"). Nonetheless, there are a number of cases where the attitude of the Court has been similar to that which it has taken with regard to the raising of new grounds; alterations of the conclusions are permitted insofar as they remain within the scope of the original conclusions. A less than obvious example is Case 80/63 *Degreef* v. *Commission* [1964] E.C.R. 391, where the applicant sought, *inter alia*, the annulment of a decision to dismiss him, and the payment of a specified sum by way of damages. During the oral procedure, he purported to amend the latter claim, asking for payment of damages limited to his salary up to the date of the judgment. The Court accepted this amendment, but not in the form in which it was put forward. It held that a necessary consequence of the annulment of the decision to dismiss the applicant would be that he became entitled to payment of arrears of his salary; hence the conclusion seeking such payment was by implication contained in those seeking the annulment of the decision, rather than in the initial claim for damages, which was treated as withdrawn. A simpler illustration is Case 28/64 *Müller* v. *Council* [1965] E.C.R. 237. The applicant initially sought the annulment of an implied decision rejecting his request to be classified in a particular career bracket, but in the reply he modified his conclusions so as to request that the defendant be ordered to classify him in a higher grade. The Court found that the new conclusions did not amount to a "substantial modification" of the conclusions contained in the application, stating that they were confined to clarifying the scope of the previous conclusions in respect of the foreseeable result of the application of the rules of the Staff Regulations; they were thus admissible. In the actions for damages in Joined Cases 29, 31, 36, 39 to 47, 50 and 51/63 *Usines de la Providence* v. *H.A.* [1965] E.C.R. 911, the applicants initially calculated their claims on the basis of a "transport parity grant" which the defendant alleged should not have been paid to them, but in their reply they recalculated the sums on the basis of the difference between the cost of the amount of shipyard scrap they had acquired and the cost of the same tonnage of imported ferrous scrap. On analysing the application, the Court found that in substance they claimed that without the "transport parity grant" the cost of shipyard scrap was higher that that of imported ferrous scrap, so that all the applicants had done in the reply was to rectify their calculations, without changing the subject-matter of the dispute or introducing fresh "moyens." Hence the amendment was admissible. Indeed, the defendant also took a new point in its comments on an expert's report: in these comments, it was observed that if the applicants had bought imported ferrous scrap, they would have been liable to pay an increased ferrous scrap equalisation contribution. Despite the objections of the applicants, the Court also held this point admissible, since it merely went to the calculation of the damage which the applicant claimed to have suffered. On the other hand, in Case 186/80 *Suss* v. *Commission* [1981] E.C.R. 2041, where the applicant's original "conclusions" sought the removal of the doctor nominated by the Commission from the medical board considering the extent of the applicant's invalidity, the Second Chamber took the view that a claim put forward by the applicant in his reply that the findings of this board should be communicated to him had no connection with his other claims and was therefore inadmissible.

4-79   There is indeed one case in which it was held expressly that article 42(2) applied to new "conclusions" as much as to new "grounds." In Case 83/63 *Krawczynski* v. *Commission* [1965] E.C.R. 623, the Court (First Chamber) found of its own motion that the reply set out the conclusions in an amended form without justifying such an amendment, and held that if, under article 42(2) of the Rules, no fresh issues ("moyen") may be raised unless it is based on matters of law or fact which come to light in the course of the written procedure, "this condition governs *a fortiori* any amendment to the conclusions." However, in Case 125/78 *Gema* v. *Commission* [1979] E.C.R. 3173

149

there is a dictum to the effect that article 42(2) "does not in any way provide for the possibility of an applicant's introducing fresh conclusions." This is a view which hardly accords with what has actually happened in a number of decided cases, and it may be submitted that *Gema* was in fact concerned with an attempt to change the whole subject matter of the action (see para. 4–82 below).

4–80   By way of contrast, there are cases where a notable modification of the "conclusions" appears to have been permitted. In Joined Cases 18 and 19/64 *Alvino* v. *Commission* [1965] E.C.R. 789, the original conclusions had challenged a number of separate measures which were not of equal concern to the 22 (in total) applicants. The Court (Second Chamber), however, without commenting on its admissibility, approved the fact that during the proceedings, the applicants amended their conclusions so as to refer only to identical measures or to measures which concerned them all equally. In Case 92/78 *Simmenthal* v. *Commission* [1979] E.C.R. 777, the application was originally drafted so as to seek the annulment of a Commission Decision, two notices of invitation to tender, and to Commission Regulations. However, although the Court itself did not comment upon the point, it is recorded both in the "Facts" part of the judgment and in A.G. Reischl's Opinion that during the course of the proceedings Simmenthal amended their conclusions to state that their action was for the annulment as such only of the Commisson Decision, and that they wished rather to plead the illegality of the invitations to tender and the Regulations under article 184 of the EEC Treaty (see para. 1–09 above). Finally, in Case 162/78 *Wagner* v. *Commission* [1979] E.C.R. 3467, the applicants initially sought the annulment of two Commission Regulations, 1182/78 and 1392/78. Three days after the proceedings were instituted, the Commission adopted Regulation 1837/78, which repealed Regulation 1182/78 and supplemented Regulation 1392/78, and in the light of this the applicants amended their conclusions so as to seek the annulment of article 1 of the new Regulation, stating that it was no longer necessary for the Court to pronounce upon its original conclusions. The Commission did not object to what it described as the amendment of the "subject-matter" of the application, and the Court did not consider it further.

4–81   On the other hand, a bare assertion as to the scope of the conclusions cannot be regarded as amending their content; in Case 33/59 *Chasse* v. *H.A.* [1962] E.C.R. 381 and Joined Cases 46 and 47/59 *Meroni* v. *H.A.* [1962] E.C.R. 411, the Court interpreted the conclusions (in actions for damages) as relating to liability for a particular set of acts of fraud, and refused to accept an assertion by counsel, who nonetheless refrained from putting forward any formal amendment, that the conclusions related to other acts of fraud as well.

What appears to be the real limitation on modification of the conclusions is that it must not amount to an alteration of the substance or subject-matter of the action. An early example is Case 17/57 *Steenkolenmijnen* v. *H.A.* [1959] E.C.R. 1; the applicants brought their action for the annulment, under Article 33 of the ECSC Treaty, of an alleged decision, but in their reply, they stated that if the High Authority was held by the Court not to have taken a decision, they sought the annulment of its implied decision of refusal to take a decision under Article 35 of that Treaty. The Court held that the basis of an action cannot be changed, even by way of an alternative, in the reply. Conversely, in Case 125/78 *Gema* v. *Commission* [1979] E.C.R. 3173, the applicants, acting on the basis of Article 175 of the EEC Treaty, challenged the Commission's failure to issue a decision with regard to certain practices by Radio Luxembourg which were alleged to be an abuse of a dominant position, but they later lodged certain "additional conclusions" seeking in the alternative the annulment under article 173 of the EEC Treaty of the Commission's decision not to continue with proceedings against Radio Luxembourg. The Court had no hesitation in holding that there was no possibility of transforming an application on grounds of failure to act into an application for annulment, although it also asserted, as has already been noted, that article 42(2) of the Rules does not provide for the possibility of introducing fresh conclusions at all.

4–82   A somewhat different type of situation was at issue in Case 232/78 *Commission* v. *France* [1979] E.C.R. 2729. The Commission had originally sought a declaration under article 169 of the EEC Treaty that France was in breach of its Treaty obligations by continuing to apply its restrictive national system to the importation of mutton and lamb from the United Kingdom "after 1 January 1978." As a result, however, of its interpetation of the judgment of the Court in Case 231/78 *Commission* v. *U.K.* [1979] E.C.R. 1447, the Commission amended its conclusions during the oral procedure so as to request a declaration that the breach had occurred in certain respects as from July 1, 1977, in other respects as from January 1, 1975 and in yet other respects as from Accession. The Court held these amended conclusions to be inadmissible, on the basis that a party may not alter the actual subject-matter of the dispute during the proceedings, a view which was reiterated in Case 124/81 *Commission* v. *United Kingdom* (February 8, 1983).

Insofar as the case law may be synthesised, it would appear to be fairly well established that detailed amendments falling within scope of the original conclusions are admissible, and it may be that broader modifications are also admissible, subject to the overall limitation that they must not have the effect of altering the subject-matter or substance of the action.

(c) Procedure where article 42(2) of the Rules is invoked

4–83   The procedure where a party raises a new issue claiming that it falls within the exception in article 42(2) is clearly set out in that provision itself. An example of its use can be found with regard to the points put forward by the applicant in an addendum to the reply in Case 30/78 *Distillers* v. *Commission* [1980] E.C.R. 2229, 2265. It is, however, clear that a judgment of the Court holding that there is nothing to invalidate an act of a Community institution does not constitute "a matter of law or fact which comes to light in the course of the written procedure." In

Case 11/81 *Dürbeck* v. *Commission* (April 1, 1982) it was held that a new fact must be something which the applicant did not know about at the time the application was lodged or indeed which did not then exist, but since Community acts were presumed valid until the contrary was held, a judgment upholding their validity merely confirmed an existing situation.

C. Procedural Time-Limits

4–84   The time-limits for lodging the defence, reply and rejoinder have been discussed in the context of these pleadings (see paras. 4–59, 4–65 above). Under article 40(1) of the Rules, the defence must be lodged within one month of the service of the application, subject to the power of the President under article 40(2) to extend this period on a reasoned application. The time-limits for lodging the reply and rejoinder are, under article 41(2) of the Rules, fixed by the President, subject to his general power under article 82 to extend any time-limit prescribed by him.

As in the case of the limitation periods for commencing proceedings (see para. 2–04 above), by virtue of article 80 of the Rules, the day of the event from which the period is to run is excluded from the calculation of the time-limits, and the period is extended until the end of the first following working day if it would otherwise end on a Sunday or on an official holiday, but time continues to run during vacations. Similarly the extensions on account of distance allowed for in article 81(2) and Annex II of the Rules, also apply to procedural time-limits.

D. Procedural Issues

Rules of Procedure

Article 91

4–85   1. A party wishing to apply to the Court for a decision on a preliminary objection or on any other procedural issue shall make the application by a separate document.

The application must state the grounds of fact and law relied on and the form of order sought by the applicant; any supporting documents must be annexed to it.

2. As soon as the application has been lodged, the President shall prescribe a period within which the opposite party is to lodge a document containing that party's submissions and the grounds for them.

3. Unless the Court decides otherwise, the remainder of the proceedings shall be oral.

4. The Court shall, after hearing the Advocate-General, decide on the application or reserve its decision for the final judgement.

If the Court refuses the application or reserves its decision, the President shall prescribe new time-limits for the further steps in the proceedings.

4–86   Article 91 enables the Court to decide procedural issues or preliminary objections before, or without, going into the substance; it is in fact most frequently used where a decision on the procedural issue may be sufficient to dispose of the case, in the vast majority of cases where the defendant claims that the action is inadmissible. So in an action for annulment of a Regulation brought by a private litigant under Article 173 of the EEC Treaty, the Council or Commission may claim that the Regulation is not of "direct and individual concern" to the applicant and ask for the point to be decided under article 91, as in the five *Japanese ball bearing* cases (see [1979] E.C.R. at pp. 1192, 1283, 1310, 1343 and 1370). Similarly, the defendant institution may ask for the admissibility of an action for damages to be considered under article 91. as in Joined Cases 56 to 60/74 *Kampffmeyer and others* v. *Commission and Council* [1976] E.C.R. 711, 740.

This does not, however, mean that it is only points going to the admissibility of the application which may be considered under article 91. In Case 28/65 *Fonzi* v. *Commission* [1966] E.C.R. at p. 506, a rare instance of an order under article 91 being fully reported, the defendant sought the exclusion from the proceedings of certain documents which had been annexed by the applicant to his reply. In the event, the Court ordered the removal from the file of a draft of the minutes of a Commission meeting on condition that the Commission produced an authentic text of the decision taken at that meeting concerning the applicant, reserving its decision as to two other documents. In its jugment in the main action ([1966] E.C.R. at pp. 492–493), it further ordered the removal from the file of one of those two documents. The procedure under article 91 of the Rules has even been invoked where one party has sought to have an offending passage in the other party's pleadings struck out. In Case 44/76 *Eier-Kontor* v. *Council and Commission* [1977] E.C.R. 393, as is reported in the Opinion of A.G. Reischl, the Commission observed in its defence that the applicant's counsel had represented the applicant "in a whole series of dubious export transactions." The applicant asked that this should be struck out as being irrelevant, incorrect and defamatory, but the Commission then redrafted the sentence in such a way that the Court did not find it necessary to pronounce upon the applicant's request under article 91.

4–87   With regard to the actual procedure under article 91, it may be noted that a formal application must be made, separately from the basic pleadings, and that this application must state the grounds of fact and law relied on and the form of order sought (terminology redolent of that used to prescribe the contents of the defence in article 40(1)(b) and (c) of the Rules). Hence a request for a decision on a procedural issue, even expressed to be made under article 91, will be inadmissible if it does not state the form of order sought. In Case 55/64 *Lens* v. *Court of Justice* [1965] E.C.R. 837, in a document stated to be an application under article 91, the applicant stated that it seemed "preferable" to dispose of two questions before any discussion of the substance of the case, but without stating any formal conclusions. The Court (First Chamber) took the view that this document simply expressed a wish, and was inadmissible since it failed to bring a clearly stated application on a procedural issue before the Court. Nonetheless, since the points taken

153

by the applicant related to admissibility, the Court held that it could consider them under article 92 of the Rules (see para. 4–68 above) enabling it at any time of its own motion to consider whether there exists any absolute bar to proceeding with a case.

4–88   It might further be observed that even where the application on a procedural issue is admissible, the Court is, by virtue of article 91(4), under no obligation to decide the point in advance of its judgment in the main action. In Case 113/74 *NTN Toyo* v. *Council* [1979] E.C.R. 1135 and other *Japanese ball bearing* cases, for example, the Court held a separate hearing on the question of the admissibility of the actions, after having received the observations of all the parties, but then made an order reserving its decision on the objection of inadmissibility for the final judgment.

REFERENCES FOR PRELIMINARY RULINGS

A. ORDER FOR REFERENCE AND ITS NOTIFICATION

EEC Statute of the Court of Justice

Article 20

4–89   In the cases governed by article 177 of this Treaty the decision of the Court or tribunal of a Member State which suspends its proceedings and refers a case to the Court shall be notified to the Court by the court or tribunal concerned. The decision shall then be notified by the Registrar of the Court to the parties, to the Member States and to the Commission, and also to the Council if the act the validity or interpretation of which is in dispute originates from the Council.

(Article 21 of the Euratom Statute is in identical terms except that it refers to article 150 of the Euratom Treaty).

Protocol concerning the interpretation by the Court of Justice of the Convention of 27 September 1968 on jurisdiction and the enforcement of civil and commercial judgments.

Article 5

1. Except where this Protocol otherwise provides, the provisions of the Treaty establishing the European Economic Community and those of the Protocol on the Statute of the Court of Justice annexed thereto, which are applicable when the Court is requested to give a preliminary ruling, shall also apply to any proceedings for the interpretation of the Convention and the other instruments referred to in article 1.

(Article 3 of the Protocol on the interpretation by the Court of Justice of the Convention of February 29, 1968 on the Mutual Recognition of Companies and Legal Persons is in virtually identical terms).

Rules of Procedure

Article 103

4–90   1. (Relates to references under the EEC and Euratom Treaties.)

154

2. (Relates to references under the two Protocols.)

3. In cases provided for in article 41 of the ECSC Treaty, the text of the decision to refer the matter shall be served on the parties in the case, the Member States, the High Authority and the Special Council of Ministers.

Article 104

1. The decisions of national courts or tribunals referred to in article 103 of these rules shall be communicated to the Member States in the original version, accompanied by a translation into the official language of the State to which they are addressed.

Although there may be differences under the various treaties and conventions as to which national courts can make references to the European Court and as to the matters on which they may seek preliminary rulings, the procedure, once the reference has been made, is the same irrespective of the treaty or convention under which it arises, and it may be doubted whether any different provision will be made for references under article 73 of the Convention of December 15, 1975 for the European Patent for the Common Market, or, further in the future, under the Convention on the law applicable to contractual obligations opened for signature in Rome on June 19, 1980.

1. *Nature and Form of the Reference*

4–91 Since a reference for a preliminary ruling is not in concept an action between the parties but a request for assistance from one court to another, the commencement of proceedings is ultimately out of the hands of the parties; it is for the national court, not the parties, to decide whether to seek a preliminary ruling and on what question. Hence, in Case 44/65 *Hessische Knappschaft* v. *Singer* [1965] E.C.R. 965, it was held that where the national court had referred a question merely as to the interpretation of a provision in a Regulation, it was not open to one of the parties to raise the question of the validity of that provision since the right to determine the questions to be brought before the European Court devolved upon the national court alone. Similarly, in Case 5/72 *Grassi* v. *Italian Finance Administration* [1972] E.C.R. 443, where an Italian court referred questions to the European Court on the interpretation of the provisions governing the grant of export refunds on exports of cereals during the period before July 1, 1967, it was held that it was not open to one of the parties to ask the Court also to give a ruling on the system of refunds applicable since that date.

4–92 No provision of community law lays down any requirements as to the form of the reference. In the first reference for a preliminary ruling, Case 13/61 *de Geus* v. *Bosch* [1962] E.C.R. 45, after noting the absence of any prescriptions as to form, the European Court held that "it is permissible for the national court to formulate its request in a simple and direct way, leaving to this Court the duty of rendering a decision on that request only in so far as it has jurisdiction to do so." Perhaps the height of informality is to be found in Case 101/63 *Wagner* v. *Fohrmann* [1964] E.C.R. 195 where, in a defamation action, the Tribunal d'Arrondissement of Luxembourg referred the *parties* to the European Court for an interpretation of the Treaties (including the ECSC Treaty) "on the points and provisions . . . which determine the duration of the sessions of the Assemblies of the European Communities and thus to settle the question of the parliamentary immunity of the defendants." The European Court held that despite the fact that the Luxembourg court had, in terms, referred the parties to it, rather than directly making a reference itself, a request for a preliminary ruling had been laid before it since the registrar of the Luxembourg court had transmitted the judgment and the file of the case to the Registrar of the European Court.

4–93   This absence of formalism is not, however, reflected in the United Kingdom rules governing references from the English Court of Appeal (Civil and Criminal Divisions), High Court, Crown Court and County Court, the Scottish Court of Session, High Court of Justiciary and Sheriff Court, and the Northern Irish Court of Appeal, Court of Criminal Appeal, High Court and County Court. The English and Northern Irish rules set out a two-part form, containing an order that the matter be referred, and a schedule setting out the request for a preliminary ruling, as in Form 109 annexed to the Rules of the Supreme Court:

Order or Reference to the European Court (Ord. 114, r. 2)

[Heading as in Cause or Matter]

It is ordered that the question[s] set out in the Schedule hereto concerning the interpretation [*or* validity] of [*specific Treaty provision or Community instrument or act concerned*] be referred to the Court of Justice of the European Communities for a preliminary ruling in accordance with article 177 of the Treaty establishing the European Economic Community [*or* article 150 of the Treaty establishing the European Atomic Energy Community *or* article 41 of the Treaty establishing the European Coal and Steel Community *as the case may be*].

And it is ordered that all further proceedings in the above-named cause [*or* matter] be stayed until the said Court of Justice has given its ruling on the said question[s] or until further order.

Schedule

REQUEST FOR PRELIMINARY RULING OF THE COURT OF JUSTICE OF THE EUROPEAN COMMUNITIES

[*Here set out a brief statement of the case giving rise to the request for the ruling of the European Court, giving particulars of the parties and the proceedings, indicating the nature of the issues between the parties, and specifying the Treaty provisions or other acts, instruments or rules of Community law concerned.*]

The preliminary ruling of the Court of Justice of the European Communities is accordingly requested on the following questions:

1, 2 etc. [*here set out the questions on which the ruling is sought*].
Dated the   day of   19 .

The Scottish rules, on the other hand, simply prescribe forms for the schedule containing the request for the preliminary ruling, similar, but not identical in wording, to that in Form 109, and using three different headings, depending on the court involved.

4-94 So far as the contents of the reference are concerned, it would appear to be sufficient in Community law that, on the face of it, it relates to a matter on which the European Court is competent to give a preliminary ruling. In Case 26/62 *Van Gend and Loos* v. *Nederlandse Adminstratie der Belastingen* [1963] E.C.R. 1, it was said that "it is necessary only that the question raised should clearly be concerned with the interpretation of the Treaty," a dictum which could be extended where appropriate to questions as to the validity of secondary legislation or as to the interpretation of other acts on which a preliminary ruling may be given. Once such a question is referred to the Court, "the procedure laid down for the settlement of preliminary questions is automatically set in motion," as was pointed out in Joined Cases 28–30/62 *Da Costa* v. *Nederlandse Administratie der Belastingen* [1963] E.C.R. 31, where the Court decided that it must answer questions identical to those already answered in *Van Gend and Loos*.

2. Admissibility

4-95 This practice of answering any question which on the face of it relates to a matter on which the Court may give a preliminary ruling, has been applied even when the question referred also relates to the *application* of Community law (as in the *Bosch* case itself) or to the interpretation of national law, in which the Court has held that it has no authority to pronounce. A formula apt to resolve such problems was devised in Case 6/64 *Costa* v. *ENEL* [1964] E.C.R. 585, where it was stated that although the Court has "no jurisdiction either to apply the Treaty to a specific case or to decide upon the validity of a provision of domestic law in relation to the Treaty . . . Nevertheless, the Court has power to extract from a question formulated by the national court those questions which alone pertain to the interpretation of the Treaty." Subject to verbal alterations, the principle underlying the forumla has been, and still has to be, repeated in a remarkably large number of preliminary rulings. With regard to questions relating to the application of Community law, a more recent version in, to take a random example, Case 49/76 *Uberseehandel* v. *Handelskammer Hamburg* [1977] E.C.R. 41, reads "although the Court has no jurisdiction under article 177 of the EEC Treaty to apply a provision of Community law to actual cases, it may nevertheless furnish the national court with the interpretative criteria necessary to enable it to dispose of the dispute," and similarly with regard to questions relating to national law, in Case 63/76 *Inzirillo* v. *Caisse d'allocations familiales* [1976] E.C.R. 2057, amongst others, the Court stated that although it has "no jurisdiction to pronounce on a provision of national law with regard to a Community rule, it can,

157

however, provide the national court with the factors of interpretation depending on Community law which might be useful to it in evaluating the effects of such provision."

4–96   It must, however, be said that the interpretation of Community law in some modern preliminary rulings appears to fall little short of an application of Community law to the facts of the case or of a pronouncement on the compatibility of a provision of national law with Community law. In Case 177/78 *Pigs and Bacon Commission* v. *McCarren* [1979] E.C.R. 2161, for example, it was quite simply stated in the judgment that "a system such as that practised by the Pigs and Bacon Commission in Ireland in reality conflicts in two separate ways with the rules relating to the free movement of goods and the common organisation of the market in pigmeat," which left little in the way of application for the Irish court making the reference.

On the other hand, where the question referred does not on the face of it relate to the interpretation or, as the case may be, validity of a provision of Community law, there is modern authority to the effect that the Court may, of its own motion, hold the reference inadmissible once it has been lodged, without going through the preliminary ruling procedure. The Court had previously held in its judgment giving the preliminary ruling in Case 93/75 *Adlerblum* v. *Caisse Nationale d'Assurance Vieillesse* [1975] E.C.R. 2147 that since the question, relating to the classification of a German benefit under French social security legislation, pertained to national law alone, it did not come within its jurisdiction. In Case 105/79 *Reference by the Acting Judge at the Tribunal d'instance, Hayange* [1979] E.C.R. 2257, however, where the reference was dated June 10, 1979, the Court made an order on June 27, 1979 to the effect that the question referred in no way concerned either the interpretation of the EEC Treaty or the validity or interpretation of an act of an institution of the Community, and hence that it had no jurisdiction to reply to the question raised. The same approach has also been used where the Court has taken the view that the body making the reference is not, or is not acting as, a court or tribunal within the meaning of Article 177 of the EEC Treaty: in Case 138/80 *Borker* [1980] E.C.R. 1975 a reference from the 'Conseil de l'Ordre des Avocats á la Cour de Paris' was received at the Court on June 9, 1980, and on June 18, 1980 the Court made an order stating that it had no jurisdiction to reply to the question put to it since the "Conseil" did not have before it a case which it was under a legal duty to try. Although article 92(2) of the Rules, enabling the Court at any time to consider of its own motion whether there exists any absolute bar to proceeding with a case (see para. 4–67 above), would appear to be appropriate to cover references for preliminary rulings as well as direct actions, it was expressly alluded to only in the second of these cases, although it was used to reject an application to *intervene* in a reference for a preliminary ruling in Case 6/64 *Costa* v. *ENEL* [1964] E.C.R. at p. 614. On the other hand, in Case 102/81 *Nordsee* v. *Nordstern* (March 13, 1982), a German arbitrator specifically asked the Court if he was entitled to make a reference, and in deciding after full argument that it had no jurisdiction to rule on the questions submitted to it, the Court effectively answered the German arbitrator's questions.

4–97   If the Court may look to see if the reference is admissible on its face, on the other hand for many years it refused to look behind the order for reference. In Case 20/64 *Albatros* v. *Sopéco* [1965] E.C.R. 29, it was stated that "article 177, being based on a clear separation of functions between national courts or tribunals and the Court of Justice, does not permit the latter to take cognizance of the facts of the case or to find fault with the grounds for making the request for interpretation" where, in its observations on a reference from an Italian court, the French government claimed that the questions referred could not assist the resolution of the dispute since it was not for an Italian court to pronounce upon the legality of a measure taken by the French public authorities. This view has been repeated in more recent decisions, *e.g.* Case 5/77 *Tedeschi* v. *Denkavit* [1977] E.C.R. 1555: "Article 177 is based on a distinct separation of functions between national courts and tribunals on the one hand and the Court of Justice on the other, and it does not give the Court jurisdiction to take cognizance of the facts of the case, or to criticize the reasons for the reference." However, a different view emerged in Case 104/79 *Foglia* v. *Novello* [1980] E.C.R. 745, where, on a reference from an Italian court the European Court, following A.G. Warner, found that the parties to the main action were concerned to obtain a ruling that the French consumption tax on liqueur wines and invalid under Article 95 of the EEC Treaty by the expedient of proceedings before an Italian court between two private individuals who were in agreement as to the result to be obtained, and held that "the duty of the Court of Justice under Article 177 of the EEC Treaty is to supply all courts in the Community with the information on the interpretation of Community law which is necessary to enable them to settle *genuine* disputes which are brought before them" (emphasis added), concluding that in the circumstances it had no jurisdiction to give a ruling on the questions referred.

4–98   It might, on the other hand, be submitted that a distinction between genuine and artificial disputes relates to the admissibility of the main action before the national court rather than to the admissibility of the questions referred, and that the only way in which the European Court can avoid seeming to encroach upon matters which should be subject to the control of the national courts is for it to continue to observe the "curtain" principle enounced in the earlier case law and look only to the matters referred, even if occasionally it may doubt whether the national court has exercised its control correctly. Indeed, in Case 126/80 *Salonia* v. *Poidomani* [1981] E.C.R. 1563, the Court stated that "a request from a national court may be rejected *only* if it is quite obvious that the interpretation of Community law or the examination of the validity of a rule of Community law sought by that court bears no relation to the actual nature of the case or to the subject-matter of the main action." In *Foglia* v. *Novello* itself, the Italian court ordered a second reference (Case 244/80), and in his Opinion, A.G. Slynn suggested that the basic requirement for the admissibility of a reference was that the national court should have considered whether a decision on the question was necessary to enable it to give judgment.

4–99 However, in its second ruling [1981] E.C.R. 3045, the Court stated that no new element had appeared to cause it to change its view, and that it was for the Italian Court to indicate if there was any such element, and in later judgments the Court has continued to enquire whether there was a "genuine" dispute before the national court, as in Case 261/81 *Rau* v. *De Smedt* (November 10, 1982). There, however, it simply asserted that there was nothing in the file on the case which provided grounds for doubting that the dispute was genuine.

4–100 It is clear from the judgment in Joined Cases 28, 29 and 30/62 *Da Costa* v. *Nederlandse Belastingadministratie* [1963] E.C.R. 31 that in the context of the interpretation of Community law, a national court remains at liberty to refer questions identical to those already answered by the Court in an earlier case; this is particularly relevant if it wishes to persuade the European Court to change its mind. However, where the Court has declared an act of a Community institution invalid on an earlier reference, it would appear from the judgment in Case 66/80 *International Chemical Corporation* v. *Italian Finance Administration* [1981] E.C.R. 1191 that the national court should first consider whether there is any real interest in making a further reference with regard to the validity of that act, and that such an interest could relate to the grounds for invalidity, the scope of the invalidity and, where appropriate, its consequences.

3. *Notification of the Reference*

4–101 Article 20 of the EEC Statute envisages two types of notification: notification of the reference by the national court to the European Court, and notification by the Registrar of the European Court to the Member States, institutions and parties. No specific form is laid down in Community law for the notification of the reference by the national court to the European Court; indeed, on a literal reading of article 20, it is not even required that the reference should actually be addressed to the *Registrar* of the Court, unlike the application commencing a direct action. However, for each of the United Kingdom courts for which rules governing references have been laid down, express mention is made of the officer who is to transmit the reference to the European Court. In Scotland, the reference is to be transmitted by the clerk of the relevant court, and in Northern Ireland by the Registrar or clerk of the relevant court, but in England all the courts for which rules have been made, the Court of Appeal, the High Court, County Court and Crown Court (see para. 4–93 above), are required to channel their references through the Senior Master of the Supreme Court (Queen's Bench Division). Insofar as the English system requires a reference to be transmitted by a person who is not an officer of the court making the reference, it may be doubted whether it is in compliance with article 20 of the EEC Statute requiring notification "by the court or tribunal concerned," although it is unlikely that anyone would have an interest in taking the point. Those United Kingdom courts for which no rules have been laid down remain free to comply directly with article 20, and references have been made, by the way of example, by a National Insurance Commissioner, in Case 17/76 *Brack* v. *Insurance Officer* [1976] E.C.R. 1429, by the House of Lords in Case 34/79 *R.* v. *Henn and Darby* [1979] E.C.R. 3795, by the Employment Appeal Tribunal in Case 96/80 *Jenkins* .v. *Kingsgate* [1981] E.C.R. 911, by the Special Commissioners in Case 208/80 *Bruce of Donington* v. *Aspden* [1981] E.C.R. 2205, by a stipendiary magistrate in Case 30/77 *R.* v. *Bouchereau* [1977] E.C.R. 1999, and by a Northern Irish resident magistrate in Case 83/78 *Pigs Marketing Board* v. *Redmond* [1978] E.C.R. 2347. Indeed, in the *Redmond* case, the resident magistrate sent with his judgment a covering letter explaining the local background to the case and setting out a number of further questions, which the European Court held it could consider together with those set out in the magistrate's judgment.

4–102   The notification of the reference to the parties, Member States and relevant institutions is the responsibility of the Registry, and has been considered in that context (see paras. 4–09, 4–10). One practical difficulty which does not arise in direct actions is that there is no Community law requirement that the parties to the main action in which the reference is made should state an address for service. Hence, finding an address to which to notify the reference can require active investigation on the part of the Registry, particularly if one of the parties is a litigant in person, quite apart from the fact that national procedural rules may mean that it is not immediately apparent who the real parties are, as in Case 41/77 *R.* v. *National Insurance Commissioner, ex p. Warry* [1977] E.C.R. 2085. The registry may also have to play an active role in determining whether it is "appropriate" to notify the Council on the ground that the validity or interpretation of one of the Council's acts is at issue. There is, however, no time-limit within which the registry must carry out its notification, just as there is no time-limit within which the national court must communicate the reference in the first place, and it would appear that if it becomes apparent in the course of the proceedings that an act of the Council is in reality at issue, it could be notified at that stage, the time-limit for the submission of its observations running from the date of its notification.

It might finally be observed that although neither Article 20 of the EEC Statute, and the parallel provision under the other treaties, nor article 16(6) of the Rules of Procedure, expressly envisage the publication of references in the *Official Journal*, in practice the name of the national court, the names of the parties, and the question or questions referred are published in the "C" series of the *Official Journal*, once the reference has been registered.

B. APPEALS AGAINST REFERENCES FOR PRELIMINARY RULINGS

4–103   The possibility of an appeal against a national court's decision to order a reference to the European Court does not appear to have been foreseen in the relevant Community legislation. Nevertheless, an appeal was lodged against the earliest reported order for reference in Case 13/61 *De Geus* v. *Bosch* [1962] E.C.R. 45, and the European Court thus found itself having to consider the effects of such an appeal. In his Opinion, A.G. Lagrange, after having concluded from a comparative survey of the then Member States that there was no general rule preventing appeals against orders analogous to references to the European Court, suggested that it was not for that Court to consider the effects in national law of an appeal against the national court's order for reference; in his view, the question was rather whether the European Court still had good "title" to give judgment, and its "title" would only cease to exist if the superior court quashed the judgment of the court which had made the reference. This had not yet happened, and so A.G. Lagrange said that the European Court should give judgment on the reference, even if there was a risk that the order for reference might later be quashed. The Court, for its part, merely said that "the Treaty makes the jurisdiction of this Court dependent solely on the existence of a request for a preliminary ruling within the meaning of article 177," which effectively seems to follow from the view of A.G. Lagrange, This view, subject to a further qualification expressed in Case 127/73 *BRT* v. *SABAM* [1974] E.C.R. 51, has become the practice of the Court. In his Opinion in that case, A.G. Mayras, after repeating that the consequences in national law of an appeal were not for the European Court to consider, stated that there were two situations where the European Court should not give judgment in a reference: where the higher court has previously quashed the order for reference, but also where the court which made the reference has itself expressly withdrawn it. This appears to be reflected in the brief statement by the Court in its judgment that the procedure on the reference "continues as long as the request of the national court has neither been withdrawn nor become devoid of object."

4–104   The fact that the court which made the reference may itself withdraw it may help explain the Court's order in Case 31/68 *Chanel* v. *Cepeha* [1969] E.C.R. 403. There, the European Court was informed by the court which made the reference that an appeal had been lodged against its decision, and therefore that "execution of the judgment is deferred"; as a result the European Court ordered the procedure on the reference to be suspended pending notification that the appeal had been decided. It did so, however, after A.G. Roemer had delivered an Opinion suggesting that the Court should take account of the consequences of an appeal in (in that case) Dutch law, with the result that this has been taken to be an example of the Court taking account of national rules (see, *e.g.* the Opinion of A.G. Warner in Case 166/73 *Rheinmühlen* v. *Einfuhr- und Vorratsstelle Getreide* [1974] E.C.R. 33, 45). However, if the Opinion of A.G. Roemer, which hardly accords with the rest of the case law, is discounted, *Chanel* can be construed as an example of the Court taking heed of a request from the national court which made the reference. This view perhaps gains support from the fact that in its judgment in *BRT* v. *SABAM* [1974] E.C.R. at page 61, the European

Court expressly mentioned as a justification for giving judgment on the reference the fact that the Belgian court which made the reference had stated that it did not wish the procedure to be suspended despite the fact that an appeal had been brought against the order.

4–105   By way of contrast, in his Opinion in the *Rheinmühlen* case, [1974] E.C.R. 33, 43–47. A.G. Warner argued forcefully that national legislation cannot effectively provide for a right of appeal against an order of a lower court referring a question to the European Court, as a logical corollary to the view he had expressed on the question directly raised in that case, that a national court bound on points of law by the judgments of superior courts may still make a reference. The Court accepted this view on the narrow question, stating that "a rule of national law whereby a court is bound on points of law by the rulings of a superior court cannot deprive the inferior courts of their power to refer to the Court questions of interpretation of Community law involving such rulins," but its practice has not followed his view on the broader question of the legality of appeals against orders for reference. A.G. Warner did, however, recognise that even if an appeal against the order for reference were not to be permitted, it would still be possible for an appeal to be lodged against the judgment given by the national court, once it had received the European Court's ruling on the reference, and in his opinion in the *B.R.T* case delivered the same day as that of A.G. Warner in *Rheinmühlen,* A.G. Mayras used this as an argument against holding that an order for reference should not in itself be subject to appeal.

4–106   The current practice may be summarised as being that the European Court will give judgment on any order for reference which has been communicated to it, and will only take account of the fact that an appeal has been lodged if the national court which made the reference asks for it to be withdrawn or suspended or if the appeal court quashes it. Hence, it can be seen from the report in Case 48/75 *Royer* [1976] E.C.R. 497, 507 that an appeal was lodged against the order for reference by the Tribunal de première instance of Liège, the order being eventually confirmed by the Cour d'Appel of Liège, but that this in itself had no apparent effect on the disposal of the reference by the European Court. On the other hand, in Case 65/77 *Razanatsimba* [1977] E.C.R. 2229, 2237, a reference by the Cour d'Appel of Douai, it is recorded that an earlier reference (Case 3/77) was made on the same questions by the Conseil de l'ordre des avocats de Lille, that the Cour d'Appel had quashed the decision of the Conseil de l'ordre on the ground that it was not acting as a court and therefore not able to make a reference, and that the European Court had therefore ordered Case 3/77 to be removed from the register.

4–107   It may be doubted whether the United Kingdom statutory instruments governing references from named English, Scottish and Northern Irish courts are consonant with this practice, insofar as, whilst expressly providing, where appropriate, for a right of appeal (without leave, in the case of the English and Northern Irish High Courts and the Scottish Court of Session) they also prohibit the transmission of the reference to the European Court until (in the phraseology used in RSC Ord. 114, r. 5) "the time for appealing against the order has expired or, if an appeal is entered within that time, until the appeal has been determined or otherwise diposed of." These rules effectively prevent the court which made the reference being able itself to determine whether the procedure on the reference should continue despite the lodging of an appeal. Nonetheless, a court which is not subject to these rules may decide that it is more practical or convenient not to communicate its reference until a possible appeal has been disposed of: in Case 83/78 *Pigs Marketing Board* v. *Redmond* [1978] E.C.R. 2347, the Resident Magistrate, County Armagh, decided to make a reference in September 1977, but did not notify it to the European Court until March 1978, after the Court of Appeal for Northern Ireland had rejected an appeal against his order for reference.

C. REPRESENTATION OF THE PARTIES

Rules of Procedure

Article 104

4–108   2. As regards the representation and attendance of the parties to the main proceedings in the preliminary ruling procedure the Court shall take account of the rules of procedure of the national court or tribunal which made the reference.

Unlike the parties to a direct action (see para. 4–15 above), the parties to an action in which a reference has been made to the European Court for a preliminary ruling are not required by any provision of Community law to be legally represented before that Court, although the provision currently contained in article 104(2) of the Rules of Procedure expressly requiring the Court to take account of national rules as to representation and attendance was only introduced in the December 1974 version of the Rules. Even before then, however, a similar attitude prevailed, the logical extension no doubt of the view expressed in Case 62/72 *Bollmann* v. *HZA Hamburg-Waltershof* [1973] E.C.R. 269, that proceedings under Article 177 of the EEC Treaty "are in the nature of a step in the action pending before a national court." Indeed, in Case 33/74 *Van Binsbergen* v. *Bedrijfsvereniging Metaalnij-verheid* [1974] E.C.R. 1299, a reference from a Dutch social court heard earlier in 1974, an unqualified "legal representative" was allowed to represent Van Binsbergen before the European Court, even though the question referred for a preliminary ruling did not relate to the substance of the case but asked whether, by virtue of the EEC rules on freedom to supply services, such a "legal representative" could continue to act before the Dutch court despite the fact that he no longer complied with Dutch rules requiring him to be established in the Netherlands, having during the course of the proceedings transferred his residence from the Netherlands to Belgium.

164

4–109   The principle laid down in article 104(2) of the Rules has two main consequences. The first is that if a reference is made by a national court which allows litigants to appear in person or before which the parties may be represented by unqualified advisers, the litigant in person or the unqualified adviser may also act before the European Court. Hence, in Case 39/75 *Coenen* v. *Sociaal-Economische Raad* [1975] E.C.R. 1547, another reference from a Dutch social court, Mr. Coenen was able to appear in person. The second consequence of article 104(2) of the Rules is the converse of the first: if the reference is from a national court before which only a limited category of lawyers has a right of audience, then the parties must be represented by such a lawyer before the European Court, if they wish to enter an appearance; in this respect the rules governing references are more severe than those governing direct actions, which allow representation by any lawyer entitled to practise before a court of a Member State. Such a situation arose, although it does not appear in the report, in Case 126/77 *Frangiamore* v. *Office National de l'Emploi* [1978] E.C.R. 725, a reference from the Belgian Cour de Cassation, before which only *avocats* have a right of audience. The appellant in the main action inquired whether she could be represented before the European Court by a legal representative who had appeared on references from lower Belgian social courts, but was informed that she would have to be represented by an *avocat*.

4–110   This result was in fact anticipated in the agreement drawn up by representatives of the Bar and Law Society in England and Wales in 1971, providing that:

> In the European Court at Luxembourg both barristers and solicitors should for the purpose of the protocol have the same rights as a French 'avocat' but solicitors would by practice rule be prohibited.
>
> (I) from taking part in the oral presentation in cases referred under Article 177 (and like provisions relating to the Steel and Coal Community and Euratom) from the Supreme Court of the House of Lords and, in any such case in which a barrister is instructed on the reference, from undertaking the written presentation except in conjunction with the barrister.

Although no such practice rule was issued, article 104(2) of the Rules of Procedure ensures that it is respected to all intents and purposes, and the formal rescission of the 1971 agreement in 1981 would appear to be of little practical effect in the context of references for preliminary rulings.

Finally it might be noted that the Member States and the Commission and the Council, insofar as they are entitled to participate in the proceedings on a reference for a preliminary ruling by virtue of article 20 of the EEC Statute, even though they are not parties to the main action before the national court, are in practice represented by agents in such proceedings, just as in direct actions (see para. 4–15 above).

D. Observations

EEC Statute of the Court of Justice

Article 20

4–111   Within two months of this notification, the parties, the Member States, the Commission and, where appropriate, the Council, shall be entitled to submit statements of case or written observations to the Court.

(The second paragraph of Article 21 of the Euratom Statute is in identical terms, and both Article 5(1) of the Protocol on the interpretation of the 1968 Judgments Convention and Article 3 of the Protocol on the interpretation of the 1968 Companies Recognition Convention state that the relevant provisions of the EEC Statute are to apply.)

Rules of Procedure

Article 103

3. In the case provided for in Article 41 of the ECSC Treaty, the text of the decision to refer the matter shall be served on the parties in the case, the Member States, the High Authority and the Special Council of Ministers.

These parties, States and institutions may, within two months from the date of such service, lodge written statements of case or written observations.

1. *General Requirements*

4–112   The fundamental distinction between the written procedure in a direct action and the written procedure on a reference for a preliminary ruling is that on a reference there is no obligation to produce any written documents at all, except for the original order for reference, whereas in a direct action there must always be a written application and a written defence (see paras. 4–28, 4–55 above). Although the parties, the Member States, the Commission and, where appropriate, the Council are given the right to submit written observations, no duty is imposed on them so to do. Furthermore, it is clear that a failure to produce written observations does not preclude a party from appearing at the hearing to put his argument orally, as in Case 48/74 *Charmasson* v. *Minister for Economic Affairs* [1974] E.C.R. 1383, 1391 where Charmasson's case was put for the first time at the hearing. However, since the written procedure on a reference comprises only a single set of observations from those concerned, with no right of reply or rejoinder, it is advisable, in order to have two opportunities to present a particular argument, both to submit written observations and to appear at the hearing. The importance of submitting written observations is perhaps even greater for parties using a "minority" language who are thus reliant on translation and interpetation (see para. 3–10 above) to be understood by the majority of the judges.

4–113   Although there is no compulsion to produce written observations, it is the practice of the Registry when notifying the reference to those concerned to ask whether they intend to submit written observations; if the Registry knows that certain parties, states or institutions are not going to submit observations, it becomes easier to determine when the written procedure has ended. With regard to the number of copies of observations which should be lodged, article 37(1) of the Rules of Procedure requiring five copies of every pleading to be lodged together with a copy for every other party is couched in language appropriate only to direct actions, since it requires also signature of every pleading by the party's agent or lawyer; the practice of the Registry, however, is to indicate when notifying the reference the number of copies of the observations which are requested. Once the observations have been lodged, the Registry sends copies to all those who were entitled to be notified of the original reference, although there appears to be no legal rule which actually requires this: under article 17 of the Rules of Procedure the Registrar is responsible for effecting "such service as is provided for by these rules," but the rules do not in fact provide for the service of observations, and under article 3(3) of the Instructions to the Registrar it is stated that "the parties" shall be served with "the pleadings" and other documents relating to the proceedings, which is hardly terminology appropriate to observations in references for preliminary rulings. However, the absence of any express provision may be a hangover from article 79 of the 1953 Rules of Procedure, which provided for the blanket application of the rules governing direct actions in references under Article 41 of the ECSC Treaty.

4–114   Just as there is no obligation to submit observations, so there are no binding requirements as to the form and content of the observations if they are submitted, although obviously they are most readily comprehensible if they are related to the way in which the questions were framed by the national court, although that might not always be possible. One particular distinction from direct actions is that the way in which the written observations are drafted would not appear to restrict the scope of the arguments which can be raised later in the oral procedure: since a relevant party, state or institution can always appear for the first time at the hearing, and hence by definition arise points which the others may not be prepared to deal with, there would appear to be no objection in principle to raising new points where written observations have been lodged, as in Case 172/80 *Züchner* v. *Bayerische Vereinsbank* [1981] E.C.R. 2021, where the defendant bank took the point at the hearing that it operated services of "general economic interest" under article 90(2) of the EEC Treaty.

4–115   The real limitation on the issues which may be raised in the observations is that enounced in Case 44/65 *Hessische Knappschaft* v. *Singer* [1965] E.C.R. 965, which is that the parties to the main action may not raise questions of Community law which are not raised by the national court itself; in effect, the scope of the action is determined by the order for reference, not by the observations which may be submitted. In that case, the national court had referred questions as to the interpretation of article 52 of Regulation 3 on social security for migrant workers, and the defendant in the main action claimed that the provision was invalid; it was held that it was not open to the defendant to raise the point since "the right to determine the questions . . . devolves upon the court or tribunal of the Member State alone," and the parties "are merely invited to be heard" in the course of "a non-contentious procedure excluding any initiative of the parties." *A fortiori,* it would appear that the Member States and Community institutions submitting observations are subject to the same limitation.

On the other hand, since it is the order for reference which determines the scope of the observation, the Second Chamber did point out in Joined Cases 141–3/81*Holdijk and others* (April 1, 1982) that such an order should contain sufficient information to enable those entitled to submit observations actually to exercise that right, although it did also take account of the fact that the written observations could be supplemented at the hearing.

2. *Parties*

4–116 The parties entitled to submit written observations are the parties entitled to be notified of the reference, *i.e.* the parties to the main action before the national court. This was stated by the Court in so many words in Case 62/72 *Bollmann* v. *HZA Hamburg-Waltershof* [1973] E.C.R. 269, 275. Indeed, in its order on the application by the Edison company to intervene in Case 6/64 *Costa* v. *ENEL* [1964] E.C.R. at p. 614, the Court stated that the provisions of article 20 of the EEC Statute determining who is entitled to submit observations would be pointless if a person able to intervene in a direct action by virtue of article 37 of the Statute (see para. 11–02 below) could also intervene in references for preliminary rulings. Similarly, in Case 19/68 *De Cicco* v. *LVA Schwaben* [1968] E.C.R. 473, where the defendant German social security institution asked that the competent Italian social security institution should be joined as a party, the Court stated that it could not agree to the participation in the proceedings of persons or institutions other than those referred to in article 20 of the Statute.

3. *Member States*

4–117 The privileged position of Member States in being entitled to submit observations on any reference can be justified in current practice by the fact that a reference for the interpretation of a Community act can often in reality concern the compatibility of national legislation with that Community act, as was noted in the context of notification (see para. 4–102 above). However, the possibility of using Community law to challenge national legislation is the result of the doctrine of the development of the doctrine of "direct effects" by the Court, and it may be wondered how far this was the situation envisaged by the draftsmen of the Treaty. For its part, the Court treats article 20 as entitling Member States to make their views known on the provision of Community law at issue, irrespective of any direct involvement. In Case 12/76 *Tessili* v. *Dunlop* [1976] E.C.R. 1473, a reference was made for a preliminary ruling on the interpretation of the 1968 Judgments

Convention; by virtue of article 5(1) of the Protocol on the interpretation of that Convention, the relevant provisions of the EEC Statute apply unless otherwise provided, and both the Republic of Ireland and the United Kingdom submitted observations under article 20 of the EEC Statute, even though they had not yet acceded to the Judgments Convention at issue. It was held that they were entitled nonetheless to submit observations by virtue of his provisions, although the Court did point out that since by virtue of article 3(2) of the Act of Accession they were required to become parties to the Judgments Convention, they did have an interest in expressing their views.

4. Institutions

4–118   Although the Commission is empowered rather than required to submit observations on any reference, in practice it appears to regard itself as being under a duty to do so, and it invariably does submit observations; it is not unknown for the observations of the Commission to be the only written observations to be received by the Court, as for example in Case 266/78 *Brunori* v. *LVA Rheinprovinz* [1979] E.C.R. 2705 where, in the absence of any observations from the parties, the Court eventually asked the defendant in the main action to give a written answer to two specific questions.

The Council, on the other hand, may only submit observations "where appropriate," which in the scheme of article 20 of the Statute is when the Registrar has notified the reference to the Council on the basis that the act the validity or interpretation of which is in dispute originates from the Council. It has been suggested in the context of notification that if it only becomes apparent during the course of the proceedings that an act of the Council is in reality at issue, it could be notified at that stage, but it remains to be seen what would happen if a serious dispute as to whether such an act is at issue did arise between the Registry and the Council (which can be hardly be unaware of any reference, since they are automatically notified to the Member States whose representatives constitute the Council).

One institution which is not given any power to submit observations is the European Parliament; on the other hand, under Article 177 of the EEC Treaty, the Court may give preliminary rulings on the acts of the "institutions" of the Community, and in the context of direct actions, the Parliament has now been held in Case 138/79 *Roquette* v. *Council* [1980] E.C.R. 3333, 3357, to be one of the "institutions" of the Community able to intervene under article 37 of the EEC Statute in cases before the Court without needing to prove an interest in the result. Hence the anomalous situation would appear to exist whereby, in so far as the Budget can be regarded as an act of the Parliament, the Court could give a preliminary ruling on its interpretation or validity, but the Parliament itself could not submit any observations, even though it could have intervened if the matter had arisen in a direct action. It remains to be seen whether the problem can be resolved by "purposive" interpretation.

E. Procedural Time-Limits

4–119   In references for preliminary rulings under all three treaties and under the later Conventions which adopt the procedure under the EEC Treaty, those entitled to submit observations must do so within two months of receiving notification of the reference (EEC Statute, article 20, Euratom Statute, article 21, Rules of Procedure, article 103(3), Protocol on the Interpretation of the 1968 Judgments Convention, article 5(1), Protocol on the Interpretation of the 1968 Companies Recognition Convention article 3 (see para. 4–89 above). As in direct actions, by virtue of article 80 of the Rules of Procedure, the day of the event from which the period is to run, *i.e.* receipt of the notification, is excluded from the calculations, and the period is extended until the end of the first following working day if it could otherwise end on a Sunday or an official holiday, but time continues to run during vacations. Similarly, the extensions on account of distance allowed for in article 81(2) and Annex II of the Rules also apply to the time-limit for submitting observations on references for preliminary rulings. The essential difference from procedural time-limits in direct actions is that, at least on references under the EEC and Euratorm Treaties, the time limit for submitting observations cannot be extended. There is no express provision for extension, and since the time-limits for the submission of observations on references under the EEC and Euratom Treaties are set out in their respective Protocols on the Statute of the Court, they do not fall within the general power set out in article 82 of the Rules of Procedure allowing any time-limit prescribed "pursuant to these rules" to be extended by whoever prescribed it. In the case of references under the ECSC Treaty, the time limits are set out in article 103(3) of the Rules of Procedure (in themselves easier to amend than the Statutes), but even then it may be doubted whether they may strictly be regarded as prescribed "pursuant" to the Rules. On the other hand, although there is no published authority on the point, it may be submitted that article 42 of the EEC Statute (Euratom Statute, article 43; ECSC Statute, article 39) providing that "no right shall be prejudiced in consequence of the expiry of a time-limit if the party concerned proves the existence of unforseeable circumstances or of force majeure," could be invoked in appropriate circumstances with regard to a failure to submit observations within the time-limit.

In any event, a failure to submit written observations in time is not irredeemable. Since there is no obligation to submit written observations, and their submission is not a precondition to appearing at the hearing, there is nothing to prevent written observations submitted or prepared outside the time-limit being read out word for word at the hearing, if it is felt that that would serve a useful purpose.

F. Procedural Issues

4–120   Since references for preliminary rulings are essentially conceived as a method of co-operation between national courts and the European

Court, and since it has been consistently held that proceedings in references are non-contentious, the parties merely being invited to state their case within the legal limits laid down by the national court (see Case 62/72 *Bollmann* v. *HZA Hamburg-Waltershof* [1973] E.C.R. 269, 275), the scope for raising procedural issues is somewhat restricted. However, given that the Court has in recent years begun actively to consider the admissibility of references for preliminary rulings (see para. 4–97 above), it may be suggested that it is open to any of those entitled to submit observations to bring matters of admissibility to the Court's attention in their observations, even if it may be doubtful whether they have any entitlement on a reference to submit an application separate from their observations under article 91 of the Rules, governing procedural issues in direct actions (see para. 4–86 above). This is despite the passage in Case 44/65 *Hessische Knappschaft* v. *Singer* [1965] E.C.R. 965, to the effect that the parties may not have the questions determined by the national court "declared to be without purpose," which in its context appears to mean only that it is not open to the parties to challenge the validity of a measure of which the interpretation is sought by the national court.

4–121 Insofar as a procedural issue relates to admissibility of the reference, it would appear to fall within the scope of article 92(2) of the Rules of Procedure allowing the Court of its own motion to consider whether there exists any absolute bar to proceeding with a case and to give a decision in accordance with article 91(3) and (4), concerned with the resolution of procedural issues in direct actions, Article 92(2) has also been used, however, where an incidental matter has arisen on a reference rather than a question of admissibility of the reference as such. In Case 6/64 *Costa* v. *ENEL* [1964] E.C.R. 614, the Edison company applied to intervene in the proceedings on the reference before the European Court in support of Costa, and the European Court rejected this application in an order made under article 92 of the Rules. In terms of the English-language text of Article 92(2) this might seem a rather cavalier approach, since the provision is expressed to relate to "any absolute bar to proceeding with a case" rather than to a bar to an incidental application. However, the French text refers to "les fins de non-recevoir d'ordre public," which might more accurately be construed as any procedural bar (be it to the case or to any incidental plea) which cannot be opted out of. If that is the meaning of article 92(2), then the order in *Costa* v. *ENEL* falls clearly within it.

ALLOCATION OF CASES

A. CHAMBERS OF THE COURT

EEC Treaty

Article 165

5–01   The Court of Justice shall sit in plenary session. It may, however, form chambers, each consisting of three or five Judges, either to undertake certain preparatory inquiries or to adjudicate on particular categories of cases in accordance with rules laid down for these purposes.

Whenever the Court of Justice hears cases brought before it by a Member State or by one of the institutions of the Community or, to the extent that the Chambers of the Court do not have the requisite jurisdiction under the Rules of Procedure, has to give preliminary rulings on questions submitted to it pursuant to Article 177, it shall sit in plenary session.

(The second and third paragraphs of Article 137 of the Euratom Treaty and of Article 32 of the ECSC Treaty are in parallel terms.)

EEC Statute of the Court

Article 15

Decisions of the Court shall be valid only when an uneven number of its members is sitting in the deliberations. Decisions of the full Court shall be valid if seven members are sitting. Decisions of the Chambers shall be valid only if three Judges are sitting; in the event of one of the Judges of a Chamber being prevented from attending, a Judge of another Chamber may be called upon to sit in accordance with conditions laid down in the rules of procedure.

(Article 15 of the Euratom Statute of the Court and article 18 of the ECSC Statute of the Court are in identical terms.)

Article 16

A party may not apply for a change in the composition of the Court or of one of its Chambers on the grounds of either the nationality of a Judge or the absence from the Court or from the Chamber of a Judge of the nationality of that party.

(The last paragraph of article 16 of the Euratom Statute and of article 19 of the ECSC Statute are in identical terms.)

Rules of Procedure

Article 9

5–02 1. The Court shall set up Chambers in accordance with the provisions of the second paragraph of Article 32 of the ECSC Treaty, the second paragraph of Article 165 of the EEC Treaty and the second paragraph of Article 137 of the Euratom Treaty and shall decide which judges shall be attached to them.

The composition of the Chambers shall be published in the *Official Journal of the European Communities.*

2. As soon as an application originating proceedings has been lodged, the President shall assign the case to one of the Chambers for any preparatory inquiries and shall designate a Judge from that Chamber to act as Rapporteur.

3. The Court shall lay down general principles governing the assignment of cases to Chambers.

4. These rules shall apply in a corresponding manner to proceedings before the Chambers.

In cases assigned to or devolving upon a Chamber the powers of the President of the Court shall be exercised by the President of the Chamber.

Article 10

1. The Court shall appoint for a period of one year the Presidents of the Chambers and the First Advocate-General.

Article 26

3. If in any Chamber the quorum of three Judges has not been atttained, the President of that Chamber shall so inform the President of the Court who shall designate another Judge to complete the Chamber.

Article 44

2. Where the Court orders a preparatory inquiry and does not undertake it itself, it shall assign the inquiry to the Chamber.

Article 46

1. A Chamber to which a preparatory inquiry has been assigned may exercise the powers vested in the Court by Articles 45 and 47 to 53 of these rules; the powers vested in the President of the Court may be exercised by the President of the Chamber.

(Article 45 of the Rules of Procedure relates to the ordering of measures of enquiries, and articles 47 to 53 relate to the summoning and examination of witnesses and experts.)

Article 95

5–03 1. The Court may assign to a Chamber any reference for a preliminary ruling of a kind mentioned in Article 103 of these rules as well as any action instituted by a natural or legal person under Article 33(2), Article 34(2), Article 35, Article 36(2), Article 40(1) and (2), and Article 42 of the ECSC Treaty, Article 172, Article 173(2), Article 175(3), Article 178 and Article 181 of the EEC Treaty, and Article 144, Article 146(2), Article 148(3), Article 151 and Article 153 of the Euratom Treaty, in so far as the difficulty or the importance of the case or particular circumstances are not such as to require that the Court decide it in plenary session.

2. The decision so to assign a case shall be taken by the Court at the end of the

written procedure upon consideration of the preliminary report presented by the Judge-Rapporteur and after the Advocate-General has been heard.

However, a case may not be so assigned if a Member State or an institution of the Communities, being a party to the proceedings, has requested that the case be decided in plenary session. In this Subparagraph the expression "party to the proceedings" means any Member State or any institution which is a party to or an intervener in the proceedings or which has submitted written observations in any reference of a kind mentioned in Article 103 of these rules.

3. Proceedings commenced by an official or other servant of an institution against the institution shall, with the exception of applications for the adoption of interim measures, be tried by a Chamber designated each year by the Court for that purpose. Such allocation shall not preclude the adoption of appropriate measures in cases whose subject-matter is related.

4. A Chamber may at any stage refer to the Court any case assigned to or devolving upon it.

5–04   Once an application or reference has been registered, the case is allocated by the President to one of the Chambers of the Court. As was noted by the House of Lords Select Committee (Session 1979—80, 23rd Report), these Chambers might more appropriately be termed "divisions" of the Court. Under the ECSC system, the six judges other than the President were divided into two Chambers of three judges, by virtue of the original article 18 of the ECSC Statute and article 21(1) of the 1953 Rules of Procedure, and each of the Advocates-General was also appointed to a Chamber. Following the entry into force of the EEC and Euratom Treaties, and the amendment of Article 32 of the ECSC Treaty by the Convention on Common Institutions, the possibility of Chambers of three or five judges was created. However, in practice the Court remained divided into two Chambers of three judges. Following the first enlargement in 1973 and the creation of a Court of nine judges and four Advocates-General, it continued to be divided into two Chambers, this being expressly provided for in the original article 9 of the 1974 Rules of Procedure. In practice, four judges and two Advocates-General were allocated to each Chamber, the work of the Chamber in each action being performed by three judges and one Advocate-General. Fundamental changes were, however, brought about by the 1979 amendment to the Rules of Procedure. The Rules no longer specify the number of Chambers into which the Court may be divided, and Advocates-General are no longer members of the Chamber. The discretion which the Court has with regard to the number and composition of the Chambers is however limited by the fact that the composition of the Chambers is required to be published in the *Official Journal*; it would appear that certain Member States, notably the Federal Republic of Germany, attach great importance to fixing the composition of the Court in advance (the principle of *der gesetzliche Richter*) so as to avoid any hint that the judges may have been specially selected to hear a particular case.

5–05   From October 1979 until Greek Accession, the Court sat in three Chambers of three judges, with the President of the Court acting as President of the new Third Chamber, which gave its first judgment on

February 14, 1980 in Case 53/79 *ONPTS* v. *Damiani* [1980] E.C.R. 273. However, following the increase in the number of judges to 10 under article 135 of the Greek Act of Accession, the President is no longer a member of the Chamber, which once again consists only of the other judges. After the further increase in the number of judges to 11 in March 1981, it was decided to appoint an additional judge to the Second Chamber for the year 1981 to 1982 (O.J., C.265/3). By a decision of October 6, 1982 (O.J. 1982 C299/6), it was decided for the first time to constitute Chambers of five judges as well as the traditional Chambers of three judges. The Court was thus divided into three Chambers of three judges, as before, and two Chambers of five judges (known as the Fourth and Fifth Chambers respectively). In principle, the President does not sit in these five-judge Chambers, but if a member of one of them is absent, he may sit, and in such a case he will act as the President of the Chamber.

Every case must be assigned to a Chamber even if in substance it falls within the exclusive jurisdiction of the Full Court. The only published rules governing the assignment of cases to Chambers however, relate to proceedings commenced by officials of Community institutions, which may be heard by a Chamber under article 95(3) of the Rules of Procedure. Here a distinction has traditionally been drawn between actions commenced by officials and other servants of the Commission, and actions commenced by officials and other servants of the other institutions. In the days when there were two Chambers, there was a simple system of alternation between these two categories each year, so that each Chamber heard cases falling within one category for one year, the roles being reversed the next year. With three Chambers, the rotation of staff cases is somewhat more difficult; by way of example, for the year 1980–1981, proceedings commenced by officials or other servants of the Commission were heard by the First and Second Chambers alternately in order of registration of the applications, and proceedings commenced by officials and other servants of institutions other than the Commission were heard by the Third Chamber (O.J. 1980, C263/6), but in 1981–1982 it was agreed simply to deal with staff cases in rotation (O.J. 1981, C265/3). Otherwise, cases appear to be distributed in rotation in order of registration, with the aim of creating a reasonably equitable workload and avoiding the impression that a particular Chamber specialises in a particular type of case.

5–06   Assignment of a case to a particular Chamber necessarily comports the selection of a Judge Rapporteur from that Chamber, (see para. 5–09 below) and used also to result in the selection of an Advocate-General from that Chamber. However, the basic function of a Chamber envisaged in the original 1953 Rules of Procedure (articles 21 and 35) was to conduct any necessary preparatory inquiries, *i.e.* to implement the Court's fact-finding procedures (see para. 6–08 below). This is still what is foreseen in article 9(2) of the current Rules, and it is indeed still the practice that such preparatory inquiries as are thought necessary are normally conducted by the Chamber. However, many cases may in fact be determined by a Chamber alone. The 1959 Rules of Procedure gave the Chambers power to try proceedings commenced by an official or other servant of an institution against that institution (generally referred to as "staff cases") in a provision corresponding to the current article 95(3), the first judgment of a Chamber being given in Joined Cases 27 and 39/59 *Campolongo* v. *H.A.* [1960] E.C.R. 391. The 1974 Rules amended article 95 so as to allow Chambers to determine references for preliminary rulings of a technical nature or on matters on which there was an established body of case law, provided any Member State submitting observations consented and no Community institution objected. Given these restrictive conditions, the references heard by Chambers tended to be on matters such as classification under the Common Customs Tariff, as in Case 120/75 *Riemer* v. *HZA Lübeck-West* [1976] E.C.R. 1003, the first example. Even where there were no institutional objections, theCourt was reluctant to assign a case relating, *e.g.* to the principle of the protection of legitimate expectation to a Chamber, as was noted by A.G. Mayras in Case 78/77 *Lührs* v. *HZA Hamburg - Jonas* [1978] E.C.R. 169, 182. Under the 1979 amendments, however, article 95(1) of the Rules provides in effect that a Chamber may try any reference for a preliminary ruling, and any direct action which may be brought by a "natural or legal person" (which in this instance appears to mean any litigant other than a Member State or a Community institution) whether it be an action for annulment, an action in relation to a failure to act, an action challenging a penalty, an action for damages or an action arising under an arbitration clause. Since the introduction of the reform, it would appear that about half the cases before the Court have been tried by a Chamber.

5–07   There are still, however, restrictions on the scope of the Court's descretion to allow such actions to be heard by a Chamber. Under article 95(2) of the Rules any Member State or Community institution which is a party (as defined in that provision) to the proceedings may still require the case to be determined by the Full Court, and even in the absence of such a request, the Court must still take account of the difficulty or importance of the case or "particular circumstances" a highly subjective test. Once the case has been assigned to a Chamber for determination, the Chamber still has the power under article 95(4) of the Rules to refer it back to the Full Court, and this provision also effectively enables a Chamber to refer a staff case, which under article 95(3) should in principle be heard by a Chamber, to the Full Court if the circumstances warrant it. So, in Case 110/75 *Mills* v. *European Investment Bank* [1976] E.C.R. 955, the First Chamber referred the case to the Full Court because, *inter alia*, it raised for the first time the question whether the Court actually did have jurisdiction to entertain actions brought by officials of the European Investment Bank against that institution.

5–08   The increased use of Chambers to some degree alleviates the burden of the judges, who, in cases not heard by the Full Court, need only concern themselves in detail with cases before their own particular Chamber; this is necessarily at the expense of a narrowing of the range of legal systems represented on the bench at any one time although

176

article 16 of the EEC Statute makes it clear that this is not a matter to which a litigant may object. On the other hand, the system provides no real relief for the Advocates-General, who must still deliver an Opinion in every case assigned to them (see para. 5–16 below), irrespective of whether it is heard by the Full Court or a Chamber.

B. JUDGE RAPPORTEUR

EEC Statute of the Court

Article 18

5–09   The oral procedure shall consist of the reading of the report presented by a Judge acting as Rapporteur, the hearing by the Court of agents, advisers and lawyers entitled to practise before a court of a Member State and of the submissions of the Advocate-General, as well as the hearing,if any, of witnesses and experts.

(The final paragraphs of article 18 of the Euratom Statute and article 21 of the ECSC Statute are in identical terms.)

Rules of Procedure

Article 9

2. As soon as an application originating proceedings has been lodged, the President shall assign the case to one of the Chambers for any preparatory inquiries and shall designate a Judge from that Chamber to act as Rapporteur.

Article 44

1. After the rejoinder provided for in Article 41 (1) of these rules has been lodged, the President shall fix a date on which the Judge-Rapporteur is to present his preliminary report to the Court. The report shall contain recommendations as to whether a preparatory inquiry or any other preparatory step should be undertaken and whether the case should be referred to the Chamber to which it has been assigned under Article 9 (2).
The Court shall decide, after hearing the Advocate General, what action to take upon the recommendations of the Judge-Rapporteur.
The same procedure shall apply:
   (a) where no reply or no rejoinder has been lodged within the time limit fixed in accordance with Article 41 (2) of these rules;
   (b) where the party concerned waives his right to lodge a reply or rejoinder.'

Article 45

3. The measures of inquiry which the Court has ordered may be conducted by the Court itself, or be assigned to the Judge Rapporteur.

5–10   In most actions before the Court, the allocation of the case to a Chamber under article 9(2) of the Rules of Procedure results in the selection of a Judge Rapporteur from that Chamber. This procedure is, however, reversed where an application is made for legal aid under article 76 of the Rules of Procedure before the commencement of proceedings (see para. 16–06). Here, article 76(3) provides for the appointment of a judge as Rapporteur, and for the decision on the grant of legal aid to be made by the Chamber to which that judge belongs. There are also special provisions for the appointment of a Rapporteur in certain special types of proceeding which are not allocated to Chamber for any purpose: article 105(3) of the Rules of Procedure provides for the appointment of a Rapporteur in the case of an application under article 103 of the Euratom Treaty for the Court to adjudicate upon the compatibility of a proposed agreement or contract with the Treaty, used for the first time in Ruling 1/78 [1978] E.C.R. 2151, and article 108(1) provides for the designation of a judge to act as Rapporteur on requests for an opinion under Article 228 of the EEC Treaty as to whether an envisaged international agreement is compatible with the provisions of the Treaty, used for the first time in Opinion 1/75 [1975] E.C.R. 1355.

5–11   The primary function of the Judge Rapporteur envisaged in the Statutes of the Court is that of preparing the report for the hearing. This effectively sets out what can be "taken as read" at the hearing. It sets out the facts of the case and summarises the submissions lodged with the Court. It will have been sent to the parties before the hearing, and is available to the public at the hearing; subject to any corrections requested by the parties, this becomes the "facts" part of the judgment. The Rules of Procedure also envisage that at the end of the written procedure, the Rapporteur will prepare a preliminary report stating whether in his view any preparatory inquiry (*i.e.* any investigation of the facts) is necessary and whether the case is suitable for determination by the Chamber rather than the Full Court. Although a formal report is not required from the Rapporteur on most other procedural matters, in the nature of things it is likely that his views will be sought since he is likely to have the most detailed knowledge of the case; a formal report is however required under article 42(2) of the Rules of Procedure (see para. 4–66) where a fresh issue is raised which is claimed to be based on matters of law or of fact which have come to light in the course of the written procedure.

5–12   The Rules also envisage that the Rapporteur may himself be empowered to undertake measures of inquiry, under article 45(3), though this has rarely occurred in practice, and under article 49(2) (see para. 6–37) it is the Rapporteur who is entrusted with the supervision of experts appointed by the Court. It is not unknown, however, for other roles to be deputed to the Rapporteur: for example, in the *Japanese ball bearing* cases, parties who were claiming that certain documents were confidential and should not be revealed to the interveners (see the order of November 16, 1977 allowing the intervention of FERMA in Case 119/77 *NSK* [1979] E.C.R.1303) appeared before the Judge Rapporteur, and in Case 155/79 *A.M. & S.* v. *Commission*, (May 18, 1982) the sealed envelope containing documents for which privilege was claimed, produced pursuant to the Order of February 4, 1981, was opened by the Judge Rapporteur and the Advocate-General.

However, neither the Statute nor the Rules make any mention of what is probably in practical terms the most important and influential role of the Rapporteur, which is the fact that he prepares the first draft of the judgment upon which the judges deliberate and normally continues to act as draftsman, taking account of the views of his colleagues, until the final version of the judgment is agreed. This does not necessarily mean that the Rapporteur will always manage to convince a majority of his colleagues, and he may eventually have to draft a judgment with which he does not agree; hence, to avoid giving the impression that the Rapporteur is in some way specially responsible for the substance of the Court's judgment, it has been the practice of the official European Court Reports, from the end of October 1975, not to indicate his name. The dividing line appears to be October 30, 1975: the judgment delivered that day in Case 33/75 *Galati* v. *LVA Schwaben* [1975] E.C.R. 1323 indicates the Rapporteur, whilst that delivered in Case 23/75 *Rey Soda* v. *Cassa Conguaglio Zucchero* [1975] E.C.R. 1279 does not.

C. ADVOCATE-GENERAL

EEC Treaty

Article 166

5–13   The Court of Justice shall be assisted by five Advocates-General.

It shall be the duty of the Advocate-General, acting with complete impartiality and independence, to make, in open court, reasoned submissions on cases brought before the Court of Justice, in order to assist the Court in the performance of the task assigned to it in Article 164.

Should the Court of Justice so request, the Council may, acting unanimously, increase the number of Advocates-General and make the necessary adjustments to the third paragraph of Article 167.

(Article 138 of the Euratom Treaty and Article 32a of the ECSC Treaty are in identical terms.)

EEC Statute of the Court

Article 18

The oral procedure shall consist of the reading of the report presented by a Judge acting as Rapporteur, the hearing by the Court of agents, advisers and lawyers entitled to practise before a court of a Member State and of the submissions of the Advocate-General, as well as the hearing, if any, of witnesses and experts.

(The final paragraphs of article 18 of the Euratom Statute and article 21 of the ECSC Statute are in identical terms.)

Rules of Procedure

Article 10

5–14   2. The First Advocate-General shall assign each case to an Advocate-General as soon as the Judge-Rapporteur has been designated by the President. He shall take the necessary steps if an Advocate-General is absent or prevented from attending.

Article 59

1. The Advocate-General shall deliver his opinion orally at the end of the oral procedure.

5–15   Until the 1979 amendments to the Rules of Procedure, the Advocates-General, like the judges, were attached to the Chambers of the Court, and an Advocate-General was designated by the President from the Chamber to which the case was assigned. Since, before the first enlargement in 1973, there were only two Advocates-General (in practice one French and one German, there being two Italian judges) and only two Chambers, the assignment to a Chamber automatically comported the selection of the Advocate-General. With the appointment of four Advocates-General from 1973 onwards (in practice one each from France, Germany, Italy and the United Kingdom), two Advocates-General were appointed to each of the two Chambers. This system, however, was found to lack flexibility if one Advocate-General fell ill or was otherwise unavailable, because in principle his workload fell entirely upon his colleague in that Chamber, the second sub-paragraph of article 26(3) of the Rules of Procedure only allowing the assignment of a case to an Advocate-General in the other Chamber "where *both* Advocates-General attached to a Chamber are absent or prevented from attending at the same time." An attempt was made to overcome this problem by interpreting "prevented from attending" as including the circumstance where an Advocate-General's workload was too great for him to be able to deal with the case. The solution adopted in the version of article 10(2) of the Rules of Procedure introduced in 1979 allows complete flexibility: the Advocates-General are not attached to a particular Chamber, and the designation of an Advocate-General for a particular case is made by the First Advocate-General from his colleagues. This system had no difficulty adapting to the appointment of a fifth Advocate-General in 1981 (the first holder of that post, Professor VerLoren van Themaat, being the first national of a smaller Member State to become an Advocate-General).

5–16   As in the case of the Judge Rapporteur (see para. 5–10 above) there is a special provision in the amended article 105(3) of the Rules of Procedure for the designation of an Advocate-General in an application under article 103 of the Euratom Treaty. Unlike the case of a Judge Rapporteur, however, there is no specific provision for the appointment of an Advocate-General on a request for an Opinion under Article 228 of the EEC Treaty; this is presumably because under article 108(2) of the Rules of Procedure, the Court delivers its Opinion after hearing the Advocates-General (the singular form occurs only in the English-language version), a provision which precludes individual designation.

The role ascribed to the Advocates-General in the Treaties is to deliver an Opinion (the term used in the English-language version of Rules of Procedure and in normal usage within the Court in preference to the term "submissions" used in the English-language versions of the Treaties and the Statutes) in each and every action before the Court, setting out a personal view of how the case should be decided; the function and nature of this Opinion will be examined in more detail in its context (see para. 7–40 below). Apart from this Opinion on the substance, an Opinion of the Advocate-General is also required on the whole gamut of procedural issues and special forms of procedure before the Court. Dealing with them in the order in which they appear in the Rules of Procedure, the Advocate-General must be heard before the Court may authorise the use of a language other than the language of the case at the request of one of the parties (article 29(2)(c), before a lawyer or adviser may be excluded from the proceedings for conduct incompatible with the dignity of the Court (article 35(1)); before an application commencing proceedings is rejected for want of form (article 38(7)), before the President allows the other party time to respond to a fresh issue raised in the course of proceedings (article 42(2)); before cases are dealt with jointly (article 43); before the Court decides whether to hold a preparatory inquiry (article 44(1)) or to assign a case to be determined by a Chamber (articles 44(1) and 95(2)); before particular measures of inquiry are prescribed (articles 45(1) and 60); before ordering certain facts to be proved by witnesses (article 47(1)) and before reporting a witness to the competent authority for perjury (Supplementary Rules, article 6); before ordering a measure of inquiry to be repeated or expanded (Rules of Procedure article 60); before reopening the oral procedure (article 61); before rectifying a judgment (article 66(3)) or supplementing it (article 67); before ordering a party to refund "avoidable costs" (article 72(a)); before the Chamber makes an order as to recoverable costs (article 74(1)); before a Chamber decides whether to grant legal aid (article 76(3)); before the Court decides on a application for interim measures where the matter is not determined by the President alone (article 85); before determining a preliminary objection or other procedural issue (article 91(4)); before determining an application to intervene (article 93(3)), before giving judgment by default (article 94(2)); before determining the admissibility of an application for revision of a judgment (article 100(1)); and before interpreting a judgment (article 102(2)).

5–17   As has already been indicated, the Advocate-General must also be heard before a decision is taken on an application under Article 103(2) of the Euratom Treaty with regard to the compatibility of a proposed international agreement or contract with that Treaty (article 105(4) of the Rules) and all the Advocates-General must be heard (although they may in practice endeavour to co-ordinate their views) before the Court gives an Opinion under Article 228 of the EEC Treaty as to the compatability of an international agreement with that Treaty (article 108(2) of the Rules), and article 109 of the Rules extends the same requirement to requests for an Opinion under Article 95 of the ECSC Treaty with regard to proposed adaptations of the rules for the High Authority's exercise ofits powers (a procedure first used in Opinion 1/59 [1959] E.C.R. 259). Historically, of course, the procedure under Article 95 of the ECSC Treaty antedates that under Article 228 of the EEC Treaty, and the obtaining of the opinion of all the Advocates-General was from the outset required by article 82(3) of the 1953 Rules of Procedure.

5–18 It might finally be noted that, as well as it being necessary for the Advocate-General to be heard before measures of inquiry are prescribed, the effect of article 45(3) of the Rules of Procedure is to require the participation of the Advocate-General in all measures of inquiry, be they conducted by the Court, a Chamber, or the Judge Rapporteur.

JOINDER OF CASES

Rules of Procedure

Article 43

5–19 The Court may, at any time, after hearing the parties and the Advocate-General, order that for the purpose of the written or oral procedure or of its final judgment, a number of related cases concerning the same subject matter shall be dealt with jointly. The decision to join the cases may subsequently be rescinded.

Article 103

1. In cases governed by Article 20 of the EEC Statute and Article 21 of the Euratom Statute, the provisions of Article 43 *et seq.* of these rules shall apply after the statements of case or written observations provided for in the said Articles 20 and 21 have been lodged.

The same provisions shall apply even where such documents are not lodged within the time prescribed in those Articles 20 and 21, or where the parties to the main action, the Member States, the Commission or, as the case may be, the Council declare an intention to dispense with them.

2. [Relates to references made under specific conventions.]

3. [In cases provided for in Article 41 of the ECSC Treaty.] . . . After these documents have been lodged, or where they have not been lodged within the time prescribed in the preceding subparagraph, the provisions of Article 43 *et seq.* of these rules shall apply.

5–20 Article 43 of the Rules of Procedure, allowing cases to be joined, appears in the context of the rules governing direct actions, and is applied to references for preliminary rulings by article 103 of these Rules. However, article 103 was in fact only amended so as to make express mention of article 43 in 1979; previously it referred to "Article 44 *et seq.* . . . ." of the Rules. Nonetheless, the Court has acted from the outset on the basis that it does have power to join references for preliminary rulings: the earliest example is to be found in the third preliminary ruling given by the Court, in Joined Cases 28, 29 and 30/62 *Da Costa en Schaake* v. *Nederlandse Belastingadministratie* [1963] E.C.R. 31. This was a fairly straightforward example of three references asking the same questions made by the same court, and the European Court joined the cases for the purposes of the oral procedure and judgment. Indeed, although article 43 allows cases to be joined for written procedure, or for oral procedure, or for the final judgment, article 103 only enables it to be used in references for preliminary rulings after the written observations have been lodged or the time-limit for lodging them has expired. Hence, in practice, references for preliminary rulings can only be joined for the oral procedure and/or the judgment. Within that limit, examples can be found of the joinder of cases emanating from diferent courts, as in Joined Cases 124/76 and 20/77 *Moulins de Pont-à-Mousson* v. *ONIC* [1977] E.C.R. 1795, where it was said that "since the questions submitted by the two national courts are identical in content and purpose, it is proper to join the cases . . . ."

5–21   In direct actions, joinder remains possible for all three phases of the procedure before the Court. Perhaps the most obvious example is where the Commission issues a decision under the competition rules addressed to a number of different undertakings, and each of these undertakings commences an action for the annulment of that decision; the modern practice of the Court is to join such cases for the whole of the procedure before it—although it might be submitted that it would be preferable for the applicants to combine to bring a single action in the first place (see para. 4–35 above). This may occur even though more than one language of the case is involved, as in Joined Cases 36 to 82/78 of Joined Cases 32/78 and 36 to 82/78 *BMW* v. *Commission* [1979] E.C.R. 2435 where the proceedings had to be conducted in Dutch and French. A more extreme illustration of the language problems encountered in joining actions occurred in the famous sugar cases, Joined Cases 40 to 48, 50, 54 to 56, 111, 113 and 114/73 *Suiker Unie* v. *Commission* [1975] E.C.R. 1663, where, although the joinder was only for the oral procedure and the judgment, four languages of the cases were involved: Dutch, French, German and Italian.

5–22   Under the ECSC Treaty, the first joinders were of successive actions brought by the same applicant against the same defendant, as in Joined Cases 7 and 9/54 *Groupement des Industries Sidérurgiques Luxembourgeouises* v. *H.A.* [1954 to 1956] E.C.R. 175, but joinder for the whole procedure of actions brought by separate applicants seeking annulment of the same decision can be found from Joined Cases 16, 17 and 18/59 *Geitling* v. *H.A.* [1960] E.C.R. 17. Joinder for all three phases of the procedure can be found in modern actions for annulment under the EEC Treaty, as in Joined cases 789 and 790/79 *Calpak* v. *Commission* [1980] E.C.R. 1949 where both applicants sought the annulment of the same Regulations, and in actions for damages, as in Joined Cases 67 to 85/75 *Lesieur Cotelle* v. *Commission* [1976] E.C.R. 391, where the harm suffered by all the applicants was alleged to result from the same wrongful act.

5–23   It is also possible for cases to be joined for just one phase of the procedure, most commonly the oral procedure, where although they are concerned with the same general subject-matter, they raise different points of detail, and hence cannot be determined by a single judgment. This may be the case where courts in different Member States make a reference for a preliminary ruling on essentially the same matter, but do not ask identical questions, as in the *EMI* v. *CBS* cases [1976] E.C.R. 811, 871 and 853; such partial joinder allows for a single hearing or a single Opinion by the Advocate-General—although it must be said that the differences between the judgments in these cases are very minor. Examples can also be found of direct actions joined only for a limited part of the procedure; in the competition field, the *Dyestuffs* cases [1972] E.C.R. 619, 713, 745, 787, 845, 851, 887, 927 and 933 were joined for the purposes of the experts' report and the oral procedure, the judgments being tailored to the individual circumstances of each applicant (*e.g.* the *ICI* case [1972] E.C.R. 619 raised problems of the Community's jurisdiction in international law); similarly, for example, actions for damages in Case 238/78 *Ireks Arkady* v. *Council and Commission* [1979] E.C.R. 2955 and in Joined Cases 241, 242 and 245 to 250/78 *DGV* v. *Council and Commission* [1979] E.C.R. 3017 were heard at the same time and dealt with in a single Opinion by the Advocate-General, but not joined for the judgment, the former being concerned with a claim arising from a failure to provide for a production refund on quellmehl, the latter cases being concerned with claims arising from a failure to provide for a production refund on gritz. The actions for annulment in the *Japanese ball bearing* cases [1979] E.C.R. 1185, 1277, 1303, 1377 and 1363 were dealt with in the same way, though there it might be noted that in Case 119/77 *NSK* v. *Council and Commission* [1979] E.C.R. 1303 there was also a claim for damages.

5–24   Indeed, in practice it has occurred that entirely different forms of action relating to the same subject-matter have been dealt with together for the purposes of the oral procedure, if not strictly joined. Hence, Case 61/77 *Commission* v. *Ireland* [1978] E.C.R. 417, a direct action brought under Article 169 of the EEC Treaty for a declaration that Ireland had breached its Treaty obligations by introducing certain fisheries measures, was heard on the same day as Case 88/77 *Minister for Fisheries* v. *Schonenberg* [1978] E.C.R. 473, a reference for a preliminary ruling arising out of a prosecution under these fisheries measures. A. G. Reischl delivered his Opinions on both cases successively on the same day, dealing with the substance in his Opinion in Case 61/77 and making a global reference thereto in his Opinion in Case 88/77 (a technique used also by the Court in drafting its judgment). Similarly, Case 114/76 *Behla-Mühle* v. *Grows-Farm* [1977] E.C.R. 1211, and three other references for preliminary ruling on the validity of a Regulation requiring the compulsory purchase of skimmed-milk powder for use in animal feeding-stuffs, were heard at the same time as the actions for damages in Joined Cases 83 and 94/76, 4, 15/77 *Bayerische HNL and Others* v. *Council and Commission* [1978] E.C.R. 1209 on the question of the validity of the Regulation, and A.G. Capotorti dealt with that question in all the cases in a single Opinion [1977] E.C.R. 1211, 1222.

The Court does have power under article 43 of the Rules to change its mind as to the desirability of dealing with cases jointly, although rescission of a joinder is not normally encountered in practice. An example may however be found in Case 261/78 *Interquell Stärke-Chemie* v. *Council and Commission* (October 6, 1982) and Case 262/78 *Diamalt* v. *Council and Commission* (October 6, 1982) which were disjoined for the final judgments on damages. On the other hand, it is not unknown for an Advocate-General, to choose a random illustration, to find himself charged with delivering a single Opinion in a group of related cases the detailed differences between which are such that this single Opinion is in reality a succession of separate Opinions as, *e.g.* the Opinion of A.G. Warner in Cases 112/76 *Manzoni* v. *F.N.R.O.M.*, 22/77 *F.N.R.O.M.* v. *Mura*, 32/77 *Giuliani* v. *LVA Schwaben* and 37/77 *Greco* v. *F.N.R.O.M.* [1977] E.C.R. at p. 1657.

ADMINISTRATIVE MEETINGS

Rules of Procedure
Article 27

5–25   7. Where the deliberations of the Court concern questions of its own administration, the Advocates-General shall take part and have a vote. The Registrar shall be present, unless the Court decides to the contrary.

The only meetings of the Court at which article 27(7) of Rules expressly envisages the presence of the Advocates-General and of the Registrar are those concerned with the Court's "own administration," a phrase somewhat narrower in concept perhaps than the French "questions administratives." On the other hand, the only expressly restrictive provision in article 27, its second paragraph (see para. 8–02 below), which restricts participation in the deliberations to "these Judges who were present at the oral proceedings," on the face of it only applies to deliberations leading to a formal judgment or formal order which follow oral proceedings. In practice, the normal incidents of procedure before the Court are considered at administrative meetings. Perhaps most important in this context is the fact that it is at an administrative meeting that the Judge Rapporteur and Advocate-General will present their views on whether or not preparatory inquiries are necessary in a particular case or whether it may be determined by a Chamber.

5–26   Furthermore, with regard to preparatory inquiries, even if the Court does desire further elucidation, in the vast majority of cases it will not formally order measures of inquiry. Rather, the administrative meeting may decide informally to put specific questions to the parties, or to ask them to produce specific documents, or to enter into a particular point in more detail (to give the usual examples) and will instruct the Registrar to write to the parties to that effect, as with regard to the matters to be dealt with at the second hearing in Case 155/79 *A.M. & S.* v. *Commission*.

More impotantly for the development of practice rules before the Court, such administrative meetings may well determine procedural points of general interest for which no specific mechanism is provided in the Rules of Procedure and with regard to which the machinery of article 91 of the Rules (see para. 4–86 above) has not been invoked. The result of this determination will be communicated to the party or parties concerned by unpublished Registrar's letter, which may make it difficult for the Court's practice to become public knowledge. As a simple illustration, Case 126/77 *Frangiamore* v. *Office Nationale de l'Emploi* [1978] E.C.R. 725 was a reference from the Belgian Cour de Cassation, before which only "avocats" have a right of audience. The claimant's advisers asked the Court whether he could be represented on the reference by an adviser who was not an "avocat," as had occurred on references from lower Belgian social security courts. The European Court decided, in administrative meeeting, that a person having no right of audience before the court making the reference cannot appear before the European Court on the reference, and this was communicated to the claimant's adviser by the Registrar. Although it is a point of considerable general importance, it is nowhere mentioned in the E.C.R. report of the case.

CHAPTER 6

PREPARATORY INQUIRIES

QUESTIONS OF FACT

A. DIRECT ACTIONS

6–01   In the vast majority even of direct actions before the European Court the real dispute concerned a question of law rather than the underlying facts. Indeed, in actions for annulment it might at first sight appear that since the European Court has jurisdiction only on grounds of "lack of competence, infringement of an essential procedural requirement, infringement of [the] Treaty or of any rule of law relating to its application, or misuse of powers" it can only consider questions of law in this context. However the dividing line between law and fact is not always easy to discern, and a material error of fact may mean that an act based on it has no legal foundation: in the *Sugar Cases* [1975] E.C.R. 1663, 1924 it was in effect held that a Commission decision based on an incorrect finding should be classified as an ingringement of the Treaty. The relevance of questions of fact, or more frequently of the inferences to be drawn from the primary facts, can be illustrated in the context of actions for the annulment of Commission competition decisions.

6–02   In Case 22/78 *Hugin* v. *Commission* [1979] E.C.R. 1869, in annulling a Commission decision holding that a manufacturer of cash registers had abused a dominant position under Article 86 of the EEC Treaty by refusing to supply spare parts to an independent repairer, the Court found the business of the maintenance, repair and renting-out of cash registers to be localised even within a Member State, and concluded therefore that the failure to supply spare parts did not affect trade between Member States within the meaning of Article 86 of the EEC Treaty. In Case 77/77 *BP* v. *Commission* [1978] E.C.R. 1513, the Commission had held in its decision that Dutch BP had abused a dominant position with regard to a purchasing co-operative referred to as "ABG" during the period November 1973 to March 1974 in that, following the Arab embargo on supplies of oil to the Netherlands, it had applied a greater rate of reduction of supplies to ABG than to other traditional customers. After analysing the history of the trading relationship, the Court came to the conclusion that in fact ABG was not a regular customer of BP by the time the crisis occurred but was an occasional customer, and therefore held that BP could not be accused of having applied to it during the crisis less favourable treatment than that which it reserved for its traditional customers. Finally an example might be taken from the *Sugar Cases* [1975] E.C.R. 1663 themselves. The Commission had there found in its decision, *inter alia*, that there had

187

been a concerted practice having as its object the protection of the Italian market; in relation to this, the Court looked at the relevant Italian legislation (which must be a question of fact for the European Court in the context of an action under Article 173 of the EEC Treaty), finding that the field for the operation of the Community competition rules was to a great extent fundamentally restricted in its scope by the special organisation of the Italian market, and concluded that the conduct complained of could not therefore appreciably impede competition and hence did not come within the prohibition of Article 85 of the EEC Treaty. It is thus clear that inferences of fact can be vitally important.

6–03   In actions for damages, on the other hand, the European Court may well be concerned with establishing the primary facts, as well as the legality of the act alleged to have caused the harm. In particular, the existence and extent of the harm will be at issue. Thus, in its second judgment in Case 74/74 *CNTA* v. *Commission* [1976] E.C.R. 797, having held in its first judgment that the Commission would be liable to the applicant for any loss suffered by the applicant as a result of its having been re-exposed to an exchange risk following the withdrawal of certain monetary compensatory amounts in breach of the applicant's legitimate expectations, the Court investigated both the terms of the contract governing the exports affected and the way in which that contract had been performed, finding that although the purchaser had a choice of paying in dollars or French francs, all the payments under it were made in French francs so that in fact no exchange risk materialised for the applicant, itself a French undertaking. Hence the applicant could not be regarded as having suffered loss.

B. REFERENCES FOR PRELIMINARY RULINGS

6–04   The jurisdiction of the European Court on references for preliminary rulings is at most, depending on the provision under which the reference is made, either to interpret a provision of Community law or to pronounce upon the validity of an item of Community secondary legislation, which are quintessentially matters of law. Indeed, from its very first preliminary ruling in Case 13/61 *De Geus* v. *Bosch* [1962] E.C.R. 45, 53, the Court has consistently stated that it is not for it to investigate or establish the facts underlying the litigation before the national court. Those facts would appear to be of direct interest to the Court only in so far as they might establish that the question referred bears no relation to the objectives of the national litigation, so that the European Court might reject the reference as being inadmissable, as was suggested in Case 126/80*Salonia* v. *Poidomani* [1981] E.C.R. 1563. However, the fact that the Court will not normally concern itself with the facts underlying the national litigation—even where, as in Case 309/81 *Klughardt* v. *HZA Hamburg-St. Annen* (December 9, 1982), the reference appears to be based on a factual assumption disputed by both the Council and the Commission—does not mean that questions of fact can never arise on references for a preliminary ruling; as was noted in the context of direct actions for annulment, a material error of fact may mean that a Community act based on it has no legal foundation. This was recognised by A.G. Warner in his Opinion in Case 51/75 *EMI* v. *CBS* [1976] E.C.R. 811, 854, and an example occurred in Case 131/77 *Milac* v. *HZA Saarbrücken* [1978] E.C.R. 1041. This concerned the validity of a Commission Regulation applying monetary compensatory amounts to powdered whey. Under the parent Council Regulation, monetary compensation amounts may only be applied to products covered by intervention arrangements under the common organisations of agricultural markets and to products whose price depends on the price of such products. Milac imported into Germany a quantity of powdered whey on which it had to pay monetary compensation amounts at the rate laid down in the Commission Regulation. In fact, under the common organisation of the market in milk and milk products, intervention prices are fixed only for butter, skimmed milk powder and certain cheeses, and Milac brought an action before the Finanzgericht of the Saar to recover the monetary compensation amounts it had paid, claiming that the price of powdered whey was not dependent on the price of any intervention product. The Finanzgericht referred to the European Court the specific question whether the Commission Regulation was contrary to the parent Council Regulation in that the price of powdered whey did not in fact depend on the price of skimmed milk powder. The Court held that the test of dependency was whether the price of the non-intervention product varied perceptibly under the influence of variations in the price of the intervention product. This could only be determined on the evidence of the recorded prices of skimmed milk powder and powdered whey. This evidence was put before the Court, and from it the Court found not only that there was no correlation between the two prices but also that there was a growing divergence. It was therefore held that the Commission Regulation was invalid in so far as it imposed monetary compensation amounts on powdered whey.

6–05 Hence it is the facts underlying the Community act rather than the national litigation which are likely to be at issue in references for preliminary rulings.

Indeed, it is not unknown for preliminary rulings to be given on alternative hypotheses, since there is no obligation for national courts to have reached a final decision on the facts before making a reference as, *e.g.* in Case 36/74 *Walrave and Koch* v. *Union Cycliste Internationale* [1974] E.C.R. 1405 where a Dutch court put alternative sets of questions based on the assumptions in the first set that the plaintiffs before it were employed persons and in the second set that they were providing services.

C. CONDUCT OF PRELIMINARY INQUIRIES

Rules of Procedure

Article 44

6–06 2. Where the Court orders a preparatory inquiry and does not undertake it itself, it shall assign the inquiry to the Chamber

Where the Court decides to open the oral procedure without an inquiry, the President shall fix the opening date.

Article 45

1. The Court, after hearing the Advocate-General, shall prescribe the measures of inquiry that it considers appropriate by means of an order setting out the issues of fact to be determined. The order shall be served on the parties.

2. Without prejudice to Articles 24 and 25 of the ECSC Statute, Article 21 and 22 of the EEC Statute or Articles 22 and 23 of the Eurotom Statute, the following measures of inquiry may be adopted.
   (a) the personal appearance of the parties;
   (b) a request for information and production of documents;
   (c) oral testimony;
   (d) experts' reports;
   (e) an inspection of the place or thing in question.

3. The measures of inquiry which the Court has ordered may be conducted by the Court itself, or be assigned to the Judge Rapporteur.

The Advocate-General shall take part in the measures of inquiry.

4. Evidence may be submitted in rebuttal and previous evidence may be amplified.

(Article 21 of the EEC Statute and the corresponding provisions of the ECSC and Euratom Treaties expressly empower the Court to order the parties, Member States or institutions to provide certain information; article 22 *et al* empowers the Court to obtain an expert opinion.)

Article 46

1. A Chamber to which a preparatory inquiry has been assigned may exercise the powers vested in the Court by Articles 45 and 47 to 53 of these rules; the powers vested in the President of the Court may be exercised by the President of the Chamber.

2. Articles 56 and 57 of these rules shall apply in a corresponding manner to proceedings before the Chamber.

3. The parties shall be entitled to attend the measures of enquiry.

(Articles 56 and 57 are concerned with the conduct of oral proceedings.)

6–07 The preliminary inquiries, where they are held, are perhaps the most overtly inquisitorial aspect of the procedure before the European Court: it is the Court itself which decides which documents are to be produced, which witnesses are to be called, whether an expert, should be appointed or whether an inspection should be carried out. Hence it is the Court, not the parties, that decides how the facts are to be investigated. However, article 47 of the Rules expressly allows a party to apply for certain facts to be proved by witnesses, and under article 50 the parties may object to a witness or an expert. In practice, parties do commonly also ask the Court to order other measures of inquiry, in particular to order the other party to produce documents (there being no "discovery" as such). As an example, in Case 110/75 *Mills* v. *European Investment Bank* [1976] E.C.R. 1613 the applicant requested that the Bank should disclose a report on his superior, which gave rise to a question of privilege (see para. 6–49 below). It would appear, however, that a party seeking measures of inquiry to be ordered should be able to furnish a *prima facie* justification for the measure: in Case 51/65 *ILFO* v. *H.A.* [1966] E.C.R. 87, the applicant requested the appointment of an expert, and its application was refused on the grounds that no evidence had been offered to justify the measure.

6–08   By the combined effect of articles 44(2), 45 and 46 of the Rules, the preparatory inquiry may be conducted by the Court or a Chamber (in practice, as has been noted, normally by a Chamber), and individual measures of inquiry may be conducted by the Court, a Chamber or the Judge Rapporteur (see para. 5–12 above). Mention might also be made of the fact that article 44(2) clearly envisages that the preparatory inquiry is distinct from the oral procedure, a view confirmed by article 54, which requires the date for the opening of the oral procedure to be fixed after the preparatory inquiry has been completed, whereas article 18 of the EEC Statute (and its parallel provisions) envisages that the hearing of witnesses and exports is part of the oral procedure. This will be considered further in the context of the oral procedure, but it might be said that in practice the strictness of the separation between these stages in the procedure depends very much upon the complexity (and nature) of the case, but that the basic rule is that the preparatory inquiry, including the hearing of witnesses and experts, is separate from the oral procedure, a system which was clearly established even in articles 35 to 45 of the 1953 Rules of Procedure. The other basic rule underlying the conduct of a preparatory inquiry is that the procedure remains contradictory in the sense that the parties should have the opportunity to comment on the material which emerges as the result of the inquiry. Article 45(1) of the 1953 Rules of Procedure in fact expressly required a period to be fixed for the parties to submit their final written arguments at the end of the preparatory inquiry; article 54 of the current Rules, (see para. 7–01 below) is not couched in obligatory terms, but recognises that the parties may be given a period to lodge written observations, and this remains the normal practice.

EVIDENCE

A. Burden of Proof

6–09   Although it is the Court itself which directs the preparatory inquiry, and although it remains free to pursue lines of inquiry not suggested by the parties, nevertheless problems as to the burden of proof remain with regard to allegations made by the parties. Under articles 38(1)(e), 40(1)(d) and 93(2)(f) of the Rules of Procedure, applicants, defendants and interveners in direct actions are respectively required to indicate in the application, defence, or application to intervene, the nature of any evidence founded upon by them. The onus rests with each party to prove, or make available proof of, each allegation that he makes, as was made clear by the Court in Joined Cases 42 and 49/59 *SNUPAT* v. *H.A.* [1961] E.C.R. 53. There, in an effort to show that it had retained title to certain ferrous scrap, an intervener sought to rely on a contract which it was not willing to produce and of which it had not indicated the terms. In the light of this, the Court refused to order its production, stating that "it is not acceptable to rely on the Court to take the initiative in obtaining for itself by measures of inquiry information intended to prove the cogency of the argument relied upon by the intervener, which itself possesses that information," and concluded that the intervener had not adduced proof of its allegation. Although the real question in this case was one of confidentiality, on which nowadays a different view might be taken under the amended article 93(4) of the Rules of Procedure (see para. 6–47 below), the principle remains that the Court is unlikely to order measures of inquiry to establish facts supporting a party's contention when that party could have proved those facts by means which were under its control. On the other hand, the Court did make an order in Case 19/77 *Miller* v. *Commission* [1978] E.C.R. 131. In this case, the applicant argued that a fine of 0.73 per cent. of the turnover should be reduced since its policy of low prices left it with only a narrow profit-margin. Since it had not produced documents in support of this allegation, the Court requested it to produce its accounts for the year 1974 to 1976. Miller replied that it was unable to comply with this request since it did not want the figures disclosed. The Court did not insist on production of the accounts, but concluded that in their absence there was no evidence on which the fine could be reduced.

6–10   Although in principle each party must prove his own case, in actions for the annulment of Commission competition decisions it would appear that the applicant does not have to disprove the facts and inferences on which the Commission's decision is based so much as to show that they do not support, or are not sufficient to support, that decision: *i.e.* the burden of proving a breach of Articles 85 or 86 of the EEC Treaty, remains with the Commission. Many decisions have been wholly or partially annulled on this basis. Thus in Case 27/76 *United Brands* v. *Commission* [1978] E.C.R. 207 at 303, the Court annulled the section of the Commission's decision relating to "unfair" prices on the ground that the Commission had not adduced "adequate legal proof"of the facts and evaluations which formed the foundation of its finding that United Brands had infringed Article 86 of the EEC Treaty by imposing unfair selling prices for bananas; in the famous *Sugar Cases* [1975] E.C.R. 1663, 1988 the Court annulled a finding that two undertakings had committed infringements of Article 86 by bringing economic pressure to bear on Dutch importers with the object of compelling them to restrict their imports, on the grounds that the facts alleged by the Commission had not been sufficiently proved; and in Case 6/72 *Continental Can* v. *Commission* [1973] E.C.R. 215, 245 the Commission's decision was annulled because it had not, as a matter of law, sufficiently shown the facts and assessments on which it was based.

Whilst the parties may be able, and expected, to produce a document to which they have access without a Court order, there is no way in the Court's procedure in which they can call their own witnesses, although they may well annex affidavits to their written pleadings (see *e.g.* Case 42/75 *Delvaux* v. *Commission* [1976] E.C.R. 167, 179). They must therefore request the Court to order their appearance. By analogy with the decision in Case 51/65 *ILFO* v. *H.A.* [1966] E.C.R. 87 where a request for the appointment of an expert was rejected on the ground that no evidence had been offered to justify the measure, it would seem that even here the parties must furnish sufficient evidence to justify an order by the Court, and in particular that they should indicate what in their view the witness will be able to prove (as indeed required under article 47(1) of the Rules). A similar view appears to be taken when a party requests the Court to order the production of documents: in Case 119/81 *Klöckner-Werke* v. *Commission* (July 7, 1982) the Court refused to order production of certain Council minutes where the applicant had made what it regarded as a vague allegation. On the other hand, where the Court orders a measure of inquiry simply to inform itself as to the background to the dispute, it may be doubted whether the question of the burden of proof imposed on the parties is relevant.

B. DOCUMENTARY EVIDENCE

EEC Statute of the Court

Article 21

6–11   The Court may require the parties to produce all documents and to supply all information which the Court considers desirable. Formal note shall be taken of any refusal.

The Court may also require the Member States and institutions not being parties to the case to supply all information which the Court considers necessary for the proceedings.

(Article 22 of the Euratom Statute and article 24 of the ECSC Statute are in similar terms.)

Rules of Procedure

Article 45

6–12   2. . . . the following measures of inquiry may be adopted
(a) . . . .
(b) a request for information and production of documents

6–13   Although the Court has power to order the parties to produce documents, in most cases they themselves will already have produced those on which they rely as annexes to their written pleadings (see para. 4–25 above). Insofar as it does order the parties to produce documents, however, the Court, unlike the Commission investigating alleged breaches of the competition rules under Regulation 17, has no power to impose a sanction or penalty if its order is disobeyed. It can only take formal note of a refusal. This may explain why in practice the parties are often asked to produce a document by informal request rather than as a specific measure of inquiry; in both cases, the only real sanction is likely to be the failure of any argument which relies on that document, as in Case 19/77 *Miller* v. *Commission* [1978] E.C.R. 131 where the Court refused to reduce a fine alleged to be excessive in relation to the applicant's profit margins, after the applicant refused to produce its accounts to justify this assertion

There is no restriction on the Court's power to obtain information from Member States and Community institutions other than its own assessment of what is necessary for the proceedings, and this method is often used to obtain elucidation as to the legal background of the dispute before the Court. For example, in Joined Cases 110 and 111/78 *Ministère public* v. *van Wesemael* [1979] E.C.R. 35 the Commission was asked to supply details of the legislation governing employment agencies in the Member States, and in Case 155/78 *M* v. *Commission* [1980] E.C.R. 1797, 1811 the Commission was requested to draw up a study of comparative law on the question of the confidentiality of medical findings under the laws of the various Member States. More specifically, in Case 132/81 *Rijksdienst voor Werknemerspensioenen* v. *Saelens née Vlaeminck* (September 16, 1982), the French government, which neither was a party to the proceedings (which originated from a Belgian court) nor had submitted observations, was requested under article 21 of the EEC Statute to explain how a French social security institution had calculated a pension paid to the claimant. On the other hand, the Court may well seek such information in a form which is not technically evidence, and thus neither shown to nor commented on by the parties, by requesting the research to be carried out by its own documentation service. Thus in Case 17/74 *Transocean* v. *Commission* [1974] E.C.R. 1063 the information on the right to be heard in administrative proceedings in the laws of the Member States used by A.G. Warner in his Opinion was supplied in an internal research note by the Court's documentation service, and not discovered by a measure of inquiry.

6–14 Given the importance of written procedure before the Court, it is hardly surprising that most of the factual information put before the Court is in written form. Indeed, article 42(1) of the Rules of Procedure expressly permits parties to a direct action to indicate further evidence in the Reply or Rejoinder, provided reasons are given for the delay, despite the general prohibition on raising new issues in article 42(2) of the Rules (see para. 4–66 above).

The acceptance of documentary evidence is rendered easier by the fact that evidence which in English law might be regarded as hearsay or *res inter alios* will be accepted by the Court if it is thought to be credible. In the *Sugar Cases* [1975] E.C.R. 1663, 1940 the Court asserted that "there is no reason why the . . . Court should not accept as evidence of an undertaking's conduct correspondence exchanged between third parties provided that the content thereof is credible to the extent to which it refers to the said conduct."

To give a random illustration of the nature of the documentary evidence the parties may be asked to produce, in Case 85/76 *Hoffman-La Roche* v. *Commission* [1979] E.C.R. 461, the Commission produced, *inter alia*, minutes of a meeting between Unilever and Roche mentioned in the recitals to its decision, documents relating to price

194

trends in the Member States, and reports of investigations carried out by its officials with certain of Roche's customers in order to ascertain how contracts between Roche and its customers were performed; the Commission and Roche together produced a joint document containing the statistical data on which they had reached agreement in relation to Roche's market shares within the EEC (reproduced on pp. 504–505 of the E.C.R. report), and also indicating the points on which they did not agree; and Roche produced copies of certain new contracts which it had entered into.

C. ORAL EVIDENCE

EEC Statute of the Court
Article 29

6–15   During the hearings the Court may examine the experts, the witnesses and the parties themselves. The latter, however, may address the Court only through their representatives.

(Article 30 of the Euratom Statute and article 28(3) of the ECSC Statute are in similar terms.)

Rules of Procedure
Article 45

2. Without prejudice to Article 24 and 25 of the ECSC Statute, Article 21 and 22 of the EEC Statute or Articles 22 and 23 of the Euratom Statute, the following measures of inquiry may be adopted.
(a) the personal appearance of the parties;
(b) . . . .
(c) oral testimony.

6–16   Article 29 of the Statute and article 45(2) of the Rules of Procedure make a clear distinction between parties and witnesses. The fundamental concept underlying this distinction is that a party cannot be a witness and cannot make a recorded statement under oath. In principle a party may only give unsworn answers to the questions put to him: article 29 of the Statute makes it clear that he should not use his personal appearance to argue his case, although of course the requirement that parties should only address the court through their representative would appear to be relevant only to direct actions, since under article 104(2) of the Rules of Procedure, litigants in person may appear on reference for preliminary rulings if the rules of the national court making the reference so allow. Indeed, since the Court has consistently held that a reference for a preliminary ruling is merely a step in the procedure before the national court (see Case 62/72 *Bollmann* v. *HZA Hamburg-Waltershof* [1973] E.C.R. 269), it may be doubted whether the European Court should prevent a party from giving evidence if the national rules would allow him to do so; in practice, however, as has been indicated, the primary facts underlying the national litigation are unlikely to be at issue before the European Court.

195

6–17   The personal appearance of the parties is most frequently encountered in staff cases, and it is not unknown for the applicant and a witness appearing at the behest of the defendant institution to be asked to give their accounts of the same event. So in case 102/75 *Petersen* v. *Commission* [1976] E.C.R. 1777 the applicant and a Commission official called as a witness were both asked to give their own account of a conversation between them three years earlier. Their conflicting accounts were considered in detail by A.G. Warner in his Opinion and more briefly by the Court in its judgment, and in neither instance did the point that only the other official could technically be a witness appear to be taken into account as a factor in determining the credibility of what they said. Similarly, in Case 43/74 *Guillot* v. *Commission* [1977] E.C.R. 1309, 1337, conflicts between the statements made by the applicant on a personal appearance and the evidence of four witnesses were resolved on the basis of the credibility of what was said rather than the fact that the applicant's statement was unsworn. It may perhaps be concluded from this that in practice the distinction between parties and witnesses in the context of oral evidence is more formal than real, except that under article 6 of the Supplementary Rules (see para. 6–32 below), only witnesses would appear to run the risk of being reported for perjury.

6–18   The real problem with any oral evidence (using that term loosely) before the European Court is that of language, as was well illustrated in *Petersen's* case. A witness may well not speak the language of the case, and even if he does, that language may be one which is not understood by the judges, who are then reliant on simultaneous interpretation. In *Petersen*, the applicant was Danish, the language of the case was Danish, but the witness was Dutch and none of the three judges of the First Chamber who heard the case understood Danish. In order to avoid the problems of simultaneous interpretation, exacerbated by the fact, noted in the context of the language of the case, that the Court did not employ its own interpreters and had to borrow them from the European Parliament, the applicant and the witness elected to speak in English. This was not totally inappropriate, since the earlier conversation of which they were giving an account had in fact also been in English, but as A.G. Warner pointed out (at p. 1802), neither of them spoke that language perfectly, so there was room for misunderstanding.

WITNESSES

A. WHOSE WITNESSES?

Rules of Procedure

Article 47

6–19   1. The Court may, either of its own motion or on application by a party, and after hearing the Advocate-General, order that certain facts be proved by witnesses. The order of the Court shall set out the facts to be proved.

The Court may summon a witness of its own motion or on application by a party or at the instance of the Advocate-General.

An application by a party for the examination of a witness shall state about what facts and for what reasons the witness should be examined.

2. The witness shall be summoned by an order of the Court containing the following information:

(a) the surname, forenames, description and address of the witness;

(b) an indication of the facts about which the witness is to be examined;

(c) where appropriate, particulars of the arrangements made by the Court for reimbursement of expenses incurred by the witness, and of the penalties which may be imposed on defaulting witnesses.

The order shall be served on the parties and the witness.

3. The Court may make the summoning of a witness for whose examination a party has applied conditional upon the deposit with the cashier of the Court of a sum sufficient to cover the taxed costs thereof; the Court shall fix the amount of the payment.

The cashier shall advance the funds necessary in connection with the examination of any witness summoned by the Court of its own motion.

Article 50

1. If one of the parties objects to a witness or to an expert on the ground that he is not a competent or proper person to act as witness or expert or for any other reason, or if a witness or expert refuses to give evidence, to take the oath or to make a solemn affirmation in lieu thereof, the matter shall be decided upon by the Court.

2. An objection to a witness or to an expert shall be raised within two weeks after service of the order summoning the witness or appointing the expert; the statement of objection must set out the grounds of objection and indicate any evidence founded upon.

Article 51

1. Witnesses and experts shall be entitled to reimbursement of their travel and subsistence expenses. The cashier of the court may make a payment to them towards these expenses in advance.

2. Witnesses shall be entitled to compensation for loss of earnings, and experts to fees for their services.

The cashier of the Court shall pay witnesses and experts their compensation or fees after they have carried out their respective duties or tasks.

Instructions to the Registrar

Article 21

6–20 1. Where pursuant to article 47 (3), 51 (1) and 76 (5) of the Rules of Procedure an application is made to the cashier of the Court for an advance payment, the Registrar shall direct that particulars of the costs for which the advance payment is required be delivered.

Witnesses must supply evidence of their loss of earnings and experts must supply a note of fees for their services.

2. The Registrar shall order payment by the cashier of the Court of sums payable pursuant to the preceding paragraph, against a receipt or other proof of payment.

Where he is of the opinion that the amount applied for is excessive, he may of his own motion reduce it or order payment by instalments.

6–21   Although it is the Court which formally summons witnesses, the parties may, under article 47(1) of the Rules of Procedure, request that a particular witness be heard or, under article 50 of the Rules, object to a particular witness. It is expressly required that a party should state about what facts and for what reasons a witness should be called, and it would appear from Case 51/65 *ILFO* v. *H.A.* [1966] E.C.R. 87 (which concerned a request for the appointment of an expert) that that party must furnish sufficient evidence to justify calling that witness. On the other hand, the Court has rarely pronounced upon the criteria it will use in determining whether to accede to that request. However, in Case 35/67 *Van Eick* v. *Commission* [1968] E.C.R. 329 the Court considered the calling of witnesses at the request of a party by a staff disciplinary board, on the basis that the board was bound to observe "the fundamental principles of the law of procedure," which are presumably also binding on the European Court itself. It held that these principles required the board to comply with an application for the examination of witnesses once that application clearly indicated both the facts on which the witness or witnesses should be heard and the reasons justifying their examination (*i.e.* once the application complies with the requirements of article 47(1)), but that it was for the board to assess both the relevance of the application to the subject-matter of the dispute and the necessity actually to examine the witnesses. Applying these principles to the Court, although it is prima facie bound to accede to a request complying with article 47(1) of the Rules, it may refuse to call witnesses if it considers that their evidence will not be relevant to the resolution of the dispute or if it considers there is no need actually to examine the witnesses. There is, however, nothing to prevent a party who fears that his suggested witness will not be called from annexing a written statement of the witnesses' statement, or an affidavit, to his written pleadings, as in Case 42/75 *Delvaux* v. *Commission* [1976] E.C.R. 167. There, in a decision for expatriation allowance which turned on the applicant's previous residence, his divorced wife swore an affidavit as to the reasons why the applicant had first gone to Denmark which was put in on behalf of the applicant as an annex to the Reply. The same technique may be used where a witness is physically unable to appear, and in Joined Cases 19 and 65/63 *Prakash* v. *EAEC Commission* [1965] E.C.R. 533, where the applicant wished a witness to be called who was resident in the United States, which was treated as preventing his appearance, the Court allowed an unsworn written statement by this person to be used in the oral proceedings (see p. 555).

6–22   It may be noted that under the scheme of article 47, witnesses are heard only in relation to specified facts; a party wishing to have a witness called must indicate the facts in relation to which he is to be heard, and the Court itself, whether acting of its own motion or at the behest of a party must indicate the facts to be proved by the witness both in the order instituting the measure of inquiry and in the order summoning the witness. So, in Case 102/75 *Petersen* v. *Commission* [1976] E.C.R. 1777, the witness and the applicant were heard in order to establish the content of one specific conversation; in Case 188/73 *Grassi* v. *Council*

[1974] E.C.R. 1099 three witnesses were heard on the specific question of the meaning of the expression "thorough knowledge" in one particular notice of vacancy. On the other hand, in the *Sugar Cases* [1975] E.C.R. 1663, 1694 four witnesses were heard on the more general question whether economic pressure was brought to bear by two sugar manufacturers on Dutch importers of sugar.

Since all witnesses are ultimately called by the Court on matters decided upon by the Court, distinctions known to common lawyers between witnesses called by one side or the other are not recognised. In particular, as will be seen, there is no real distinction between examination-in-chief and cross-examination, and no prohibition on leading witnesses. However, there is one sense in which witnesses who are officials of Community institutions remain that institution's witnesses. Although article 51 of the Rules and article 21 of the Instructions to the Registrar regulate the payment of witnesses' expenses in considerable detail, there is authority to the effect that, insofar as the institutions are in general liable to meet their own costs in staff cases under article 70 of the Rules of Procedure (see para. 17–19 below), those costs include the expenses of all witnesses who are officials of that institution giving evidence as officials of that institution, even if evidence was against the interests of the institution and in favour of the applicant. This was decided in Joined Cases 19 and 65/63 *Prakash* v. *Commission* [1965] E.C.R. 533, 561–562 and confirmed in Case 34/65 *Mosthaf* v. *Commission* [1966] E.C.R. 521, 532. On the other hand, in Case 43/74 *Guillot* v. *Commission* [1977] E.C.R. 1309, 1338, although the Commission was ordered to pay its own costs, the unsuccessful applicant was ordered to bear the costs of hearing the witnesses, apparently on the grounds that the witnesses were only called because the applicant's account of the facts conflicted with that put forward by the Commission, and his account ultimately was not accepted by the Court.

B. EXAMINATION OF WITNESSES

1. *Before the European Court*

EEC Statute of the Court

Article 23

6–23　Witnesses may be heard under conditions laid down in the rules of procedure.

Article 25

Witnesses and experts may be heard on oath taken in the form laid down in the rules of procedure or in the manner laid down by the law of the country of the witness or expert.

Article 29

During the hearings the Court may examine the experts, the witnesses and the parties themselves. The latter, however, may address the Court only through their representatives.

Article 30

Minutes shall be made of each hearing and signed by the President and the Registrar.

(Articles 24, 26, 30 and 31 of the Euratom Statute of the Court, and articles 27 and 28(2) and (3) of the ECSC Statute are in similar terms).

Rules of Procedure

Article 47

6–24 4. After the identity of each witness has been established, the President shall inform him that he will be required to vouch the truth of his evidence in the manner laid down in these rules.

The witness shall give his evidence to the Court, the parties having been given notice to attend. After the witness has given his main evidence the President may, at the request of a party or of his own motion, put questions to him.

The other Judges and the Advocate-General may do likewise.

Subject to the control of the President, questions may be put to witnesses by the representatives of the parties.

5. After giving his evidence, the witness shall take the following oath:

"I swear that I have spoken the truth, the whole truth and nothing but the truth."

The Court may, after hearing the parties, exempt a witness from taking the oath.

6. The Registrar shall draw up minutes in which the evidence of each witness is reproduced. The minutes shall be signed by the witness and by the Registrar. They shall constitute an official record.

Article 48

1. Witnesses who have been duly summoned shall obey the summons and attend for examination.

2. . . . .[imposes penalties].

Article 53

1. The Registrar shall draw up minutes of every hearing. The minutes shall be signed by the President and by the Registrar and shall constitute an official record.

2. The parties may inspect the minutes and any expert's report at the Registry and obtain copies at their own expense.

Article 110

1. The President shall instruct any person who is required to take an oath before the Court, as witness or expert, to tell the truth or to carry out his task conscientiously and impartially, as the case may be, and shall warn him of the criminal liability provided for in his national law in the event of any breach of this duty.

2. The witness shall take the oath either in accordance with the first subparagraph of Article 47(5) or in the manner laid down by his national law.

Where his national law provides the opportunity to make, in judicial proceedings, a solemn affirmation equivalent to an oath as well as or instead of taking an oath, the witness may make such an affirmation under the conditions and in the form prescribed in his national law.

Where his national law provides neither for taking an oath nor for making a solemn affirmation, the procedure described in paragraph 1 shall be followed.

6–25   To judge from the weight given to the matter in the Rules of Procedure, the fundamental characteristic of a witness is that he gives evidence on oath or by a solemn affirmation. It may, however, be doubted whether in practice the Court gives any less weight to unsworn written statements, as in Joined Cases 19 and 65/63 *Prakash* v. *Commission* [1965] E.C.R. 533, 555, or to unsworn statements by parties, as in Case 102/75 *Petersen* v. *Commission* [1976] E.C.R. 1777. In any event, the possibility of making a solemn affirmation rather than swearing an oath, recognised in article 110 of the Rules of Procedure, was introduced into the Rules in 1974 apparently out of respect for Danish scruples in the matter.

What appears to be envisaged in article 47(4) and (6) is that the witness will make a statement on the matter on which he was asked to give evidence, and that there should be a written record of that statement to be entered in the file of the case. The importance of this written record is heightened by the fact that even in cases heard by the Full Court the preparatory inquiry will normally be conducted by a Chamber (see para. 5–06 above) and the witness will therefore have been seen and heard only by three of the judges, so that personal impression may count for relatively little. This view is reinforced by the fact that the previous version of article 47(6) of the Rules, requiring the drawing-up of minutes of the evidence of each witness, used to be applied so as to require the Registrar to take down a long-hand summary of what the witness said, a procedure likely to discourage vigorous questioning, the witness being required to read out and sign this summary, which had also to be signed by the President (normally of the Chamber) or Judge Rapporteur as well as by the Registrar. However, in the *Sugar Cases* [1975] E.C.R. 1663, where the witnesses were examined by the Second Chamber although the case was heard by the Full Court, Lord Mackenzie Stuart as President of the Second Chamber made an innovation which has subsequently become the universal practice: he took advantage of the fact that everything that is said in open court in the European Court is recorded on tape, and ordered that the recordings of what the witnesses said should be immediately transcribed and that each witness should then sign the transcript of the recording. The sheerly administrative nature of the preparation of such a transcript is emphasised by the fact that article 47(6) of the Rules was amended in 1979 to define the drawing-up of the minutes as being the responsibility of the Registrar, who is the only officer of the Court whose signature is now required.

6–26   A further obstacle to direct questioning arose from the fact that between 1959 and 1974 the Rules of Procedure only provided for questions to be put to the witness through the Court. Since 1974, article

47(6) of the Rules has stated that subject to the control of the President, questions may be put to the witnesses by the representatives of the parties, thus restoring the position which originally existed under article 42 of the 1953 Rules of Procedure. Although it is still usual for the questions to be put for the most part by the President of the Chamber or by the Judge Rapporteur, it is not unknown (or indeed prohibited) for a witness to be led through his evidence by counsel. Furthermore, since all witnesses are the Court's witnesses then, as has been mentioned, any clear distinction between examination-in-chief and cross-examination disappears. The real problem encountered in examining witnesses before the European Court remains however that of language. If there is a witness who cannot speak the same language as the lawyer examining him, then the cross-examination, if such it is meant to be, is likely to lose some of its edge, however good the interpretation. Similarly, even if the lawyer and the witness speak the same language, that language may not be understood by the judges of the Chamber conducting the preparatory inquiry, so that the witness may feel that every nuance of what he is saying is not fully conveyed by the interpretation. Hence, in Case 102/75 *Petersen* v. *Commission* [1976] E.C.R. 1777, where the language of the case was Danish, evidence (using that term to cover statement by a party) was given in English, even though the command of that language of the person involved was not perfect.

With regard to the admissibility of oral evidence, there are no stated rules of evidence as such, and there would appear to be no reason why the basic test of credibility enounced in the *Sugar Cases* [1975] E.C.R. 1663, 1940 with regard to documentary evidence should not apply also to oral evidence, even if in other systems it would be classified as hearsay or *res inter alios*. The Court there said "there is no reason why the . . . Court should not accept as evidence of any undertaking's conduct correspondence exchanged between third parties provided that the content thereof is credible to the extent to which it refers to the said conduct."

2. By Letters Rogatory

EEC Statute of the Court

Article 26

6–27   The Court may order that a witness or expert be heard by the judicial authority of his place of permanent residence.

The order shall be sent for implementation to the competent judicial authority under conditions laid down in the rules of procedure. The documents drawn up in compliance with the letters rogatory shall be returned to the Court under the same conditions.

The Court shall defray the expenses, without prejudice to the right to charge them, where appropriate, to the parties.

(Article 27 of the Euratom Statute of the Court is in identical terms; the ECSC Statute contains no corresponding provision).

Rules of Procedure

Article 52

6–28   The Court may, on application by a party or of its own motion, issue letters rogatory for the examination of witnesses or experts, as provided for in the supplementary rules mentioned in Article 111 of these rules

Supplementary Rules

Article 1

6–29   Letters rogatory shall be issued in the form of an order which shall contain the names, forenames, description and address of the witness or expert, set out the facts on which the witness or expert is to be examined, name the parties, their agents, lawyers or advisers, indicate their addresses for service and briefly describe the subject matter of the dispute.

Notice of the order shall be served on the parties by the Registrar.

Article 2

The Registrar shall send the order to the competent authority named in Annex I of the Member State in whose territory the witness or expert is to be examined. Where necessary, the order shall be accompanied by a translation into the official languages of the Member State to which it is addressed.

The authority named pursuant to the first paragraph shall pass on the order to the judicial authority which is competent according to its national law.

The competent judicial authority shall give effect to the letters rogatory in accordance with its national law. After implementation the competent judicial authority shall transmit to the authority named pursuant to the first paragraph the order embodying the letters rogatory, any documents arising from the implementation and a detailed statement of costs. These documents shall be sent to the Registrar of the Court.

The Registrar shall be responsible for the translation of the documents into the language of the case.

Article 3

The Court shall defray the expenses occasioned by the letters rogatory without prejudice to the right to charge them where appropriate to the parties.

ANNEX 1

List referred to in the first paragraph of Article 2

Belgium
  The Minister of Justice

Denmark
  The Minister of Justice

France
  The Minister of Justice

Germany
  The Federal Minister of Justice

Greece
  The Minister of Justice

Ireland
  The Minister for Justice

Italy
  The Minister of Justice

Luxembourg
  The Minister of Justice

Netherlands
  The Minister of Justice

United Kingdom
  The Secretary of State

Instructions to the Registrar

Article 21

3. The Registrar shall order the cashier of the Court to refund the costs of letters rogatory payable in accordance with Article 3 of the Supplementary Rules to the authority designated by the competent authority referred to in Article 2 of those rules, in the currency of the State concerned against proof of payment.

6–30   The detail with which the rules on letters rogatory are drafted, and the complexity of the system they create, would appear to be in inverse proportion to the use actually made of them. The aim of these rules is to provide a method by which sworn evidence can be obtained from a witness without requiring the physical presence of the witness in Luxembourg. In most cases, however, that aim can be achieved much more simply, insofar as one of the parties wishes the witness to give evidence, by obtaining an affidavit from the witness and annexing it to the written pleadings (see, *e.g.* Case 42/75 *Delvaux* v. *Commission* [1976] E.C.R. 167, 179), and indeed the Court may even accept an unsworn written statement as in Joined Cases 19 and 65/63 *Prakash* v. *Commission* [1965] E.C.R. 533, 555. This case also illustrates a problem which the rules on letters rogatory as drafted cannot resolve. These rules only allow letters rogatory to be issued to the competent authority of a Member State, whereas in practice there is normally little difficulty, except in cases of physical incapacity, in obtaining the presence in Luxembourg of a witness resident in a Member State. On the other hand, in *Prakash*, the absent witness was resident in the United States of America, and the Court allowed an unsworn written statement in the form of a letter from the witness to be used in the proceedings.

C. SANCTIONS

EEC Statute of the Court

Article 24

6–31   With respect to defaulting witnesses the Court shall have the powers generally granted to courts and tribunals and may impose pecuniary penalties under conditions laid down in the rules of procedure.

Article 27

A Member State shall treat any violation of an oath by a witness or expert in the same manner as if the offence had been committed before one of its courts with jurisdiction in civil proceedings. At the instance of the Court, the Member State concerned shall prosecute the offender before its competent court.

(Articles 25 and 28 of the Euratom Statute of the Court, and article 28(4) and (5) of the ECSC Statute, are in similar terms).

Rules of Procedure

Article 48

2. If a witness who has been duly summoned fails to appear before the Court,

the Court may impose upon him a pecuniary penalty not exceeding 250 EMA units of account and may order that a further summons be served on the witness at his own expense.

The same penalty may be imposed upon a witness who, without good reason, refuses to give evidence or to take the oath or where appropriate to make a solemn affirmation in lieu thereof.

3. If a witness upon whom a penalty has been imposed proffers a valid excuse to the Court, the penalty may be cancelled.

4. Penalties imposed and other measures ordered under this Article shall be enforced in accordance with Articles 44 and 92 of the ECSC Treaty, Articles 187 and 192 of the EEC Treaty and Articles 159 and 164 of the Euratom Treaty.

(These Treaty provisions relate to the enforcement by national authorities of judgments of the European Court.)

Article 110

1. The President shall instruct any person who is required to take an oath before the Court, as witness or expert, to tell the truth or to carry out his task conscientiously and impartially, as the case may be, and shall warn him of the criminal liability provided for in his national law in the event of any breach of this duty.

Supplementary Rules

Article 6

6–32   The Court, after hearing the Advocate-General, may decide to report to the competent authority referred to in Annex III of the Member State, whose courts have penal jurisdiction in any case of perjury on the part of a witness or expert before the Court, account being taken of the provisions of Article 110 of the Rules of Procedure.

Article 7

The Registrar shall be responsible for communicating the Decision of the Court.

The Decision shall set out the facts and circumstances on which the report is based.

European Communities Act 1972

6–33   **11.**—(1) A person who, in sworn evidence before the European Court, makes any statement which he knows to be false or does not believe to be true shall, whether he is a British subject or not, be guilty of an offence and may be proceeded against and punished—

(a) In England and Wales as for an offence against section 1(1) of the Perjury · Act 1911; or

(b) in Scotland as for an offence against section 1 of the False Oaths (Scotland) Act 1933; or

(c) in Northern Ireland as for an offence against section 1(1) of the Perjury Act (Northern Ireland) 1946.

Where a report is made as to any such offence under the authority of the European Court, then a bill of indictment for the offence may, in England or

ANNEX III
List referred to in Article 6

Belgium
The Minister of Justice

Denmark
The Minister of Justice

France
The Minister of Justice

Germany
The Federal Minister of Justice

Greece
The Minister of Justice

Ireland
The Attorney General

Italy
The Minister of Justice

Luxembourg
The Minister of Justice

Netherlands
The Minister of Justice

United Kingdom
Her Majesty's Attorney General, for witnesses or experts resident in England or Wales

Her Majesty's Advocate, for witnesses or experts resident in Scotland

Her Majesty's Attorney General, for witnesses or experts resident in Northern Ireland

Wales or in Northern Ireland, be preferred as in a case where a prosecution is ordered under section 9 of the Perjury Act 1911 or section 8 of the Perjury Act (Northern Ireland) 1946, but the report shall not be given in evidence on a person's trial for the offence.

6–34   The Statutes and the Rules of Procedure distinguish between, on the one hand, failure by a witness to appear, refusal by a witness to give evidence and refusal to take the oath or solemn affirmation, and on the other hand perjury by a witness. In the former cases the Court itself may impose a penalty, although like any other judgment of the European Court, it will ultimately be enforced by the national authorities, whereas in the latter case the European Court may only report the matter to the competent national authorities, the prosecution of the offender and imposition of any penalty being treated as a matter of national law. The distinction may well derive from the fact that in the case of perjury it is envisaged that physical sanctions rather than merely pecuniary ones may be imposed upon an offender, and the European Court itself has no powers of imprisonment: indeed, article 9(1) of the 1954 Supplementary Rules (O.J. 1954, p.302), authorising the Court to impose penalties on witnesses for failure to appear, refusal to give evidence or refusal to take the oath, expressly stated that, although the penalties were to be derived from national legislation, imprisonment was excluded. In any event, the provisions governing perjury have not so far been used.

6–35   The maximum penalty for failure to appear or refusal to give evidence or to take the oath was fixed at 250 EMA units of account in the 1959

Rules. The unit of account of the European Monetary Agreement (EMA), which succeeded the European Payments Union at the end of 1958, corresponded to the gold value of the U.S. dollar and was converted at official parities. Following the demise of the EMA at the end of 1972 in the wake of the general floating of currencies, this unit of account became totally artificial, but article 48(2) has not been formally amended—perhaps because of its lack of use in practice. On the literal reading, however, it may be doubted whether it has been replaced by the European Monetary System unit of account (ECU) used generally in the Communities, since Council Regulation 3308/80 on the replacement of the European unit of account by the ECU in Community legal instruments (O.J. 1980, C345/1) applied on the face of it only to legal instruments which already referred to the European unit of account (EUA) based on the value of a "basket" of currencies and used originally in the context of the first Lomé Convention.

It might finally be observed that even in theory, the European Court only has power to sanction defaulting witnesses, and that a failure to produce documentary evidence may, under article 21 of the EEC Statute and corresponding provisions in the other Statutes, only result in formal note being taken of such failure. The only real sanction here is likely to be the failure of any argument which relies on that documentary evidence, as in Case 19/77 *Miller* v. *Commission* [1978] E.C.R. 131 where the Court refused to reduce a fine alleged to be excessive in relation to the applicant's profit margins, after the applicant had refused to produce its accounts, which would have allowed this allegation to be verified.

EXPERTS

EEC Statute of the Court

Article 22

6–36   The Court may at any time entrust any individual, body, authority, committee or other organization it chooses with the task of giving an expert opinion.

(Article 23 of the European Statute of the Court and article 25 of the ECSC Statute are in similar terms.)

Article 25

(Hearing on oath—see para. 6–23 above.)

Article 26

(Letters rogatory—see para. 6–23 above.)

Article 27

(Violation of oath—see para. 6–31 above.)

Article 29

(Examination by Court—see para. 6–23 above.)

207

Rules of Procedure
Article 49

6–37
1. The Court may order that an expert's report be obtained. The order appointing the expert shall define his task and set a time limit within which he is to make his report.

2. The expert shall receive a copy of the order, together with all the documents necessary for carrying out his task. He shall be under the supervision of the Judge-Rapporteur, who may be present during his investigation and who shall be kept informed of his progress in carrying out his task.

3. At the request of the expert, the Court may order the examination of witnesses. Their examination shall be carried out in accordance with Article 47 of these rules.

4. The expert may give his opinion only on points which have been expressly referred to him

5. After the expert has made his report, the Court may order that he be examined, the parties having been given notice to attend

Subject to the control of the President, questions may be put to the expert by the representatives of the parties.

6. After making his report, the expert shall take the following oath before the Court:

"I swear that I have conscientiously and impartially carried out my task"

The Court may, after hearing the parties, exempt the expert from taking the oath.

Article 50

(Objections to witness or expert, and refusal to give evidence or take oath—see para. 6–19 above.)

Article 51

1. . . . (Expenses—see para. 6–19 above.)
2. Witnesses shall be entitled to compensation for loss of earnings, and experts to fees for their services.

The cashier of the Court shall pay witnesses and experts their compensation or fees after they have carried out their respective duties or tasks.

Article 52

(Letters rogatory—see para. 6–28 above.)

Article 110

2. The witness shall take the oath either in accordance with the first subparagraph of Article 47(5) or in the manner laid down by his national law.

Where his national law provides the opportunity to make, in judicial proceedings, a solemn affirmation equivalent to an oath as well as or instead of taking an oath, the witness may make such an affirmation under the conditions and in the form prescribed in his national law.

Where his national law provides neither for taking an oath nor for making a solemn affirmation, the procedure described in paragraph 1 shall be followed.

3. Paragraph 2 shall apply *mutatis mutandis* to experts, a reference to the first subparagraph of Article 49(6) replacing in this case the reference to the first subparagraph of Article 47(5) of these Rules of Procedure.

Supplementary Rules

Articles 1, 2 and 3

6–38   (Letters rogatory—see para. 6–29 above.)

Articles 6 and 7

(Reports of perjury—see para. 6–32 above.)

Instructions to the Registrar

Article 21

1. and 2. (Advance payments—see para. 6–20 above.)
3. (Costs of letters rogatory—see para. 6–30 above.)

6–39   The rules governing experts are for the most part identical with those governing witnesses. Apart from the rather technical points that an expert is paid a fee rather than compensation for loss of earnings under article 51 of the Rules of Procedure, and that no fixed penalty is envisaged in article 48 of those Rules with regard to a refusal by an expert to give evidence, to take the oath or to make a solemn affirmation (although the Court may still take a decision under article 50(1)), the chief exceptions relate to the appointment of experts, the preparation of their reports, and the exercise of other powers specific to them.

Although article 50 of the Rules allows a party to object to an expert, there is no express provision enabling a party to request the appointment of an expert. Nevertheless, it would appear from Case 51/65 *ILFO* v. *.H.A.* [1966] E.C.R. 87, 96 that the Court will accede to a party's request for the appointment of an expert where evidence is offered to justify such a measure: this was not forthcoming in that case. Such a request was, however, acceded to in Case 785/79 *Pizziolo* v. *Commission* [1981] E.C.R. 969. On the other hand, as with other evidence, there is nothing (except expense) to prevent a party commissioning its own expert's report on a particular matter which is then annexed to its written pleadings. In Joined Cases 19 and 20/74 *Kali und Salz and Kali-Chemie* v. *Commission* [1975] E.C.R. 499, for example, the applicant put forward an expert's report on the interchangeability of straight potash fertilizers and compound potash fertilizers, and a report of a geological expert on the probable duration of the life of one of Kali-Chemie's potash mines, in the context of an agreement whereby Kali und Salz marketed part of Kali-Chemie's production of potash. It can indeed happen that the Court will appoint experts in a case in which a party has already produced its own experts' opinion. In Case 48/69 *ICI* v. *Commission* [1972] E.C.R. 619, which involved concerted practices in the dyestuffs industry, the applicant annexed to its application, *inter alia,* a report by two professors from the University of Basle on the European dyestuffs industry, but the Court ordered an expert's report essentially on the questions whether a dyestuffs producer could in practice have increased prices on a variable basis in relation to each customer and product, and whether dyestuffs other than speciality dyes were in practice interchangeable. The form of order (p. 647) invited the parties to propose the name of an agreed expert by a fixed date, and the parties in fact proposed the appointment of two experts, professors respectively at the Universities of Bonn and Tübingen.

6–40   Experts have in fact been appointed in very few cases, but they appear largely to have been employed either with regard to questions of economic analysis or with regard to matters requiring scientific knowledge (usually under the Euratom Treaty). The *ICI dyestuffs* case falls clearly within the former category, as do, for example, Joined Cases 24 and 34/58 *Chambre Syndicale de la Sidérurgie de l'Est de la France.* v. *H.A.* [1960] E.C.R. 281. There, the French applicants sought the annulment of a High Authority decision upholding certain German railway tariffs for the carriage of mineral fuels for the iron and steel industry; in the view of the applicants these tariffs offered preferential rates to German iron and steel undertakings, and in particular they challenged the High Authority's assertion that the tariffs were justified on grounds of competition. In order to investigate the facts on which these assertions were based, the Court appointed the Director of the Central Office for International Railway Transport in Berne, a person agreed upon by all the parties, to prepare a report on the matter: he in fact found that there was actual or potential competition from inland waterways, but that certain of the tariffs were not correctly aligned on the internal waterways rates, a view which the Court stated it adopted as its own. Questions of scientific knowledge have usually arisen in Euratom staff cases. In Joined Cases 19 and 65/63 *Prakash* v. *EAEC Commission* [1965] E.C.R. 533, where the applicant alleged that the apparatus and laboratory space at his disposal were insufficient for him to begin the experiments he was asked to carry out, the First Chamber stated that it was not for the Court to decide whether or not a particular set of apparatus was sufficient for undertaking a given piece of research and that, if necessary, it would have to appoint an expert for that purpose. However, anticipating the rule stated in Case 51/65 *ILFO* v. *H.A.* [1966] E.C.R. 87 with regard to a request by a party for the appointment of an expert, the First Chamber held that such a step could only be justified if the facts already proved raised a presumption in favour of the applicant's argument, since the general burden of proof rested with him. In Case 785/79 *Pizziolo* v. *Commission* [1981] E.C.R. 969, however, where a Euratom official who had been given a year's leave of absence and had not been re-employed thereafter by the Commission brought an action claiming, *inter alia*, that he should have been offered any one of a number of specified vacant posts, the Second Chamber decided that it was necessary to obtain an expert's report on the question whether the applicant had the necessary qualifications and aptitudes to take up these specific posts, (a measure which the applicant had in fact requested in his reply) since that question involved highly technical matters. Where the appointment of an expert is regarded as appropriate, it would appear that it may even be ordered as an interim measure, as in Case 318/81R *Commission* v. *Codemi* (order of April 28,

1982, O.J. C135/6), where an expert was appointed to inspect the progress of building work as an interim measure.

6–41   As a halfway house between the appointment of an expert by the Court and the production by a party of an expert's report as an annex to its pleadings, it is not unknown for an expert whose report was produced by a party to be called as a witness by the Court. In Case 43/74 *Guillot* v. *Commission* [1977] E.C.R. 1309, another Euratom case, where the accuracy of the results of certain experiments carried out by the applicant was at issue, the Commission had, during the course of its internal proceedure, instructed an independent research organisation to carry out an inquiry into these experiments, and its reports were annexed to the Commission's pleadings. Although A.G. Capotorti recognised that "the probative value of an investigation carried out extra-judicially is not, of course, the same as that of an inquiry directly ordered by the Court in the course of an action" (at p. 1347), one of the scientific officers of the research organisation was called as a witness by the Court, effectively to confirm the contents of that organisation's reports. In Case 261/78 *Interquell* v. *Council and Commission* (October 6, 1982), on the other hand, the experts who had investigated the applicant's production figures simply answered questions at the Hearing.

6–42   The expert evidence put forward by the parties themselves in the written procedure has not always been limited to economic or scientific questions; indeed, opinions of eminent lawyers have been annexed to the pleadings. In Case 48/69 *ICI* v. *Commission* [1972] E.C.R. 619, ICI annexed to its application an opinion by Professor R.Y.Jennings, Q.C., of Cambridge University, on the question whether, according to recognised principles of international law and practice, the Commission had jurisdiction to make a "cease and desist" order or to impose a fine on ICI, a company registered in a non-Member State. Incidentally, this does illustrate how the legal advice of a person who is not a lawyer entitled to practise before a court of a Member State (the United Kingdom not having been a Member State at that time) may be brought before the European Court in a direct action, even though by virtue of article 17 of the EEC Statute, such a person would not be able to represent a party in those proceedings.

INSPECTIONS

Rules of Procedure

Article 45

6–43   2. . . . , the following measures of inquiry may be adopted:
  (a) .. ..
  (b) .. ..
  (c) .. ..
  (d) .. ..
  (e) an inspection of the place or thing in question.

6–44   Inspection, or "descente sur les lieux" to use the more colourful French expression, has the distinction of being the least used of the measures of inquiry available under article 45. It normally involves the Members of the Court hearing the case, together with the representives of the parties, visiting a particular location, and appears only to have been used in cases under the ECSC Treaty where a manufacturing process or system of production was relevant to the legal issues. In Case 14/59 *Fonderies de Pont-àMousson* v. *H.A.*[1959] E.C.R. 215, the applicant sought exemption from the ferrous scrap equalisation levy, since the finished products made at its works were iron castings, which fell outside the scope of the ECSC Treaty and hence of the levy. However, producers of pig-iron fell within the scope of the Treaty and of the levy, and the applicant produced pig-iron in its own blast furnaces which was used directly in its molten state for the manufacture of iron castings. The applicant's argument was, in part, that it was not a "producer" of pig-iron since that was merely an intermediate product in the manufacture of iron castings. Before deciding this point, the Court inspected the applicant's works at Pont-à-Mousson in order to see its manufacturing process for itself; it concluded, however, that an intermediate and even short-lived product could fall within the scope of the Treaty, adding that there was no evidence that the applicant's pig-iron could be used only for iron castings: it could have been marketed in lumps or blocks or even in its molten state.

6–45   Similarly, the degree of integration was relevant in Joined Cases 42 and 49/59 *SNUPAT* v. *H.A.* [1961] E.C.R. 53. Under the rules governing the ferrous scrap equalisation scheme, a levy was payable on "bought scrap" but not on scrap which was "own resources"; the applicant sought to challenge a decision, which had exempted a Dutch undertaking and an Italian undertaking fron the levy on the basis that they and their ferrous scrap suppliers were in a state of "local integration." These two undertakings both intervened in the action, and the Court decided to inspect their factories. However, the case was decided on a point of law, in that, however great their economic interdependence, these undertakings and their ferrous scrap suppliers were separate legal persons annd therefore the scrap could not be regarded as the "own resources" of the undertakings.

PRIVILEGE AND CONFIDENTIALITY

EEC Statute of the Court

Article 21

6–46   The Court may require the parties to produce all documents and to supply all information which the Court considers desirable. Formal note shall be taken of any refusal.

The Court may also require the Member States and institutions not being parties to the case to supply all information which the Court considers necessary for the proceedings.

212

(Article 22 of the Euratom Statute of the Court and article 24 of the ECSC Statute are in similar terms.)

ECSC Statute of the Court

Article 23

Where proceedings are instituted against a decision of one of the institutions of the Community, that institution shall transmit to the Court all the documents relating to the case before the Court.

(There is no corresponding provision in the EEC and Euratom Statutes, although article 26 of the Staff Regulations requires the personal file of an official to be forwarded to the Court if an action concerning that official is brought before the Court. Nonetheless, it would appear to be normal practice in actions involving *individual* decisions under the EEC Treaty, notably in the area of competition law, for the file to be forwarded to the Court.)

Rules of Procedure

Article 93

1, 2 and 3. . . . (Relate to applications to intervene.)
4. If the Court allows the intervention, the intervener shall receive a copy of every document served on the parties. The Court may, however, on application by one of the parties, omit secret or confidential documents.

6–47   Although the terms "privilege" and "confidentiality" do not yet appear to have acquired precise technical meanings in proceedings before the European Court, two distinct problems can be identified. The first arises when a party wishes to produce certain evidence or information, but does not wish it to be disclosed to other parties (here referred to as "confidentiality"), and the second arises when a party or witness is requested or ordered by the Court to produce certain information or evidence, whether or not at the behest of another party, and claims to be legally entitled not to produce that information or evidence (here referred to as "privilege" although of course it may well be that a claim of privilege rests upon the alleged confidentiality of the information at issue. In both cases the Court is faced with a conflict between the protection of confidential or privileged information and the principle that judicial decisions should be based on material of which the parties have been able to take cognisance (Joined Cases 42 and 49/59 *SNUPAT* v. *H.A.* [1961] E.C.R. 53, 84). The Court's Statutes clearly favour disclosure, but the Court's own approach has altered over the years.

6–48   With regard to confidentiality, in the *SNUPAT* case, an intervener wished to rely on the terms of a contract between itself and another undertaking, but did not wish its terms to be disclosed to the applicant or the other intervener, who were its competitors. Although the intervener was willing to make the contract available to "any person bound by professional secrecy" in the presence if need be of the Judge Rapporteur, the Court held quite simply that "it would infringe a basic principle of law to base a judicial decision on facts and documents of which the parties themselves, or one of them, have not been able to take cognizance and in relation to which they have not therefore been able to formulate an opinion." Since it was the intervener itself which relied on the contract, the Court refused to *order* its production, and simply held that the intervener had failed to adduce proof of its allegations. On the other hand, in Case 119/77 *NSK* v. *Council and Commission* [1979] E.C.R. 1303, where an application to intervene by the Federation of European Bearing Manufacturers' Associations was opposed by the applicants on the grounds, *inter alia*, of the confidentiality of many of the facts likely to be placed before the Court, the intervention was allowed by an order dated November 16, 1977 which stated in its final recital that "if any confidential information is produced as evidence in the course of the proceedings, the applicants are empowered to request that such information shall not be communicated to the intervener." This ruling has now been given legislative effect in the amended article 93(4) of the Rules of Procedure. In its order of March 30, 1982 in Case 236/81 *Celanese Chemical* v. *Council and Commission* (O.J.1982, C127/3), where it was held that certain documents could be treated as confidential, in the sense of being revealed only to the principle parties and the Court's officers, either where the parties agreed on the status of the documents or the President so determined after examination of them, the Court did however state that such documents must be excluded from the file completely insofar as their confidentiality would conflict with the requirement that the Court should give a public statement of reasons for its judgments. In other words, a judgment cannot be based on confidential information. There has been no clear statement as to how far the *SNUPAT* principle remains in force where it is sought to prevent disclosure of confidential information to parties other than an intervener. An analogy may perhaps be sought from the Court's view of the manner in which the Commission should conduct competition proceedings: in Case 85/76 *Hoffmann-La Roche* v. *Commission* [1979] E.C.R. 461, the Court held that the commission may not use, to the detriment of undertakings involved in competition proceedings, facts, circumstances or documents which it cannot in its view disclose, "if such a refusal of disclosure adversely affects the undertaking's opportunity to make known effectively its views on the truth or implications of these circumstances, on those documents or again on the conclusions drawn by the Commission from them." Adopting this to procedure before the Court, it might be suggested that it leads to an adaption of the *SNUPAT* principle so that the use of undisclosed information is not absolutely prohibited but prohibited only insofar as it prevents the proper presentation of the other party's case, *i.e.* minor deletions would be permitted.

6–49   Claims for privilege encountered before the European Court can loosely be classified into three main categories—institutional, medical and legal professional privilege. In principle the Statutes require the Community institutions to produce any relevant information in their possession either of their own initiative or when ordered by the Court, but the Court has been prepared to recognise a limited degree of protection from disclosure where protection of confidential information is required for the proper functioning of the institution. The problem was discussed in one of the earliest judgments in Case 2/54 *Italy* v. *H.A.* [1954–56] E.C.R. 37, 54–55, where the Court held that under article 23 of the ECSC Statute, the High Authority could be required to produce both its minutes and those of the Council of Ministers relating to the case, but that it was willing to authorise the names of the speakers to be omitted and to order the documents to be examined *in camera;* nonetheless it was held not to be necessary to order the production of the minutes in that case.

The question of privilege for a whole document was considered in Case 110/75 *Mills* v. *European Investment Bank* [1976] E.C.R. 1613. There, the Bank was ordered by the Court to produce a report on the applicant's superior; eventually, after the Court insisted, it was produced but the Bank indicated that it did not wish to have it disclosed to the applicant or his legal advisers. A.G. Warner discussed the matter in some detail in his Opinion (at pp. 1634–1635) and suggested, as the House of Lords decided with regards to claims of "Crown privilege" in *Conway* v. *Rimmer* [1968] A.C. 910, that in cases where there was doubt as to whether a document should be disclosed, the Court itself should look at the document to see whether its evidentiary value outweighed the harm that its disclosure might do. It appears from the Opinion that the report was in fact seen by the Members of the First Chamber hearing the case and by A.G. Warner, and his own conclusion was that the report added nothing to what was known from other evidence and that justice did not therefore require its disclosure. This view would appear to have been followed by the First Chamber.

6–50   Claims of privilege by medical witnesses were encountered in Case 155/78*M.* v. *Commission* [1980] E.C.R. 1797. Effectively, the applicant in this case was challenging the finding of a medical board composed of three medical officers of the Commission that she was unfit to take up a post with the Commission, apparently on psychological or psychiatric grounds. The Second Chamber ordered the doctors who had examined the applicant to appear as witnesses, hearing them *in camera.* However, they refused to give any information concerning the conduct of their examination of the applicant, relying on "the confidentiality of medical findings," even though the applicant formally released them from their obligation to observe it. The Second Chamber thereupon requested the Commission to carry out a comparative study of the confidentiality of medical findings in the law of the Member States, and concluded that such confidentiality ceases to be protected where the person concerned has given his consent, where the doctor's involvement is in the context of administrative checking procedures, and where reliance on such confidentiality would have the result of obstructing the normal course of justice. In this case the applicant had given her consent and the examinations had been carried out in an administrative recruitment procedure, so that confidentiality was not protected. The Second Chamber then penalised the doctors' refusal to give information as to

215

the conduct of their examinations by formally holding that this refusal had the result of making it impossible for the Court to carry out the judicial review entrusted to it and by thereupon annulling the Commission's implied decision rejecting the applicant's complaint against the medical board's finding

6–51   Questions of legal professional privilege have not been raised directly in proceedings before the European Court, but in Case 155/79 *A.M. & S.* v. *Commission* (May 18, 1982), the Court was faced with an application for the annulment of a Commission decision requiring the applicant to produce certain documents which it had failed to produce after an on-the-spot investigation under the competition rules, claiming that these documents were "covered by the doctrine of legal privilege"; they included solicitors' instructions to counsel, communications between an outside solicitor and A.M. & S. or one of its parent companies containing legal advice or requests for legal advice, documents containing legal advice or requests for legal advice from an "in-house" lawyer employed by A.M. & S. or by one of its parent companies, and communications between executives of A.M. & S. or one of its parent companies recording legal advice or requests for legal advice. One point at issue in this case is of relevance to procedure before the Court itself rather than simply competition proceedings before the Commission is the very existence of a concept of "legal professional privilege" in Community law. The conclusion of the Court in this case was that what was common to the national laws of the Member States, and hence should be taken into account in Community law, was the protection of the confidentiality of written communications between lawyer and client provided that, on the one hand, such communications are made "for the purposes and in the interests of the client's rights of defence" and on the other hand "they emanate from independent lawyers, that is to say, lawyers who are not bound to the client by a relationship of employment," provided that such lawyer is "entitled to practise his profession in one of the Member States." The solution offered in this case, which was by an order dated February 4, 1981 to require, as a measure of inquiry, the production of the documents in question to the Court in sealed envelopes so that the Court might establish the precise status of the writers of the documents and of their recipients, the time and place at which they were drawn up, and adequate information as to the nature of their contents, would appear to be apposite to proceedings before the Court itself and analogous to the method by which a claim of institutional privilege was dealt with in Case 110/75 *Mills* v. *European Investment Bank* [1976] E.C.R. 1613. It would appear from the judgment in *A.M. & S.* that in the view of the Court, legal professional privilege, like medical privilege, exists for the client, since it was stated that "the principle of confidentiality does not prevent a lawyer's client from disclosing the written communications between them if he considers that it is in his interests to do so."

CHAPTER 7

ORAL PROCEDURE

NATURE OF ORAL PROCEDURE

EEC Statute of the Court

Article 18

7–01   The oral procedure shall consist of the reading of the report presented by a judge acting as Rapporteur, the hearing by the Court of agents, advisers and lawyers entitled to practise before a court of a Member State and of the submissions of the Advocate-General, as well as the hearing, if any, of witnesses and experts.

(Article 18 (last paragraph) of the Euratom Statute and article 21 (last paragraph) of the ECSC Statute are in similar terms.)

Rules of Procedure

Article 54

Unless the Court prescribes a period within which the parties may lodge written observations, the President shall fix the date for the opening of the oral procedure after the preparatory inquiry has been completed.

Where a period had been prescribed for the lodging of written observations, the President shall fix the date for the opening of the oral procedure after that period has expired.

Article 55

1. Subject to the priority of decisions provided for in Article 85 of these rules, the Court shall deal with the cases before it, in the order in which the preparatory inquiries in them have been completed. Where the preparatory inquiries in several cases are completed simultaneously, the order in which they are to be dealt with shall be determined by the dates of entry in the register of the applications originating them respectively.

The President may in special circumstances order that a case be given priority over others.

2. On a joint application by the parties the President may order that a case in which the preparatory inquiry has been completed be deferred. In the absence of agreement between the parties the President shall refer the matter to the Court for a decision.

(Article 85 relates to applications for interim measures.)

7–02   On the face of it, there is a clear incompatibility between the drafting

217

of article 18 of the Statute and article 54 of the Rules of Procedure. The Statute expressly includes the hearing of witnesses and experts in its definition of the oral procedure, whereas the Rules of Procedure treat the oral procedure as a separate stage beginning after the completion of the preparatory inquiries, which are defined in article 45(2) of the Rules as including the hearing of witnesses and experts. This dichotomy has existed ever since the adoption of the original Rules of Procedure in 1953: article 21 of the ECSC Statute was in similar terms to article 18 of the EEC Statute, whereas articles 35 to 45 of the 1953 Rules treated the hearing of experts and witnesses as part of the preparatory inquiries and separate from the oral procedure. Indeed, article 45(1) of the 1953 Rules was more definite than the current article 54, in that it required the Court to allow the parties to lodge written observations at the end of the preparatory inquiry before fixing the date of the opening of the oral procedure, thus marking a clear break between the two, whereas the current article 54 merely allows this to be done (although it remains the normal practice).

7–03   The basic rule actually followed by the Court is that the preparatory inquiry, including the hearing of witnesses and experts, is separate from the oral procedure, which consists of the presentation of the Report for the hearing, oral argument before the Court, and the delivery of an Opinion by the Advocate-General. Thus in the *Sugar Cases* [1975] E.C.R. 1663, it is reported (at p. 1694) that the witnesses were heard by the Second Chamber about one month before oral argument was heard by the Full Court. Nevertheless, in practice the strictness of the separation between these stages in the procedure depends very much upon the complexity and nature of the case, and in relatively straightforward cases in which there is an issue of fact, particularly in staff cases, it is normal for the witnesses to be heard on the same day (and at the same time) as that set for the hearing of oral argument. As an example of this, in Case 188/73 *Grassi* v. *Council* [1974] E.C.R. 1099, the Court issued an order (at p. 1102) formally deciding "to fix the hearing of the witnesses for the day . . . set for the oral procedure." Similarly, in Case 102/75 *Petersen* v. *Commission* [1976] E.C.R. 1777, the Court decided to order the personal appearance of the applicant, and also hear a witness, at the time set for the oral argument. Indeed, bearing in mind that the Court may, under article 60 of the Rules, order any measure of inquiry at any time (see para. 7–46 below), there are instances where, after having decided to open the oral procedure without preparatory inquiry, the Court has changed its mind during the hearing. In Case 34/77 *Oslizlok* v. *Commission* [1978] E.C.R. 1099, it is reported (at p. 1101) that the Court decided to open the oral procedure without holding any preparatory inquiry, but that the applicant's former Director-General gave evidence during the oral procedure (at p. 1112). It would appear that the witness was in the party accompanying the Commission's legal representative at the hearing, and that, in the light of the oral argument, it was decided, with the consent of counsel, that it would be useful to hear him on certain specific matters. In Case 261/78 *Interquell* v. *Council and Commission* (October 6, 1982), on the other

218

hand, the experts who had investigated the applicant's production figures simply answered questions at the Hearing. Where a witness is not so conveniently available, but it becomes clear from the information presented at the hearing that oral evidence should be taken, the Court may order the witnesses to be heard at a later date, after the hearing, but before the delivery of the Advocate-General's Opinion, as in Case 43/74 *Guillot* v. *Commission* [1977] E.C.R. 1309, 1323–1323.

7–04   Returning to the oral procedure *stricto sensu*, article 55 of the Rules sets out the simple rule that cases come on for hearing in the order in which preparatory inquiries are completed (although it would perhaps be more accurate to say in the order in which it is determined that preparatory inquiries are not necessary, under article 44(2) of the Rules). Where under this rule the cases would come on at the same time, they are dealt with according to the order of registration (see para. 4–07 above). However, under article 55(1) of the Rules, the President does have a certain discretion to accord priority to certain cases, and the practice of successive Presidents has been, at all stages of the procedure, to give priority to references for preliminary rulings so far as practicable, given that the national court which has made the reference will be unable to resolve the dispute before it until it has received the ruling of the European Court. This, of course, is subject to the absolute priority of applications for interim measures under article 85(3) of the Rules.

7–05   Although it is the normal practice in direct actions for the parties to present oral argument, there is no obligation to attend the hearing, unless the personal appearance of a party on that date has been ordered as a measure of inquiry. Hence, for example, in Case 121/76 *Moli* v. *Commission* [1977] E.C.R. 1971, 1976 the parties waived their right to submit oral observations at a hearing. In references for preliminary rulings it is not uncommon for the Commission's agent alone to attend the hearing. On the other hand, since there is no obligation to present written observations on references for preliminary rulings (see para. 4–112 above), it is clear that a failure to produce written observations does not preclude a party from appearing at the hearing to put his argument orally, as in Case 48/74 *Charmasson* v. *Minister for Economic Affairs* [1974] E.C.R. 1383, 1391, where Charmasson's case was put for the first time at the hearing. Similarly, on a reference for a preliminary ruling, there is nothing to prevent written observations submitted or prepared outside the two-month time-limit (see para. 4–119 above) being read out word for word at the hearing, if it is felt that would serve a useful purpose. In any event, in both types of action, it is only in exceptional cases that the parties tend to be present or represented at the delivery of the Advocate-General's Opinion, which is clearly part of the oral procedure as defined both in the Statutes and in the Rules of Procedure.

219

LEGAL REPRESENTATION

A. BASIC RULES

EEC Statute of the Court

Article 29

7–06   During the hearings the Court may examine the experts, the witnesses and the parties themselves. The latter, however, may address the Court only through their representatives.

(Article 30 of the Euratom Statute and article 28(3) of the ECSC Statute are in similar terms.)

Rules of Procedure

Article 58

A party may address the Court only through his agent, adviser or lawyer.

Article 104

2. As regards the representation and attendance of the parties to the main proceedings in the preliminary ruling procedure the Court shall take account of the rules of procedure of the national court or tribunal which made the reference.

7–07   Despite their apparent generality, article 29 of the EEC Statute and article 58 of the Rules of Procedure, requiring the parties to address the Court through their legal representatives, are clearly only appropriate to direct actions, and must be read subject to article 104(2). In fact, the rules governing legal representation in the oral procedure are the same as those prevailing in the written procedure: in direct actions, Member States and Community institutions must be represented by an agent, who may be assisted by an adviser or practising lawyer, and private litigants must be represented by a lawyer entitled to practise before a court of a Member State; in references for preliminary rulings, on the other hand, the rules governing representation before the national court making the reference apply. Hence a litigant in person or an unqualified adviser may appear before the European Court if they could appear before the relevant national court. Conversely, if the reference is from a national court before which only a limited category of lawyers has a right of audience, then the parties must be represented by such a lawyer if they wish to take part in any stage of the procedure. In so far as Member States, the Commission and the Council are entitled to submit observations and participate in the oral argument in references for preliminary rulings, even though they are not parties to the national proceedings, they are in practice represented by agents, who may be assisted by advisers or lawyers, as in direct actions.

7–08   The details of these rules governing representation are considered in the context of the written procedure (see para. 4–15 above). However, the rules governing the rights and obligations of legal representatives

220

are drafted in a manner which is peculiarly apposite to their physical attendance before the Court during the oral procedure. Hence their inclusion here.

B. RIGHTS AND OBLIGATIONS OF LEGAL REPRESENTATIVES

EEC Statute of the Court

Article 17

7–09   Such agents, advisers and lawyers shall, when they appear before the Court, enjoy the rights and immunities necessary to the independent exercise of their duties,under conditions laid down in the rules of procedure.

As regards such advisers and lawyers who appear before it, the Court shall have the powers normally accorded to courts of law, under conditions laid down in the rules of procedure.

University teachers being nationals of a Member State whose law accords them a right of audience shall have the same rights

Before the Court as are accorded by this Article to lawyers entitled to practise before a court of a Member State.

(Article 17 of the Euratom Statute and article 20 of the ECSC Statute are in similar terms.)

Rules of Procedure

Article 32

7–10   1. Agents representing a State or an institution, as well as advisers and lawyers, appearing before the Court or before any judical authority to whom the Court has addressed letters rogatory, shall enjoy immunity in respect of words spoken or written by them concerning the case or the parties.

2. Agents, advisers and lawyers shall enjoy the following further privileges and facilities:

    (a) papers and documents relating to the proceedings shall be exempt from both search and seizure; in the event of a dispute the customs officials or police may seal those papers and documents; they shall then be immediately forwarded to the Court for inspection in the presence of the Registrar and of the person concerned;

    (b) agents, advisers and lawyers shall be entitled to such allocation of foreign currency as may be necessary for the performance of their duties;

    (c) agents, advisers and lawyers shall be entitled to travel in the course of duty without hindrance.

Article 33

In order to qualify for the privileges, immunities and facilities specified in Article 32, persons entitled to them shall furnish proof of their status as follows:

    (a) agents shall produce an official document issued by the State or institution which they represent; a copy of this document shall be forwarded without delay to the Registrar by the State or institution concerned;

    (b) advisers and lawyers shall produce a certificate signed by the Registrar. The validity of this certificate shall be limited to a specified period, which may be extended or curtailed according to the length of the proceedings.

Article 34

The privileges, immunities and facilities specified in Article 32 of these rules are granted exclusively in the interests of the proper conduct of proceedings.

The Court may waive the immunity where it considers that the proper conduct of proceedings will not be hindered thereby.

Article 35

1. Any adviser or lawyer whose conduct towards the Court, a Chamber, a Judge, an Advocate-General or the Registrar is incompatible with the dignity of the Court, or who uses his rights for purposes other than those for which they were granted, may at any time be excluded from the proceedings by an order of the Court or Chamber, after the Advocate-General has been heard; the person concerned shall be given an opportunity to defend himself.

The order shall have immediate effect.

2. Where an adviser or lawyer is excluded from the proceedings, the proceedings shall be suspended for a period fixed by the President in order to allow the party concerned to appoint another adviser or lawyer.

3. Decisions taken under this Article may be rescinded.

Article 36

The provisions of this Chapter shall apply to university teachers who have a right of audience before the Court in accordance with Article 20 of the ESCS Statute and Articles 17 of the EEC and Euratom Statutes.

Instructions to the Registrar

Article 9

Certificates as provided for in Article 33(b) of the Rules of Procedure shall be delivered to the adviser or lawyer concerned if he so requests, where this step is required for the proper conduct of proceedings.

The certificates shall be drawn up by the Registrar.

Article 10

For the purposes of Article 32 of the Rules of Procedure, an extract from the cause list shall be transmitted in advance to the Minister of Foreign Affairs of the place where the Court is sitting.

7–11   The provisions contained in article 32 to 36 of the Rules of Procedure were originally introduced a year after the basic 1953 Rules of Procedure by the first set of Additional Rules of Procedure adopted in 1954 (J.O. 1954, p. 302). These also included the requirement that a lawyer should lodge a certificate of entitlement to practise before a court of a Member State, now contained in article 38 of the Rules, specifying the contents of an application commencing a direct action and the documents which must accompany such an application (see paras. 4–18 and 4–29 above). In fact, articles 32 to 36 of the Rules are still drafted so as to refer to the types of legal representative listed in article 17 of the Statute as having capacity to appear before the Court in direct actions, and although the vast majority of parties to references for preliminary rulings tend to be represented by practising lawyers, the situation of litigants in person or unqualified advisers having the right of audience on a reference is not dealt with expressly. It could be suggested that in principle the privileges (under article 32(2)) and controls (under article 35) specific to travel to and appearance before the European Court in Luxembourg should be extended to them, whereas the general question of immunity for words spoken or written concerning the case or the parties should, since the proceedings before the European Court are in the nature of a step in the action pending before a national court (Case 62/72 *Bollmann* v. *HZA Hamburg-Waltershof* [1973] E.C.R. 269, 275), be governed by the relevant national rules. Indeed, the national rules may offer greater protection to those involved in litigation than the Community rules: under article 34 of the Rules, the Court may waive the immunity granted by article 32(1) if it considers that the proper conduct of the proceedings will not be hindered thereby, whereas in English law it is well established that what is said in judicial proceedings is protected absolutely. In the words of Lord Mansfield in *R.* v. *Skinner* (1772) Lofft 55, 56, "neither party, witness, counsel, jury, or judge, can be put to answer civilly, or criminally, for words spoken in office."

7–12 The immunity which is available under article 32(1) of the Rules, originally described in the 1954 Additional Rules as "immunité de juridiction" would appear to apply to both civil and criminal proceedings. What is however specific to these provisions in the Rules of Procedure is their recognition that lawyers appearing before the European Court will usually have to travel from another Member State. Hence article 32(2) deals with searches by customs officials or police, the availability of foreign currency and freedom of movement. To some extent, however, article 32(2) has been overtaken by the direct effect of the EEC Treaty provisions relating to free movement for persons and freedom to supply services, and for most Member States article 32(2) has been overtaken by the relaxation of exchange control restrictions. Nonetheless, it remains the practice of the Registry to issue the certificates under article 33.

7–13 The corollary of the privileges and immunities granted under article 32 is that their use is subject to the control of the Court under article 35, which does not however appear to have been used in practice. Indeed, article 35(1) confers a more general power on the Court to control the conduct of advisers or lawyers towards its members. However, article 17 of the EEC Statute only empowers the Court to control the "advisers and lawyers" who appear before it, and it may be wondered how far a broad interpretation could be given to an essentially penal provision to allow it to be applied, *e.g.* to litigants in person or unqualified advisers. In any event, no provision confers upon the Court a general power to punish contempt, and it has never purported to exercise such a power; on the other hand, at a rather mundane level, it is not unknown for an usher, at the request of the President or another member of the Court, to tell a member of the general public to refrain from smoking (in particular) or talking during a hearing.

One final practical point which might be mentioned is that counsel are normally gowned as they would be before national courts—and that wigs are not readily compatible with earphones.

223

HEARINGS

A. CONDUCT

EEC Statute of the Court

Article 28

7–14   The hearing in court shall be public, unless the Court, of its own motion or on application by the parties, decides otherwise for serious reasons.

(Article 29 of the Euratom Statute and article 26 of the ECSC Statute are in similar terms.)

Article 30

Minutes shall be made of each hearing and signed by the president and the Registrar.

(Article 31 of the Euratom Statute and article 27 of the ECSC Statute are in similar terms.)

Article 31

The cause list shall be established by the President.

(Article 32 of the Euratom Statute and article 28(1) of the ECSC Statute are in identical terms.)

Rules of Procedure

Article 54

7–15   Unless the Court prescribes a period within which the parties may lodge written observations, the President shall fix the date for the opening of the oral procedure after the preparatory inquiry has been completed.
Where a period has been prescibed for the lodging of written observations, the President shall fix the date for the opening of the oral procedure after that period has expired.

Article 56

1. The proceedings shall be opened and directed by the President, who shall be responsible for the proper conduct of the hearing.
2. The oral proceedings in cases which are heard *in camera* shall not be published.

Article 62

1. The Registrar shall draw up minutes of every hearing. The minutes shall be signed by the President and by the Registrar and shall constitute an official record.
2. The parties may inspect the minutes at the Registry and obtain copies at their own expense.

Instructions to the Registrar

Article 7

7–16   1. Before every public hearing of the Court or a Chamber the Registrar shall draw up a cause list in the respective language of each case.

224

This list shall contain:
—the date, hour and place of the hearing,
—the references to the cases which will be called,
—the names of the parties;
—the names and descriptions of the parties' agents, advisers and lawyers.
   The cause list shall be displayed at the entrance to the courtroom.
   2. The Registrar shall draw up in the respective language of each case the minutes of every public hearing.
   The minutes shall contain:
—the date and place of the hearing,
—the names of the Judges, Advocates-General and Registrar present,
—the reference to the case,
—the names of the parties,
—the names and descriptions of the parties' agents, advisers and lawyers,
—the names, forenames, descriptions and permanent addresses of the witnesses or experts examined,
—an indication of the evidence produced at the hearing,
—an indication of the documents lodged by the parties in the course of the hearing,
—the decisions of the Court, the Chamber or the President of the Court or Chamber, given at the hearing.
   If the oral procedure in the case extends over several successive hearings, it may be reported in a single set of minutes.

7–17   The fundamental characteristics of hearings before the European Court which emerge from the above provisions are that they take place at a fixed time on a fixed date, that they are in principle held in public, that they are controlled by the President, and that a formal record is kept of them.

The principle that hearings should be held at a time fixed in advance is of particular importance in the procedure of a court to which counsel will have to make a special, and often lengthy, journey. The usual practice of the Registry is to inform potential participants of the time of the hearing about three weeks in advance, though in the case of applications for interim measures (see para. 10–16 below) counsel may be informed by telephone only a few days in advance. No formal machinery is provided to enable an adjournment to be requested, and indeed the fact that counsel may have other commitments would not generally be regarded as an adequate reason for granting an adjournment; counsel who is aware that he will be unavailable at a particular period would be well advised to inform the Registry of that fact at an early stage in the proceedings, before the date for the hearing is fixed. If counsel feels that there are other reasons for requesting an adjournment, the recommended practice is to inform the Registry by telephone (or telex), followed by a written request. However, a joint application for an adjournment by all the parties could perhaps be construed as an application for the case to be deferred under article 55(2) of the Rules (see para. 7–01 above). Oral argument has traditionally been heard by the Court at sittings on Tuesdays, Wednesdays, and Thursdays, normally held from 10.00 a.m. to 1.00 p.m., and from 3.00 p.m. onwards. Earlier sittings are not, however, unknown, and afternoon sittings may well continue until fairly late in the evening so as to avoid the need for those involved to spend an extra day in Luxembourg. Sittings on other days will be arranged where pressure of business or administrative convenience so require. Hence, in the *Sugar Cases* [1975] E.C.R. 1663, 1694, where it was expected that oral argument would take five days, the whole of the week April 14–18, 1975 was set aside for the hearing. Indeed in applications for interim measures involving some special degree of urgency, the Court has been known to sit on Saturday and Sunday: in Case 61/77R *Commission* v. *Ireland* [1977] E.C.R. 937, the hearing took place and A.G. Reischl delivered his Opinion on Saturday, May 21, 1977, and the Court issued its Order on Sunday, May 22, 1977.

7–18   As well as informing the parties of the time of the hearing, the cause list serves a double purpose: under article 10 of the Instructions, an extract is sent to the Luxembourg Minister of Foreign Affairs (see para. 7–10 above) so that legal representatives may more easily obtain the immunities and privileges under article 32, and under article 7(1) of the Instructions it is displayed at the entrance to the courtroom so that the public at large may be informed of the hearings. It should, however, be borne in mind that, as in other courts, if successive hearings are scheduled for the same day, it is quite likely that the later hearings will not begin precisely at the advertised time.

7–19   Although most of the cases heard by the Court are not of a nature to attract the attendance of the local population, the Court receives large numbers of visitors—*e.g.* lawyers, law students, and other interest groups—and hence many of the public hearings are attended by interested outsiders; certain cases of particular political or commercial significance may be attended by press reporters, and indeed television film crews have on occasion been admitted to the courtroom and allowed to film the proceedings. In order to help the public follow the proceedings, the Court's practice goes well beyond displaying the cause list. The Report for the hearing is made available outside the courtroom shortly before the hearing (always at least in the language of the case and in French, if that is not the language of the case), so that it can be read by interested members of the public, and all the public seats in the courtrooms are equipped with earphones and selector switches allowing access to the simultaneous interpretation (which, however, may not always be available in every official language—see below para. 7–34). On occasions when it has been known in advance that a hearing would be attended by more people than could be accommodated in the relevant courtrooms, arrangements have been made for the proceedings to be relayed by closed-circuit television to a conference room elsewhere in the Court's building. In the light of this, it is hardly perhaps surprising that the Court has evinced a considerable reluctance to allow hearings in the course of ordinary direct actions or references for preliminary rulings to be heard *in camera*. It has, however, shown a greater willingness to conduct measures of inquiry *in camera*, a point which shows the practical importance of the distinction between the oral procedure and measures of inquiry as such. In Case 2/54 *Italy* v. *H.A.*

[1954 to 1956] E.C.R. 37, 55, the Court stated that if it had been necessary to require the production of certain minutes of the Council of Ministers and the High Authority, it would have been willing to order them to be examined *in camera*, and more recently in Case 155/78 *M.* v. *Commission* [1980] E.C.R. 1797, the applicant appeared in person and four doctors gave evidence at a sitting held *in camera*, but oral argument was presented at a public hearing a month later (which was followed by a second hearing at which counsel dealt with a specific question put by the Court).

7–20   On the other hand, private hearings are the normal rule in certain exceptional forms of procedure: oral argument (if any) in most applications for interim measures (see para. 10–17 below) is heard in a separate room on the same floor as the judges' Chambers, and the public is not normally admitted. In the context of a request for an Opinion under Article 228 of the EEC Treaty, in relation to which no express provision is made for oral argument (see para. 13–04 below), it is reported in Opinion 1/78 [1979] E.C.R. 2871, 2902 that the legal representatives of the Council and the Commission attended a hearing in closed session, of which the Member States has also been informed.

7–21   The management of the oral procedure, and in particular the hearing, is very much in the hands of the President or the President of the relevant Chamber where the case is being heard by a Chamber. He fixes the opening of the oral procedure (effectively the date of the hearing) under article 54 of the Rules, even if the preparation of the detailed cause list is delegated to the Registrar under article 7(1) of the Instructions, he opens and directs the proceedings under article 56(1) of the Rules, and, although it is not expressly stated in the Rules or the Statutes, except insofar as it can be implied in the preparation of a cause list, he determines, in consultation with the Advocate-General, when the Advocate-General's Opinion will be delivered. However, although the President is responsible for "the proper conduct of the Hearing" under article 56(1) of the Rules, he does not have any general power to deal with contempt. Under article 35 of Rules (see para. 7–10 above), the Court, but not the President alone, may exclude from the proceedings an adviser or lawyer whose conduct is incompatible with the dignity of the Court or who uses his privileges and immunities for purposes other than those for which they were granted, but there is no provision allowing recalcitrant members of the public to be dealt with. Nonetheless, a member of the public smoking or talking during a hearing will usually be requested to refrain by an usher acting at the behest of the President (or another member of the Court).

7–22   The Statutes and Rules envisage the preparation of minutes of the hearing which constitute a formal record of the proceedings. As well as the information required to be included in the minutes by article 7(2) of the Instructions to the Registrar, such details as the time counsel commenced speaking and finished speaking are also reported. However, what the minutes do not contain is any indication as to the substance of what was said; nevertheless, the members of the Court are not left totally reliant upon their notes, since in practice the hearing is recorded on tape, and a transcript (together with a transcript of at least the interpretation into French, where appropriate) is made available shortly afterwards. Indeed, article 53(2) of the original 1953 Rules of Procedure expressly required that a shorthand note of the oral arguments and, where appropriate, of the interpretation, should be annexed to the minutes. Although article 56(2) of the Rules effectively allows the oral arguments in public hearings to be published, the Court itself does not usually even summarise them in the official European Court Reports; the exceptions to this would appear to be where a new point is raised at the hearing, as in Joined Cases 67 to 85/75 *Lesieur Cotelle* v. *Commission* [1976] E.C.R. 391, 405, or where, in a reference for a preliminary ruling, a party's observations are presented for the first time at the hearing, as in Case 48/74 *Charmasson* v. *Minister for Economic Affairs and Finance* [1974] E.C.R. 1383, 1392. On the other hand, although article 56(1) prohibits publication of the oral proceedings in cases heard *in camera*, in the report of Opinion 1/78 [1979] E.C.R. 2871, 2879 a summary is given of the matters dealt with by counsel for the Council and Commission at a hearing held in closed session.

B. Report for the Hearing

EEC Statute of the Court

Article 18

7–23   The oral procedure shall consist of the reading of the report presented by a Judge acting as Rapporteur, the hearing by the Court of agents, advisers and lawyers entitled to practise before a court of a Member State and of the submissions of the Advocate-General, as well as the hearing, if any, of witnesses and experts.

(Article 18 (last paragraph) of the Euratom Statute and article 21 (last paragraph) of the ECSC Statute are in similar terms.)

Notes for the Guidance of Counsel at Oral Hearings

The Report for the Hearing

As this document will normally form the first part of the Court's jugement, Counsel are asked to read it with care and, if they find any inaccuracies, to inform the Registrar before the hearing. At the hearing they will be able to put forward any amendment which they propose for the drafting of the part of the judgment headed "Facts and Issues."

7–24   As has been noted in describing the Judge Rapporteur (see para. 5–11 above), the Report for the hearing sets out the facts of the case and summarises the submissions and observations lodged with the Court. Despite the wording of article 18 of the Statute it is not in fact read out at the hearing; rather, it is "taken as read." In order to enable this to be done, it is distributed to the participants and to the Members of the Court a few days before the hearing, and made available to the public outside the courtroom. As the Notes for the Guidance of Counsel at Oral Hearings emphasise, the Report becomes the "Facts" part of the judgment, hence accuracy is essential. These Notes are issued by the Court "with the object of making it possible, with the assistance of counsel for the parties, to ensure that the Court can dispose of its business in the most effective and expeditious manner possible." Hence, although paragraph 3 of these Notes is not legally binding, it is regarded as courteous, and will avoid embarrassment, if counsel inform the Registrar in advance of any alleged errors in or omissions from the Report. Nonetheless, such a point may be a useful peg on which to hang further oral argument.

C. ADDRESSES BY COUNSEL

Notes for the Guidance of Counsel at Oral Hearings

1. *Estimates of time*

7–25   The Registrar of the Court always requests from Counsel an estimate in writing of the length of time for which they wish to address the Court. It is most important that this request be promptly complied with so that the Court may arrange its time-table. Moreover, the Court finds that Counsel frequently underestimate the time likely to be taken by their address—sometimes by as much as 100 per cent. Mistaken estimates of this kind make it difficult for the Court to draw up a precise schedule of work and to fulfill all its commitments in an orderly manner. Counsel are accordingly asked to be as accurate as possible in their estimates, bearing in mind that they may have to speak more slowly before this Court than before a national court for the reasons set out in point 4 below.

(Point 4 relates to problems of interpretation)

2. *Length of address to the Court*

This inevitably must vary according to the complexity of the case but Counsel are requested to remember that:
  (i) the Members of the Court will have read the papers;
  (ii) the essentials of the arguments presented to the Court will have been summarized in the Report for the Hearing; and
  (iii) the object of the oral hearing is, for the most part, to enable Counsel to comment on matters which they were unable to treat in their written pleadings or observations
Accordinly, the Court would be grateful if Counsel would keep the above considerations in mind. This should enable Counsel to limit their address to the essential minimum. Counsel are also requested to endeavour not to take up with their address the whole of the time fixed for the hearing, so that the Court may have the opportunity to ask questions.

6. *Citations*

Counsel are requested, when citing in argument a previous judgment of the Court, to indicate not merely the number of the case in point but also the names of the parties and the reference to it in the Reports of Cases before the Court (the ECR). In addition, when citing a passage from the Court's judgment or from the opinion of its Advocate-General, Counsel should specify the number of the page on which the passage in question appears.

7. *Documents*

The Court wishes to point out that under Article 37 of the Rules of Procedure all documents relied on by the parties must be annexed to a pleading. Save in exceptional circumstances and with the agreement of the parties, the Court will not admit any documents produced after the close of pleadings, except those produced at its own request; this also applies to any documents submitted at the hearing.

Since all the oral arguments are recorded, the Court also does not allow notes of oral arguments to be lodged.

7–26   Estimates of time are requested so as to enable the Court to make reasonably efficient use of its sittings; they will, for example, help the President in determining whether there will be time for the Opinion of the Advocate-General in one case to be given after the hearing of oral argument in another case—although in the light of experience of the accuracy or otherwise of these estimates of time, Opinions are often delivered *before* such hearings. In effect, paragraph 1 of the Notes for Guidance admits that the estimates are not always adhered to, and indeed there is no legal obligation on counsel to adhere to them. However, counsel whose address greatly exceeds the estimate is likely to be interrupted by the President to have that fact pointed out to him, and as a matter of practice it would appear to be preferable to overestimate rather than underestimate, particularly bearing in mind the problems of interpretation to which attention is drawn in paragraphs 4 and 5 of the Notes for the Guidance of Counsel (see below para. 7–32).

7–27   One fundamental point which is not regulated by the Statutes, Rules or Notes for the Guidance of Counsel is the order in which oral arguments are presented. Usually this will finally be indicated at a brief meeting between the President and counsel in the judges' retiring room immediately before the hearing, but the normal order of speeches in a direct action is applicant, defendant and intervener, if any, although an intervener supporting the applicant may be heard immediately after the applicant, and in references for preliminary rulings the normal order is plaintiff in the national proceedings, defendant in these proceedings, Member States if represented, Council if represented and the Commission: it has been the invariable practice of the Commission to send a lawyer to appear at the hearing in every reference, for a preliminary ruling even if only to say, in the absence of any other participants, that he has nothing to add to his written observations. In more complex cases, however, the Court may decide to hear argument on a series of specific topics dealt with separately by each counsel, rather than hearing a series of compendious speeches, and counsel may well agree amongst themselves that each of them will deal only with a limited aspect of the cases. In any event, all those presenting oral arguments are given a right of reply, normally exercised in the same order as the main addresses were given.

7–28 So far as the contents of the speeches is concerned, a distinction may be made between direct actions and references for preliminary rulings. In direct actions there will by definition have been a written application and a written defence (see paras. 4–28, 4–55 above) and in the vast majority of cases there will also have been a written reply and a written rejoinder. Hence, bearing in mind the strictures of paragraph 2(i) and (ii) of the Notes for the Guidance of Counsel, there will often be little left to say at the hearing, unless the Court has asked for a specific question to be dealt with. If that is the case, it might be suggested that it is preferable to recognise the fact than to repeat in not quite such a well-prepared form what has already been stated in the written pleadings. On the other hand, if counsel uses it as an opportunity to reply to the rejoinder or to ensure that the Court is given a chance to see the wood rather than the trees in his argument, or indeed to put forward the main aspects of his argument with a new or interesting emphasis, then the oral hearing can be very effective.

7–29 Although paragraph 2(iii) of the Notes for the Guidance of Counsel states that "the object of the oral hearing is, for the most part, to enable counsel to comment on matters which they were unable to treat in their written pleadings," it should be remembered that article 42(2), prohibiting the raising of any fresh issue in the course of proceedings unless it is based on matters of fact or law which come to light in the course of the written procedure, continues to apply. The precise scope of this rule has been considered in detail in the context of the written procedure (see para. 4–67 above), but essentially it would appear to mean that oral argument may not do more than amplify the points already raised in the application or defence. The policy objection to raising new issues at the hearing was stated by A.G. Warner in Case 46/75 *IBC* v. *Commission* [1976] ECR 65 to be that "the raising of a fresh ground at the Hearing may catch the defendant unprepared to deal with it." On the other hand, although the Court did not find it necessary to decide the point, in Case 139/79 *Maizena* v. *Council* [1980] E.C.R. 3393 the applicant claimed for the first time at the hearing that there was a material error in the calculation of its production quota, justifying its lateness on the ground that it was only in the rejoinder that the Council had revealed certain of the factors it had taken into account in calculating the quota. It is also still relevant in this context that under article 92(2) of the Rules of Procedure, the Court, may "at any time" of its own notion consider whether there exists any absolute bar to proceeding with a case. This has meant that the Court has been prepared to consider challenges to its jurisdiction even when they are raised during a hearing. In Joined Cases 67 to 85/75 *Lesieur Cotelle* v. *Commission* [1976] E.C.R. 391, 405, the admissibility of the applications was contested by counsel for the Commission only towards the end of the hearing. The applicants claimed that it was too late to take the point, but the Court held that "that argument is irrelevant because the admissibility of the proceedings must be examined by the Court of its own motion," and found the applications to be inadmissible in part (albeit laying down a test for the admissibility of actions for unliquidated damages which was reversed after full argument in Case 126/76 *Dietz* v. *Commission* [1977] E.C.R. 2431).

7–30   In references for preliminary rulings, however, there is no obligation to submit written observations (see para. 4–112 above), although it is the usual practice so to do, in which case paragraph 2(i) and (ii) of the Notes for the Guidance of Counsel will again be relevant. It is therefore possible for a party to remain silent during the written procedure, whilst still receiving the written observations submitted by other parties, and then put in an appearance at the hearing and let the Court hear his arguments for the first time there. This was the technique successfully used by the *avocat* appearing for the plaintiff in Case 48/74 *Charmasson* v. *Minister for Economic Affairs* [1974] E.C.R. 1383, 1391. Similarly, even if written observations have been lodged in a reference for a preliminary ruling, there would appear to be no bar in principle to raising new points at the hearings: in Case 172/80 *Züchner* v. *Bayerische Vereinsbank* [1981] E.C.R. 2021 the defendant bank, which had submitted written observations, took a new point at the hearing to the effect that banks should be considered to be undertakings entrusted with the operation of services of general economic interest under Article 90(2) of the EEC Treaty and hence subject to the competition rules only to a limited extent; the Court devoted much of its judgment to dealing with this point. However, in considering whether, in a reference for a preliminary ruling, it is advisable to rely upon being able to present fresh arguments at the hearing, in practice account should also be taken of the problems of interpretation.

D. INTERPRETATION

Rules of Procedure

Article 22

7–31   The Court shall set up a translating service staffed by experts with adequate legal training and a thorough knowledge of several official languages of the Court.

Article 29

3. The language of the case shall in particular be used not only in parties' written statements and oral addresses to the Court and in supporting documents but also in the minutes and decisions of the Court. . . .

Notwithstanding the foregoing provisions, a Member State shall be entitled to use its official language when intervening in a case before the Court or when taking part in any reference of a kind mentioned in Article 103. This provision shall apply both to written statements and to oral addresses. The Registrar shall cause any such statement or address to be translated into the language of the case. . . .

5. The President of the Court and the Presidents of Chambers in conducting oral proceedings, the Judge Rapporteur both in his preliminary report and in his

232

report at the hearing, Judges and Advocates-General in putting questions and Advocates-General in delivering their opinions may use a language referred to in paragraph 1 of this Article other than the language of the case. The Registrar shall arrange for translation into the language of the case.

Article 30

1. The Registrar shall, at the request of any Judge, of the Advocate-General or of a party, arrange for anything said or written in the course of the proceedings before the Court or a Chamber to be translated into the languages he chooses from those referred to in Article 29 (1).

Notes for the Guidance of Counsel at Oral Hearings

4. *Simultaneous translation*

7–32   Depending on the language of the case not all the Members of the Court will be able to listen directly to the Counsel. Some will be listening to an interpreter. The interpreters are highly skilled but their task is a difficult one and Counsel are particularly asked, in the interests of justice, to speak *slowly* and into the microphone. Counsel are also asked so far as is possible to simplify their presentation. A series of short sentences in place of one long and complicated sentence is always to be preferred. It is also helpful to the Court and would avoid misunderstanding if, in approaching any topic, Counsel would first state very briefly the tenor of their arguments, and, in an appropriate case, the number and nature of their supporting points, before developing the argument more fully.

5. *Written texts*

For simultaneous translation it is always better to speak *freely* from notes rather than to read a prepared text. However, if Counsel has prepared a written text of his address which he wishes to *read* at the hearing it assists the simultaneous translation if the interpreters can be given a copy of it some days before the hearing. It goes without saying that this recommendation does not in any way affect Counsel's freedom to amend, abridge, or supplement his prepared text (if any) or to put his points to the Courts as he sees fit. Finally it should be emphasized that any reading should not be too rapid and that figures and names should be pronounced clearly and slowly.

7–33   As has been noted in the context of the written procedure (see para. 3–12 above), the term "translation" is used in articles 29 and 30 of the Rules of Procedure in relation both to written and oral procedure. However, the translating service established by the Court under article 22 of the Rules was until 1981 concerned solely with the translation of the written word. Translation of the spoken word is referred to as "interpretation," and the Court did not employ its own interpretation service. As appears from the Report of the House of Lords Select Committee on the European Communities on the European Court (Session 1979–80, 23rd Report, para. 46, and Minutes of Evidence, para. 265), the Court has been refused the finance necessary to employ such a service, and had to "borrow" interpreters from the European

Parliament who were not necessarily legally qualified. Given the generality of the term "translation" as used in the Rules of Procedure, it may perhaps be doubted whether such a situation complied with the requirements of article 22 of those Rules. The practical consequence has been to enhance even further the importance of the written procedure as opposed to the oral procedure, particularly where the litigants speak a minority language.

7–34   Interpretation may be required both out of and into the language of the case. The fundamental function of the interpretation service is to enable the members of the Court to follow the oral argument, and to that end there is invariably interpretation from the language of the case into French, if French is not the language of the case, and also interpretation into other languages if requested by Members of the Court, interpretation into other languages being more frequently requested than translation into other languages during the written procedure (see para. 3–10 above). Interpretation into other languages may also be required where the Court has authorised their use for part of the proceedings under article 29(2)(b) or (c) of the Rules or where a Member State has intervened in a direct action or presented observations in a reference for a preliminary ruling and is using its own official language rather than the language of the case under article 29(2) of the Rules; in each of these relatively rare cases, the party or State using another language would be entitled to request interpretation from the language of the case into the language used by them. Indeed, although there is no obligation so to do, interpretation into a particular language may even be provided when it is known in advance that a group of visitors speaking that language will be attending the hearing.

7–35   It is interpretation from the language of the case into languages understood by Members of the Court which is the primary concern of paragraphs 4 and 5 of the Notes for the Guidance of Counsel: the fundamental rule therein laid down is that counsel should speak slowly and into the microphone placed in front of them (use of the microphone also being essential for the tape-recording of the proceedings), and failure to comply with this suggestion is likely to give rise to protest on the part of the interpreters which will be communicated to counsel through such of the Members of the Court as are listening to the interpretation. It would also appear that in practice interpreters do find it very useful to be supplied with a written text or outline in advance so that, even if it is not followed word-for-word, they do have an overall view of the address. As is implied in paragraph 4 of the Notes, florid or dramatic language loses much of its impact in interpretation, and simple language in short sentences comes across more clearly.

Particularly complex problems of cross-interpretation can arise where cases involving the use of different languages are joined for the purposes of the oral procedure, since in practice addresses in any one of the languages will have to be interpreted into all the others. Thus in the *Sugar Cases* [1975] E.C.R. 1663, the languages of the various joined cases were Dutch, French, German and Italian, and the problem can even arise in references for preliminary rulings, as when Case 51/75 *EMI*

v. *CBS United Kingdom* [1976] E.C.R. 811, in which the language of the case was English, Case 86/75 *EMI* v. *CBS Grammofon* [1976] E.C.R. 871, in which the language of the case was Danish, and Case 96/75 *EMI* v.*CBS Schallplatten* [1976] E.C.R. 913, in which the language of the case was German, were joined for the purposes of the oral procedure.

7–36   Although in this type of joinder, interpretation from the language of one case will necessarily involve interpretation into the language of another case, in more straightforward actions the fundamental function of intepretation into the language of the case is to enable the members of the Court to communicate with counsel. Counsel are, of course, expected to use the language of the case, although permission has been given for counsel in cases involving a minority language, *e.g.* Danish, to use a language which will be understood by the majority of the members of the Court without interpretation, *e.g.* English, but the members of the Court may, by virtue of article 29(5) of the Rules, use any of the languages listed in article 29(1) during the oral proceedings. Thus the President of the Court may well direct the proceedings in a language other than the language of the case, the other judges and the Advocate-General may well put questions in their own languages, and, which is also a part of the oral procedure, the Advocate-General will almost invariably deliver his or her Opinion in his or her native language, even if that is not the language of the case (see para. 3–09 above). Where this occurs, there is a need not only for interpretation into the language of the case, for the benefit of counsel, but also into French, for the benefit of the other members of the Court and into any other language into which interpretation has been requested under article 30(1) of the Rules. Interpretation into the language of the case (and French and any other relevant language) will also be required during the addresses by counsel for parties authorised to use another language under article 29(2) of the Rules and by counsel for a Member State using its official language under article 29(3) of the Rules.

7–37   The extent to which the members of the Court are reliant upon the interpretation depends very much upon the language of the case: it is probably true to say that only French or English could be understood directly by the majority of the Full Court, although it may be possible that, depending on its composition, two if not all three of the judges of a Chamber may be able to understand German. For other languages, the majority of the members of the Court will normally have to rely on interpretation. So far as the mechanics of interpretation are concerned, each of the courtrooms is equipped with soundproof interpreters' cabins, communication with which is by means of earphones and microphones. All the seats in each courtroom, even those occupied by the general public, are equipped with earphones and a selector switch allowing passive access to the interpretation. All the judges and the Advocate-General have direct access to a microphone, enabling them to speak to, or rather through, the interpreters; microphones are also placed in front of the lecterns at which counsel stand to deliver their addresses, and only words spoken directly into these microphones will be heard by the interpreters—an arrangement which can mean that a spontaneous interjection by a counsel will have lost some of its spontaneity by the time he has made his way to the microphone. As has already been indicated (see para. 7–35 above), words spoken into these microphones are recorded on tape and thereafter transcribed for the use of the members of the Court.

E. Questions

Rules of Procedure

Article 57

7–38   The President may in the course of the hearing put questions to the agents, advisers or lawyers of the parties
The other Judges and the Advocate-General may do likewise.

7–39   Although article 57 gives the members of the Court an unfettered power to put questions to counsel, it is relatively unusual for them to interrupt counsel during their main addresses. To what extent this is tradition and to what extent it is due to problems of interpretation is difficult to assess, but it would appear to be the case that interruptions are less infrequent if the language of the case is French or English. The normal practice is for questions, if any, to be put at the end of the counsel's address, and in the nature of things these tend to be put by the Judge Rapporteur or the Advocate-General, both of whom will by definition have taken a special interest in the case. To take a random example, in Joined Cases 110 and 111/78 *Ministère Public* v. *Van Wesemael* [1979] E.C.R. 35, 48 it is reported that the Judge Rapporteur asked counsel for the Belgian Government to explain the effect of a particular phrase in the Belgian legislation at issue in that case. Quite frequently, however, the Court may decide in administrative meeting before the hearing (see para. 5–76 above) to ask a party to answer a specific question at the hearing. So, in Case 98/78 *Racke* v. *HZA Mainz* [1979] E.C.R. 69, 79, the Court had asked the Commission to answer a specific question asking how it could be "ascertained and proved at what time an issue of the Official Journal was actually available at the sales office in Luxembourg," where the date of publication of a Regulation was at issue. Conversely, it may only become apparent during the course of oral argument that a particular question requires an answer which can only be given after further research; in this case, the Court may request a written answer to be supplied after the hearing, or may indeed fix a further hearing at which argument can be heard on the question, as in Case 115/78 *M.* v. *Commission* [1980] E.C.R. 1797, 1806 where, following the presentation of oral argument on November 8, 1979, the Second Chamber decided on November 14, 1979 to ask the parties to discuss the question of the confidentiality of medical findings under the laws of the various Member States, fixing a second hearing on February 7, 1980 to allow them to present oral argument on this matter.

236

OPINION OF THE ADVOCATE-GENERAL

Rules of Procedure

Article 59

7–40   1. The Advocate-General shall deliver his opinion orally at the end of the oral procedure.

2. After the Advocate-General has delivered his opinion, the President shall declare the oral procedure closed.

Apart from the procedural issues and special forms of procedure in which an Opinion of the Advocate-General in required (see para. 5–16 above), his or her essential role is to deliver an Opinion in each and every action before the Court, setting out a personal view of how the case should be decided. The requirement that the Opinion should be delivered at the end of the oral procedure does not, of course, mean that it must be delivered at the hearing at which oral argument is presented, since that hearing is only a part of the oral procedure. On the other hand, there are examples of unreserved Opinions being delivered where the Advocate-General is of the view that the point at issue has been settled in an earlier case, as A.G. Warner in Case 68/74 *Alaimo* v. *Préfet du Rhône* [1975] E.C.R. 109, 115, or where he or she wishes to adopt entirely the arguments of one of the parties, as A.G. Reischl in Case 260/78 *Maggi* v. *HZA Münster* [1979] E.C.R. 2693, 2702. The general practice of the Advocates-General appears to be to aim to deliver an Opinion two to three weeks after the hearing, so as to allow time both for the preparation of the Opinion and its translation into the language of the case and into French (where that is not the language of the case), if these languages are not used by the Advocate-General in his original text. Nevertheless, pressure of work may lead to this period being considerably extended, *e.g.* four months in Case 115/76 *Leonardini* v. *Commission* [1978] E.C.R. 735, 752.

7–41   Under article 59(1) the duty of the Advocate-General is to deliver his or her Opinion *orally*, a rule which is adhered to irrespective of the length of the Opinion; hence, in the *Sugar Cases* [1975] E.C.R. 1663 it took A.G. Mayras two days to deliver his Opinion. The requirements of a spoken Opinion no doubt helps explain why it is the virtually invariable practice of Advocates-General to deliver their Opinions in their native languages, the only exceptions usually being brief unreserved Opinions in a language of the case which the Advocate-General knows well as, *e.g.* in the *Alaimo* case [1975] E.C.R. 109, 115. This is also the reason why the text of an Opinion will not normally be released until the Advocate-General has finished reading it out, so as to take account of any adjustments made during the course of its delivery. Similarly, although a translation of the written text of a reserved Opinion into the language of the case and French, where appropriate, will be prepared in advance by the Court's own translation service (see para. 3–09 above), these translations are read out during the delivery of

237

the Opinion as simultaneous interpretations, the interpreters being expected to follow any deviations from the text.

7–42   On the other hand, although it is part of the oral procedure, it is not the usual practice of counsel to attend the delivery of the Opinion, presumably because their role would be entirely passive and they will in any event be sent a copy by the Registry. It is not, however, uncommon for counsel to telephone members of the Advocate-General's staff to find out the gist of the Opinion.

7–43   So far as the substance of the Opinion is concerned, it will normally discuss the facts and arguments (often in much greater detail than the judgment), analyse the relevant authorities (which only occurs to a limited extent in judgments) and reach a conclusion as to how the case should be decided; once delivered the Opinion itself becomes citeable authority in subsequent cases. The analogy seized upon by the first Advocate-General from the United Kingdom, A.G. Warner, was that of an English or Scottish first-instance judgment ([1976] *Journal of the Society of Teachers of Public Law* 18). He noted however that there were at least four essential differences, in that the Advocate-General hears the case at the same time as the judges who deliver the final judgment, his Opinion is never decisive, his Opinion can never be commented on by the parties, and it is delivered standing up instead of sitting down. It is the absence of a direct opportunity to comment on the Opinion of the Advocates-General which has given rise to most debate on their role, particularly in view of the fact that the Opinion may well not be limited to the arguments presented by the parties. Such a situation is perhaps unavoidable given that in many Member States counsel are under no professional obligation in civil cases to cite all relevant authority whether in their favour or not, whilst the courts are deemed to become the law. With this in view, indeed, the Court has established a documentation service within its Library and Research Division, an important function of which is, when requested by Members of the Court, to provide notes of authorities relevant to particular cases (a similar service on occasion being provided for individual Members of the Court by their legal secretaries). A familiar example of its use is in Case 17/74 *Transocean* v. *Commission* [1974] E.C.R. 1063 where the applicants based their arguments on the express provisions of a specific Regulation, and did not take the point that there had been a breach of the general principle of *audi alteram patern*.

7–44   A.G. Warner, however, formed the view that the case rested on this general principle, and requested a study by the documentation service on the right to be heard in administrative proceedings in the laws of the Member States, concluding on the basis of this study that such a right was recognised in most Member States and that its observance should be ensured by the Court. The Court in turn thereupon held that there was a "general rule that a person whose interests are perceptibly affected by a decision taken by a public authority must be given the opportunity to make his point of view known." Such studies of comparative law are relatively common and rarely contentious, even though the parties will not have had the opportunity to comment thereon, and even though it might be suggested that national law is a question of fact before the European Court. It may, however, be noted that more recently, in Case 155/78 *M.* v. *Commission* [1980] E.C.R. 1797, 1811, the Second Chamber, in the light of the first hearing, requested the *parties* to draw up a study of comparative law on the question of the confidentiality of medical findings under the laws of the various Member States and ordered a second hearing for the presentation of oral argument thereon, and in Case 115/79 *A.M. & S.* v. *Commission* (May 18, 1982), having ordered a second hearing (order of February 4, 1981), the Full Court requested the parties to state at that hearing their views on the protection of certain correspondence, *inter alia*, between lawyers and between lawyers and clients, under the laws of the Member States. It remains to be seen whether this will become the pattern.

7–45   If counsel wishes to challenge an alleged error or omission in the Advocate-General's Opinion, the only remedy would appear to be to request the Court to reopen the oral procedure under article 61 of the Rules of Procedure (see para. 7–47 below); so far the Court has evinced considerable reluctance to exercise this power at the behest of a party. In Case 51/76 *Nederlandse Ondernemingen* v. *Inspecteur der Invoerrechten* [1977] E.C.R. 113, 123 it is reported that the Belgian Government requested the reopening of the oral procedure because it disputed the Advocate-General's interpretation of a particular provision, and that this request was refused on the ground that every factor needing to be considered had been taken into account. Although it does not appear in the report, counsel for the applicant in Case 27/76 *United Brands* v. *Commission* [1978] E.C.R. 207 has written (Van Bael, "EEC Antitrust Enforcement and Adjudication as seen by Defence Counsel" [1979] *Revue Suisse du droit internationale de la concurrence* 24) that the applicant there requested the reopening of the oral procedure on the grounds of alleged factual errors and selective quotations in the Advocate-General's Opinion, and that in refusing this request, the Court referred to the "complete independence" of the Advocate-General. It further appears from the judgment in Case 206/81 *Alvarez* v. *European Parliament* (October 6, 1982) that the European Parliament there sought the re-opening of the oral procedure on the ground that the Advocate-General had taken a point not raised by the applicant. This request was rejected, both because "to grant such a request would be tantamount to enabling the parties to discuss the Advocate-General's Opinion," and because the Third Chamber took the view that the Parliament had in fact had the opportunity of dealing with the point at the Hearing. It may be noted, however, that in its Report on the proposals for the reorganisation of the Court (Session 1979–80, 23rd Report), the House of Lords Select Committee on the European Communities recommended that a liberal attitude should be taken to such requests.

REOPENING THE ORAL PROCEDURE AND FURTHER MEASURES OF INQUIRY

Rules of Procedure

Article 60

7–46   The Court may at any time, after hearing the Advocate-General, order any measure of inquiry to be taken or that a previous inquiry be repeated or expanded. The Court may direct the Chamber or the Judge Rapporteur to carry out the measures so ordered.

Article 61

The Court may after hearing the Advocate-General order the reopening of the oral procedure.

7–47   Although articles 60 and 61 of the Rules only allow further measures of inquiry to be taken or the reopening of the oral procedure to be ordered "after hearing the Advocate-General," and although they follow immediately the provision governing the delivery of the Advocate-General's formal Opinion, it is clear both in practice and from the other language versions (*e.g.* "l'avocat général entendu" in French) that the precondition for the exercise of these powers is not that the Advocate-General should have delivered his Opinion, but that he or she should be consulted, although on a literal interpretation of article 61, it is only possible to "reopen" the oral procedure once it has closed, which under article 59(2) of the Rules occurs after the Advocate-General has delivered his Opinion. Nevertheless, the Court has ordered further measures of inquiry and ordered a further hearing for the presentation of oral argument both before and after the delivery of the formal Opinion, and has indeed taken a very broad view of the concept of reopening the "oral" procedure.

7–48   Thus in Case 43/74 *Guillot* v. *Commission* [1977] E.C.R. 1309, 1323 it was decided to hear oral evidence after the hearing of oral argument but before the delivery of the Opinion, whereas in Case 785/79 *Pizziolo* v. *Commission* [1981] E.C.R. 969 the preparation of an expert's report was ordered in the judgment; in Case 155/78 *M.* v. *Commission* [1980] E.C.R. 1797, 1806 it was decided, after the presentation of oral argument, to hear further oral argument on a particular point, whereas in Case 155/79 *A.M. & S.* v. *Commission* (order of February 4, 1981) the Court decided, after the delivery of the Advocate-General's Opinion, both to require the production of certain documentary evidence and to hear further oral argument at a later hearing. Indeed, since the Advocate-General's Opinion is part of the oral procedure, it is possible for an order reopening the oral procedure simply to require the Advocate-General to deliver a second Opinion: in Case 127/73 *BRT* v. *SABAM* [1974] E.C.R. 51, 64 the Court disagreed with A.G. Mayras' Opinion that the national court had no jurisdiction to make the reference for a preliminary ruling there at issue, and ordered him to deliver a second Opinion on the substance of the matter (reported at

[1974] E.C.R. 320). The Court has, however, so far been reluctant to exercise this power at the behest of one of the parties (see para. 7–45 above).

7–49   Although the Court has no express power to reopen the written procedure, it has exercised its power to reopen the *oral* procedure by inviting the parties to submit *written* observations. In Joined Cases 253/78 and 1 to 3/79 *Procureur de la République* v.*Giry* [1980] E.C.R. 2327, 2359 the Court decided, after the delivery of the Advocate-General's Opinion, to order the reopening of the oral procedure by inviting the parties, the Member States, the Council and the Commission to state their views on certain specific questions; written replies were received from most of those concerned, and this was followed by a second hearing for the presentation of oral argument, and the delivery of a "Supplementary Opinion" by A.G. Reischl ([1980] E.C.R. 2393) on those specific questions. In cases 4/79, 109/79 and 145/79 *Providence Agricole de la Champagne etc.* v. *ONIC etc.* [1980] E.C.R. 2823 a similar pattern was followed: after the delivery of the Opinion of A.G. Mayras, the oral procedure was reopened by requesting the plaintiff in the main action, the French and Italian governments (the latter having only presented oral arguments), the Council and the Commission to reply *in writing* to certain questions. This was again followed by a second hearing and a second Opinion of A.G. Mayras, in which he described the expedient of reopening the oral procedure by inviting the submission of written observations as "a most unusual step."

In the result, therefore, the Court appears to be willing to use its power to reopen the oral procedure as a method of inviting both further oral argument and further written argument.

CHAPTER 8

JUDGMENT

DELIBERATION AND DRAFTING

EEC Statute of the court

Article 15

8–01   Decisions of the Court shall be valid only when an uneven number of its members is sitting in the deliberations. Decisions of the Full Court shall be valid if seven members are sitting. Decisions of the Chambers shall be valid only if three judges are sitting; in the event of one of the judges of a Chamber being prevented from attending, a judge of another Chamber may be called upon to sit in accordance with conditions laid down in the rules of procedure.

(Article 15 of the Euratom Statute and article 18 of the ECSC Statute are in identical terms.)

Article 32

The deliberations of the Court shall be and shall remain secret.

Article 33

Judgments shall state the reasons on which they are based. They shall contain the names of the Judges who took part in the deliberations.

(Articles 33 and 34 of the Euratom Statute and articles 29 and 30 of the ECSC Statute are in identical terms.)

Rules of Procedure

Article 26

8–02   1. Where, by reason of a Judge being absent or prevented from attending, there is an even number of Judges, the most junior Judge within the meaning of Article 6 of these rules shall abstain from taking part in the deliberations.

Article 27

1. Deliberations of the Court and Chambers shall take place in the Deliberation Room.

2. Only those Judges who were present at the oral proceedings and the Assistant Rapporteur, if any, entrusted with the consideration of the case may take part in the deliberations.

3. Every Judge taking part in the deliberations shall give his view and the reasons for it.

4. Any Judge may require that any question be formulated in the language of his choice and be communicated in writing to the Court or Chamber before being put to the vote.

5. The opinion reached by the majority of the Judges after final discussion shall determine the decision of the Court. Votes shall be cast in reverse order to the order of precedence laid down in Article 6 of these rules.

6. Differences of view of the substance, wording or order of questions, or on the interpretation of the voting shall be settled by decision of the Court or Chamber.

Article 63

The judgment shall contain:

— a statement that it is the judgment of the court,
— the date of its delivery,
— the names of the President and of the Judges taking part in it,
— the name of the Advocate-General,
— the name of the Registrar,
— the description of the parties,
— the names of the agents, advisers and lawyers of the parties,
— the submissions of the parties,
— a statement that the Advocate-General has been heard,
— a summary of the facts,
— the grounds for the decision,
— the operative part of the judgment, including the decision as to costs.

8–03 What is nowhere stated in the Statutes and Rules of the Court, even though it is a matter of fundamental importance, is that it is the responsibility of the Judge Rapporteur to prepare the first draft of the judgment, *i.e.* the text upon which the deliberations of the Court will be centred, and that he normally continues to act as draftsman, taking account of the views of the other judges, until the final version of the judgment is approved. As has been noted in the context of the role of the Rapporteur (see para. 5–12 above), this does not necessarily mean that he will always manage to convince a majority of his colleagues, and he may eventually have to draft a judgment with which he does not agree. In order therefore to avoid giving the impression that the Rapporteur is in some way specially responsible for the substance of the judgment, it has become the practice of the official European Court Reports not to indicate his name. The dividing line appears to be October 30, 1975: the judgment delivered that day in Case 33/75 *Galati* v. *LVA Schwaben* [1975] E.C.R. 1323 indicates the name of the Rapporteur, whilst that delivered in Case 23/75 *Rey Soda* v. *Cassa Conguaglio Zucchero* [1975] E.C.R. 1279 does not.

8–04 Judgments of the Court are normally divided into two parts, the current English-language usage being to label the first part "Facts and Issues" and the second part "Decision." The "Facts and Issues" in practice reproduces the report for the hearing, setting out the facts of the case and summarising the submissions or written observation lodged with the Court, and will not normally be discussed in the deliberations. Indeed, an internal minute of the Court requires the Rapporteur not to alter the report for the hearing except in so far as it is essential, so as to avoid unnecessary work for the translation service. The only alterations usually made are corrections requested by the parties, and the addition

243

of a section stating that the oral procedure took place. This account of the hearing tends to be merely formal, but a summary of the oral arguments presented may also be inserted in cases where it is felt that they go beyond the written arguments (see para. 7–22 above), *e.g.* if a new point is taken or, in a reference for a preliminary ruling, argument is presented for the first time at the hearing by a party or institution which has not submitted written observations. Similarly, where the oral procedure is reopened to enable argument to be presented on specific questions, the "Facts and Issues" part of the judgment is likely to include a summary of the views presented to the Court, as *e.g.* in Case 4/79 *Providence Agricole de la Champagne* v. *ONIC* [1980] E.C.R. 2823, 2835–2836.

The "Decision" part of the judgments, as its name implies, sets out the decision of the Court both as to the law and, where appropriate, as to the facts. It is this latter consideration which led to the adoption of the heading "Decisions" in the English-language versions of the Court's judgments rather than the previous heading "Law." The change appears to have occurred in March 1977: the judgment in Case 93/76 *Liègeois* v. *ONPTS* [1977] E.C.R. 543 delivered on March 16, 1977 uses the heading "Law." whereas the judgment in Case 74/76 *Iannelli and Volpi* v. *Meroni* [1977] E.C.R. 557 delivered on March 22, 1977 uses the heading "Decision"; nonetheless, in French the second part of the judgment is still described, less than accurately, as being "En droit."

8–05   It is this second part of the judgment which is in practice the object of the judges' deliberations. These deliberations culminate in the adoption of a judgment which is given as the judgment of the Court or of the Chamber, as the case may be. No provision is made for the publication of dissenting opinions and the obligation of secrecy has prevented any public indication of those judgments which were reached by a majority decision. Nonetheless, it would appear to have been the practice of the Court to endeavour to achieve unanimity on a certain minimum rather than to push through a stronger judgment on a majority vote wherever possible. Under article 27(5) of the Rules, voting is in inverse order of seniority, the aim being to prevent the more recently appointed judges from being unduly influenced by their colleagues with greater experience of the Court and to ensure that each judge does have the opportunity to express a view. In order to ensure that a majority can be obtained, if necessary, article 26(1) of the Rules requires, subject to the quorum of seven for the Full Court or three for a Chamber, that the most junior judge should not take part in the deliberations if there would otherwise be an even number of judges present. This does not, however, prevent an even number of judges sitting at the hearing, something which allows a margin of safety if one of the judges becomes indisposed between the hearing and the deliberation. Indeed, although article 27(2) only allows the judges who were present at the oral proceedings to take part in the deliberations, it is normal practice where a judge becomes unavailable between the hearing and the deliberation, but has to be replaced so as to maintain the quorum, for the parties to be asked if they are willing to forego a second hearing, given that a full transcript will exist of the original hearing, and in most cases it would appear that the parties are willing to assent to this arrangment. Conversely, where the court decides to hold a second hearing for substantive reasons, and the composition of the Court has changed between the hearings, the parties may be invited, if they consider it appropriate, to "put afresh at the next Hearing the arguments in relation to fact and law which they advanced during the first Hearing" (Registrar's letter to counsel in Case 155/79 *A.M. & S.* v. *Commission*).

8–06   Since the provisions relating to Assistant Rapporteurs have never been used in practice, it is only the relevant judges who take part in the deliberations, and the requirement of secrecy in article 32 of the Statute has been taken to the extent that it is only these judges who may be present at the deliberations. Hence they meet without the assistance of the Registrar or of any interpreters, which obviously may give rise to linguistic problems. To meet this difficulty, article 27(2) of the original 1953 Rules of Procedure expressly empowered the Court to choose the language in which the judgment would be drafted, allowing for its subsequent translation into the language of the case. This provision has not been reproduced in the current Rules of Procedure, but the reality remains that the judges must deliberate and initially draft the judgment in a language which they can all understand. In the case of the Full Court, this has usually meant that the judgment is drafted in French and then translated into the language of the case. Nonetheless, under article 31 of the rules of Procedure (see para. 3–01 above), it is only the text in the language of the case that is "authentic"and the French original (if such it be) upon which the judges agreed will be published as a "translation" if that is not the language of the case, even though the Judge Rapporteur primarily responsible for its drafting may not be a native speaker of French.

8–07   Although article 33 of the Statute and article 63 of the Rules set out certain formal requirements as to the information which must be contained in the judgment, it may well be that it was the use of French rather than a legal requirement which led to judgments taking the form which, apart from the early years of the ECSC, they did until the middle of May 1979, which was that of a formal French-style judgment, drafted in that language version as a series of "attendu que . . . ." At least this system had the merit of making it clear when the Court was repeating the parties' arguments and when it was putting forward its own views, the two being normally separated by an "alors que . . . ." However, a less formal style has now been adopted, the dividing line apparently being May 16, 1979, when an "old" formal judgment was delivered in Case 84/78 *Tomadini* [1979] E.C.R. 1801, and "new" informal judgments were delivered in Case 2/78 *Commission* v. *Belgium* [1979] E.C.R. 1761 and in Case 236/78 *Mura* [1979] E.C.R. 1819.

Although the Court is not bound by its earlier decisions, it is generally difficult to persuade it to change its mind, and in a consistent line of case law it may be found on close analysis that certain passages in later judgments are taken verbatim from earlier judgments. In recent years, it has become more common to cite earlier decisions by name in

245

judgments which follow them (and even occasionally distinguish them) and in some modern judgments virtually every proposition of law is supported by citation of an earlier authority, as in, to take a modern example, Case 113/80 *Commission* v. *Ireland* [1981] E.C.R. 1625. On the other hand, the Court does not seem to be willing to indicate in its judgments when it is effectively reversing its earlier decisions, *e.g.* there is no mention of Joined Cases 67 to 85/75 *Lesieur Cotelle* v. *Commission* [1976] E.C.R. 391 in the "Decision" part of the judgment in Case 126/76 *Dietz* v. *Commission* [1977] E.C.R. 2431. in relation to the admissibility of actions for damages.

DELIVERY AND PUBLICATION

EEC Statute of the Court
Article 34

8–08 Judgments shall be signed by the President and the Registrar. They shall be read in open court.

(Article 35 of the Euratom Statute is in identical terms; article 31 of the ECSC Statute requires signature also by the Judge Rapporteur.)

Rules of Procedure
Article 64

1. The judgment shall be delivered in open court; the parties shall be given notice to attend to hear it.
2. The original of the judgment, signed by the President, by the Judges who took part in the deliberations and by the Registrar, shall be sealed and deposited at the Registry; the parties shall be served with certified copies of the judgment.
3. The Registrar shall record on the original of the judgment the date on which it was delivered.

Article 68

The Registrar shall arrange for the publication of reports of cases before the Court.

Instructions to the Registrar
Article 24

There shall be published in the languages referred to in Article 1 of Council Regulation No. 1 "Reports of Cases before the Court" which shall, subject to a decision to the contrary, contain the judgments of the Court together with the submissions of the Advocates-General and the opinions given and the interim orders made in the course of the calendar year.

Article 25

The Registrar shall cause the following to be published in the *Official Journal of the European Communities*:

246

. . . . . .
    (c) subject to a decision by the Court to the contrary, the operative part of every judgment and interim order;

8–09   The collegiate nature of the Court's judgment is emphasised by article 64(2) of the Rules of Procedure which, going beyond the prescriptions even of the ECSC Statute, requires signature of the judgment by *all* the judges who took part in the deliberations. This is normally done in the robing-room just before the judgment is delivered. Furthermore, going beyond the requirements of the Rules of Procedure, the formula "Delivered in open court in Luxembourg on . . . " is practice signed both by the Registrar and the President (or President of the relevant Chamber), as will be evident even to the casual reader of the European Court Reports. Despite the terms of article 34 of the Statute, the only part of the judgment which is usually read out in court is the "operative part," the part which under article 25 of the Instructions to the Registrar is required to be published in the *Official Journal*, and which is printed in heavy type in the European Court Reports. This is read out in the language of the case, in principle by the President, but he may ask another judge more conversant with that language to do so.

    Judgments of the European Court are always reserved, for both practical and legal reasons. The requirement that the judgment must be signed necessarily implies the existence of a written text; the provisions of the Rules of Procedure on the deliberation obviously treat it as a separate step in the procedure, and by its very nature the achievement of a collegiate judgment is a time-consuming process. Furthermore, only the text of the judgment in the language of the case is authentic, and it will therefore be necessary to allow time for translation if the judgment was not drawn up in that language. Although these processes can be considerably accelerated in applications for interim measure (see para. 10–16 below), it would be unusual for a judgment to be delivered less than about three or four weeks after the Advocate-General's Opinion, and the delay may be considerably longer than this—six months in the *Sugar Cases* [1975] E.C.R. 1663, which may be contrasted with the one day in the next case in the Reports, Case 93/75 *Alderblum* v. *Caisse Nationale* [1975] E.C.R. 2147, where it was held that the question referred was a matter of national law, not Community law.

8–10   It is relatively unusual for counsel themselves to travel to Luxembourg for the reading of the judgment, although they more often ask their Luxembourg agent (see para. 4–32 above) to collect a copy or telephone the Court to enquire as to the result. In any event a certified copy will be sent to the parties, and duplicated copies are made available to the public outside the courtroom as soon as the judgment has been read. These may also be obtained on request from the Registry, and on payment of an appropriate fee, they may be obtained on a regular basis. The official reports of cases before the Court are published by virtue of article 24 of the Instructions to the Registrar, in all the languages which could be used before the Court except Irish (see para. 3–11 above). The English version is entitled "European Court

Reports," and, at least since publication of the official versions of the pre-Accession judgments was completed in 1979 (the actual process of translation having been completed in 1977), it alone should be cited in proceedings before the Court.

8–11 The European Court Reports are required to contain the judgments, opinions and interim orders of the Court and the opinions of the Advocates-General, but they may well contain other orders which are felt to be of general interest. Orders for costs are regularly published, *e.g.* Case 126/76—Costs *Dietz* v. *Commission* [1979] E.C.R. 2131, and although orders relating to applications to intervene seem to be published less frequently than was once the case, such of them as are felt to deal with matters of principle are published, as in Joined Cases 116, 124 and 143/77 *Amylum* v. *Council and Commission* [1978] E.C.R. 893. On the other hand, orders joining cases do not seem to have been reported *in extenso*, and it appears to be the view of the Court that the innate confidentiality of the matter precludes publication of orders allowing or refusing applications for legal aid, although the grant of legal aid may be mentioned in subsequent orders as to costs or in the part of the main judgment dealing with costs, as the Case 25/68 *Schertzer* v. *Parliament* [1977] E.C.R. 1729, 1745–1746.

ENFORCEMENT AND BINDING EFFECT

EEC Treaty
Article 171

8–12 If the Court of Justice finds that a Member State has failed to fulfil an obligation under this Treaty, the State shall be required to take the necessary measures to comply with the judgment of the Court of Justice.

(Article 143 of the Euratom Treaty is in identical terms, and Article 86 of the ECSC Treaty imposes a general duty on Member States "to ensure fulfilment of the obligations resulting from decisions . . . of the institutions of the Community.")

Article 176

The institution whose act has been declared void or whose failure to act has been declared contrary to this Treaty shall be required to take the necessary measures to comply with the judgment of the Court of Justice.

This obligation shall not affect any obligation which may result from the application of the second paragraph of Article 215.

(Article 149 of the Euratom Treaty is in parallel terms, and Article 34(1) of the ECSC Treaty is to similar effect, except that it contains express provisions allowing for the payment of damages.)

Article 187

The judgments of the Court of Justice shall be enforceable under the conditions laid down in Article 192.

Article 192

Decisions of the Council or of the Commission which impose a pecuniary obligation on persons other than States shall be enforceable.

Enforcement shall be governed by the rules of civil procedure in force in the State in the territory of which it is carried out. The order for its enforcement shall be appended to the decision, without other formality than verification of the authenticity of the decision, by the national authority which the Government of each Member State shall designate for this purpose and shall make known to the Commission and to the Court of Justice.

When these formalities have been completed on application by the party concerned, the latter may proceed to enforcement in accordance with the national law, by bringing the matter directly before the competent authority.

Enforcement may be suspended only by a decision of the Court of Justice. However, the courts of the country concerned shall have jurisdiction over complaints that enforcement is being carried out in an irregular manner.

(Articles 159 and 164 of the Euratom Treaty and Articles 44 and 92 of the ECSC Treaty are to similar effect, except that Article 92 of the ECSC Treaty is *not* restricted to pecuniary obligations "on persons other than States.")

Protocol on the Privileges and Immunities of the European Communities

Article 1

8-13   The premises and buildings of the Communities shall be inviolable. They shall be exempt from search, requisition, confiscation or expropriation. The property and assets of the Communities shall not be the subject of any administrative or legal measures of constraint without the authorization of the Court of Justice.

Rules of Procedure

Article 65

The judgment shall be binding from the date of its delivery.

European Communities (Enforcement of Community Judgments) Order 1972
S.I. 1972 No. 1590

Interpretation

8-14   **2.**—(1) In this Order—

"Community judgment" means any decision, judgment or order which is enforceable under or in accordance with Article 187 or 192 of the EEC Treaty, Article 18, 159 or 164 of the Euratom Treaty or Article 44 or 92 of the ECSC Treaty;

"Euratom inspection order" means an order made by or in the exercise of the functions of the President of the European Court or by the Commission of the European Communities under Article 81 of the Euratom Treaty;

"order for enforcement" means an order by or under the authority of the Secretary of State that the Community judgment to which it is appended is to be registered for enforcement in the United Kingdom; and

"the High Court" means in England and in Northern Ireland the High Court and in Scotland the Court of Session.

(2) The Interpretation Act 1889 shall apply to the interpretation of this Order as it applies to the interpretation of an Act of Parliament.

249

Registration of Community judgment and orders

3.—(1) The High Court shall, upon application duly made for the purpose by the person entitled to enforce it, forthwith register any Community judgment to which the Secretary of State has appended an order for enforcement or any Euratom inspection order.

(2) Where a sum of money is payable under a Community judgment which is to be registered, the judgment shall be registered as if it were a judgment for such sum in the currency of the United Kingdom as, on the basis of the rate of exchange prevailing at the date when the Community judgment was originally given, is equivalent to the sum so payable.

(3) Rules of court shall be made requiring notice to be given of the registration of a Community judgment or Euratom inspection order to the persons against whom the judgment was given or the order was made.

(4) Where it appears that a Community judgment under which a sum of money is payable has been partly satisfied at the date of the application for its registration, the judgment shall be registered only in respect of the balance remaining payable at that date.

(5) Where, after the date of registraion of a Community judgment under which a sum of money is payable, it is shown that at that date the judgment had been partly or wholly satisfied, the registration shall be varied or cancelled accordingly with effect from that date.

Effect of registration of Community judgment

4. A Community judgment registered in accordance with Article 3 shall, for all purposes of execution, be of the same force and effect, and proceedings may be taken on the judgment, and any sum payable under the judgment shall carry interest, as if the judgment had been a judgment or order given or made by the High Court on the date of registration.

Suspension of enforcement of Community judgments

5. An order of the European Court that enforcement of a registered Community judgment be suspended shall, on production to the High Court, be registered forthwith and shall be of the same effect as if the order had been an order made by the High Court on the date of its registration staying or sisting the execution of the judgment for the same period and on the same conditions as are stated in the order of the European Court; and no steps to enforce the judgment shall thereafter be taken while such an order remains in force.

(Detailed rules for the implementation of this order were made by S.I. 1972 No. 1898 adding rules 15 to 24 to Order 71 of the Rules of the Supreme Court, by S.I. 1972 No. 1982 adding Chapter V B to the Act of Sederunt, and by S.R. & O. 1972 No. 317 adding Order 93 to the Rules of the Supreme Court of Northern Ireland.)

8–15   In principle, the question of the enforcement of the European Court's judgments should be of relevance only in the context of direct actions, since in references for preliminary rulings the final judgment requiring enforcement will be that of the national court; hence the provisions above are drafted in terms appropriate to direct actions. It will be seen, however, that certain of them have in fact been applied by analogy in references for preliminary rulings.

The precise form of enforcement differs according to the status of the party against whom enforcement is sought, and the nature of the judgment. Where the judgment is given against a Community institution, a distinction can be drawn between annulment, the taking of consequential measure, and the award of damages. A declaration of annulment as such hardly needs further enforcement. Indeed, in Case 49/70 *Bode* v. *Commission* [1971] E.C.R. 465, 475, the application was held to be inadmissible on the ground, *inter alia*, that since the decision there challenged was merely confirmatory of an earlier decision against which an action had already been brought, if the Court annulled that earlier decision, the institution which issued it was "under an obligation to revoke or at least not to apply a subsequent decision which simply confirms the first one." However, Article 176 of the EEC Treaty and the parallel provisions of the other Treaties, enable the Court, when wholly or partially annulling an act or declaring that an institution has failed to act, to require that institution to take the necessary consequential measures. The Court has consistently held since Case 2/56 *Geitling* v. *H.A.* [1957] E.C.R. 3, 15 that its judgment cannot anticipate the measures which the institution may be required to adopt, and since Case 30/59 *Gezamenlijke Steenkolenmijnen* v. *H.A.* [1961] E.C.R. 1, 17 that it may not dictate to the institution the decisions which should be consequent upon the judgment. On the other hand, it may indicate fairly precisely to the institution the area within which and criteria under which the new act must be adopted. In Case 17/74 *Transocean Marine Paint Association* v. *Commission* [1974] E.C.R. 1063, 1081 the Court annulled one particular condition attached to a decision exempting an agreement under Article 85(3) of the EEC Treaty, and stated that "the Commission must be given the opportunity to reach a fresh decision on this point after hearing the observations or suggestions of [the applicants]."

–16   Although Article 176 of the EEC Treaty is drafted in terms appropriate only to direct actions, the need for consequential measures has become apparent also in the context of declarations of invalidity on references for preliminary rulings: where the national proceedings are based on a claim that a payment under Community law was too low or that a charge under Community law was too high, a simple declaration of invalidity will not in itself enable the national court to determine the correct level of the payment or charge. Hence, in Joined Cases 124/76 and 20/77 *Moulins de Pont-à-Mousson* v. *ONIC* [1977] E.C.R. 1795, 1814, having held that ceretain Council Regulations were incompatible with the principle of equality in so far as they retained a production refund on some maize products but not others, the Court quite simply declared that the institutions must take the necessary steps to remedy the incompatibility, and in Case 4/79 *Providence Agricole de la Champagne* v. *ONIC* [1980] E.C.R. 2823, 2853, where it was held that certain monetary compensatory amounts had been wrongly calculated although it was legitimate to impose them, the Court cited its 1977 judgment as authority for holding that the principle underlying Article 176 could be applied in references for preliminary rulings.

8–17   The second paragraph of Article 176 of the EEC Treaty makes it clear that the duty to take consequential measures is without prejudice to the award of damages under Article 215 of that Treaty (in the French version "cette obligation ne préjuge pas celle qui peut résulter de l'application de l'art. 215 alinéa 2"), although Article 34(1) of the ECSC Treaty expressly envisages the payment of damages as an appropriate consequential measure to be taken by the Commission. With regard to the enforcement of an award of damages against a Community institution, it would appear that the judgment of the European Court is both necessary and sufficient, since under article 1 of the Protocol on the Privileges and Immunities of the Communities, the property and assets of the Communities may only be subject to administrative or legal measures of constraint with the authorisation of the Court of Justice. In practice, however, it would appear that the Community institutions meet awards of damages with reasonable promptitude.

8–18   Judgment against Member States give rise to an obligation of compliance which is not, under the EEC and Euratom Treaties, subject to any direct sanctions. This obligation was defined by the Court in Case 6/60 *Humblet* v. *Belgium* [1960] E.C.R. 559, 569 as being that "if the Court rules in a judgment that a legislative or administrative measure adopted by the authorities of a Member State is contrary to Community law, that Member State is obliged . . . to rescind the measure in question and to make reparation for any unlawful consequences which may have ensued," and, in Case 48/71 *Commission* v. *Italy* [1972] E.C.R. 527, 532 it added that the Member State is also obliged "to take all appropriate measures to enable Community law to be fully applied." Despite the absence of sanctions, judgments against Member States have generally been obeyed, even if sometimes after a considerable delay: in Case 48/71 itself, Italy was held to be in breach of its Treaty obligation in failing to comply with the judgment given against it in December 1968 in Case 7/68 *Commission* v. *Italy* [1968] E.C.R. 423. However, when France failed to give effect, within what the Commission regarded as a reasonable time, to the judgment in Case 232/78 *Commission* v. *France* [1977] E.C.R. 2729 condemning its import restrictions on sheepmeat, the Court, whilst recognising that a second action could be brought, refused in Joined Cases 24 and 97/80R *Commission* v. *France* [1980] E.C.R. 1319 to grant an interim order which would merely repeat the substance of an already binding judgment. Although direct enforcement against Member States may not be possible, the concept that certain provisions of Community may produce "direct effect" and hence be enforceable by interested individuals before their national courts may lead to indirect enforcement. In the leading case, Case 26/62 *Van Gend en Loos* v. *Nederlandse Administratie der Belastingen* [1963] E.C.R. 1, 13, the Court expressly recognised that "the vigilance of individuals concerned to protect their rights amounts to an effective supervision in addition to the supervision entrusted . . . to the diligence of the Commission and of the Member States," and in Case 39/72 *Commission* v. *Italy* [1973] E.C.R. 101, 112, it was held that even where there had been belated compliance with the

Community obligation, "a judgment by the Court under Articles 169 and 171 of the [EEC] Treaty may still be of substantive interest as establishing the basis of a responsibility that a Member State can incur as a result of its default, as regards other Member States, the Community or private parties." Nevertheless, it was emphasised in Joined Cases 314–316/81 and 83/82 *Procureur de la République* v. *Waterkeyn and others* (December 14, 1982) that in such a case enforceable individual rights flow from the direct effect, if such there be, of the relevant provisions of Community law rather than from the judgment of the European Court under Articles 169 and 171.

3–19   There is no provision for the enforcement of money judgments against Member States under the EEC or Euratom Treaties, even though such a judgment could be given in the private context of jurisdiction conferred by an arbitration clause under Article 181 of the EEC Treaty as well as the public context of, *e.g.* failure to pay budget contributions. On the other hand, under Article 92 of the ECSC Treaty pecuniary obligations on the States are not expressly excluded from enforcement. Furthermore, unlike the corresponding provisions of the EEC and Euratom Treaties, Article 88 of the ECSC Treaty (see para. 2–45 above) enables the Commission, with the assent of the Council, to impose pecuniary sanctions on a Member State which continues in its breach of a Treaty obligation, although this possibility has not so far been invoked in practice. However, since enforcement under Article 92 of the ECSC Treaty, as under the corresponding provisions of the other Treaties, is by the appropriate national procedure, it may be doubted how far a money judgment may be effectively enforced against a recalcitrant Member State: in the United Kingdom section 25 of the Crown Proceedings Act 1947 requires damages and costs to be paid by the appropriate government department, but it does not allow execution to be levied against the Crown. In reality, however, it may be hoped that governments will obey the Court's judgments imposing pecuniary obligations.

3–20   The real concern of the Treaty provisions, however, appears to be with the enforcement of judgments imposing pecuniary obligations on private litigants, *i.e.* litigants other than Community institutions or Member States. The archetype of such a judgment would be one in which the Court exercised its unlimited jurisdiction under Article 172 of the EEC Treaty (see para. 1–13 above) to alter the amount of a fine imposed on an undertaking by the Commission in relation to a breach of the competition rules, the amended fine thereby being imposed by the Court's judgment. However, it should also be noted that under articles 63 and 69 of the Rules of Procedure every judgment is required to include a decision as to costs, although the quantum may be decided later under article 74 of the Rules (see para. 17–24 below), and this will be enforceable against a private litigant as a judgment imposing a pecuniary obligation.

So far as the detailed implementation of these provisions in the United Kingdom is concerned, "verification" is carried out by the Secretary of State appending an "order for enforcement" to the judgment. It may, however, be doubted whether article 3(2) of the Order, providing for the conversion of pecuniary obligations into United Kingdom currency at the rate prevailing on the date of the original judgment, is compatible with the decision of the Court in Joined Cases 41, 43 and 44/73—Interpretation *S.A. Generale Sucrière* v. *Commission* [1977] E.C.R. 445, 463 to the effect that the conversion of national currencies must be carried out "at the exchange rate on the free foreign exchange market applicable on the *day of payment.*"

8–21 In references for preliminary rulings, the final judgment requiring enforcement will be that of the national court making the reference, and enforcement is therefore a matter of national law. However, it has been noted that in Case 4/79 *Providence Agricole de la Champagne* v. *ONIC* [1980] E.C.R. 2823 the Court held that the principle underlying Article 176 of the EEC Treaty, allowing it to require an institution whose act has been annulled to take the necessary consequential measures, could also be invoked in the context of a declaration of invalidity given on a reference for a preliminary ruling. Furthermore, preliminary rulings produce other effects which might be mentioned in the present context. In Joined Cases 28, 29 and 30/62 *Da Costa* v. *Nederlandse Belastingadministratie* [1963] E.C.R. 31, it was held that the existence of a preliminary ruling as to the interpretation of a Community act may relieve a national court against whose decisions there is no judicial remedy under national law from the obligation under the third paragraph of Article 177 of the EEC Treaty to make a further reference on a materially identical question, even if it remains at liberty to do so, and in Case 66/80 *International Chemical Corporation* v. *Italian Finance Administration* [1981] E.C.R. 1191 the Court indicated that a declaration of invalidity given in a preliminary ruling constituted a sufficient reason for any and every national court to consider the act as not being valid, although further references might be made as to the grounds for invalidity, its scope, and where appropriate, its consequences. It may be wondered whether this ruling will be enforced by holding inadmissible further references as to the validity of an act already declared invalid.

RECTIFICATION AND SUPPLEMENTATION

Rules of Procedure

Article 66

8–22 1. Without prejudice to the provisions relating to the interpretation of judgments the Court may, of its own motion or on application by a party made within two weeks after the delivery of a judgment, rectify clerical mistakes, errors in calculation and obvious slips in it.

2. The parties, whom the Registrar shall duly notify, may lodge written observations within a period prescribed by the President.

3. The Court shall make its decision in the Deliberation Room after hearing the Advocate-General.

4. The original of the rectification order shall be annexed to the original of the

rectified judgment. A note of this order shall be made in the margin of the original of the rectified judgment.

Article 67

If the Court should omit to give a decision on a particular point at issue or on costs, any party may within a month after service of the judgment apply to the Court to supplement its judgment.

The application shall be served on the opposite party and the President shall prescribe a period within which that party may lodge written observations.

After these observations have been lodged, the Court shall, after hearing the Advocate-General, decide both on the admissibility and on the merits of the application.

8–23   Although the system of rectification envisaged in article 66(1) is stated to relate, *inter alia*, to "clerical mistakes" and "errors of calculation," in practice errors such as the wrong numbering of paragraphs, incorrect numerals, the omission of words such as "not," and even the replacement of an obviously incorrect word by the correct one tend to be dealt with by an informal "corrigendum," and it appears rather to be in cases where the correction requires the rewriting of a passage that a formal order for rectification is used, as in Case 27/76 *United Brands* v. *Commission* [1978] E.C.R. 207, 345 and 349, where there was not only an order for rectification but also an order for the rectification of the first order for rectification. Where the rectification is to the operative part of the judgment, which has been published in the *Official Journal*, the order for rectification will also be published in the *Offical Journal*, as in Case 158/80 *Rewe Nord* v. *HZA Kiel* (O.J. 1981, C219/3).

It is well established that applications for rectification or supplementation may not be used to short-circuit the procedural requirements relating to applications for the interpretation of judgments under article 102 of the Rules or to applications for the revision of judgments under articles 98 to 100 of the Rules, both of which must comply with the formal prescriptions of articles 37 and 38 of the Rules relating to the written pleadings in direct actions (see paras. 4–22, 4–29 above). Thus in Joined Cases 4 to 13/59 *Mannesmann* v. *H.A.* [1960] E.C.R. 113, 161 the Court held that an application to strike out a particular phrase in the judgment was inadmissible as a request for rectification since in reality it rested upon the interpretation to be given to that phrase. Similarly, in its order in Joined Cases 19 and 21/60, 2 and 3/61 *Fives Lille Cail* v. *H.A.* [1961] E.C.R. 281, 315–316, the Court held that an application seeking rectification of the passages in its judgment setting out the criteria for the assessment of damages by the substitution of other criteria was inadmissible as being intended to seek the amendment or revision of its decision.

8–24   It is also clear that an application for supplementation of a preliminary ruling may not be made by a party to the national proceedings in which the reference was made. In Case 13/67 *Becher* v. *München* [1968] E.C.R. 187, 197, where the plaintiff before the national court sought supplementation of the judgment given by the European Court on a reference for a preliminary ruling, it was held that since the system of such references established a direct form of co-operation between the European Court and national courts or tribunals, in which the parties to the main action could not take any initiative, it followed that it was exclusively for the national courts or tribunals to decide whether they had received adequate clarification in the preliminary ruling. It was suggested that if this was not the case, it was for the national court to make a further reference if it so desired. This reasoning would appear to be equally applicable to requests for rectification by parties to the national proceedings; however, under article 66 of the Rules of Procedure, the Court may order rectification of its own motion, and it does in practice exercise this power in relation to judgments delivered on references for preliminary rulings, as in its order of July 15, 1981 in Case 158/80 *Rewe Nord* v. *HZA Kiel* (O.J. 1981, C219/3). It might be suggested that the fact that an error is brought to the Court's attention by a party not entitled to request rectification directly would not preclude the Court from exercising this power. It may also be wondered whether the fact that the Court may order rectification of its own motion may enable the two-week limitation period to be overcome, just as in Joined Cases 67 to 85/75 *Lesieur Cotelle* v. *Commission* [1976] E.C.R. 391 the Court allowed a late challenge to its jurisdiction on the ground that it was a matter which it could examine of its own motion (see para. 4–67 above).

INTERPRETATION

EEC Statute of the Court

Article 40

8–25   If the meaning or scope of a judgment is in doubt, the Court shall construe it on application by any party or any institution of the Community establishing an interest therein.

(Article 41 of the Euratom Statute and article 37 of the ECSC Statute are in identical terms.)

Rules of Procedure

Article 102

1. An application for interpretation of a judgment shall be made in accordance with Articles 37 and 38 of these rules. In addition it shall specify:
   (a) the judgment in question;
   (b) the passages of which interpretation is sought.
   The application must be made against all the parties to the case in which the judgment was given.
2. The Court shall give its decision in the form of a judgment after having given the parties an opportunity to submit their observations and after hearing the Advocate-General.
   The original of the interpreting judgment shall be annexed to the original of the judgment interpreted. A note of the interpreting judgment shall be made in the margin of the original of the judgment interpreted.

8-26   Unlike applications for rectification and supplementation, applications for interpretation of judgments must comply with the formal requirements of artsicles 37 and 38 of the Rules of Procedure (see paras. 4–22 and 4–29 above). Hence, in Case 110/63A *Willame* v. *Commission* [1966] E.C.R. 287 the Court held that a request for interpretation of a particular point which was not mentioned in the statement of the form of order sought ("conclusions") in the application for interpretation was inadmissible. Indeed, one of the early leading cases on the question, Case 5/55 *Assider* v. *H.A.* [1954] E.C.R. 135, was registered as a separate action, even though its object was to seek the interpretation of Case 2/54 *Italy* v. *H.A.* [1954–56] E.C.R. 37. The fundamental problem here was that the applicant for interpretation was not a party to Case 2/54. However, the applicant had been a party to Case 3/54 *Assider* v. *H.A.* [1954–56] E.C.R. 63 challenging the same decision of the High Authority as was at issue in Case 2/54, and the Court held that where several actions are brought against the same decision and that decision is annulled as a result of one of these actions, the applicants in these other actions may be regarded as "parties" to that action if they have cited in their previous applications the same ground on which the judgment to be interpreted has annulled the decision or has declared the application well founded. This can be contrasted with Case 24/66 bis *Getreidehandel* v. *Commission* [1973] E.C.R. 1599, where the interpretation was sought of Joined Cases 106 and 107/63 *Toepfer* v. *Commission* [1965] E.C.R. 405, annulling a Commission Decision, and of the interlocutory judgment in Joined Cases 5, 7 and 13 to 24/66 *Kampffmeyer and others* v. *Commission* [1967] E.C.R. 245 claiming damages for the harm caused by that decision. The applicant for interpretation was a party only to the latter case, and its application for the interpretation of the former judgment was therefore held inadmissible. Although the Court did not expressly deal with the point, *Assider* was distinguished, since, although the same act was at issue in the two judgments whose interpretation was sought in *Getreidehandel*, they were not parallel actions seeking the same remedy against the same act on the same grounds. Furthermore, in *Getreidehandel* the applicant in effect requested the Court to define the effects of its judgments on parallel actions before national courts in Germany, and it was held that "since this concerns proceedings between different parties, the definition requested does not concern the scope of the judgment as regards the relationship between the parties thereto, and may not accordingly be sought under art. 40 of the Statute." Hence, apart from the privileged position of Community institutions interpretation is only available to the parties to the original judgment (as extended by *Assider*) with regard to its effect as between those parties. Since all the parties will be affected by the interpretation, article 102 of the Rules enables them all to be joined in the action as defendants if not themselves applicants; hence the list of 15 defendants in Joined Cases 41, 43 and 44/73—Interpretation *SA Générale Sucrière* v. *Commission* [1977] E.C.R. 445.

8-27   With regard to the question whether the meaning or scope of a judgment is in doubt, it was held in Case 5/55 *Assider* v. *H.A.* [1954–56]

E.C.R. 135, 142 that for the application to be admissible "it is enough that the parties in question give different meanings to the wording of that judgment" and in Case 110/63A *Willame* v. *Commission* [1966] E.C.R. 287, 292 it was suggested that "it is enough that the applicant alleges the existance of an ambiguity or of obscurity." This however is subject to the proviso noted in Case 70/63A *H.A.* v. *Collotti* [1965] E.C.R. 275, 279 (where the applicant for interpretation was the High Authority acting as an institution not as a party) that the obscurity and ambiguity must affect the meaning or scope of the judgment itself in settling the particular case before the Court and not its possible effect in other cases. The Court also indicated in *Assider* the parts of the judgment which might be the subject of interpretation, stating that it could only interpret those parts which express the decision of the Court on the matter submitted to it, *i.e.* "the operative part and such of the grounds as determine it and are essential for that purpose." On the other hand it could not interpret "ancillary matter which supplements or explains those basic grounds," nor could it give an interpretation of matters which had not in fact been decided in the original judgment.

8–28   It appears from Case 70/63A *H.A.* v. *Collotti* [1965] E.C.R. 275, 280 that an application for interpretation may not be used to obtain the opinion of the Court on the general question of the legal authority of its judgments; nor, as was held in Case 110/63A *Willame* v. *Commission* [1966] E.C.R. 287, 291, may a request for interpretation be used to obtain the application of the judgment to a given set of facts. An illustration of what does fall within the concept can be found in Joined Cases 41, 43 and 44/73—Interpretation *SA Générale Sucrière* v. *Commission* [1977] E.C.R. 445, where the applicants sought the interpretation of the operative part of a judgment imposing fines on them expressed both in units of account and French francs. The applicants in fact claimed that the fine was the sum fixed in units of account, that the sum expressed in French francs was merely an indication of its amount, and that the sum in units of account could be converted into the currency of any Member State at the old IMF parity and paid in that currency (which would have led to savings of 30 to 40 per cent. over the fine expressed in French francs if payment had been made in Italian lire). However, the Court held that the amount of the fine was the sum expressed in French francs, the reference to units of account being made only to check that the fine fell within the limits expressed in units of account in article 15(2) of Regulation 17, and conversion into another currency must be effected at the exchange rate on the free foreign exchange market applicable on the day of payment.

8–29   One similarity to an application for rectification or supplementation is that a request for interpretation of a preliminary ruling may not be made directly by the parties to the main action. This was decided in Case 13/67 *Becher* v. *HZA München* [1968] E.C.R. 187 and confirmed in the order in Case 40/70 *Sirena* v. *Eda* [1979] E.C.R. 3169, 3170–3171 on the ground that since it is for the national courts alone to decide on the principle and purpose of any reference to the European Court, it is also for such courts alone "to appraise whether they have obtained sufficient guidance from the preliminary ruling delivered in response to their question or to the question of a lower court or whether it appears to them necessary to refer the matter once more to the [European] Court." This possibility of making a subsequent reference to obtain further elucidation of a preliminary ruling already given in the same proceedings has been made use of by national courts. In Case 8/78 *Milac* v. *HZA Freiburg* [1978] E.C.R. 1721 the first question referred enquired expressly as to the scope of the preliminary ruling given in Case 28/76 *Milac* v. *HZA Freiburg* [1976] E.C.R. 1639 on a reference in the same national proceedings, and in Case 135/77 *Bosch* v. *HZA Hildesheim* [1978] E.C.R. 855 the only question referred related to the interpretation of the preliminary ruling given in the context of the same proceedings in Case 1/77 *Bosch* v. *HZA Hildesheim* [1977] E.C.R. 1473. In this latter case, the second reference was made because one particular subordinate clause in one paragraph of the judgment was omitted when the rest of the paragraph was reproduced in the "operative part," the Court holding on the second reference that the operative part must be understood in the light of the rest of the decision, and inserting the omitted passage in the operative part of the second judgment. On the other hand, it would appear that in Case 244/80 *Foglia* v. *Novello* [1981] E.C.R. 3045 a second reference was made with the underlying object of obtaining not so much the interpretation as the reversal of the preliminary ruling in Case 104/79 *Foglia* v. *Novello* [1980] E.C.R. 745 (see para. 4–99 above).

8–30   In practice, therefore, a national court which has made a reference for a preliminary ruling may seek to have that preliminary ruling interpreted by the European Court by means of a second reference. It still remains an open question, however, whether a Community institution may apply directly to the Court for the interpretation of a preliminary ruling under article 40 of the EEC Statute; the possibility appears not to have been excluded in the judgment in Case 13/67 *Becher* v. *HZA München* [1968] E.C.R. 187, 197.

REVISION

EEC Statute of the Court

Article 41

8–31   An application for revision of a judgment may be made to the Court only on discovery of a fact which is of such a nature as to be a decisive factor, and which, when the judgment was given, was unknown to the Court and to the party claiming the revision.

The revision shall be opened by a judgment of the Court expressly recording the existence of a new fact, recognizing that it is of such a character as to lay the case open to revision and declaring the application admissible on this ground.

No application for revision may be made after the lapse of ten years from the date of the judgment.

(Article 42 of the Euratom Statute and article 38 of the ECSC Statute are in identical terms).

Rules of Procedure

Article 98

An application for revision of a judgment shall be made within three months of the date on which the applicant receives knowledge of the facts on which the application is based.

Article 99

1. Articles 37 and 38 of these rules shall apply in a corresponding manner to an application for revision. In addition such an application shall:
   (a) specify the judgment contested;
   (b) indicate the points on which the judgment is contested;
   (c) set out the facts on which the application is based;
   (d) indicate the nature of the evidence to show that there are facts justifying revision of the judgment and that the time limit laid down in Article 98 has been observed.

2. The application must be made against all parties to the case in which the contested judgments was given.

Article 100

1. Without prejudice to its decision on the merits the Court sitting in the Deliberation Room shall, after hearing the Advocate-General and having regard to the written observations of the parties give in the form of a judgment its decision on the admissibility of the application.

2. If the Court finds the application admissible, it shall proceed to consider the merits of the application and shall give its decision in the form of a judgment in accordance with these rules.

3. The original of the revising judgment shall be annexed to the original of the judgment revised. A note of the revising judgment shall be made in the margin of the original of the judgment revised.

8–32   Like a request for interpretation, an application for revision must comply with the formal requirements governing applications commencing direct actions; unlike a request for interpretation, however, the subsequent procedure is divided into two phases, in that the Court is required to give a formal judgment on the admissibility of the application before considering its merits. This was explained in Case 116/78 Rev. *Bellintani* v. *Commission* [1980] E.C.R. 23 on the grounds that since revision is an exceptional procedure and not a means of appeal and it "defeats the force of *res judicata*," strict conditions must be imposed. In practice, these strict conditions are themselves strictly construed, so that, for example, an application made out of time will not be considered. Hence, in Case 40/71 *Richez-Parise* v. *Commission* [1972] E.C.R. 73, 80, an application for revision registered on July 8, 1971 in relation to facts of which the applicant had received knowledge on June 8, 1970 was dismissed as falling outside the three-month period laid down in article 98 of the Rules of Procedure without consideration of whether it complied with the other conditions.

8–33   These other conditions, apart from the overall 10-year limit from the date of the original judgment, were defined by the Second Chamber in *Bellintani* as being three in number. The first condition was stated to be the total absence of knowledge on the part of the Court and the applicant of the existence of a fact prior to the delivery of judgment, a requirement which would not be satisfied if the fact in question had been referred to in any manner, or simply known even if not expressly referred to, in the course of proceedings. The second condition was that of priority in time, *i.e.* at the time of delivery of the judgment the Court must have been unaware of a fact already in existence, and the third condition required that the unknown fact should have been of such a nature as to be a decisive factor as regards the outcome of the case, so that it was capable of altering the decision of which revision was sought. However, the second condition laid down by the Second Chamber, requiring the unknown fact to be in existence at the time of delivery of the original judgment, and the first, insofar as it implies the same priority in time, would appear to be hardly compatible with the decision of the First Chamber in Case 56/75 Rev. *Elz* v. *Commission* [1977] E.C.R. 1617, 1621 where it was held that the fact that a judgment of a national court was given *after* the original judgment of the European Court did not prevent that national judgment from being taken into account as the discovery of a new fact, although it was ultimately held not to be a new fact since it merely confirmed earlier national judgment which had been known to the Court and the parties. Similarly, in Case 28/64 Rev. *Müller* v. *Council* [1967] E.C.R. 141, where the applicant sought the revision of a judgment given in 1965, the new fact was alleged to be constituted by a notice issued in 1967, and this in itself was not treated by the then Second Chamber as rendering the application inadmissible. The application was, however, held to be inadmissible on the grounds, *inter alia,* that the notice only related to the future, and it may perhaps be deduced from this, and from *Elz*, that, despite what was said in *Bellintani*, a fact arising after the date of the original judgment may be taken into account as the discovery of a new fact on an application for revision if it relates back to the matters dealt with in the original judgment, and if it is not merely confirmatory of facts which were already known at that time.

In none of these cases, however, did the applicant succeed in convincing the Court that the new fact would have altered its original judgment, a burden which appears to fall entirely on the applicant.

CHAPTER 9

SETTLEMENT AND WITHDRAWAL OF PROCEEDINGS

RELEVANCE OF THE DISTINCTION

Rules of Procedure

Article 77

9–01   If, before the Court has given its decision, the parties reach a settlement of their dispute and intimate to the Court the abandonment of their claims,the Court shall order the case to be removed from the register.

This provision shall not apply to proceedings under Articles 33 and 35 of the ECSC Treaty, Articles 173 and 175 of the EEC Treaty or Articles 146 and 148 of the Euratom Treaty.

Article 78

If the applicant informs the Court in writing that he wishes to discontinue the proceedings, the Court shall order the case to be removed from the register.

9–02   Although there is no need for a case to go to judgment, Article 77 of the Rules of Procedure does not on the face of it allow the settlement of actions for the annulment of Community acts (ECSC Treaty Article 33, EEC Treaty Article 173, and Euratom Treaty Article 146) or of actions relating to the alleged failure to act of a Community institution (ECSC Treaty Article 35, EEC Treaty Article 175 and Euratom Treaty Article 148). Whilst it might be thought that this is because it should not be for the parties themselves to decide whether or not a particular act or failure to act should be treated as lawful, the fact remains that withdrawal of the action under article 78 of the Rules is subject to no such restriction and indeed article 81 of the 1953 Rules of Procedure, which in principle prohibited withdrawal once the defendant had entered an appearance, allowed withdrawal at any stage in the proceedings in the case of an action for annulment. It was in the light of this that in Case 13/57 *Eisen-und Stahlindustrie* v. *H.A.* [1957 and 1958] E.C.R. 265, 287 the Court held that in an action for annulment "it is unnecessary to obtain the concurrence of the defendant" if an applicant wishes to withdraw from the proceedings. Be that as it may, although the current article 78 of the Rules of Procedure is drafted in a manner which makes it appear that withdrawal is a unilateral act, the normal modern practice is to serve a request for withdrawal on the other parties so that they can state their views, particularly as to costs. Hence, in the report of the order in Joined Cases 109 and 114/75 *National Carbonising Co.* v. *Commission* [1977] E.C.R. 381, it is recorded that the applicant's request to be allowed to withdraw its applications was served on the defendant and on the interveners, and that the order was made after they had informed the Court that they had no objection to such withdrawal and did not seek an order as to costs.

9–03 Despite the failure of the Rules of Procedure to allow expressly for the settlement of actions for annulment or in relation to a failure to act, the Court has long been prepared to accept a withdrawal based in reality on a settlement between the parties. Thus, in allowing the withdrawal of a particular claim in Joined Cases 16, 17 and 18/59 *Geitling and others* v. *H.A.* [1960] E.C.R. 17, 26, the Court expressly noted the fact that by virtue of an agreement between the parties the defendant had undertaken to bear the costs attributable to that claim. This judgment also shows that no particular form is required for an application to withdraw a claim: a statement by the applicants that a particular claim had lost its purpose was construed as the withdrawal of that claim. However, in Joined Cases 5, 7 and 8/60 *Meroni* v. *H.A.* [1961] E.C.R. 107, 111 it was held that the fact that an applicant's claim has lost its purpose does not oblige the applicant to discontinue the action, but that the applicant will be liable for the costs incurred thereafter.

Settlement or withdrawal by the *parties* as envisaged in articles 77 and 78 of the Rules of Procedure is of relevance only in direct actions. Although a settlement between the parties may terminate the national proceedings in which a reference has been made, the reference itself can only be terminated if it is withdrawn by the national court which made it or by a superior court on appeal. What constitutes a settlement in this context is a matter of national law: in Case 172/80 *Züchner* v. *Bayerische Vereinsbank* [1981] E.C.R. 2021 the plaintiff sought the recovery of the commission levied by the defendant bank on the transfer of funds to another Member State on the grounds that this commission breached the EEC competiton rules; the bank in fact repaid the commission, but the German court held that the plaintiff still had an interest in continuing the proceedings, since a similar commission might be levied on him in the future, and so the reference remained before the European Court.

9–04 With regard to withdrawal as such of a reference, it is clear that this is not a matter for the parties. The practice in fact would appear to be that established in the context of appeals from references for preliminary rulings (see para. 4–103 above); the reference may be withdrawn by the national court which made it, as stated in Case 127/73 *BRT* v. *SABAM* [1974] E.C.R. 51, or by a higher court quashing the order for reference, as is recorded in Case 65/77 *Razanatsimba* [1977] E.C.R. 2229, 2237 in relation to an earlier reference in the same national proceedings

EFFECTS

Instructions to the Registrar

Article 25

9–05 The Registrar shall cause the following to be published in the Official Journal of the European Communites

263

(a) . . . . . .

(b) notices of the removal of cases from the Register:

9–06   The requirement that the removal of a case from the Register should be published in the *Official Journal* is the corollary of the obligation to publish the fact that proceedings have been commenced before the Court (see para. 4–12 above), and is drafted in terms apt to cover both direct actions and references for preliminary rulings. The removal of a case from the Register is not, however, usually printed in the European Court Reports. In the exceptional instance of Joined Cases 109 and 114/75 *National Carbonising Co.* v. *Commission* [1977] E.C.R. 381, the actions were withdrawn only after the Advocate-General had delivered his Opinion (albeit on a procedural point); that Opinion was required to be published under article 24 of the Instructions to the Registrar (see para. 3–08 above), and the order removing the cases from the register was no doubt printed to explain the context of the Opinion. On the other hand, the fact that one of a number of claims has been withdrawn will normally be noted in the judgment on the other claims.

Publication of the withdrawal or settlement of an action would appear largely to be a matter of information: in references for preliminary rulings, the fact that a reference has been withdrawn does not preclude any other national court from making a reference on the same point, and in direct actions it is now clear that settlement or withdrawal is binding only as between the parties. For example, in Joined Cases 80 and 81/77 *Ramel* v. *Receveur des Douanes* [1978] E.C.R. 927, French wine importers were able to invoke the direct effect of the relevant provisions of EEC law to challenge before the French courts, and on a reference for a preliminary ruling before the European Court, the legality of levies imposed by the French authorities on imports of Italian wine in 1975 to 1976 even though, following a political settlement, the Commission had withdrawn an action it had brought against France under article 169 alleging that the imposition of such levies was in breach of France's Treaty obligations. it might further be noted in this context that following the judgment in Joined Cases 142 and 143/80 *Italian Finance Administration* v. *Essevi* [1981] E.C.R. 1413 it is clear that an interested individual may similarly invoke the direct affects, if such there be, of the relevant Community rules with regard to conduct of a Member State against which the Commission has decided not to initiate proceedings under article 169 or which it has indeed regarded as permissible.

COSTS

Rules of Procedure

Article 69

9–07   4. A party who discontinues or withdraws from proceedings shall be ordered to pay the costs, unless the discontinuance or withdrawal is justified by the conduct of the opposite party.

If the opposite party has not asked for costs, the parties shall bear their own costs.

5. Where a case does not proceed to judgment the costs shall be in the discretion of the Court.

9–08   Although costs in general are treated as a separate topic (see Chapter 17 below), the special rules relating to costs when an action is withdrawn or settled are self-contained. The effect of article 69(4) and (5) of the Rules of Procedure is that a party which withdraws its claim or action is in principle liable to pay the costs, whereas in a settlement the Court has a general discretion—although in practice settlements will deal express-ly with the matter of costs. Where one of a number of applicants withdraws from a case, its liability would appear to be limited to the costs arising from its participation: in Case 13/57 *Eisen-und Stahlindus-trie* v. *H.A.* [1958] E.C.R. 265, where one of the applicants withdrew at the hearing, its liability to costs was fixed (rather generously?)at one-half of that of the other applicants who unsuccessfully continued to judgment. On the other hand, the Court has been willing to give effect to agreements under which the applicant has withdrawn the action or a particular claim on terms that the defendant will meet the costs, as in Joined Cases 16, 17 and 18/59 *Geitling and others* v. *H.A.* [1960] E.C.R. 17, 26–27, and it appears from Joined Cases 109 and 114/75 *National Carbonising Co.* v. *Commission* [1975] E.C.R. 381 that the costs will not have to be borne by an applicant which withdraws its application where the other parties state at the time of withdrawal that they do not seek an order as to costs, irrespective of whether they claimed costs in their original "conclusions."

9–09   Finally, it may be noted that where a party fails to withdraw its application when it no longer has an interest in continuing the proceedings, it may be ordered to pay the costs incurred thereafter, even if the other party is liable for the costs incurred up to that point. In Joined Cases 5, 7, and 8/60 *Meroni* v. *H.A.* [1961] E.C.R. 107, the High Authority stated in its rejoinder that it had revoked the decisions which were at issue, and offered to pay the costs up to the date of that revocation. However, the applicants did not discontinue the proceed-ings, and the Court held that although they were not olbiged to withdraw, since they no longer had any interest in continuing the proceedings, they were liable to meet the costs incurred after the notification of the revocation of the original decisions.

A more lenient view was taken in Case 179/80 *Roquette* v. *Council* (October 19, 1982), where the applicant was held to have no interest in continuing proceedings for the annulment of a Regulation which had been superseded by other Regulations, the validity of which had been upheld in other proceedings, but was merely ordered to bear its own costs.

Part III

Special Forms of Procedure

CHAPTER 10

INTERIM MEASURES

SCOPE

EEC Treaty

Article 185

10–01 Actions brought before the Court of Justice shall not have suspensory effect. The Court of Justice may, however, if it considers that circumstances so require, order that application of the contested act be suspended.

Article 186

The Court of Justice may in any cases before it prescribe any necessary interim measures.

(Articles 157 and 158 of the Euratom Treaty and Article 39 of the ECSC Treaty are to similar effect, except that Article 157 of the Euratom Treaty is prefaced by an express saving in favour of other provisions of that Treaty. In particular, Article 83(2) of that Treaty reverses the usual situation, allowing automatic suspension of the sanctions at issue unless immediate enforcement is ordered by the Court on application by the Commission or a Member State.)

The power to prescribe interim measures is one which the European Court has exercised sparingly: to the end of 1980 there would appear to have been 22 orders granting interim measures, and 62 orders refusing requests for such measures. Articles 185 and 186 effectively divide interim measures into those concerned with the suspension of an act of a Community institution, and those concerned with other matters, a classification which will be followed here.

A. SUSPENSION OF COMMUNITY ACTS

10–02 The acts whose suspension is most frequently sought are individual decisions, usually either addressed to an undertaking under the competition rules as, *e.g.* in Case 27/76R *United Brands* v. *Commission* [1976] E.C.R. 425, or to an official of the Communities by his employing institution as, *e.g.* in Case 174/80R *Reichardt* v. *Commision* [1980] E.C.R. 2665; where the applicant is the addressee of the decision, no problems of *locus standi* arise. Such problems do, however, arise where the applicant is not the addressee of the decision, or where an applicant other than a Member State or Community institution is seeking the annulment, and interim suspension, of an act of general application (see paras. 1–27 and 1–29 above). In many instances, discussion of the problem of admissibility has been avoided by rejecting the request for

269

interim measures on other grounds, as in Case 48/78R *Ooms* v. *Commission* [1979] E.C.R. 1703, 1705. However, although in Joined Cases 35/62 and 16/63R *Leroy* v. *H.A.* [1963] E.C.R. 213, 215 the then President suggested that a provision of the Staff Regulations could not be suspended, the more recent attitude, relying on the principle enounced in Case 75/72R *Perinciolo* v. *Council* [1972] E.C.R. 1201, 1203 that the judge in the interim proceedings must not prejudge questions relating to the admissibility of the main action, would appear to be that whether or not an act may be suspended depends not so much on its generality or its addressee as on a consideration of the individual harm it may cause to the applicant. Hence, in Case 26/76R *Metro* v. *Commission* [1976] E.C.R. 1353, 1356, where the applicant, which had been a complainant before the Commisssion, sought the suspension of a decision addressed to another undertaking, the President considered not the admissibility of the action but the balance of the harm that might be caused to the applicant if the decision remained in force, and to the other undertaking's distributors if it were suspended. Similarly, with regard to acts of general application, in Case 113/77R *NTN Toyo* v. *Council* [1977] E.C.R. 1721, the President suspended a provision of a Regulation at the behest of a group of companies after consideration of the harm its application would cause to the applicants, and partial suspension of a provision of a Regulation was also ordered in Case 232/81R *Agricola Commerciale Olio* v. *Commission* [1981] E.C.R. 2193 on the request of an individual trader. On the other hand, in Case 258/80R *Rumi* v. *Commission* [1980] E.C.R. 3867, 3876, the President emphasised that suspension of or derogation from a general act should be ordered only in exceptional circumstances and where it was apparent that failure to take the measures requested would cause the applicant to suffer damage so serious and irreparable that it could not be redressed even if the measure contested in the main action were annulled, holding that the applicant had not fulfilled these criteria.

10–03   Although Article 185 of the Treaty only expressly provides for the suspension of the act which is being challenged, in practice the Court has been willing also to order the suspension of other closely related acts. In Case 15/63R *Lassalle* v. *Parliament* [1964] E.C.R. 57, where in his main action the applicant sought the annulment of a notice of vacancy, the President ordered the suspension not only of that notice as such but of "any steps to fill the vacancy . . . in question." Further, in 18/65R *Gutmann* v. *Commission* [1966] E.C.R. 135, where the applicant sought in the main action the annulment of a decision relating to his suspension and transfer, the President of the First Chamber ordered the suspension of the operation of a notice of vacancy for the post the applicant had previously occupied, even though he had not yet sought its annulment, on the basis that "it would be excessively formalistic in an application for the adoption of an interim measure to compel the parties to enter multiple pleadings when the facts of the case show that the subject-matter of the main application and of the application for the adoption of the interim measure are so linked as cause and effect that the second appears as the inevitable consequence of the first."

However, in Case 258/80R *Rumi* v. *Commission* [1980] E.C.R. 3867, although the President was prepared to consider the suspension of the provisions of a general ECSC decision implemented by the contested individual decision, he was not prepared to order the suspension of provisions of that general decision which were not implemented by the contested individual decision, stating (at p. 3878) that an application for interlocutory relief may relate only to interim measures "having a direct link with the decision which is at issue in the main action."

10-04   It might finally be noted in this context that the suspension of an act of a Community institution is only that: *i.e.*, the suspension of a Community decision requiring the termination of a restrictive agreement under Article 85 of the EEC Treaty is not to be taken as a provisional validation of that agreement. This was clearly stated in Case 71/74R and RR *Frubo* v. *Commission* [1974] E.C.R. 1031, 1034, and re-emphasised in Joined Cases 209 and 215 and 218/78R *Van Landewyck and others* v. *Commission* [1978] E.C.R. 2111, 2114, where the President of the Second Chamber stated categorically that such a suspension "in no way makes provisionally valid any agreement or concerted practice declared null and void" under Articles 85(1) and (2) "since the court to which application is made for the adoption of interim measures cannot substitute its discretion for that of the Commission." The Commission's decision in fact related to certain rules of the Belgian tobacco manufacturers' association, and the President of the Second Chamber pointed out that despite his suspension of the Commission decision requiring the termination of these rules, the members of the association remained free to disregard these rules.

B. Other Measures

10-05   The power to order "any necessary interim measures" leaves the Court with a very wide range of discretion, subject only to its appreciation of what is "necessary." Thus in Case 318/81R *Commission* v. *Codemi* (order of April 28, 1982; O.J. 1982 C135/16), an expert was appointed to inspect the progress of building work by an interim order. It adds considerable flexibility to the basic power to suspend an act of a Community institution, so that in Case 3/75R *Johnson & Firth Brown* v. *Commission* [1975] E.C.R. 1, 6–7, the President, whilst refusing to order the suspension of a Commission decision authorising the British Steel Corporation to acquire a shareholding in Johnson & Firth Brown, was able to order British Steel not to exercise the voting rights attached to the shares it acquired until judgment in its main action; this in itself also clearly illustrates that interim measures may be ordered against a person other than the defendant in the main action, although British Steel did appear in these proceedings as an intervener. It would also appear to be possible to order a Community institution to make a provisional money payment: although the President refused the applicant's request for an advance on salary in Joined Cases 19 and 65/63 *Prakash* v. *Commission* [1965] E.C.R. at pp. 576, 578, he did not reject the possibility, stating rather that provisional payment could only be granted by means of an interim measure if the main application appeared prima facie to be clearly well-founded. More generally, however, the Court would appear to be reluctant to anticipate the main judgment by an interim measure which goes beyond the mere suspension of the contested act. In Case 25/62RI and R2 *Plaumann* v. *Commission* [1963] E.C.R. 123 and 126, where in its main action the applicant sought the annulment of a Commission decision refusing to authorise the German authorities to charge a lower rate of customs duty on clementines, the President twice rejected the applicant's request for an interim measure requiring the Commission to authorise the Federal Republic provisionally to suspend the application of part of the customs duties imposed on clementines, suggesting that such a far-reaching measure could be justified only by wholly exceptional circumstances. This may be contrasted with the relative willingness shown, *e.g.* in Case 113/77R *NTN Toyo* v. *Council* [1977] E.C.R. 1721 to suspend provisions of a Community act which itself imposes the duty in question, in that case anti-dumping duty on certain Japanese ball bearings. The Court is also reluctant to make an interim order which effectively anticipates a failure to comply with the judgment in the main action, or a related action. In Joined Cases 98 and 99/63R *Reynier* v. *Commission* [1964] E.C.R. at p. 276, the applicants requested the suspension of a vacancy notice for a post in Grade A3 of which they were seeking the annulment. They had previously brought two other actions, Joined Cases 79 and 82/63 [1964] E.C.R. 259, in which they claimed that they should be reclassified in Grade A3, and their argument in the application for interim measures was that if the vacancy procedure went ahead, the Commission might be able to claim that it no longer had any vacant A3 posts to which to appoint them, even if judgment were given in their favour in the reclassification proceedings. In the event, the Commission gave an undertaking to give effect to that judgment if it went in favour of the applicants, but the President did observe (at p. 278) that "there is no need to lay down in advance by means of an interlocutory order the methods for giving effect to the judgment."

10–06   Positive interim measures ordered against Community institutions have in fact extended to requiring the Commission itself to take interim measures. In Case 109/75R *NCC* v. *Commission* [1975] E.C.R. 1193, 1202, the President ordered the Commission to use its powers under Article 66(7) of the ECSC Treaty (relating to dominant positions) to take the interim measures necessary to keep two coking plants belonging to the applicants in operation. Although the competition rules of the EEC Treaty do not confer similar express powers on the Commission, the Court held in Case 792/79R *Camera Care* v. *Commission* [1980] E.C.R. 119, where the applicant had specifically requested the Court to order the Commission to take interim measures, that the Commission had an implied power "to take interim measures which are indispensable for the effective exercise of its functions" under Regulation 17 implementing the competition rules; on this occasion, however, it left the Commission itself to decide whether to order the interim measures requested by the applicant, *i.e.* the restoration of supplies at the usual price and upon the usual conditions by a manufacturer against which the applicant had lodged a complaint before the Commission.

The Commission first exercised such powers of its own notion in a decision which was challenged in Joined Cases 225 & 229/82R *Ford* v. *Commission*. In his Order of September 29, 1982, the President held that a Commission interim decision requiring a supplier to resume supplies by lifting an export restriction should be merely conservatory, *i.e.* it should be calculated to maintain the flow of trade at the level achieved when the restriction was imposed, rather than removing the restriction completely.

With regard to interim orders against Member States, it will be evident that they may be caught by an interim order made in proceedings brought against a Community defendant. Hence, in Case 88/76R *Société pour l'Exportation des Sucres* v. *Commission* [1976] E.C.R. 1585, where the applicant challenged in its main action a Regulation abolishing the right to cancellation in respect of defined export licences, the President of the First Chamber ordered the Commission, by way of an interim measure, to inform the competent Belgian authorities that the deposit paid by the applicant on certain of these licences could not be treated as forfeited so long as the judgment of the Court terminating the proceedings was still pending. Member States may, however, themselves be defendants in direct actions before the Court, and the question of principle whether interim measures could extend to requiring the suspension or termination of national legislation was settled in Joined Cases 31/77R and 53/77R *Commission* v. *U.K.* [1977] E.C.R. 921. Despite the doubts of A.G. Mayras (at pp. 934–935), the Court there ordered the United Kingdom, as an interim measure, "to cease forthwith" payment of a pigmeat subsidy introduced in breach of the requirements of Article 93(3) of the EEC Treaty governing the ratification of new state aids. This was followed in Case 61//77R *Commission* v. *Ireland* [1977] E.C.R. 1411 by an order requiring Ireland to cease the application of two statutory instruments to fishing boats registered in any of the Member States.

10–07   Whilst persons other than Community institutions or Member States are not likely to be defendants in direct actions before the European Court except in cases where that Court has jurisdiction under an arbitration clause, they also may be directly affected by interim orders in proceedings in which they are neither applicant nor defendant. In Case 3/75R *Johnson & Firth Brown* v. *Commission* [1975] E.C.R. 1, 6, the interim measures were, in fact, directed to British Steel to prevent it exercising voting rights attached to shares that it might acquire in Johnson & Firth Brown. A similar result had been achieved in Joined Cases 160, 161 and 170/73R II *Miles Druce* v. *Commission* [1974] E.C.R. 281, where, in the context of a takeover bid for Miles Druce by Guest, Keen and Nettlefolds, which required the Commission's authorisation under Article 66 of the ECSC Treaty, the Court ordered the Commission, so as to ensure compliance with a provision deferring the implementation of its decision for a fixed period, "to ensure . . .

neutral behaviour on the part of those concerned" until the expiry of that period; the neutral behaviour was in fact to be required of Miles Druce and Guest, Keen and Nettlefolds. Similarly, in Case 109/75R *NCC* v. *Commission* [1975] E.C.R. 1193, the interim measures the Commission was required to adopt in fact related to the conduct of the National Coal Board and National Smokeless Fuels Ltd.

WHO MAY APPLY?

Rules of Procedure

Article 83

10–08   1. An application to suspend the operation of any measure adopted by an institution, made pursuant to the second paragraph of Article 39 of the ECSC Treaty, Article 185 of the EEC Treaty or Article 157 of the Euratom Treaty, shall be admissible only if the applicant is challenging that measure in proceedings before the Court.

An application for the adoption of any other interim measure referred to in the third paragraph of Article 39 of the ECSC Treaty, Article 186 of the EEC Treaty or Article 158 of the Euratom Treaty shall be admissible only if it is made by a party to a case before the Court and relates to that case.

10–09   Article 83(1) of the Rules of Procedure continues the distinction between the suspension of Community acts and other interim measures. Whilst the latter may be requested by any party to a case, the former may only be requested by a party challenging the act in question. Although there is no clear authority on the point, it might be suggested that this challenge could be by way of a plea of illegality (see para. 1–33 above) or counterclaim, since the term "applicant" would appear here to be used in the context of the application for interim measures rather than of the main action. Nevertheless,in practice requests for the suspension of Community acts have usually been made by the party who is also applicant in the main action. Insofar as a party is entitled to apply for the suspension of a contested act, it was emphasised by the President of the First Chamber in Case 22/75R *Küster* v. *Parliament* [1975] E.C.R. 277, 278, that this right is granted to an applicant for the protection of his own interests, and that he may not support his application for suspension by referring to the disadvantages to third parties which might result if the measure in question were not suspended. It was suggested in Case 12/64R *Ley* v. *Commission* [1965] E.C.R. 132, 134, that it was for the defendant institution to take into consideration the harm which immediate implementation might cause to the interests of third parties in deciding whether or not to oppose the suspension of the measure in question.

10–10   Third party interests may, however, be taken into account as a factor to be balanced *against* the applicant's interest in determining whether to suspend the operation of a Community act, as in Case 26/76R *Metro* v. *Commission* [1976] E.C.R. 1353, 1356, where it was held that the suspension of the decision at issue, permitting the distribution system for "SABA" electronic equipment, would affect not only the relationship of SABA to the applicant but the relationship of SABA to all its distributors, and that this would fall outside the scope of an interim measure intended to safeguard temporarily the interests of the applicant. The same balancing of interests also occurs in considering whether to order other interim measures, and may indeed influence a decision to grant other measures rather than suspend the act in question. In Case 3/75R *Johnson & Firth Brown* v. *Commission* [1975] E.C.R. 1, the applicant sought the suspension of a Commission decision authorising British Steel to acquire a large holding of its shares from Jessel Securities, but the President held that the suspension of this decision would cause at least as much harm to the creditors of Jessel Securities as its implementation would cause to the applicant. In the result, rather than suspending the decision as such, he ordered British Steel not to exercise its voting rights with regard to the shares in question until the delivery of the main judgment.

Consideration of the applicant's own interests is not, however, appropriate where the interim measures are sought by the Commission in its capacity as guardian of the application of the Treaties against a Member State. So, in Case 61/77R *Commission* v. *Ireland* [1977] E.C.R. 1411, the Commission obtained the suspension of two Irish fisheries measures, not for its own benefit but for the benefit of "fishing boats registered in any of the Member States."

10–11   Third parties who may be affected by interim measures may protect their interests by intervening, often in practice by what appears to be a simplified procedure (*cf.* para. 11–17 below). In the *Johnson & Firth Brown* case [1975] E.C.R. 1, British Steel, against whom the interim measures in reality took effect, applied formally to intervene, and two other undertakings are described in the "Facts" part of the order as having "made what amounts to an application to intervene." Although there is nothing in the operative part of the order expressly allowing any intervention, all these would-be interveners were in fact able to present both written and oral argument, and indeed the "Facts" part of the Order also summarises the arguments presented by telex by another undertaking (at p. 5). On the other hand, by way of example, the Order in Case 109/75R *NCC* v. *Commission* [1975] E.C.R. 1193, 1200 expressly allowed the National Coal Board to intervene in the proceedings for the adoption of interim measures in support of the Commission, and the order in Cases 113/77R and 113/77R—Int. *NTN Toyo* v. *Council* [1977] E.C.R. 1721, 1726 expressly allowed the NSK Group to intervene in the interlocutory procedure in support of the applicants, since the same considerations would be at issue in its own application for interim measures in Case 119/77R *NSK* v. *Council* [1977] E.C.R. 1867. However, even where intervention is expressly allowed in the order, what distinguishes intervention in proceedings for the adoption of interim measures from intervention in the main action, apart from matters of detail, is the fact that the order allowing the intervention, if it forms part of the order dealing with the grant of interim measures, is likely to be made *after* the intervention has actually occurred. This situation is usually encountered where the request for interim measures is lodged immediately after the application commencing proceedings in the main action; in Joined Cases 209 to 215 and 218/78R *Van Landwyck and Others* v. *Commission* [1978] E.C.R. 2111, by way of comparison, where the applications commencing proceedings were lodged over a period of about a month, the Court joined the cases and allowed two trade associations to intervene in support of the applicants by an order made the day before the hearing of the applications for interim measures (see pp. 2113–2114).

AT WHAT STAGE MAY INTERIM MEASURES BE REQUESTED?

Rules of Procedure

Article 83

10–12   1. An application to suspend the operation of any measure adopted by an institution, made pursuant to the second paragraph of Article 39 of the ECSC Treaty, Article 185 of the EEC Treaty or Article 157 of the Euratom Treaty, shall be admissible only if the applicant is challenging that measure in proceedings before the Court.

An application for the adoption of any other interim measure referred to in the third paragraph of Article 39 of the ECSC Treaty, Article 186 of the EEC Treaty or Article 158 of the Euratom Treaty shall be admissible only if it is made by a party to a case before the Court and relates to that case.

10–13   The common thread underlying both sentences of article 83(1) of the Rules of Procedure is that a substantive action must have been commenced before the European Court before an application for interim measures may be made. Although the parent Treaty provisions, notably Article 186 of the EEC Treaty, are in very general terms, interim measures would appear only to have been sought in the context of direct actions before the European Court. On the basis of the rule expounded in Case 62/72 *Bollmann* v. *HZA Hamburg-Waltershof* [1973] E.C.R. 269, 275 that references for preliminary rulings are non-contentious and are in the nature of a step in the action pending before a national court, it has been generally accepted that any necessary interlocutory measures should be taken by the national court; nevertheless, it may be observed that the prospect of a national court suspending the application of a directly applicable or directly effective provision of Community law raises fundamental questions as to the relationship between Community law and national law.

In the context of direct actions,it has long been established that a request for interim measures may be made from the moment the main action has been introduced; indeed, article 63(1) of the 1953 Rules of Procedure expressly allowed the application for interim measures to be made at the same time as the lodging of the application in the main action. In Case 18/57 *Nold* v. *H.A.* [1957 and 1958] E.C.R. 121, 123, the Court held that "it is necessary and also sufficient that a main action has

276

been brought and that there is a legal representative for the purpose of the application for interim measures." Thereafter the timing of a request for interim measures is for the applicant to decide, although if the request is left until after the hearing in the main action, as in Joined Cases 3 to 18, 25 and 26/58 *Barbara Erzbergbau* v. *H.A.* [1960] E.C.R. at p. 223, it is likely to be difficult to convince the Court of its urgency. At the other extreme, there have been attempts to obtain interim measures covering the period until the interim order itself is made; however, in the context of actions for the annulment of Commission competition decisions, the President took notice in his order in Case 71/74R and RR *Frubo* v. *Commission* [1974] E.C.R. 1031, 1034 of a declaration by the Commission that "it is not its practice to force the parties concerned formally to annul their agreements or to make them conform to the Treaty when an interim application is pending against a decision declaring an agreement incompatible with article 85 [of the EEC Treaty]"; he concluded that it was therefore sufficient to make a normal interim order suspending the operation of the decision until the date of the judgment in the main action. Nevertheless, it would appear that since the end of 1981, the Commission has required undertakings which are challenging a decision imposing a fine to provide security for the payment, and in Case 107/82R *AEG Telefunken* v. *Commission* an order was made on March 29, 1982 suspending the imposition of the fine as a conservatory measure until a decision was given on the whole application for interim measures. However, the subsequent interim order of May 6, 1982 suspended the fine subject to the provision of security, and in the order of November 11, 1982 in Case 263/82R *Klöckner-Werke* v. *Commission* (O.J. 1983 C14/7) a fine was suspended subject to security both for the fine and for default interest at a rate 1 per cent. above the discount rate.

10–14 Special provisions have been enacted with regard to staff actions. Under article 91 of the Staff Regulations, an official may in principle bring an action against his employing institution before the Court only if he has previously complained to his appointing authority, and this complaint has been expressly or impliedly rejected. By way of derogation from this rule, article 91(4) of the Staff Regulations allows an official to bring an action before the European Court immediately after submitting his complaint to the appointing authority if the application this action is accompanied by a request for interim measures. Effectively this action is a fiction to allow the interim measures to be requested, since it is expressly provided that "the proceedings in the principal action before the Court of Justice shall then be suspended until such time as an express or implied decision rejecting the complaint is taken." It was in the context of this procedure that the President of the First Chamber stated in Case 75/72R *Perinciolo* v. *Council* [1972] E.C.R. 1201, 1203 that "in examining the admissibility of an application for a suspension of the operation of a measure, the judge in the interim proceedings must not prejudge questions relating to the admissibility of the main action which are within the jurisdiction of the court hearing the main action." This approach was followed in Case

714/79R *B* v. *Parliament* [1979] E.C.R. 3635, 3637 and appears to have been generalised, although problems remain with regard to the suspension of acts which are apparently of general application at the behest of individual litigants. In Case 44/75R *Könecke* v. *Commission* [1975] E.C.R. 637, 640, the President stated that "an application for the adoption of interim measures, when it may have the effect of stultifying a series of regulations, presupposes that the applicant must prove in a particularly clear fashion that he is concerned directly and individually," a test which at first sight is a more severe version of that laid down for the admissibilty of the main action under Article 173 of the EEC Treaty. However, the President then went on to consider the likelihood of harm being suffered by the applicant, and the possibility of avoiding that harm, and it might be suggested, in the light of the orders which did actually suspend the application of provisions of Regulations in the *Japanese ball bearings Cases* [1977] E.C.R. 1721, 1867 and 2107, that what the applicant has to show is the direct and individual nature of the harm he is likely to suffer rather than that the act at issue will ultimately be held to be susceptible to challenge by an individual litigant (see para. 1–27 above).

PROCEDURE

EEC Statute of the Court

Article 36

10–15   The President of the Court may, by way of summary procedure, which may, in so far as necessary, differ from some of the rules contained in this Statute and which shall be laid down in the rules of procedure, adjudicate upon applications to suspend execution, as provided for in Article 185 of this Treaty, or to prescribe interim measures in pursuance of Article 186, or to suspend enforcement in accordance with the last paragraph of Article 192.

Should the President be prevented from attending, his place shall be taken by another Judge under conditions laid down in the rules of procedure.

The ruling of the President or of the Judge replacing him shall be provisional and shall in no way prejudice the decision of the Court on the substance of the case.

(Article 37 of the Euratom Statute and Article 33 of the ECSC Statute are in corresponding terms.)

Rules of Procedure

Article 83

1. . . . (see para. 10–12 above).

2. An application of a kind referred to in paragraph 1 of this Article shall state the subject matter of the dispute, the circumstances giving rise to urgency and the factual and legal grounds establishing a *prima facie* case for the interim measures applied for.

3. The application shall be made by a separate document and in accordance with the provisions of Articles 37 and 38 of these rules.

Article 84

1. The application shall be served on the opposite party, and the President shall prescribe a short period within which that party may submit written or oral observations.

2. The President may order a preparatory inquiry.

The President may grant the application even before the observations of the opposite party have been submitted. This decision may be varied or cancelled even without any application being made by any party.

Article 85

The President shall either decide on the application himself or refer it to the Court.

If the President is absent or prevented from attending, Article 11 of these rules shall apply in a corresponding manner.

Where the application is referred to it, the Court shall postpone all other cases, and shall give a decision after hearing the Advocate-General. Article 84 shall apply in a corresponding manner.

Article 86

1. The decision on the application shall take the form of a reasoned order, from which no appeal shall lie. The order shall be served on the parties forthwith.

Article 87

On application by a party, the order may at any time be varied or cancelled on account of a change in circumstances.

Article 88

Rejection of an application for an interim measure shall not bar the party who made it from making a further application on the basis of new facts.

10–16 Although the commencement of a substantive action is an essential prerequisite to making an application for interim measures, the procedure on an application for interim measures is essentially self-contained. Hence the requirement in article 83(3) of the Rules of Procedure that the application must be made by a separate document is strictly interpreted, and in Case 108/63 *Merlini* v. *H.A.* [1965] E.C.R. 1, 9 and Case 32/64 *Italy* v. *Commission* [1965] E.C.R. 365, 372, requests for interim measures which were contained in the application commencing the main action were held to be inadmissible. Nevertheless, article 83(3) of the Rules itself requires the application for interim measures to comply both with the general rules governing written pleadings in direct actions (see para. 4–22 above) and with the specific rules governing applications commencing proceedings in direct actions (see para. 4–29 above). The summary nature of the procedure becomes apparent, however, thereafter: the defendant in the proceedings for interim measures may well be given only a matter of days to submit its observations, and in Case 3/75R *Johnson & Firth Brown* v. *Commission* [1975] E.C.R. 1, 5, account was taken of observations submitted by telex. As has been noted above (para. 10–11), a relatively informal concept of intervention has been developed to take account of the fact that parties other than the applicant and defendent may be affected by the interim measures in question. In the *Johnson & Firth Brown* case itself, two undertakings which had submitted observations were described ([1975] E.C.R. at p. 3) as having "made what amounts to an application to intervene," and in Case 109/75R *NCC* v. *Commission* [1975] E.C.R. 1193, 1200 and Cases 113/77R and 113/77R—Int. *NTN Toyo* v. *Council* [1977] E.C.R. 1721, 1726, requests to intervene were expressly acceded to in the order granting the interim measures, *i.e.* after the intervention had produced its practical results. Although article 84(1) of the Rules always requires the opposite party to be notified of a request for interim meassures, article 84(2) allows the measures to be granted before that party's observations are submitted. Nevertheless, in practice successive Presidents resisted attempts to obtain interim measures on an *ex parte* basis until 1982. However, in Case 107/82R *AEG-Telefunken* v. *Commission* (O.J. 1982 C99/5), President Mertens de Wilmars suspended the payment of a fine by an *ex parte* order dated March 29, 1982, such supervision being described as a "conservatory measure" until the interim measures as such were ordered on May 6, 1982. This was followed in Case 229/82R *Ford* v. *Commission* (O.J. 1982 C258/4) where a Commission decision ordering interim measures (see para. 10–06 above) was suspended as a "conservatory measure" by an *ex parte* order dated September 6, 1982 until the interim measures as such were ordered on September 29, 1982. Such an order was also made in a staff case by the President of the Third Chamber in Case 293/82R *De Compte* v. *European Parliament* (O.J. 1983 C14/7) on November 21, 1982, where it took the form of the "provisional" suspension of disciplinary proceedings until the termination of the interlocutory proceedings—and in fact interim measures as such were refused in an order dated December 13, 1982 (O.J. 1983 C41/9). What these cases would appear to have in common is a degree of urgency going beyond what is required simply to obtain interim measures as such.

10–17   Unlike the procedure in substantive direct actions, there is no obligation on the other party to submit written observations, although it is the normal practice given that the "other party" has usually been either a Community institution or a Member State. On the other hand, a number of examples can be found of the President deciding to dispose with oral argument, notably in staff cases, *e.g.* Case 186/80R *Suss* v. *Commission* [1980] E.C.R. 3501, 3505, and in competition cases, *e.g.* Case 27/76R *United Brands* v. *Commission* [1976] E.C.R. 425, 429. Where oral argument is heard, the practice of the Court is to sit *in camera:* although the Rules of Procedure are silent on the point, it is expressly stated in successive issues of the periodical *Information on the Court of Justice of the European Communities* published by the Court that "no visitor may be present . . . during proceedings for the adoption of interim measures."

The vast majority of applications for interim measures are determined by the President (or the President of the relevant Chamber) as envisaged under article 36 of the Statute and article 85 of the Rules. By the combined effect of articles 85, 11 and 6 of the Rules, if the President himself is unable to attend, his powers may be exercised by the Presidents of the Chambers according to their seniority, and if they are unable to attend, these powers may be exercised by one of the other judges according to their seniority. This last situation is most frequently encountered when an application for interim measures is made during a vacation, as *e.g.* in Case 174/80R *Reichardt* v. *Commission* [1980] E.C.R. 2665 where the application was made in the month of August. Although the decision under this procedure is that of the President or judge acting as President alone, it is common practice if a hearing is held for the President to be accompanied at that hearing by the Judge Rapporteur and the Advocate-General acting in that case.

10–18   Where the application for interim measures is referred to the Full Court by the President, an essential difference in the procedure is that the last paragraph of article 85 of the Rules requires the Advocate-General to be heard, and in the modern examples the Advocate-General has delivered a formal Opinion which has been published in the Reports. In Joined Cases 31/77R and 53/77R *Commission* v. *U.K.* [1977] E.C.R. 921 and in Case 61/77R *Commission* v. *Ireland* [1977] E.C.R. 937 the respective Advocates-General delivered their Opinions on the day on which oral argument was presented by the parties, and in Joined Cases 24 and 97/80R *Commission* v. *France* [1980] E.C.R. 1319 the Advocate-General delivered his Opinion the day after that on which oral argument was presented, as he did also in Case 42/82R *Commission* v. *France* (March 2, 1982). It may also be observed from these cases that the modern tendency is to refer applications for interim measures against Member States to the Full Court. Applications for interim measures are also heard by the Full Court where a novel point of general importance arises, as in Case 729/79R *Camera Care* v. *Commission* [1980] E.C.R. 119, where the Commission's competence to take interim measures in competition proceedings was at issue for the first time. Article 85 of the Rules also expressly provides that applications for interim measures heard by the Full Court must be given priority over all other cases. In practice, of course, priority is also given to applications determined by the President alone, but it was presumably not thought necessary to include a specific provision in the Rules since it remains feasible for a quorate Full Court or Chamber to continue with its ordinary business whilst the President is dealing with the request for interim measures.

10–19   Whichever procedure is followed, no appeal is permitted against the resultant order, and in Joined Cases 12 and 29/64 *Ley* v. *Commission* [1965] E.C.R. 107, 121 this was held to mean that if the interim order required the applicant to bear his costs on the application for interim measures, a request in the main action for a new ruling on these costs was inadmissible. The more usual practice with regard to costs, however, is to reserve them until judgment in the main action. Nevertheless, although an appeal as such is not possible, article 87 of the Rules allows an order to be varied or cancelled on account of a change in circumstances, and if the President were to make an interim order under article 84(2) of the Rules before the observations of the opposite party had been submitted he would be empowered to vary or cancel it of his own motion. Furthermore, although an order refusing interim measures cannot be challenged directly, the unsuccessful applicant remains at liberty to submit a further request for interim measures at a later stage in the proceedings if he considers that the circumstances justify it. Hence, although the application for interim measures failed in Joined Cases 160 and 161/73R *Miles Druce* v. *Commission* [1973] E.C.R. 1049 on the grounds that the *status quo* was not threatened, a few months later in Joined Cases l60 and 161/73R II *Miles Druce* v. *Commission* [1974] E.C.R. 281, the President did formally order the Commission to take steps to ensure the neutral behaviour of its undertakings concerned for a stated period, given that its decision under the ECSC Treaty concerning the takeover of one of the undertakings by the other was imminent.

CONDITIONS ATTACHED TO THE GRANT OF INTERIM MEASURES

Rules of Procedure

Article 86

10–20   2. The enforcement of the order may be made conditional on the lodging by the applicant of security, of an amount and nature to be fixed in the light of the circumstances.

3. Unless the order fixes the date on which the interim measure is to lapse, the measure shall lapse when final judgment is delivered.

4. The order shall have only an interim effect, and shall be without prejudice to the decision of the Court on the substance of the case.

10–21   Although it is not unknown, it would appear to be unusual for an interim order suspending an act of a Community institution to require the lodging of a security by the applicant. Such a requirement has, however, been imposed where the order has the effect of suspending a pecuniary obligation, as in the *Japanese ball bearing* cases: in Case 113/77R *NTN Toyo* v. *Council* [1977] E.C.R. 1721, for example, a provision in a Regulation requiring the definitive collection of anti-dumping duties was suspended with regard to the applicants on condition that they continued to provide security for the amounts they were liable to pay under the provision in question. A similar view has been taken with regard to the suspension of a fine, as in Case 263/82R *Klöckner-Werke* v. *Commission* (order of November 11, 1982), where security was required both for the fine and for default interest.

Where however the interim order in reality limits the activities of a business enterprise, it would appear that an undertaking in damages may be required from the applicant. In Case 109/75R *NCC* v. *Commission* [1975] E.C.R. 1193, 1202, the President ordered the Commission to take the necessary measures of conservation (which would effectively relate to the pricing policy of the National Coal Board) "subject to all appropriate guarantees"; the Commission's decision pursuant to this order required the National Coal Board to reduce the price of coal sold by it to NCC for the production of domestic hard coke by a fixed sum for a limited period, subject to the provision by NCC of security for the repayment by NCC of an amount corresponding to the total price reductions plus interest (O.J. 1976, 235/6).

GROUNDS ON WHICH INTERIM MEASURES WILL BE GRANTED

Rules of Procedure

Article 83

10–22   2. An application of a kind referred to in paragraph 1 of this Article shall state the subject matter of the dispute, the circumstances giving rise to urgency and the factual and legal grounds establishing a prima facie case for the interim measures applied for.

10–23   The only indication given in the Rules of Procedure with regard to the criteria to be taken into account in granting interim measures is that the applicant miust show "circumstances giving rise to urgency." This is of particular importance in the context of the timing of the application (see para. 10–13 above), and it is well established that interim measures will not be granted where the matter is not urgent, as in Case 61/76R II *Geist* v. *Commission* [1976] E.C.R. 2075, where the applicant unsuccessfully sought the suspension of the decision which he was challenging in his main action some six months after the commencement of proceedings.

The criteria by which the Court will determine whether there are factual and legal grounds establishing a prima facie case for the interim measures have evolved through the case law, although their application is perhaps inevitably dependent upon an appreciation of the facts of each individual case.

10–24   What is perhaps the fundamental criterion has been reported from the earliest cases onwards: this is the requirement that the applicant must show that "irreparable" harm (or "irreversible" damage) will occur unless the interim measures are granted. Thus in Case 19/59R *Geitling* v. *H.A.* [1960] E.C.R. 34, 37, the Court held that the applicants had not shown that a provision prescribing certain inspections would cause them damage which could not be redressed if that provision were annulled in the main action. This criterion has been regularly invoked in subsequent orders, *e.g.*, to take random examples, in Case 17/64R *Suss* v. *H.A.* [1964] E.C.R. 617, 618, in Case 71/74R *Frubo* v. *Commission* [1974] E.C.R. 1031, 1034, and in Case 258/80R *Rumi* v. *Commission* [1980] E.C.R. 3867, 3876. Irreparable or irreversible harm in this context would appear essentially to mean harm against which it is impossible to provide retroactive safeguards, as was expressly stated in Case 29/66R *Gutmann* v. *Commission* [1966] E.C.R. 241, 242. On the other hand, it would appear from the modern case law that the applicant is not required to show that such harm will inevitably occur but that there is a reasonable likelihood of its occurring. In Case 113/77R *NTN Toyo* v. *Council* [1977] E.C.R. 1721, the applicant claimed that it would incur additional financing costs if it had to pay the anti-dumping duties in question immediately rather than continuing to provide security for their payment, and indeed the Council did not contest this. The President, however, was prepared to suspend the provision requiring payment of the duty even on the basis that "it has not been possible to establish conclusively within the context of the present proceedings whether, in the event of NTN's being successful in the main action, this expenditure would be wholly recouped," but it should be borne in mind that in this case the interests of the defendant could be adequately protected by requiring the continuance of the security provided by the applicant for the payment of the duty, a factor which was expressly pointed out by the President in his order in the parallel application in Case 121/77R *Nachi Fujikoshi* v. *Council* [1977] E.C.R. 2107, 2110. In this latter case, however, the President refused to order the repayment by the national authorities of duty already paid by the applicants, on the grounds that the charges incurred by the public budget as a result of an order for repayment would exceed the harm suffered by the applicants as a result of the failure of their application.

10–25   There is a long line of authority to the effect that the harm likely to be suffered by the applicant should be "serious" as well as irreparable, and this was particularly emphasised in Case 258/80R *Rumi* v. *Commission* [1980] E.C.R. 3867, 3876 in the context of a request for the suspension of a measure of general application. Nevertheless, in Case 113/77R *NTN Toyo* v. *Council* [1977] E.C.R. 1721, the President used a subtly different approach, stating that the harm there at issue could not be regarded as negligible. Although in the order in Case 31/59 *Acciaieria di Brescia* v. *H.A.* [1960] E.C.R. 98, 99, the requirement that the harm should be serious is expressed as an alternative to the requirement that it should be irreparable in a passage which states that the applicant should show "irreparable or at least serious damage," this approach does not appear to have been followed in the modern case law. In one of the most usual situations, that of an undertaking seeking the suspension of a Commission competition decision addressed to it, however, it may be noted that the immediate unravelling of a network of agreements or practices held by the Commission in a contested decision to be in breach of the competition rules may be regarded as likely to cause both serious harm (*e.g.* Case 45/71R *Gema* v. *Commission* [1971] E.C.R. 791, 794) and irreparable harm (*e.g.* Case 71/74R *Frubo* v. *Commission* [1974] E.C.R. 1031, 1034) to the undertakings involved.

Where the interim measure sought is the suspension of a Community act, it is in principle necessary to show that the harm arises from that act. There are, however, rare instances of extrinsic factors being put forward insofar as they form part of the relevant legal or factual circumstances. Thus in Case 20/74R *Kali-Chemie* v. *Commission* [1974] E.C.R. 337 and Case 20/74R II *Kali-Chemie* v. *Commission* [1974] E.C.R. 787, where the President accepted that immediate compliance with a Commission decision, requiring the termination of an agreement by which another undertaking marketed pure potassic fertilizers produced by the applicant, could cause irreparable damage to the applicant, particularly if it undertook a hurried reconversion of its business, one of the factual circumstances put forward by the applicant was that the continued exploitation of the potash mine was in any event in doubt, and it produced an expert's report on the condition of its mine as an annex to its second application for interim measures.

10–26   One matter on which there remains some doubt, although in most orders it has not been found necessary to mention it, is whether the applicant needs to show that the main action is likely to succeed. In an early staff case, Joined Cases 43 to 45/79 *Lachmüller and others* v. *Commission* [1960] E.C.R. 489, 492, it was suggested by the President in an order dated October 20, 1959 that "it should be clearly apparent that there exists a strong presumption that the application in the main action is well-founded." Subsequently, in an order dated October 1, 1960 in Case 44/59 *Fiddelaar* v. *Commission* [1960] E.C.R. at pp. 555, 556, following the award of damages to the other two applicants in their main actions, the President did award an interim payment to the applicant on the basis that he could reasonably expect to receive comparable damages. However, the interim measure sought in these cases involved payments by the defendant to the applicants, and it would appear from the express authority of the order in Joined Cases 19 and 65/63 *Prakash* v. *Commission* [1965] E.C.R. at pp. 576, 578, that "a provision for immediate sustenance can only be granted by means of an interim measure if the original application appears *prima facie* to be clearly well-founded" (see para. 10–05 above). It might be suggested that where the applicant is seeking interim measures which do not involve payments in his favour, the relevant test is that enounced in Case 3/75 *Johnson & Firth Brown* v. *Commission* [1975] E.C.R. 1, 6, *i.e.* that the grounds on which the substantive application is made should not appear to be manifestly without foundation.

Nevertheless, although it may not in itself lead to the failure of an application for interim measures, the fact that the main action appears to have little chance of success may well be taken into account in balancing the interests of the parties where the interim measures sought are likely to cause serious harm to the defendant, as in Case 91/76R *De Lacroix* v. *Court of Justice* [1976] E.C.R. 1563, 1565. There the application was dismissed because the suspension requested would involve serious difficulties both for the defendant and third parties whilst the main action appeared to be based on "questionable" grounds.

10–27   Although it may be concluded from this that the usual practice of the Court is to require an applicant for interim measures to show the likelihood of irreversible harm of a serious nature, and that the main action is not manifestly unfounded, there is nothing to preclude the

Court from taking account of other legal or factual circumstances or applying other criteria. Such an exceptional approach has in particular been encountered in the context of interim measures ordered against Member States. In its order in Joined Cases 31/77R and 53/77R *Commission* v. *U.K.* [1977] E.C.R. 921, 924, the Court held that disregard of the rules in Article 93 of the EEC Treaty governing the introduction of national aids, requiring Member States to obtain the approval of the Commission (or possibly of the Council) before introducing such aids, was "capable by itself of giving rise to the application of Article 186." Similarly, in Case 61/77R *Commission* v. *Ireland* [1977] E.C.R. 937, 942, the Court decided in principle to suspend the Irish fisheries measures in question on the ground that they might jeopardise the elaboration of a common fishing policy, that the status quo should not be altered by divergent national provisions, and that the measures were capable of prejudicing the position of the Community in international negotiations. It did not, however, discuss whether this harm was irreparable, which had been doubted by A.G. Reischl ([1977] E.C.R. at 937, 954). On the other hand, whatever the likelihood of harm, it would appear from the order in Joined Cases 24 and 97/80R *Commission* v. *France* [1980] E.C.R. 1319, 1333, that the Court is not willing in subsequent proceedings to order interim measures against a Member State which has failed to obey a judgment given against it where the tenor of the interim measures would be the same as that of the already binding earlier judgment.

10–28   More generally, in determining whether there is a need formally to order interim measures, the Court will take account of undertakings offered to it by the parties. Thus, the first application for interim measures in the *Miles Druce* case [1973] E.C.R. 1049, 1053–1054, was rejected in the light of an undertaking by GKN (which appeared as an intervener, not the defendant) not to use its shares in Miles Druce to summon a general meeting within the next six months, and a declaration by the Commission that it would act if the status quo appeared to be threatened. Similarly, in Case 71/74R and RR *Frubo* v. *Commission* [1974] E.C.R. 1031, 1034, the President found that it was not necessary formally to suspend the decision at issue for the period before the making of the order on the application for interim measures, following a declaration by the Commission that it was not its practice to force the parties concerned formally to annul their agreements or to make them conform to the Treaty whilst an interim application was pending against a decision declaring an agreement incompatible with Article 85 of the EEC Treaty. Account has also been taken of the likelihood of the substantive dispute being settled. This may lead either to the interim measures being restricted to a relatively short period, as in Case 20/74R *Kali-Chemie* v. *Commission* [1974] E.C.R. 337, or to the postponement for a fixed period of their entry into force, as in Case 61/77R *Commission* v. *Ireland* [1977] E.C.R. 937.

APPLICATION OF THE INTERIM MEASURES PROCEDURE TO OTHER CIRCUMSTANCES

Rules of Procedure

Article 89

10–29   The provisions of this Chapter shall apply in a corresponding manner to applications to suspend the enforcement of a decision of the Court or of any measure adopted by another institution, submitted pursuant to Articles 44 and 92 of the ECSC Treaty, Articles 187 and 192 of the EEC Treaty or Articles 159 and 164 of the Euratom Treaty. The order granting the application shall fix a date on which the interim measure is to lapse.

Article 90

1. An application of a kind referred to in the third and fourth paragraphs of Article 81 of the Euratom Treaty shall contain:
   (a) the names and addresses of the persons or undertakings to be inspected;
   (b) an indication of what is to be inspected and of the purpose of the inspection.
2. The President shall give his decision in the form of an order. Article 86 of these rules shall apply in a corresponding manner.

If the President is absent or prevented from attending, Article 11 of these rules shall apply.

10–30   By virtue of article 89 of the Rules of Procedure, the procedure governing applications for interim measures is used also where it is sought to suspend the enforcement of a judgment of the Court (see para. 8–12 above) or of a decision of the Council or Commission, or of the Euratom Arbitration Committee. With regard to the suspension of the enforcement of a judgment, a special provision is obviously needed since there is no way in which a substantive action could be brought to challenge the judgment; with regard to the decisions of the other institutions, there is no authority on the question whether Article 192 of the EEC Treaty and the parallel provisions of the other Treaties create an independent remedy allowing the enforcement of the decision to be suspended without there being any need for the applicant to challenge that decision in a substantive action. It is, however, submitted that an applicant with doubts as to the legality of such a decision would be well advised to challenge it in a substantive action and then request interim measures in the normal way.

Article 90 of the Rules similarly applies the interim measure procedures where an inspection under Article 81 of the Euratom Treaty is opposed. Here speed is of the essence, since Article 81(3) of the Euratom Treaty requires that where the Commission applied to the Court for an order that the inspection be carried out compulsorily, the President must give a decision within three days, and article 81(4) allows the Commission itself to order an inspection, if there is danger in delay, subject to submitting this order to the President of the Court "without delay" for subsequent approval.

The interim measures rules have indeed been applied by analogy by

287

the Court itself. In Case 4/73—Enforcement *Nold* v. *Ruhrkohle A.G.*
[1977] E.C.R. 1, the applicant asked the Court to declare the
enforcement of an order requiring it to pay the intervener's costs ([1975]
E.C.R. 985) "inadmissible" on the grounds that this debt was
extinguished by renunciation or waiver. It was held that in the absence
of any provision expressly governing such an application, the procedure
relating to the suspension of the enforcement of a judgment of the Court
under article 89 of the Rules should be followed (in a passage which is
unfortunately omitted from the printed English version of the Report),
which in turn refers back to the procedure on an applilcation for interim
measures. In the result, however, it was, hardly surprisingly, held that
the Court had no jurisdiction to try the application.

CHAPTER 11

INTERVENTION

BY WHOM AND ON WHAT BASIS?

EEC Statute of the Court

Article 37

11–01   Member States and institutions of the Community may intervene in cases before the Court.

The same right shall be open to any other person establishing an interest in the result of any case submitted to the Court, save in cases between Member States, between institutions of the Community or between Member States and institutions of the Community

Submissions made in an application to intervene shall be limited to supporting the submissions of one of the parties

(Article 38 of the Euratom Statute is in identical terms.)

ECSC Statute of the Court

Article 34

Natural or legal persons establishing an interest in the result of any case submitted to the Court may intervene in that case.

Submissions made in an application to intervene shall be limited to supporting or requesting the rejection of the submission of one of the parties.

Article 41

[Where a dispute between Member States is brought before the Court under Article 89 of this Treaty. . . .]

. . . Each Member State shall have the right to intervene in the proceedings.

A. THE CONCEPT OF INTERVENTION

11–02   In the practice of the European Court, intervention is a method by which a third party may intervene voluntarily in proceedings between other parties. As explained in Joined Cases 42 and 49/59—Third Party Proceedings *Breedband* v. *Acieries du Temple* [1962] E.C.R. 145, 158.

> "the efficient administration of justice and the need for certainty in legal relationships demand that persons interested in the result of an action pending before the Court be precluded from asserting their rights once a judgment has been delivered settling the question in dispute. It is precisely in order to meet this requirement that [article 34 of the ECSC Statute] makes available to third

parties whose interests are involved in an action pending before the Court the right of voluntary intervention."

As a right of voluntary intervention, however, it is dependent upon the initiative of the interested third party; there is no mechanism of compulsory intervention by which a third party may be joined to the proceedings against his will. Hence, in Case 12/69 *Wonnerth* v. *Commission* [1969] E.C.R. 577, 584, an application for the compulsory intervention of a third party was held inadmissible as being a form of action not provided for in the Rules of Procedure.

B. WHO MAY INTERVENE?

11–03   Article 37 of the EEC Statute expressly provides for intervention by Member States and Community institutions on the one hand, and "any other person" on the other, "any other person" being required to show an interest in the result of the case (see para. 11–07 below). Article 34 of the ECSC Statute, however, uses the general phrase "natural or legal persons"; in the context of the ECSC Treaty, which confers direct rights of action only on Member States, Community institutions, and undertakings or associations of undertakings in the coal and steel sectors, this phrase would appear to be intended to allow for a wide definition of possible interveners. In Case 20/59 *Netherlands* v. *H.A.* [1960] E.C.R. 355, 388, it was stated that this provision "enables any natural or legal person without any distinction whatever to appear before the Court as an intervener." Indeed, the first order allowing an intervention was made at the behest of a Member State, when Luxembourg applied to support the defendant in Joined Cases 7 and 9/54 *Industries Sidérurgiques Luxembourgeoises* v. *H.A.* [1954–1956] E.C.R. 175, 223, and the question of its capacity so to do appears to have given rise to no comment, except with regard to its interest in the result, which was held to be "incontestable." Nevertheless, intervention by a Member State is expressly provided for in article 41 of the ECSC Statute in the context of an action brought by one Member State against another under Article 89 of the ECSC Treaty. In such a dispute, the remaining Member States are entitled to intervene as of right.

11–04   In practice, however, intervention by Member States has tended to be more common in actions governed by the EEC statute. In Case 231/78 *Commission* v. *United Kingdom* [1979] E.C.R. 1447, for example, France intervened to support the United Kingdom's unsuccessful contention that under article 60(2) of the 1972 Act of Accession it could maintain the control of imports in the context of its national organisation of the market in potatoes until that organisation was replaced by a common organisation, despite the expiry of the basic Accession transitional period laid down in article 9 of that Act. The apparent reason for this intervention was that France wished to take the same points with regard to its national organisation of the market in sheepmeat in Case 232/78 *Commission* v. *France* [1979] E.C.R. 2729. Examples can also be found of Member States intervening to support a

Community institution, as in Case 804/79 *Commission* v. *United Kingdom* [1981] E.C.R. 1045, where France and Ireland intervened to support the Commission, or even to support a private litigant as when Germany and Italy intervened to support the applicants in Joined Cases 56 and 58/64 *Consten & Grundig* v. *Commission*[1966] E.C.R. 299.

It is now clear that the phrase "institutions of the Community" in article 37 of the EEC Statute is not limited to those institutions entitled to bring a direct action for annulment or to submit observations on a reference for a preliminary ruling. This appears from the judgment in Case 138/79 *Roquette* v. *Council* [1980] E.C.R. 3333, 3357, where it was stated that the right to intervene was available to all the institutions of the Community, and where the European Parliament was permitted to intervene to support the private applicant. It may also be noted that in that case the Commission intervened to support the defendant Council. The Commission has also intervened in a direct action to which no Community institution was originally a party in Case 141/78 *France* v. *United Kingdom* [1979] E.C.R. 2923, where it supported the French Government.

11–05   Intervention by natural persons is most frequently encountered in staff cases, as in Case 130/75 *Prais* v. *Council* [1976] E.C.R. 1589, where the official appointed as a result of the competition challenged by the applicant intervened to support the defendant institution. Intervention by legal persons (in the sense of business enterprises) has occurred particularly in competition cases, where, for example, a complainant before the Commission may well wish to intervene to support the Commission in subsequent judicial proceedings, as in the first application for the annulment of a competition decision to be heard by the Court in Joined Cases 56 and 58/64 *Consten & Grundig* v. *Commission* [1966] E.C.R. 299, 385. Similarly, in an action for failure to act, a potential addressee of the requested decision may wish to intervene, as Hasselblad Limited intervened to support the Commission in Case 792/79R *Camera Care* v. *Commission* [1980] E.C.R. 119, 124.

11–06   In this context, the Court has often been faced with the question whether an intervener other than an institution, Member State, or natural person must be recognised as having separate legal personality in the strict sense, and it has consistently taken the view that the legal classification of the intervener is not conclusive. In Joined Cases 16 and 17/62 *Confédération nationale des producteurs de fruits et légumes* [1962] E.C.R. 471, 487, the Court took the view that the expression "any other person" in article 37 of the EEC Statute was drafted in the widest possible terms, and included a professional association such as the "Assemblée permanente des présidents de chambre d'agriculture" recognised under French law as a representative organisation concerned with agricultural interests. Criteria for determining whether a body not having legal personality may intervene were eventually set out in the *Sugar Cases* [1973] E.C.R. 1465, 1468, where the Italian consumers' union was allowed to intervene in support of the Commission. It was stated that "bodies not having legal personality may be permitted to intervene if they display the characteristics which are at the foundation

291

of such personality, in particular, the ability, however circumscribed, to undertake autonomous action and to assume liability." Subsequently, even an international professional representative body has been permitted to intervene: the Commission Consultative des Barreaux de la Communauté Européenne (CCBE), a representative body of the legal profession in the European Community, was, by order dated May 7, 1980, permitted to intervene in support of the applicant in Case 155/79 *A. M & S.* v. *Commission* (May 18, 1982). The European Court may in particular take account of the national law under which such a body is constituted, if that law allows it to participate in legal proceedings. In the order of November 16, 1977 in Case 119/77 *NSK* v. *Council* [1979] E.C.R. 1303, the Federation of European Bearing Manufacturers' Associations (FEBMA) was treated as having capacity to intervene in support of the Council largely on the basis that according to German law, under which it was constituted, it had capacity to intervene in court proceedings, and costs could be recovered against it.

A more specific problem has been encountered with regard to collective intervention in staff cases. In Case 15/63 *Lassalle* v. *Parliament* [1964] E.C.R. 31, 50, an application by the Staff Committee of the European Parliament, established under article 9 of the Staff Regulations, to intervene in support of the applicant was rejected on the grounds that the Staff Committee was a mere internal agency of the institution, and it lacked independence and even a limited degree of responsibility. However, in Case 72/74 *Union Syndicale* v. *Council* [1975] E.C.R. 401, 410, it was expressly stated that the right to intervene is available to trade unions representing staff, presumably on the basis, accepted earlier in Case 175/73 *Union Syndicale* v. *Council* [1974] E.C.R. 917, 925, that their structure was "such as to endow [them] with the necessary independence to act as a responsible body in legal matters."

C. BASIS FOR INTERVENTION

11–07 The EEC and Euratom Statutes make a fundamental distinction between intervention by Member States and Community institutions on the one hand, and by "any other person" on the other, in that only the latter are required to show an interest in the result of the case. Hence, in Case 138/79 *Roquette* v. *Council* [1980] E.C.R. 3333, 3357–3358, it was held that the European Parliament when intervening, did not have to show it had an interest in the outcome of the proceedings. On the other hand, although in the specific context of disputes between Member States article 41 of the ECSC Statute enables other Member States to intervene as of right, in general article 34 of the ECSC Statute would appear to require any intervener to show an interest in the result, a test applied without comment on application to intervene by Luxembourg in Joined Cases 7 and 9/54 *Industries Sidérurgiques Luxembourgeoises* v. *H.A.* [1954–1956] E.C.R. 175, 223 and on an application to intervene by Germany in Case 30/59 *Steenkolenmijnen* v. *H.A.* [1961] E.C.R. 1, 48, to give two examples. This view is also supported by the finding in

Joined Cases 9 and 12/60—Third Party Proceedings *Belgium* v. *Vloeberghs and H.A.* [1962] E.C.R. 171, 183 that the Belgian Government had no "direct and specific interest" in intervening in Case 9/60. Be that as it may, the concept of an interest in the result of a case has been interpreted in a manner which closely relates to the requirement that all interveners must support the submission (*i.e.* "conclusions") of the parties. In Case 111/63 *Lemmerz-Werke* v. *H.A.* [1965] E.C.R. 677, 717, it was held that "result" meant "the operative part of the final judgment which the parties ask the Court to deliver," and in Joined Cases 56 and 58/63 *Consten & Grundig* v. *Commission* [1966] E.C.R. 299, 383, the Court stated that the interest in the result of a case must relate "to the actual conclusions of a party to the main action." Hence the distinction between Member States and Community institutions under the EEC and Euratom Statutes, and other interveners, is that whilst the former need only support the submissions of one of the parties, the latter must also show that they have an interest in these submissions.

11-08   The use of the word "submissions" in the English versions of the Statutes is unfortunate, since the term used in the other versions is the same as that which in article 38(1)(d) of the Rules of Procedure relating to the contents of an application is rendered into English as the statement of the "form of order sought" by the applicant (see para. 4–40 above), and it is clear from the case law that it is this statement of the form of order sought (called "conclusions" even in Enlish in the European Court Reports from mid-1974) which the intervener must support. Hence, in the *Lemmez-Werke* case [1965] E.C.R at 718, the application to intervene was rejected on the basis that the would-be intervener wished to support the arguments put forward by the applicant rather than the conclusions supported by those arguments. More recently, the same view was expressed in Joined Cases 116, 124 and 143/77 *Amylum* v. *Council and Commission* [1978] E.C.R. 893, 895, where it was held that the applicants to intervene were interested only in supporting certain arguments of the defendants rather than their conclusions. On the other hand, in the *Grundig* case [1966] E.C.R. at 384 and 386, it was found that the interveners did indeed wish to support the conclusions of the defendant since, in the view of the Court, the acceptance or rejection of those conclusions would exercise a decisive influence on national litigation in which the interveners were parties

11-09   That the intervener must support the formal statement of the order sought by a party is further emphasised by the statement in Joined Cases 9 and 12/60—Third Party Proceedings *Belgium* v. *Vloeberghs and H.A.* [1962] E.C.R. 171, 182 that "in view of the fact that the written procedure is not of a public nature, it is only possible to determine an interest establishing a right to intervene in the case from the subject matter and conclusions of the application as published in the Official Journal," since until the 1979 amendments to the Rules of Procedure, the only published indications of the substance of the case were the statement of the subject-matter of the dispute and of the form of order sought in the application. Taken literally, the view that intervention is based on published information would make it difficult to intervene in support of the defendant under the EEC and Euratom Statutes, since the conclusions of the defence are not published; however, in practice the defendant usually seeks the rejection of the applicant's conclusions, and an intervener may determine whether to support this rejection from the statement of the original conclusions. Nonetheless, perhaps as a corollary to the imposition of time-limits on the right to intervene, the 1979 amendments have broadened the scope of the published information (although it still only relates to the application) and have put the Commission and the Council (and hence presumably the Member States) in a privileged position. As amended, article 16(6) of the Rules of Procedure (see para. 4–12 above and para. 12–04 below) requires the publication not only of the subject-matter of the dispute and of what are now termed "the claims made in the application," but also a summary of the contentions and of the main arguments adduced in support, information intended to help place the conclusions in their context even if, as has been seen, an interest in the arguments does not confer an entitlement to intervene. The privileged treatment of the Council and Commission arises from the amended article 16(7) of the Rules, which requires copies of the application and defence to be forwarded to either of those institutions in any case to which it is not a party. Ostensibly this is to enable the institution to study whether one of its acts is being indirectly challenged by a plea of illegality (see para. 1–33 above), but since the Council consists of representatives of the Member States, it is not improbable that the contents of these documents will be communicated to the national authorities, who will then be better equipped to decide whether to intervene

11–10   So far as the arguments put forward by the parties are concerned, just as support for the arguments of one party is not sufficient to justify intervention, so also a third party who has been permitted to intervene is not limited to supporting the arguments of the party whose conclusions he supports. In Case 30/59 *Steenkolenmijnen* v. *H.A.* [1961] E.C.R. 1, 17–18 the German Government, in intervening to support the conclusion of the defendant, used arguments conflicting with those of the defendant and with which it expressly disagreed. Nevertheless, the Court held that "the intervention procedure would be deprived of all meaning if the intervener were to be denied the use of any argument which had not been used by the party which it supported," despite the doubts of A.G. Lagrange. This view was confirmed shortly afterwards in Joined Cases 42 and 49/59 *SNUPAT* v. *H.A.* [1961] E.C.R. 53, 75. Indeed, in Joined Cases 16 and 17/62 *Producteurs de Fruits* v. *Council* [1963] E.C.R. 471, 488, where the defendant argued that the intervention should not be allowed on the grounds that the intervener had no separate interest in the case, the Court, although it held that there was no requirement that the interest of the intervener should be distinct from that of the party whom he supports, put forward a further justification for allowing the intervention the fact that "even in this case the purpose of the intervention is to allow the intervener to put forward *its own arguments* in support of the common cause" (emphasis added).

A more recent example of an intervener using arguments opposed by the party whose conclusions it supported is to be found in Case 155/79 *A.M. & S. Europe Ltd.* v. *Commission* (May 18, 1982) where the French Government intervened, technically in support of the Commission's conclusions, to argue that there was no concept of "legal professional privilege" or "confidentiality" in Community law, whereas A.M.& S. and the Commission were in agreement that the dispute between them related to the procedure whereby it should be determined whether a document was protected from disclosure, not to the existence of such protection.

D. TYPES OF ACTION IN WHICH INTERVENTION MAY BE PERMITTED

11–11 Although article 37 of the EEC Statute and article 38 of the Euratom Statute do not allow the intervention of a person other than a Member State or Community institution "in cases between Member States, between institutions of the Community or between Member States and institutions of the Community," there is no such restriction expressed in article 34 of the ECSC Statute. Nevertheless, the European Court has taken the view that there must be limits on the intervention of private litigants under the ECSC Statute in disputes between Member States and/or Community institutions. In Case 20/59 *Netherlands* v. *H.A.* [1960] E.C.R. 355, 389, in the context of an application to intervene in an action brought by a Member State under Article 88 of the ECSC Treaty seeking the annulment of a High Authority decision finding that State (among others) in breach of certain Treaty obligations, it was stated that:

> "such intervention can . . . be for the sole purpose of obtaining an interpretation of the Treaty, to the exclusion of any consideration of determination of the time-limit which the High Authority can set that State for the fulfilment of its obligations or the detailed rules for the application of any restrictive decision by the Authority against that State since, in these various cases, the very nature of these acts, which take place at the level of the relationship between States, public authorities and the High Authority as the Community agency, precludes the intervention of private persons."

This view that the details of the relationships between Member States and/or Community institutions are not the concern of private litigants no doubt underlay the total exclusion of intervention in such disputes by "other persons" under the EEC and Euratom Statutes. It is not, however, totally impossible for a private litigant to have his arguments taken into account under the EEC and Euratom Statutes. He may, for example, be a party in a reference for a preliminary ruling which is heard at the same time as, for example, an action brought by the Commission against a Member State with regard to the same matter. Thus Case 88/77 *Minister for Fisheries* v *Schonenberg* [1978] E.C.R. 473, a reference from an Irish criminal court, and Case 61/77*Commission* v. *Ireland* [1978] E.C.R. 417, which both involved questions of the legality of certain Irish fisheries measures, were heard on the same day.

11–12   At the other extreme from these institutional disputes, it is also now well established that intervention is not possible in a reference for a preliminary ruling. As a matter of principle, if, as was held in Case 62/72 *Bollmann* v. *HZA Hamburg-Waltershof* [1973] E.C.R. 269, 275 a reference is merely a step in an action already before a national court, it cannot be open to the European Court to let new parties join in. The matter was, however, decided in Case 6/64 *Costa* v. *ENEL* [1964] E.C.R. at p. 614 on the simple basis that Article 20 of the EEC Statute, allowing parties to the main action, the Member States, the Commission and, where appropriate, the Council, to submit observations to the Court (see para. 4–111 above) "would be pointless if the right to participate in the procedure under Article 177 of the Treaty were conferred on all persons interested under article 37 of the Statute."

11–13   With regard to direct actions under the EEC and Euratom Treaties which are not between Member States and/or Community institutions, it was stated in Joined Cases 9 and 12/60—Third Party Proceedings *Belgium* v. *Vloeberghs and H.A.* [1962] E.C.R. 171, 182 that voluntary intervention cannot be justified in any and every action and that "the interest in intervention in proceedings pending before the Court must be justified as much by reference to the nature of the proceedings in which the intervener asks to be allowed to take part as by reference to the conclusions of one of the parties." In that case, the main action sought the payment of damages by the High Authority, and the Court took the view that it was "unreasonable" to assert that either the subject-matter or the conclusions stated in the original application disclosed a specific and direct interest on the part of the potential intervener in intervening voluntarily in order to support or reject the applicant's conclusions. This would appear to mean that a person independent of the original parties will normally be unable to intervene in an action for damages, since no-one other than the parties is likely to have an interest in the payment or non-payment of damages. Thus in the order in Joined Cases 116, 124 and 143/77 *Amylum* v. *Council and Commission* [1978] E.C.R. 893, 895, where certain professional associations of sugar producers sought to intervene in support of the defendants, in the context of an action for damages brought by manufacturers of isoglucose, it was held that the applicants to intervene had not proved that they had a "direct and present interest" in the acceptance of the defendants' conclusions. Nevertheless, it is not impossible to prove such an interest in the conclusions presented in an action for damages. In Joined Cases 197 to 200, 243, 245 and 247/80 *Walzmühle Erling & others* v. *Council and Commission* [1981] E.C.R. 3211, a group of actions claiming damages for the harm caused to the applicants by Community institutions in fixing the threshold price for durum wheat at a level which was alleged to be too high, two undertakings which milled imported durum wheat were allowed to intervene in support of an applicant which manufactured pasta and noodles, and three French professional associations concerned with the milling, pasta and cereals trades, and the Italian Government were allowed to intervene in support of the defendants. It remains to be seen, however, whether those orders indicate an overall change in attitude to the possibility of intervention in actions for damages, or indeed whether the original *Vloeberghs* decision was itself an exceptional case, given that the Court was there concerned with an application for third party proceedings by the Belgian Government, and under article 97 of the Rules of Procedure (see para. 12–03 below) such an application would have been barred if it was found that the Belgian Government could have been expected to have taken part in the original case.

THE APPLICATION TO INTERVENE

Rules of Procedure

Article 16

11–14   6. Notice shall be given in the *Official Journal of the European Communities* of the date of registration of an application originating proceedings, the names and permanent residences of the parties, the subject-matter of the dispute, the claims made in the application and a summary of the contentions and of the main arguments adduced in support.'

Article 93

1. An application to intervene must be made within three months of the publication of the notice referred to in Article 16(6) of these rules.

2. The application shall contain:
(a) the description of the case;
(b) the description of the parties;
(c) the name and permanent residence of the intervener;
(d) the reasons for the intervener's interest in the result of the case, having regard to Article 37 of the EEC Statute and Article 38 of the Euratom Statute;
(e) submissions supporting or opposing the submissions of a party to the original case;
(f) an indication of any evidence founded upon and, in an annex, the supporting documents;
(g) the intervener's address for service at the place where the Court has its seat.

The intervener shall be represented in accordance with the first and second paragraphs of Article 20 of the ECSC Statute and with Article 17 of the EEC and Euratom Statutes.

Articles 37 and 38 of these rules shall apply in a corresponding manner.

3. The application shall be served on the parties to the original case. The Court shall give the parties an opportunity to submit their written or oral observations and shall, after hearing the Advocate-General, give its decision in the form of an order.

A. TIMING OF THE APPLICATION

11–15   The time-limit for intervention has been changed twice since the Court's inception. Under article 71(1) of the 1953 Rules of Procedure, an application to intervene had to be lodged before the end of the written procedure, *i.e.* before the rejoinder was lodged or the time-limit for its lodging expired. Article 93(1) of the 1959 Rules, re-enacted in the 1974 Rules, extended this period by requiring the application to intervene to be made before the opening of the oral procedure, a change which allowed interventions to be made during the preparatory inquiries and until the hearing. Thus, in Case 30/59 *Steenkolenmijnen* v. *H.A.* [1961] E.C.R. 1, 18, it is reported that the German Government intervened after delivery of the rejoinder, to give one early example. It further appears from the report in Case 26/76 *Metro* v. *Commission* [1977] E.C.R. 1875, 1894 that a professional association of self-service wholesalers intervened in support of the applicant not only after the written procedure had terminated, but also after the Court had asked the parties to reply to a number of specific questions. However, the possibility of late intervention would seem to have given rise to the fear that it could be used as a tactical device to prolong the proceedings, and in the 1979 amendments to the Rules of Procedure, article 93(1) was altered so as to impose a fixed time-limit for intervention of three months from the publication of the notice of commencement of proceedings in the *Official Journal*. This provision was invoked by the Court in an order dated May 7, 1980 to dismiss an application to intervene in Case 809/79 *Pardini* v. *Commission* (subsequently withdrawn) where the notice of commencement of proceedings had been published on January 11, 1980. Like other procedural time-limits, this limit may be extended on account of distance under Annex II to the Rules (see para. 2–02 above), and it could be argued that the policy considerations underlying article 81(1) of the Rules, which provides that in an action challenging a published act of an institution the limitation period begins to run from the fifteenth day after its publication in the *Official Journal*, are equally relevant here, although the point does not appear to have been taken.

11–16   There is, on the other hand, no restriction on making an early application to intervene other than the fact that the proceedings in the main action must have been commenced. It is also possible to intervene in an early application for interim measures by what amounts to a simplified procedure, in that observations presented by interested third parties may be treated as applications to intervene, as in Case 3/75R *Johnson & Firth Brown* v.*Commission* [1975] E.C.R. 1, 3, and the formal order allowing intervention may form part of the order regulating the grant of interim measures, hence being made after the intervention has actually occurred, as in Cases 113/77R and 113/77R— Int. *NTN Toyo* v. *Council* [1977] E.C.R. 1721, 1726; this matter is further discussed in the context of interim measures (see para. 10–11 above). The order in this last case also shows that an application to intervene may be limited to the proceedings for interim measures, where the intervener's interest relates to the interim measures as such.

B. Making the Application

11–17 The formal requirements relating to an application to intervene are broadly similar to those relating to an application commencing proceedings under articles 37 and 38 of the Rules of Procedure (see paras. 4–22, 4–29 above). What is particular to an application to intervene is that it must, where appropriate, state the reasons for the intervener's interest in the result of the case, contain conclusions ("submissions" in the official English version) supporting or opposing the conclusions of a party to the original case, and describe the case and the parties rather than simply naming the defendant. Otherwise the rules governing the number of copies, translations of documents, the statement of an address for service, and the need for legal representation are the same, although there are certain special considerations with regard to the language of the case. Since the mere making of an application to intervene does not in itself entitle the intervener to participate in the main action, it was held by the Court in Case 30/59 *Steenkolenmijnen* v. *H.A.* [1961] E.C.R. 1, 48 that an intervener may draw up his application in a language other than that of the case in the main action, and that he only becomes bound by the language of the case when his intervention has been allowed. Even then, an intervener may apply, like any other party, for permission to use another language for all or part of the procedure under article 29(2)(c) of the Rules (see above para. 3–01); in the *Steenkolenmijnen* case itself, where the language of the case was Dutch, the German Government as intervener was required to use Dutch for the written procedure but authorised to use German for the oral procedure ([1961] E.C.R. 1, 50–51). With regard to intervention by Member States, it is now expressly provided in the fourth sub-paragraph of article 29(3) of the Rules as amended in 1979 that a Member State shall be entitled to use its own official language when intervening. This, however, was already the usual modern practice of the Court even with regard to intervention by private persons, *e.g.* in Joined Cases 6 and 7/73 *Commercial Solvents* v. *Commission* [1974] E.C.R. 223, where the language of the case was English, an Italian company which intervened (albeit briefly) in support of the Commission was permitted by order of May 8, 1973 to use the Italian language.

11–18 Whilst article 93(2) of the Rules allows the parties to the original action to submit written or oral observations on the application to intervene, it does not enable the applicants to intervene to reply to these observations. This provision has been strictly applied, so that when, in Case 20/59 *Netherlands* v. *H.A.* [1960] E.C.R. 355, 387–388, those applying to intervene lodged a reply to the observations of the defendant in the original case, it was quite simply held that this reply was out of order and could not be the subject of argument, *i.e.* it was totally disregarded. Hence, the material available to the Court in determining whether to allow an intervention will normally be the application to intervene together with the observations of the original applicant and defendant on that application.

CONSEQUENCES OF INTERVENTION

Rules of Procedure

Article 93

11–19   4. If the Court allows the intervention, the intervener shall receive a copy of every document served on the parties. The Court may, however, on application by one of the parties, omit secret or confidential documents.

5. The intervener must accept the case as he finds it at the time of his intervention.

The President shall prescribe a period within which the intervener is to state in writing the grounds for his submissions.

A. PROCEEDINGS IN THE ORIGINAL ACTION

11–20   The fundamental rule laid down in article 93(5) is that the intervener must accept the case as he finds it at the time of his intervention, *i.e.* intervention does not lead to the reopening of any of the stages of the procedure which have already been completed. Nevertheless, there are two respects in which intervention may alter the normal procedure. The first is that, as has already been mentioned (see para. 11–10 above), an intervener is not bound by the arguments of the party whose conclusions he supports. This emerged from Case 30/59 *Steenkolenmijnen* v. *H.A.* [1961] E.C.R. 1, 17–18, where the applicant argued that under article 95(3), requiring the intervener to take the case as he finds it, an intervener could not raise a fundamental argument conflicting with those of the party which it supposed to support. Although this view received some sympathy from A.G. Lagrange (at p. 36),the Court's view was that the intervention procedure would be deprived of all meaning if the intervener were to be denied the use of any argument which had not been used by the party which it supported.

11–21   The second variation from the normal procedure is that intervention brings with it an additional element of written procedure, in that the intervener is permitted to state in writing the grounds for his submissions; from 1959 until the 1979 amendments to the Rules this additional written element was greater since the original parties were then entitled to comment in writing on the statement submitted by the intervener. It would appear that this right to make written comments was abolished for the same reason that the three month time-limit for intervention was introduced, *i.e.* to reduce the prolongation of the procedure caused by intervention. It might be submitted, however, that if there is a specific time-limit for intervention, then no undue delay is likely to be caused by allowing written comments; on the other hand, if no specific provision is made for written comments then the matter becomes somewhat haphazard. Given the three-month time-limit, it is quite likely that the intervener's written submissions would eventually appear between the reply and the rejoinder, so giving the defendant alone the chance to comment (indirectly if not directly) on them in writing). More specifically, it has been strongly argued (Jacobs:

"Amendments to the Rules of Procedure" (1980) 5 E.L.Rev. 52, 55) that the effect of this amendment is that whilst the intervener remains free to put new arguments in writing, the original parties will have no entitlement to comment on these arguments in writing, and will be forced to rely upon the oral hearing, which may not be the most satisfactory method of communicating their views.

Although the intervener must in principle take the case as he finds it, he is under no obligation to follow it to the end. It is perfectly admissible for an intervener to withdraw from the proceedings. As an illustration, in Joined Cases 6 and 7/73 *Commercial Solvents* v. *Commission* [1974] E.C.R. 223, 227, an Italian firm applied for leave to intervene in support of the Commission in March 9, 1973, its application was granted on April 11, 1973, it applied for leave to discontinue its intervention on May 21, 1973, and its intervention was ordered to be removed from the Register on June 20, 1973.

B. CONFIDENTIALITY

11–22 It is particularly in the context of intervention that problems of confidentiality have been encountered by the European Court, particularly in competition cases where an intervener supporting the Commission may well be a trade competitor of the applicant undertaking. The problem of preventing confidential information being communicated *to* the intervener is expressly governed by article 93(4) of the Rules of Procedure as amended in 1979, allowing the parties to apply for the omission of secret or confidential documents. This effectively puts in legislative form the view enounced in the order of November 17, 1977 allowing the Federation of European Bearing Manufacturers' Associations to intervene in Case 119/77 *NSK* v. *Council and Commission* [1979] E.C.R. 1303, where it was said that "if any confidential information is produced as evidence in the course of the proceedings, the applicants are empowered to request that such information shall not be communicated to the intervener." More problematic is the situation where the intervener wishes confidential information to be kept from the original parties. In the judgment in Joined Cases 42 and 49/59 *SNUPAT* v. *H.A.* [1961] E.C.R. 53, 84, where an intervener wished to rely on the terms of a contract between itself and another undertaking, but did not wish its terms to be disclosed to the applicant or the other intervener, who were its competitors, it was said that "it would infringe a basic principle of law to base a judicial decision on facts and documents of which the parties themselves, or one of them, have not been able to take cognizance and in relation to which they have not therefore been able to formulate an opinion." Leaving aside the question whether article 93(4) of the Rules is consonant with the principle, the Court has subsequently considered the use of undisclosed information in proceedings before the Commission in Case 85/76 *Hoffman-La Roche* v. *Commission* [1979] E.C.R. 461, stating that the fundamental question is whether "such a refusal of disclosure adversely affects the undertaking's opportunity to make known effectively its views" (see para. 6–48 above), and it may be suggested that an intervener could ask for certain information not to be disclosed to another party insofar as it did not prevent the proper presentation of that other party's case.

C. Costs

11–23 Although costs in general are considered as a separate topic (see para. 17–01 below), there are certain points specific to intervention. So far as the costs of the application to intervene are concerned, these are usually reserved if the application is successful as, *e.g.* in the order of November 16, 1977 in Case 119/77 *NSK* v. *Council and Commission* [1979] E.C.R. 1303, and borne by the applicant to intervene if the application does not succeed, as in the order of April 12, 1978 in Joined Cases 116, 124 and 143/77 *Amylum* v. *Council and Commission* [1978] E.C.R. 893, 895. Where an application to intervene has been permitted, the costs will usually follow the result of the main action although the liability of the intervener is normally limited to the costs occasioned by the intervention. Hence, the usual form of order if the intervener has supported an unsuccessful party as, *e.g.* in Case 113/77 *NTN Toyo* v. *Council* [1979] E.C.R. 1185, 1211, is that the intervener should "bear its own costs and those incurred by the [successful party] on account of its intervention" Similarly, in the *NSK* case [1979] E.C.R. 1303, 1335, where the defendants supported by the intervener had been ordered to pay two-thirds of the costs of the main action, the intervener was ordered to "bear its own costs and two-thirds of those incurred by the [successful party] on account of its intervention." Conversely, where the party supported by the intervener has been successful, the intervener may expect to obtain his costs from the unsuccessful party, if he has requested them, as in Case 130/75 *Prais* v.*Council* [1976] E.C.R. 1589, 1600. Hence, in an action where both sides are supported by interveners, the interveners supporting the unsuccessful party will usually have to pay the costs not only of the successful party but also of the intervener supporting the successful party, as in Joined Cases 197 to 200, 243, 245 and 247/80 *Walzmühle Erling* v. *Council and Commission* [1981] E.C.R. 3211, although it may be noted that in its order in that judgment, the Second Chamber made the interveners jointly liable with the applicants for the whole of the costs, rather than limiting their liability to the costs occasioned by their intervention.

11–24 Where each party succeeds on some and fails on other heads, the Court's discretion under article 69(3) of the Rules of Procedure (see para. 17–05 below) would appear to extend also to the intervener. Hence, in the *Sugar Cases* [1975] E.C.R. 1663, 2024–2026, the Italian consumers' union, although it had supported conclusions of the Commission which were not upheld, was merely ordered to pay its own costs, on the basis that "on the one hand, the intervener is an association having as its object the protection of consumers' intervention and, on the other hand, neither the costs incurred by the applicant nor by the Commission in connexion with the intervention were very large." Although circumscribed, this would appear to be a precedent for privileged treatment of those who intervene in the public interest.

Finally, it should be emphasised that even a successful intervener may only recover his costs if they have been requested, under article 69(2) of the Rules of Procedure. Hence, in Case 138/79 *Roquette* v. *Council* [1980] E.C.R. 3333, 3361, the European Parliament, which had intervened in support of the successful party, was nevertheless ordered to pay its own costs since it had failed to ask for them in its pleadings.

CHAPTER 12

THIRD PARTY PROCEEDINGS

EEC Statute of the Court

Article 39

12–01   Member States, institutions of the Community and any other natural or legal persons may, in cases and under conditions to be determined by the rules of procedure, institute third-party proceedings to contest a judgment rendered without their being heard, where the judgment is prejudicial to their rights.

(Article 40 of the Euratom Statute is in identical terms; article 36 of the ECSC Statute is similar, but contains no specific mention of Member States and omits the words "where the judgment is prejudicial to their rights.")

Rules of Procedure

Article 97

12–02   1. Articles 37 and 38 of these rules shall apply in a corresponding manner to an application originating third party proceedings In addition such an application shall:
(a) specify the judgment contested;
(b) state how that judgment is prejudicial to the rights of the third party;
(c) indicate the reasons why the third party was unable to take part in the original case.
The application must be made against all parties to the original case.
Where the judgment has been published in the *Official Journal of the European Communities*, the application must be lodged within two months of the publication.
2. The Court may, on application by the third party, order a stay of execution of the judgment. The provisions of Title 3, Chapter 1, of these rules shall apply in a corresponding manner.
3. The contested judgment shall be varied on the points on which the submissions of the third party are upheld.
The original of the judgment in the third party proceedings shall be annexed to the original of the contested judgment. A note of the judgment in the third party proceedings shall be made in the margin of the original of the contested judgment.

A. RELATIONSHIP TO INTERVENTION

12–03   Just as intervention is the method by which a third party may intervene voluntarily in proceedings between other parties, in the practice of the European Court third party proceedings are the method by which a third party may challenge a judgment given in proceedings between other parties. The relationship between the two remedies is not immediately apparent from the Statutes of the Court or the Rules of Procedure, but on such occasions as it has considered the point, the Court has interpreted the requirement in article 97(1)(c) of the Rules that an applicant in third party proceedings should indicate the reasons why he was unable to take part in the original case, which was first introduced in the 1959 version of the Rules, as meaning that such an applicant must show that he was not in a position to intervene in the original case; hence the basic remedy for third parties is intervention, with third party proceedings available only to those who were unable to intervene.

12–04　　The policy behind this interpretation was clearly stated in Joined Cases 42 and 49 to 49—Third Party Proceedings *Breedband* v. *Acieries du Temple* [1962] E.C.R. 145, 158 to be that "the efficient administration of justice and the need for certainty in legal relationships demand that persons interested in the result of an action pending before the Court be precluded from asserting their rights once a judgment has been delivered settling the question in dispute". As has been noted in the context of intervention (see para. 11–02 above), the Court went on to say that intervention was made available to third parties "precisely in order to meet this requirement." It therefore concluded that third party proceedings were only available to a person "who was not in a position to intervene in the original case" or, in the alternative, "to a third party who, though called upon to take part in the original case, was unable to do so for good and sufficient reasons." Quite what constitutes a good and sufficient reason in the latter alternative remains an open question; the Court itself has so far only had to consider the question whether the applicant in the third party proceedings had been in a position to intervene. In the *Breedband* case itself, the judgment at issue was given in Joined Cases 42 and 49/59 *SNUPAT* v. *H.A.* [1961] E.C.R. 53 in which the Hoogovens undertaking had intervened; it was found that the applicant Breedband was contractually associated with Hoogovens, and that Hoogovens' managerial staff was at the disposal of Breedband, so that Breedband could hardly be unaware of the original action and Hoogovens' intervention in it, and indeed the Court found that Breedband's conclusions in its application for third party proceedings were identical to those put forward by Hoogovens in its intervention. In the result, it was held that Breedband had not shown that it was unable to intervene in the original action. However, leaving aside the specific links between Breedband and a party which had intervened in the original action, there are passages in the judgment which appear to accept that publication in the *Official Journal* of the subject matter and conclusions of the application in the original action (see para. 4–12 above) gives notice to those concerned as to the information therein contained. This view receives support in the contemporaneous judgment in Joined Cases 9 and 12/60—Third Party Proceedings *Belgium* v. *Vloeberghs and H.A.* [1962] E.C.R. 171, 182 when it was stated that "it is only possible to determine an interest establishing a right to intervene in the case from the subject matter and conclusions of the application as published in the Official Journal." This case concerned third party proceedings commenced by the Belgian government relating to the judgment given in Joined Cases 9 and 12/60 *Vloeberghs* v. *H.A.* [1961] E.C.R. 197, and what the Court considered was "whether the subject matter and conclusions in the action in Case 9/60 as published in the Official Journal disclosed an interest which the Belgian government had in intervening to support or reject the conclusions of the applicant." In this case the applicant's conclusions sought the payment of damages, and the Court held that it was "unreasonable" to assert that either the subject-matter or the conclusions stated in the original application disclosed a specific and direct interest on the part of the Belgian government in intervening voluntarily in order to support or reject the conclusions of the applicant.

12–05 Although this judgment has given rise to doubts as to whether intervention is in fact possible in an action for damages (see para. 11–13 above), the principle underlying *Belgium* v. *Vloeberghs* appears to be that third party proceedings are only excluded where the applicant in such proceedings could reasonably have been expected to intervene on the basis of the information published in the *Official Journal* (although it should be noted that the question of knowledge of the contents of the *Official Journal* does not appear actually to have been at issue).

If the applicant in the third party proceedings succeeds in showing that he could not reasonably be expected to have intervened, then the two remedies diverge. Whereas an intervener must always support the conclusions of a party, and in many instances show an interest in the result (see para. 11–07 above), an applicant in third party proceedings must rather show, under the EEC and Euratom Statutes and under article 97(1)(b) of the Rules, that the judgment is prejudicial to his rights. This requirement is not expressly stated in article 36 of the ECSC Statute, but it was included in article 73(1) of the 1953 Rules of Procedure and was applied in an ECSC context in *Belgium* v. *Vloeberghs*. In theory, this means that a person unable to satisfy the requirements of intervention may nevertheless bring third party proceedings if the judgment adversely affects his interests. However, the only example of its use so far is in *Belgium* v. *Vloeberghs*, where it was held that the judgment in *Vloeberghs* v. *H.A.* did not in fact prejudice the rights of the Belgian Government in that judgment did not determine the legality of certain Belgian legislation but merely stated its effects in the context of a particular case. Nevertheless, it could more generally be argued that, since the time limit for commencement of third party proceedings runs from publication of the judgment in the *Official Journal*, and under article 25(c) of the Instructions to the Registrar it is only the operative part of each judgment that is published in the *Official Journal* (see para. 8–08 above), the applicant in third party proceedings must show that he is prejudiced by the operative part of the original judgment, rather than the grounds upon which it is based.

B. APPLICATION FOR THIRD PARTY PROCEEDINGS

12–06 Third party proceedings may be brought by Member States, Community institutions, and any other natural or legal persons. Member States are not mentioned expressly in article 36 of the ECSC Statute, but the expression "natural or legal persons" appears to be broad enough to include them, and indeed in Joined Cases 9 and 12/60—Third Party Proceedings *Belgium* v. *Vloeberghs and H.A.* [1962] E.C.R. 171, third party proceedings were brought by the Belgian government under the ECSC provisions. Article 97(1) of the Rules requires the application to be made against all the parties to the original case, which is taken as including those who intervened in the original case, so that in Joined Cases 42 and 49/59—Third Party Proceedings *Breedband* v. *Acieries du Temple* [1962] E.C.R. 145, the Hoogovens undertaking, which had intervened in the original proceedings, was joined as a defendant.

12–07 The application is required to be made within two months of the publication of the judgment in the *Official Journal*; under article 25(c) of the Instructions to the Registrar, what is published in the *Official Journal* is the operative part of each judgment (see para. 8–08 above), and it would appear that such publication is taken as constituting notice to those concerned of that part of the judgment. Under article 97(1) the application in third party proceedings must both comply with the general rules governing written pleadings in direct actions under article 37 of the Rules (see para. 4–22 above), and the specific rules governing applications in direct actions under article 38 of the Rules (see para. 4–29 above). It must also, however, contain the three specified additional items of information, two of which, the statement of how the original judgment is prejudicial to the rights of the third party, and the statement of the reasons why the third party was unable to take part in the original case relate to the essential preconditions for the bringing of third party proceedings, as has been noted (see para. 12–03 above.)

CHAPTER 13

REQUESTS FOR OPINIONS AND RULINGS

Rules of Procedure

Article 105

13–01 1. Four certified copies shall be lodged of an application under the third paragraph of Article 103 of the Euratom Treaty. The Commission shall be served with a copy.

2. The application shall be accompanied by the draft of the agreement or contract in question, by the observations of the Commission addressed to the State concered and by all other supporting documents.

The Commission shall submit its observations to the Court within a period of 10 days, which may be extended by the President after the State concerned has been heard.

A certified copy of the observations shall be served on that State.

3. As soon as the application has been lodged the President shall designate a Judge to act as Rapporteur. The First Advocate-General shall assign the case to an Advocate-General as soon as the Judge-Rapporteur has been designated.

4. The decision shall be taken in the Deliberation Room after the Advocate-General has been heard.

The agents and advisers of the State concerned and of the Commission shall be heard if they so request.

Article 106

1. In cases provided for in the last paragraph of Article 104 and the last paragraph of Article 105 of the Euratom Treaty, the provisions of Articles 37 *et seq* of these rules shall apply in a corresponding manner.

2. The application shall be served on the State to which the respondent person or undertaking belongs.

Article 107

13–02 1. A request by the Council for an Opinion under Article 228 of the EEC Treaty shall be served on the Commission. Such a request by the Commission shall be served on the Council and on the Member States. Such a request by a Member State shall be served on the Council, the Commission and the other Member States.

The President shall prescribe a period within which the institutions and Member States which have been served with a request may submit their written observations.

2. The Opinion may deal not only with the question whether th envisaged agreement is compatible with the provisions of the EEC Treaty but also with the question whether the Community or any Community institution has the power to enter into that agreement.

Article 108

1. As soon as the request for an Opinion has been lodged, the President shall designate a Judge to act as Rapporteur.

2. The Court sitting in the Deliberation Room shall, after hearing the Advocate-General, deliver a reasoned Opinion.

3. The Opinion signed by the President, by the Judges who took part in the deliberations and by the Registrar shall be served on the Council, the Commission and the Member States.

Article 109

Requests for the Opinion of the Court under the fourth paragraph of Article 95 of the ECSC Treaty shall be submitted jointly by the High Authority and the Special Council of Ministers.

The Opinion shall be delivered in accordance with the provisions of the preceding Article. It shall be communicated to the High Authority, the Special Council of Ministers and the European Parliament.

13–03   Articles 105, 107, 108 and 109 of the Rules lay down special procedures leading respectively to the delivery of a Ruling under Article 103 of the Euratom Treaty and of an Opinion under Article 228 of the EEC Treaty and Article 95 (fourth paragraph) of the ECSC Treaty. In substance the Euratom and EEC provisions have more in common, both being concerned with determining the compatibility of proposed international agreements with the relevant Community rules, whereas the ECSC provision is concerned with amendments to the rules governing the High Authority's (*i.e.* the Commission's) exercise of its powers. Procedurally, however, there is prima facie more in common between the EEC and ECSC provisions, since article 109 of the Rules expressly relates back to Article 108.

The drafting of Article 105 of the Rules reflects the fact that Article 103 of the Euratom Treaty only allows a proposed agreement to be referred to the Court by a Member State, after having communicated the draft to the Commission and received the Commission's comments, and it therefore assumes a dispute between that State and the Commission. However, when the procedure was used in Ruling 1/78 [1978] E.C.R. 2151, the State which referred the matter to the Court, Belgium, was in fact largely in agreement with the Commission, and the real dispute was with the Council (or in reality, a majority of its members). Since the Rules make no provision for the participation of the Council or other Member States in the procedure, the Court invited the Council to supply written information under its general power under the second paragraph of article 22 of the Euratom Statute (equivalent to article 21 of the EEC Statute—see para. 6–11 above) to require an institution which is not a party to the case to supply all information which the Court considers necessary for the proceedings, and it also requested the Council to submit oral observations and reply to questions at the hearing held under article 105(4) of the Rules ([1978] E.C.R. at p. 2157). It is nonetheless worthy of note that article 105(4) does expressly require a hearing to be held if requested, and that article 105(3) requires the appointment of an individual Advocate-General.

13–04   Article 107 of the Rules, on the other hand, reflecting the fact that a request for an Opinion under Article 228 of the EEC Treaty may be made by the Council, the Commission or a Member State provides for the request to be served on the Commission alone, if the request is made by the Council, but states that if it is made by the Commission it should be served on the Council and the Member State, and that if it is made by a Member State it should be served on both the Council and the Commission and on the other Member States. Presumably in the first situation the Council is taken to represent the Member States. In practice, in the first three instances in which this procedure has been used before the Court (Opinion 1/75 [1975] E.C.R. 1355, Opinion 1/76 [1977] E.C.R. 741, and Opinion 1/78 [1979] E.C.R. 2871) the requests for an Opinion were all submitted by the Commission, and written observations were submitted in each case by the Commission, the Council, and certain Member States. On the other hand, articles 107 and 108 of the Rules make no provision for an oral hearing, and none was held in Opinion 1/75 or Opinion 1/76. However, in Opinion 1/78, it is reported ([1979] E.C.R. at pp. 2879 and 2902) that the agents for the Council and Commission were invited to and did submit oral observations at a Hearing in closed session, of which the Member States were informed, although none of them appeared. Hence, in practice the Court appears to have equiparated the prima facie different procedures under the Euratom and EEC provisions. Nonetheless, a difference does remain, although it is not immediately apparent from the English-language text of article 108(2) of the Rules. This is the fact that, in all the other versions of article 108(2), the opinions are required of all the Advocates-General, not of a selected Advocate-General, and the practice of the Court is to follow this requirement (see [1975] E.C.R. at p. 1359, [1977] E.C.R. at p. 744, [1979] E.C.R. at p. 2880). In the light of this, the Advocates-General have met together to consider the practicability of delivering a common opinion in particular cases, but they are under no obligation to do so; furthermore, the opinion or opinions they deliver under this procedure have not been published.

13–05 Requests for Opinions under the ECSC Treaty, which relate to amendments of that Treaty, may only be presented by the High Authority (*i.e.* the Commission) and the Special Council acting jointly, so that there is less likely to be any dispute before the Court—although this, of course, does not prevent the Court itself from finding the proposed amendment incompatible with the Treaty, as in Opinion 1/59 [1959] E.C.R. 259. Where this procedure has been used (Opinion 1/59 [1959] E.C.R. 259, Opinion 1/60 [1960] E.C.R. 39, and Opinion 1/61 [1961] E.C.R. 243) the practice of the Council and the Commission has been to present joint written observations. No hearing was held in any of these instances, but all (or more accurately at that time, both) the Advocates-General were heard, without their opinions being reported.

Finally in the context of Opinions and Rulings, it might be noted that article 106 of the Rules, concerning requests for Rulings brought by the Commission under articles 104 and 105 of the Euratom Treaty in relation to agreements or contracts concluded by persons or undertakings, requires the normal procedure for direct actions to be followed (see para. 4–29), except that the application is served (by the Registrar, see para. 4–09 above) on the Member State to which the defendant "belongs"; although there is no authority on the point, it would appear from the context and the other language versions that this means the Member State able to exercise jurisdiction over the person or undertaking in question, and is not a question of nationality as such.

311

CHAPTER 14

PROCEDURES IN OTHER SPECIAL EURATOM ACTIONS

APPEALS AGAINST THE ARBITRATION COMMITTEE

Euratom Treaty

Article 18

14–01   An appeal, having suspensory effect, may be brought by the parties before the Court of Justice against a decision of the Arbitration Committee within one month of notification thereof. The Court of Justice shall confine its examination to the formal validity of the decision and to the interpretation of the provisions of this Treaty by the Arbitration Committee.

Euratom Statute of the Court

Article 20

A case governed by Article 18 of this Treaty shall be brought before the Court by an appeal addressed to the Registrar. The appeal shall contain the name and permanent address of the applicant and the description of the signatory, a reference to the decision against which the appeal is brought, the names of the respondents, the subject matter of the dispute, the submissions and a brief statement of the grounds on which the appeal is based.

The appeal shall be accompanied by a certified copy of the decision of the Arbitration Committee which is contested.

If the Court rejects the appeal, the decision of the Arbitration Committee shall become final.

If the Court annuls the decision of the Arbitration Committee, the matter may be re-opened, where appropriate, on the initiative of one of the parties in the case, before the Arbitration Committee. The latter shall conform to any decisions on points of law given by the Court.

Rules of Procedure

Article 101

14–02   1. An application originating an appeal under the second paragraph of Article 18 of the Euratom Treaty shall state:
(a) the name and permanent address of the applicant;
(b) the description of the signatory;
(c) a reference to the arbitration committee's decision against which the appeal is made;
(d) the description of the parties;
(e) a summary of the facts;
(f) the grounds of the application and the form of order sought by the applicant.

2. Articles 37(3) and (4) and 38(2), (3) and (5) of these rules shall apply in a corresponding manner.

A certified copy of the contested decision shall be annexed to the application.

3. As soon as the application has been lodged, the Registrar of the Court shall request the arbitration committee registry to transmit to the Court the papers in the case.

4. Articles 39, 40, 55 *et seq.* of these rules shall apply in a corresponding manner to these proceedings.

5. The Court shall give its decision in the form of a judgment. Where the Court sets aside the decision of the arbitration committee it may remit the case to the committee.

14–03   The Arbitration Committee was created by Article 18 of the Euratom Treaty as part of the machinery for the granting of non-exclusive licences in the absence of amicable agreement, its rules of procedure being laid down by Council Regulation 7/63—Euratom of December 3, 1963 (O.J. Sp. Ed. 1963–1964, p. 56). However, at the time of writing no appeal against its decision has been brought before the European Court; in any event, it might be suggested that the term "appeal" used in the English version is inappropriate, since what is envisaged is an action for annulment, as appears from the last paragraph of article 20 of the Euratom Statute, very similar to the basic actions for the annulment of acts of the Council and of the Commission but on grounds more specifically appropriate to the review of the decisions of a quasi-judicial body. The procedure is in fact a slight modification of the normal procedure in a direct action. So far as the written pleadings are concerned, the effect of article 101(2) of the Rules is that the usual provisions as to the date of documents, and as to annexes, apply, but the provisions as to the number of copies do not (see para. 4–22 above); with particular regard to the application, the information required in article 101(1) of the Rules is very similar to that required by article 38(1) for normal direct actions (see para. 4–29 above), except that no indication of evidence is listed, and under article 101(2) the usual rules apply as to address for service, production of a lawyers certificate of entitlement to practise and, in the case of a "legal person" (see para. 4–49 above) as to the production of its constitutive instruments and of proof that its lawyer has been duly authorised to act. By virtue of article 101(4) of the Rules, the usual provisions as to service of the application and the lodging of the defence are applied, but no provision is made for reply, rejoinder or preparatory inquiry; in effect, the action moves straight on to the oral procedure once the defence has been lodged, and then continues in the normal way to judgment.

INSPECTIONS

Euratom Treaty

Article 81

14–04   3. If the carrying out of an inspection is opposed, the Commission shall apply to the President of the Court of Justice for an order to ensure that the inspection be carried out compulsorily. The President of the Court of Justice shall give a decision within three days.

4. If there is danger in delay, the Commission may itself issue a written order, in the form of a decision, to proceed with the inspection. This order shall be submitted without delay to the President of the Court of Justice for subsequent approval.

Rules of Procedure

Article 90

1. An application of a kind referred to in the third and fourth paragraphs of Article 81 of the Euratom Treaty shall contain:
   (a) the names and addresses of the persons or undertakings to be inspected;
   (b) an indication of what is to be inspected and of the purpose of the inspection.

2. The President shall give his decision in the form of an order. Article 86 of these rules shall apply in a corresponding manner.

If the President is absent or prevented from attending Article 11 of these rules shall apply.

14–05   As has been noted in the context of interim measures, article 90 of the Rules applies part of the procedure governing application for interim measures (see para. 10–30 above) to requests for compulsory inspection under Article 81 of the Euratom Treaty, which forms part of the safeguards provisions of that Treaty. Speed is here of the essence, since article 81(3) requires that the President must give a decision within three days (whereas an interim order is rarely made less than a week after the application), article 81(4) allows the Commission itself to order an inspection, if there is danger in delay, subject to submitting this order to the President of the Court "without delay" for subsequent approval. The provision of article 86 of the Rules which is perhaps of greatest relevance here is the statement that no appeal lies against the President's order; article 11 of the Rules allows the function of the President to be exercised in his absence by a President of a Chamber or one of the other judges in descending order of seniority.

314

Part IV

Financial Aspects of Procedure before the European Court

CHAPTER 15

COURT FEES AND EXPENSES

FEES AND CHARGES

Rules of Procedure

Article 16

15–01   5. Interested persons may consult the register at the Registry and may obtain copies or extracts on payment of a charge on a scale to be fixed by the Court acting on a proposal from the Registrar.

The parties to a case may on payment of the appropriate charge also obtain copies of pleadings and authenticated copies of judgments and orders.

Article 62

1. The Registrar shall draw up minutes of every hearing. The minutes shall be signed by the President and by the Registrar and shall constitute an official record.

2. The parties may inspect the minutes at the Registry and obtain copies at their own expense.

Article 72

Proceedings before the Court shall be free of charge except that:
- (a) where a party has caused the Court to incur avoidable costs the Court may, after hearing the Advocate-General order that party to refund them;
- (b) where copying or translation work is carried out at the request of a party, the cost shall, in so far as the Registrar considers it excessive, be paid for by that party on the scale of charges referred to in Article 16(5) of these rules.

Instructions to the Registrar

Article 17

15–02   No registry charges may be imposed save those referred to in this section.

Article 18

Registry charges may be paid either in cash to the cashier of the Court or by bank transfer to the Court account at the bank named in the demand for payment.

Article 20

Registry charges shall be as follows:
- (a) for an authenticated copy of a judgment or order, a certified copy of a procedural document or set of minutes, an extract from the Court

Register, a certified copy of the Court Register or a certified copy made pursuant to Article 72(b) of the Rules of Procedure: Lfrs 60 a page;

(b) for a translation made pursuant to Article 72(b) of the Rules of Procedure: Lfrs 500 a page;

No page shall contain more than 40 lines.

This scale applies to the first copy; the charge for further copies shall be Lfrs 50 for each page or part of a page.

The charges referred to in this Article shall as from 1 January 1975 be increased by 10% each time the cost-of-living index published by the Government of the Grand Duchy of Luxembourg is increaded by 10%.

Article 22

1. [Where sums paid out by way of legal aid pursuant to Article 76(5) of the Rules of Procedure are recoverable,] payment of the sums shall be demanded by registered letter, signed by the Registrar. The letter shall state not only the amount payable but also the method of payment and the period prescribed.

The same provision shall apply to the implementation of Article 72(a) of the Rules of Procedure [and Article 21(1), (3) and (4) of these instructions.]

2. If the sums demanded are not paid within the period prescribed by the Registrar, he shall request the Court to make an enforceable Decision and to order its enforcement in accordance with Articles 44 and 92 of the ECSC Treaty, 187 and 192 of the EEC Treaty or 159 and 164 of the Euratom Treaty.

Where a party is by a judgment or order directed to pay costs to the cashier of the Court, the Registrar shall, if the costs are not paid within the period prescribed, apply for payment of the costs to be enforced.

15–03 The basic principle laid down in article 72 of the Rules of Procedure is that proceedings before the European Court are not subject to any charge for the use of the Court's services, that is there are no Court fees as such. This is subject to a general exception where the Court has been caused to incur "avoidable costs," a concept which does not appear to have been considered in any reported decision of the Court. It could be argued that any vexatious proceedings cause the Court to incur voidable costs, but in judgments in which, for the purpose of determining liability for costs as between the parties, it has characterised the conduct of one of the parties as vexatious (see paras. 17–11, 17–12 below), the Court does not appear to have required the repayment of the "avoidable costs" it has itself incurred. On the other hand, there are specific provisions governing payment for copies and translations and the payment of witnesses' expenses and experts' fees and expenses (see para. 15–06 below), and it could be suggested that article 72(a) (which originates from article 2(1) of the 1954 Rules on Costs (J.O. 1954, p. 373)) was enacted as a precaution to deal with instances which might not be caught by the more specific provisions.

15–04 Although proceedings as such are free, the Rules of Procedure are consistant in requiring payment to be made for copies or extracts from the register, and for copies of pleadings, judgments and orders under article 16(5), and for copies of the minutes of hearings under article 62(2). It might incidentally be noted that in the other language versions, the expression rendered into English as "pleadings" in article 16(5) of the Rules and as "procedural document" in article 20(a) of the

318

Instructions to the Registrar is in fact the same. In practice, the pleadings, judgments and orders will be received by all the parties to the action, so that payment will only be for additional authenticated copies. Furthermore, it could be suggested that the charge for excessive costs of copying under article 72(b) of the Rules is largely redundant, since a party is usually unlikely to wish to obtain copies of documents other than those provided for expressly in articles 16(5) and 62(2) of the Rules, and the charges imposed under article 72(b) are exactly the same as those levied under arts. 16(5) and 62(2). As has been noted in the context of the role of the Registry (see para. 4–08 above) any "interested person" may obtain copies of or extracts from the register under art 16(5) for the same charge, but the actual pleadings and other documents on the file are treated as confidential, and hence available only to those taking part in the proceedings.

15–05   The charge which may be imposed under article 72(b) of the Rules when the cost of translation work is considered excessive relates to the right of a party under article 30(1) of the Rules to request that anything said or written in the proceedings be translated into any of the other languages recognised in article 29(1) of the Rules (see para. 3–01 above), a facility which is in fact not very likely to be used except possibly, *e.g.* by an intervener using a language other than the language of the case by virtue of an order under article 29(2)(c) of the Rules. In any event, there appears to be no authority on what amounts to an "excessive" cost of translation work.

SUMS PAID OUT BY THE EUROPEAN COURT

EEC Statute of the Court

Article 26

15–06   [The Court may order that a witness or expert be heard by the judicial authority of his place of permanent residence.

The order shall be sent for implementation to the competent judicial authority under conditions laid down in the rules of procedure. The documents drawn up in compliance with the letters rogatory shall be returned to the Court under the same conditions.]

The Court shall defray the expenses, without prejudice to the right to charge them, where appropriate, to the parties.

(Article 27 of the Euratom Statute of the Court is in identical terms; the ECSC Statute contains no corresponding provision.)

Rules of Procedure

Article 47

2. The witness shall be summoned by an order of the Court containing the following information:

  (a) . . . .

  (b) . . . . . .

319

(c) where appropriate, particulars of the arrangements made by the Court for reimbursement of expenses incurred by the witness, and of the penalties which may be imposed on defaulting witnesses.

The order shall be served on the parties and the witness.

3. The Court may make the summoning of a witness for whose examination a party has applied conditional upon the deposit with the cashier of the Court of a sum sufficient to cover the taxed costs thereof; the Court shall fix the amount of the payment.

The cashier shall advance the funds necessary in connection with the examination of any witness summoned by the Court of its own motion.

Article 51

1. Witnesses and experts shall be entitled to reimbursement of their travel and subsistence expenses. The cashier of the Court may make a payment to them towards these expenses in advance.

2. Witnesses shall be entitled to compensation for loss of earnings, and experts to fees for their services.

The cashier of the Court shall pay witnesses and experts their compensation or fees after they have carried out their respective duties or tasks.

Article 73

Without prejudice to the preceding Article, the following shall be regarded as recoverable costs;

(a) sums payable to witnesses and experts under Article 51 of these rules;

(b) . . . .

Article 75

1. Sums due from the cashier of the Court shall be paid in the currency of the country where the Court has its seat.

At the request of the person entitled to any sum, it shall be paid in the currency of the country where the expenses to be refunded were incurred or where the steps in respect of which payment is due were taken.

2. Other debtors shall make payment in the currency of their country of origin.

3. Conversions of currency shall be made at the official rates of exchange ruling on the day of payment in the country where the Court has its seat.

Supplementary Rules

Article 3

The Court shall defray the expenses occasioned by the letters rogatory without prejudice to the right to charge them, where appropriate to the parties.

Instructions to the Registrar

Article 21

15–07 1. Where pursuant to Articles 47(3), 51(1) and 76(5) of the Rules of Procedure an application is made to the cashier of the Court for an advance payment, the Registrar shall direct that particulars of the costs for which the advance payment is required be delivered.

Witnesses must supply evidence of their loss of earnings and experts must supply a note of fees for their services.

2. The Registrar shall order payment by the cashier of the Court of sums payable pursuant to the preceding paragraph, against a receipt or other proof of payment.

Where he is of the opinion that the amount applied for is excessive, he may of his own motion reduce it or order payment by instalments.

3. The Registrar shall order the cashier of the Court to refund the costs of letters rogatory payable in accordance with Article 3 of the Supplementary Rules to the authority designated by the competent authority referred to in Article 2 of those rules, in the currency of the State concerned against proof of payment.

Article 22

1. [Where sums paid out by way of legal aid pursuant to Article 76(5) of the Rules of Procedure are recoverable,] payment of the sums shall be demanded by registered letter, signed by the Registrar. The letter shall state not only the amount payable but also the method of payment and the period prescribed.

The same provision shall apply to the implementation of [Article 72(a) of the Rules of Procedure and] Article 21(1), (3) and (4) of these instructions.

2. If the sums demanded are not paid within the period prescribed by the Registrar, he shall request the Court to make an enforceable Decision and to order its enforcement in accordance with Articles 44 and 92 of the ECSC Treaty, 187 and 192 of the EEC Treaty or 159 and 164 of the Euratom Treaty.

Where a party is by a judgment or order directed to pay costs to the cashier of the Court, the Registrar shall, if the costs are not paid within the period prescribed, apply for payment of the costs to be enforced.

15–08   A corollary of the fact that witnesses and experts are called by the Court rather than by the parties (see para. 6–07 above) is that, so far as the witnesses and experts are concerned, it is the Court which meets the financial consequences of calling them, even though under article 47(3) of the Rules the Court may require a deposit to be paid where a witness has been called at the request of a party. By virtue of article 47(3) and article 51 of the Rules, witnesses and experts receive travel and subsistence expenses from the cashier of the Court (and may obtain payment in advance), and the cashier also pays compensation for loss of earnings to witnesses and the fees due to experts, subject in all these cases to the power of the Registrar under article 21 of the Instructions to reduce the amount payable if he considers it excessive or to order its payment by instalments, a power whose exercise does not appear to have given rise to any reported dispute. Similarly, article 26 of the Statute and article 3 of the Supplementary Rules require the cost of letters rogatory to be met by the Court in the first place. Nevertheless, under article 73(a) of the Rules, the sums paid to witnesses and experts are recoverable costs, and under article 26 of the Statute and article 3 of the Supplementary Rules, the expenses occasioned by letters rogatory may be charged to the parties.

15–09   Although the costs relating to witnesses and experts may well go with the general costs in the action, and not be mentioned specifically, as in Case 155/78 *M.* v. *Commission* [1980] E.C.R. 1797 with regard to witnesses or in Case 48/69 *ICI* v. *Commission* [1972] E.C.R. 619 with regard to experts, there are a number of instances where the Court has dealt with the matter as a separate part of the order as to costs. In particular, insofar as the institutions are in general liable to meet their own costs in staff cases under article 70 of the Rules of Procedure (see para. 17–19 below), it was held in Joined Cases 19 and 65/63 *Prakash* v. *Commission* [1965] E.C.R. 533, 561–562 and reiterated in Case 34/65 *Mosthaf* v. *Commission* [1966] E.C.R. 521, 532 that these costs include the expenses of all witnesses who are officials of that institution giving evidence as officials of that institution, even if their evidence was against the interests of the institution and in favour of the applicant. However, in Case 43/74 *Guillot* v. *Commission* [1977] E.C.R. 1309, 1338, although the Commission had to meet its own costs, the unsuccessful applicant was ordered to bear the costs of hearing the witnesses, since the witnesses were only called because the applicant's account of the facts conflicted with that put forward by the Commission, and his account was not ultimately accepted by the court.

This view that the costs relating to witnesses should be met by the party who was unsuccessful on the point on which the witnesses were heard has been applied outside the context of staff cases in the *Sugar Cases* [1975] E.C.R. 1663, 2025 and 2027. There, after describing the points on which the witnesses were heard, the Court quite simply stated that "since the Commission failed on this head it must be ordered to pay the costs of examining these witnesses."

15–10 With regard to the costs incurred in the preparation of an expert's report, the matter was considered specifically in Joined Cases 24 and 34/58 *Chambre Syndicale de la Sidérurgie de l'Est de la France* v. *H.A.* [1960] E.C.R 281, 301 in the context of Case 24/58. In that case, each party was ordered to bear its own costs, subject to each paying half the costs of and incidental to the expert's report—which is perhaps no more than a recognition of the fact that an order requiring each party to bear its own costs is not in itself appropriate to meet the expenses initially borne by the Court.

On the other hand, there appears to be no legislative provision enabling the Court to require the parties to meet the costs incurred by the Court itself in carrying out an inspection (see para. 6–44 above), although no doubt the expenses necessarily incurred by the parties themselves and their agents or lawyers would be recoverable *inter partes* under article 73(b) of the Rules of Procedure (see below para. 17–01).

Insofar as sums paid out by the Court are to be recovered from a party, the effect of article 22 of the Instructions is that, if a request from the Registrar is not acceded to, the Court may issue a specific decision on the point, enforceable like any other judgement or order of the Court in a direct action.

CHAPTER 16

LEGAL AID

DIRECT ACTIONS

A. APPLICATION TO THE COURT

Rules of Procedure

Article 76

16–01   1. A party who is wholly or in part unable, to meet the costs of the proceedings may at any time apply for legal aid.

The application shall be accompanied by evidence of the applicant's need of assistance, and in particular by a document from the competent authority certifying his lack of means.

2. If the application is made prior to proceedings which the applicant wishes to commence, it shall briefly state the subject of such proceedings.

The application need not be made through a lawyer.

16–02   Unlike the application commencing proceedings, an application for legal aid in direct actions may be made by a litigant in person. However, in the light of the very short limitation periods governing actions for annulment, actions for failure to act and staff actions (see paras. 2–09, 2–25, 2–36 above), and in the absence of any indication by the Court that it would be prepared to regard an application for legal aid as "unforeseeable circumstances" or "force majeure" under article 42 of the EEC Statute and the corresponding provisions of the other Statutes so as to allow the time limits to be disregarded, the usual practice of applicants for legal aid would appear to be to lodge an application commencing proceedings signed by a lawyer, and then soon, if not immediately, submit an application for legal aid, a decision as to which may well take several weeks if not months. Hence, in Case 121/76 *Moli* v. *Commission* [1977] E.C.R. 1971, the application commencing proceedings was lodged on December 20, 1976, an application for legal aid was lodged on December 21, 1976, and legal aid was granted by an order of April 28, 1977; in Case 175/80 *Tither* v. *Commission* [1981] E.C.R. 2345 the application was registered on August 1, 1980, legal aid was requested on September 12, 1980 and was granted by an order dated October 2, 1980. On the other hand, for an unassisted litigant to seek legal aid before commencing proceedings is more feasible in actions for damages; in relation to non-contractual liability, the limitation period laid down in article 43 of the EEC Statute and the corresponding provisions of the other Statutes is five years, and in

323

relation to contractual liabililty it was suggested in Case 25/60 *De Bruyn* v. *Parliament* [1962] E.C.R. 21, 28 that, in the absence of any specific provision in the Treaties, what was relevant was whether the applicant's delay in bringing the matter before the Court could be interpreted as a waiver of the right of action. In that case, the applicant submitted a request for legal aid on December 7, 1960, legal aid was granted on February 16, 1961, and the application commencing proceedings was lodged towards the end of March 1961 (on March 28, according to the "Facts" part of the judgment at p. 23, on May 23, according to A.G. Lagrange at p. 35); this case involved a breach of contract alleged to have occurred in July 1959, and it was held that there was no evidence of a waiver of the right of action.

16–03   What is clearly not permissible under the current Rules is for an applicant for legal aid to lodge an application commencing proceedings which has not been signed by a lawyer acting on his behalf. In Case 10/81 *Farrall* v. *Commission* [1981] E.C.R. 717 the applicant lodged on January 19, 1981 an application commencing proceedings, an application for interim measures, and an application for legal aid, none of which had been signed by a lawyer. After he had failed to comply with a request under article 38(7) of the Rules (see para. 4–53 above) to rectify his applications by causing them to be lodged by a lawyer, the Second Chamber declared the applications inadmissible. At first sight, this might seem to conflict with the early decision in Case 10/55 *Mirossevich* v. *H.A.* [1954–1956] E.C.R. 333, where the applicant herself commenced proceedings on July 19, 1955, requested legal aid on July 29, 1955, designating her advocate at the same time, and legal aid was eventually granted on October 21, 1955; however, under article 29(1) of the 1953 Rules of Procedure, an application commencing proceedings could be signed by the applicant him or herself, and under article 62(1) of these Rules legal aid could only be requested after the application commencing proceedings had been lodged.

B. Grant of Legal Aid

Rules of Procedure

Article 76

16–04   3. The President shall designate a Judge to act as Rapporteur. The Chamber to which the latter belongs shall, after considering the written observations of the opposite party and after hearing the Advicate-General, decide whether legal aid should be granted in full or in part, or whether it should be refused. Where there is manifestly no cause of action, legal aid shall be refused.

The Chamber shall make an order without giving reasons, and no appeal shall lie there from.

4. The Chamber may at any time, either of its own motion or on application, withdraw legal aid if the circumstances which led to its being granted alter during the proceedings.

5. Where legal aid is granted, the cashier of the Court shall advance the funds necessary to meet the expenses.

Supplementary Rules

Article 4

16–05   The Court, by any order by which it decides that a person is entitled to receive legal aid, shall order that a lawyer be appointed to act for him.

If the person does not indicate his choice of lawyer, or if the Court considers that his choice is unacceptable, the Registrar shall send a copy of the order and of the application for legal aid to the authority named in Annex II, being the competent authority of the State concerned. The Court, in the light of the suggestions made by that authority, shall of its own motion appoint a lawyer to act for the person concerned.

Article 5

The Court shall advance the funds necessary to meet expenses. It shall adjudicate on the lawyer's disbursements and fees; the President may, on application by the lawyer, order that he receive an advance.
Insert table F. 484

Instructions to the Registrar

Article 21

1. Where pursuant to Articles 47(3), 51(1) and 76(5) of the Rules of Procedure an application is made to the cashier of the Court for an advance payment, the Registrar shall direct that particulars of the costs for which the advance payment is required be delivered.

2. The Registrar shall order payment by the cashier of the Courts of sums payable pursuant to the preceding paragraph, against receipt or other proof of payment.

Where he is of the opinion that the amount applied for is excessive, he may of his own motion reduce it or order payment by instalments.

4. The Registrar shall order the cashier of the Court to make the advance payment referred to in the second paragraph of Article 5 of the Supplementary Rules of Procedure, subject to the second sub paragraph of paragraph 2 of this Article.

16–06   An order granting or refusing legal aid is made by a Chamber after the parties have submitted their observations and the Advocate-General has delivered his opinion. Hence, even an application for legal aid is not dealt with on an *ex parte* basis. The order is required not to be reasoned, and there is therefore very little published indication as to the basis on which the Court acts: where the application was refused, the judgment may simply state that the Court rejected the request of the applicant for legal aid, as in Case 16/64 *Rauch* v. *Commission* [1965] E.C.R. 135, 142, and in Case 23/64 *Vandevyvere* v. *Parliament* [1965] E.C.R. 157, 163, but insofar as it may be relevant, it would appear that slightly less than half the applications made have been successful (to the end of 1980 there appear to have been 15 cases in which legal aid was granted to some extent, and 20 cases in which it was refused). It would appear that the basic evidence relied upon by the Court comprises such matters as tax assessments, and statements by social security officials or statements by employers as the case may be, which may be regarded as certifying the applicant's lack of means under article 76(1) of the Rules. Apart from the financial situation of the applicant for legal aid, the other major factor to which the Court must turn its attention under article 76(3)of the Rules is the question whether there is manifestly no cause for action; although this form of words may also require consideration of the merits of the case, it would appear to be similar in concept to the general power of the Court under article 92(1) of the Rules to declare an application inadmissible where it is clear that the Court has no jurisdiction to take cognizance of it.

16–07   Where legal aid is granted, article 76(5) of the Rules and article 5 of the Supplementary Rules, as implemented in article 21(1) and (4) of the Instructions to the Registrar, make a distinction between expenses in general, for which funds may in principle be advanced, and the lawyer's disbursements and fees, advance payment of which must be ordered by the President. However, it has been the practice for the Chamber when deciding to grant legal aid to state that a recoverable advance of a fixed global sum should be made to the applicant by the cashier, as in (to take examples where the figures are published) Joined Cases 19 and 65/63 *Prakash* v. *Commission* [1965] E.C.R. 533, 545 and in Case 68/63 *Luhleich* v. *Commission* [1965] E.C.R. 581, 591, the sum having been fixed in both these cases are 25,000 FB, or to state that legal aid will be available up to a fixed sum, as in Case 18/63 *Wollast* v. *Commission* [1964] E.C.R. 85, 95 (30,000 FB) and in Case 35/67 *Van Eick* v. *Commission* [1968] E.C.R. 329, 333 (15,000 FB), although in the latter case the First Chamber rather unusually stated that this sum should be paid only "when the case is concluded, unless special costs justify an application for an advance payment." It would appear that more recent orders granting legal aid have specified not only the sums involved but also the aspects of the procedure which they are intended to cover, distinguishing between the written procedure and the oral procedure with its concomitant travel and accommodation expenses.

C. LIABILITY FOR LEGAL AID COSTS

Rules of Procedure

Article 76

16–08   5. In its decision as to costs the Court may order the payment to the cashier of the Court of the whole or any part of amounts advanced as legal aid.

The Registrar shall take steps to obtain the recovery of these sums from the party ordered to pay them.

Instructions to the Registrar

Article 19

Where the party owing Registry charges has been granted legal aid, Article 76(5) of the Rules of Procedure shall apply.

Article 22

1. Where sums paid out by way of legal aid pursuant to Article 76(5) of the Rules of Procedure[1] are recoverable, payment of the sums shall be demanded by

registered letter, signed by the Registrar. The letter shall state not only the amount payable but also the method of payment and the period prescribed.

2. If the sums demanded are not paid within the period prescribed by the Registrar, he shall request the Court to make an enforceable Decision and to order its enforcement in accordance with Articles 44 and 92 of the ECSC Treaty, 187 and 192 of the EEC Treaty or 159 and 164 of the Euratom Treaty.

Where a party is by a judgment or order directed to pay costs to the cashier of the Court, the Registrar shall, if the costs are not paid within the period prescribed, apply for payment of the costs to be enforced.

16–09 In principle, the sums paid out by the Court as legal aid may be recovered from the party ordered to pay the costs. In so far as that party may be a Community institution, this gives rise to little difficulty, and there have been a number of cases where in a judgment ordering the Commission to pay the costs in staff cases, express mention has been made of the legal aid costs incurred by the Court, as in Case 175/80 *Tither* v. *Commission* (October 8, 1981), Case 68/63 *Luhleich* v. *Commission* [1965] E.C.R. 581, 608 and Case 18/63 *Wollast* v. *Commission* [1964] E.C.R. 85, 102, and in Case 10/55 *Mirossevich* v. *H.A.* [1954–1956] E.C.R. 333, 345, the High Authority was ordered to pay of the same proportion of the legal aid costs (four-fifths) as it was ordered to pay off the applicant's costs (which may well, of course, be greater than the amount allocated as legal aid). Conversely, it would appear to have been the normal practice of the Court to order an unsuccessful legally-aided litigant to repay the sums advanced as legal aid, even though his conduct is not characterised as vexatious or unreasonable; hence the grant of legal aid in a direct action would not appear to reduce the risks for its recipient. The effect of this is particularly striking in staff cases, where the aim of article 70 of the Rules (see para. 17–19 below) is that officials who fail in their actions are not liable to meet the costs of the institution, unless their conduct of the action has been unreasonable or vexatious. Nonetheless, unsuccessful legally-aided officials who have been required only to pay their own costs have been ordered also to repay to the Court the sums received as legal aid, as in Case 25/68 *Schertzer* v. *Parliament* [1977] E.C.R. 1729, 1745–1746 and joined Cases 19 and 65/63 *Prakash* v. *Commission* [1965] E.C.R. 533, 561–562, and in Case 12/68 *X* v. *Audit Board* [1970] E.C.R. 291, 295–296, the applicant was ordered to repay the sums received as legal aid despite the fact that his liability for his own costs was limited to those incurred up to a date just over a year before the final judgment; however, insofar as the legal aid was spent on costs incurred after that date, those costs were recoverable from the Audit Board, which was ordered to meet all such costs.

16–10 Although legal aid has rarely been granted to litigants other than officials of the Communities, the risks for such a recipient are even greater. In Case 18/60 *Worms* v. *H.A.* [1962] E.C.R. 195, 207, where legal aid was granted to a scrap-dealer who eventually failed in his action, he was quite simply ordered to pay "all the costs."

With regard to the costs of the application for legal aid, this has rarely been alluded to expressly in the final judgment, and it may be supposed that in general it is subsumed in the general order. However, in Case 16/64 *Rauch* v. *Commission* [1965] E.C.R. 135, 149 and Case 23/64 *Vandevyvere* v. *Parliament* [1965] E.C.R. 157, 168, it was specifically ordered that the applicant officials, who in the event failed in their main actions, should meet their own costs incurred in their unsuccessful applications for legal aid.

REFERENCES FOR PRELIMINARY RULINGS

Rules of Procedure

Article 104

16–11   3. It shall be for the national court or tribunal to decide as to the costs of the reference.

In special circumstances the Court may grant, as legal aid, assistance for the purpose of facilitating the representation or attendance of a party.

16–12   On the basis of the theory enounced in Case 62/72 *Bollmann* v. *HZA Hamburg-Waltershof* [1973] E.C.R. 269, 275 that a reference for a preliminary ruling is in the nature of a step in the action pending before a national court, it might be expected that it should be for the relevant national authorities to grant legal aid under their national rules to litigants in whose actions a reference is made to the European Court. In the United Kingdom, this view was accepted in *R.* v. *Marlborough Street Stipendiary Magistrate, ex p. Bouchereau* [1977] 1 W.L.R. 414 by the Queen's Bench Divisional Court, when it declared that an existing criminal legal aid certificate extended to and covered proceedings on a reference to the European Court in Case 30/77 *R.* v. *Bouchereau* [1977] E.C.R. 1999. The point is expressly recognised in regulation 6(2)(d) of the Legal Aid (General) Regulations 1971 (S.I. 1971 No. 62) as amended by the Legal Aid (General) Amendment Regulations 1977 (S.I. 1977 No. 1293), which, in England and Wales, requires the authority of an area committee before a legal aid certificate can extend to proceedings on a reference to the European Court (a provision for which no equivalent was apparently regarded as necessary under the different Scottish system).

16–13   Examples can also be found from other Member States of national legal aid extending to proceedings on a reference to the European Court. In Case 72/76 *LVA Rheinland-Pfalz* v. *Töpfer* [1977] E.C.R. 271, for example, it is reported (at p. 273) that Mme. Töpfer was in receipt of legal aid. Hence article 104(3) of the Rules which was introduced in 1974 limits legal aid granted by the European Court on references for preliminary rulings to "special circumstances." This provision is, however, by no means redundant, since national systems of legal aid tend not to be universal in scope as to persons eligible, as to the sums payable, or as to the courts and tribunals before which legal aid is available—and in any event, the European Court does not appear to have formally indicated that an applicant for legal aid on a reference for a preliminary ruling should show that he has first exhausted the possibilities of national legal aid, although it might be expected that this would be relevant to the determination of "special circumstances." The inability of a body corporate to obtain legal aid under the United Kingdom systems may well have led the respondent company in Case 96/80 *Jenkins* v. *Kingsgate (Clothing Productions) Ltd.* [1981] E.C.R. 911 to apply to the European Court for legal aid; this request was, however, rejected by the First Chamber, as is noted by A.G. Warner in his Opinion at page 932, with the result that no argument was presented on that company's behalf.

A successful claim for legal aid was however made in Case 152/79 *Lee* v. *Minister for Agriculture* [1980] E.C.R. 1495, a reference by the Irish High Court in proceedings commenced at a time when legal aid was not available for civil proceedings in Ireland (a situation which gave rise to the judgment of the European Court of Human Rights of October 9, 1979 in the *Airey* case (Series A, No. 32)).In its order of January 23, 1980 granting legal aid to the appellant in the main action, it would appear that the First Chamber awarded two fixed sums of money, the smaller of which was to be used for the purposes of the written procedure, and the larger of which was to meet the costs incurred in the oral procedure, including travel and accommodation.

16–14   There is no express provision as to how, if at all, the Court may recover sums advanced by it as legal aid in references for preliminary rulings. In direct actions, under article 76(5) of the Rules, the recovery of sums advanced as legal aid is dealt with in the order as to costs, but in references for preliminary rulings, article 104(3) of the Rules, confirming the earlier case law typified in Case 62/72 *Bollmann* v. *HZA Hamburg-Waltershof* [1973] E.C.R. 269, 275, provides that it is for the national court or tribunal to decide as to the costs of the reference. In its judgment in *Lee's* case [1980] E.C.R. 1495, 1509 the European Court in fact made no mention of the legal aid costs, simply repeating the usual formula (see para. 17–28 below) that the Commission's costs were not recoverable and that as between the parties to the main action, the decision on costs was a matter for the national court. It may perhaps therefore be concluded that, unlike the situation in direct actions, the European Court may be unable to recover sums advanced as legal aid on references for preliminary rulings unless it subjected the original grant to a specific condition regulating the matter, *e.g.* requiring repayment in the event of costs being recovered from the other party. In the result, the receipt of legal aid on a reference may present considerably less of a risk than its receipt in a direct action, but may be more liable to be restricted by the funds available to the Court.

CHAPTER 17

COSTS

DIRECT ACTIONS

A. RECOVERABLE COSTS

Rules of Procedure

Article 73

17–01   Without prejudice to the preceding Article, the following shall be regarded as recoverable costs:
  (a) sums payable to witnesses and experts under Article 51 of these rules;
  (b) expenses necessarily incurred by the parties for the purpose of the proceedings, in particular the travel and subsistence expenses and the remuneration of agents, advisers or lawyers.

17–02   Article 73 of the Rules groups together two different matters under the heading of recoverable costs. Since article 51 provides for the payment by the Court itself of witnesses' and experts' travel and subsistence expenses, and for payment by the Court itself of compensation for loss of earnings to witnesses and of fees to experts article 73(a) is effectively concerned with recovery by the Court of sums it has paid out, and is considered in this book under that heading (see para. 15–08 above). Article 73(b) on the other hand is concerned with costs as between the parties, in particular in relation to their legal advisers.

The concept of "expenses necessarily incurred by the parties for the purpose of the proceedings" has been the subject of remarkably few decisions. Nonetheless, certain guidelines do emerge. It would appear that 'the proceedings" are regarded as commencing with the formal application to the Court: in the order on costs in Case 75/69 *Hake* v. *Commission* [1970] E.C.R. 901, 902–903, it was held that expenses and fees relating to the stage prior to the application to the Court were not recoverable costs. Hence the cost of pre-trial advice would appear not to be recoverable. With regard to the remuneration of lawyers, it would appear that this is only recoverable in so far as the lawyer was acting as such in the case, so that if a party represented by another lawyer or lawyers obtains advice, *e.g.* from a Luxembourg lawyer whose office is being used as an address for service, fees payable in respect of that advice will not be recoverable, although the fees payable for the acceptance of service will be regarded as an expense necessarily incurred. This appears directly from the order in costs in Joined Cases 20 and 21/63 *Maudet* v. *Commission* [1964] E.C.R. 621, 622–623, where it was stated that "only the remuneration of the lawyer *representing* a private party in an action before the Court may be regarded as necessary expenses of legal assistance" (emphasis added), and of the fees claimed with respect to the services of the Luxembourg lawyer whose office was used as an address for service, these were held to be recoverable "only in so far as the fees for acceptance of service in the proper sense are concerned." The moral would appear to be that a party should only take remunerated advice from those he appoints to represent him, if he wishes the expenses to be recoverable. With regard to a party's personal expenses in attending a hearing at the Court, it appears from the order in Case 24/79 *Oberthür* v. *Commission* [1981] E.C.R. 2229 that these are not recoverable unless the party's presence was necessary for the purpose of the proceedings.

17–03 So far as the recovery by a Community institution of its costs when represented by its own agent in the proceedings is concerned, it would appear to have been the practice of the Commission until about 1978 to claim only travel and subsistence expenses. However, it then changed its policy in the light of the growing number of cases brought before the Court, and a claim by the Commission relating to the remuneration of a salaried agent was considered by the Court in its order in Case 126/76—costs *Dietz* v. *Commission* [1979] E.C.R. 2131. The Court there held that for a salaried official of an institution to act as its agent in proceedings before the Court fell within the scope of his employment, which was remunerated in accordance with the Staff Regulations, and the expense of this remuneration could not be regarded as an expense incurred "for the purpose of the proceedings." On the other hand, travelling expenses and a daily subsistence allowance relating to the agent's participation in the oral procedure were held to be recoverable, *e.g.* the Court's order restored what had been the Commission's previous practice. It was also recognised that the remuneration of a lawyer who is not a member of the institution's staff does fall within article 73(b) of the Rules, so that there could well be a financial inducement for a Community institution to employ outside counsel, particularly in complex cases.

17–04 With regard to the quantum of a lawyer's remuneration, it was recognised in Case 75/69 *Hake* v. *Commission* [1970] E.C.R. 901 that "Community law contains no provisions as to scale fees on which to base a calculation of the amount up to which such remuneration must always be regarded as recoverable costs." The Court therefore concluded that it must be free to consider "the facts of the case, taking particularly into account the importance of the action from the point of view of Community law and the volume of work involved for the lawyer in the proceedings before the Court." This formula has subsequently been repeated with minor variations, the version used in the orders in Case 6/72 *Europemballage and Continental Can* v. *Commission* [1975] E.C.R. 495 and Case 4/73 *Nold* v. *Commission* [1975] E.C.R. 985 adding that account should be taken of the "object and nature" of the action and "the difficulty of the case." The Rules of Procedure do not in fact provide for any specific system of taxation of costs—indeed it would hardly seem appropriate in the light of these criteria, which treat the importance of the case from the point of view of Community law as a relevant factor. Article 74 of the Rules (see para. 17–24 below) does however allow an order to be made where there is a dispute as to the costs to be recovered.

Finally, on the subject of the calculation of a lawyer's remuneration, it was held in the *Continental Can* case [1975] E.C.R. 495, 496 that since private parties may only be represented by lawyers entitled to practise before a court of a Member State, the fixing of recoverable costs "must be effected on the basis of the national currencies of the Member States."

B. LIABILITY TO MEET COSTS: BASIC PRINCIPLES

EEC Statute of the Court
Article 35

17–05   The Court shall adjudicate upon costs.

(Article 36 of the Euratom Statue and article 32 of the ECSC Statute are in identical terms.)

Rules of Procedure
Article 69

1. The Court shall give a decision as to costs in its final judgment or in the order which closes the proceedings.

2. The unsuccessful party shall be ordered to pay the costs if they have been asked for in the successfull party's pleading

Where there are several unsuccessful parties the Court shall decide how the costs are to be shared.

3. Where each party succeds on some and fails on other heads, or where the circumstances are exceptional, the Court may order that the parties bear their own costs in whole or in part.

The Court may order even a successful party to pay costs which the Court considers that party to have unreasonably or vexatiously caused the opposite party to incur.

4. A party who discontinues or withdraws from proceedings shall be ordered to pay the costs, unless the discontinuance or withdrawal is justified by the conduct of the opposite party.

If the opposite party has not asked for costs, the parties shall bear their own costs.

5. Where a case does not proceed to judgment the costs shall be in the discretion of the Court.

Article 71

Costs necessarily incurred by a party in enforcing a judgment or order of the Court shall be refunded by the opposite party on the scale in force in the State where the enforcement takes place.

Article 75

1. Sums due from the cashier of the Court shall be paid in the currency of the country where the Court has its seat.

At the request of the person entitled to any sum, it shall be paid in the currency of the country where the expenses to be refunded were incurred or where the steps in respect of which payment is due were taken.

2. Other debtors shall make payment in the currency of their country of origin.

3. Conversions of currency shall be made at the official rates of exchange ruling on the day of payment in the country where the Court has its seat.

17–06 In the terms of article 69(1) and (2) of the Rules of Procedure, the judgment or order closing the proceedings is required to rule on the question of costs, and in principle costs follow the event provided they have been asked for. Whilst it does not appear to be absolutely essential that the request for the payment of costs should be included in the initial application or the defence, since in Case 121/76 *Moli* v. *Commission* [1977] E.C.R. 1971, 1974 costs were awarded when the request was made only in the reply, it is nevertheless the usual practice to insert a request for costs in every application or defence before the European Court (see para. 4–41 above). In Case 138/79 *Roquette* v. *Council* [1980] E.C.R. 3333, the Court did in fact refuse to award costs to a successful applicant and to a successful intervener who had failed to ask for them.

Although the judgment may deal specifically with the costs incurred in relation to specific aspects of the proceedings such as an application for interim measures, an intervention, an application for legal aid, or the hearing of witnesses, matters which have been considered in their respective contexts, it may be assumed that in the absence of any such specific mention, the decision on costs relates to the whole of the costs in the proceedings. Nevertheless, examples can be found where a list of the costs involved is expressly included, as in Case 60/81 *IBM* v. *Commission* [1981] E.C.R. 2639, where it was stated that the costs included these relating to the application for interim measures and those incurred by the intervener.

17–07 The question of who is the "unsuccessful party" is determined largely on the basis of the main issue in the proceedings, where such an issue is identifiable. Hence in Joined Cases 59 and 71/69 *Brembati* v. *Commission* [1970] E.C.R. 623, 632–633, where the applicant was held to have failed in his principal head of claim but to have succeeded in alternative conclusions which could lead only to a minimal difference in the effect of the decisions he was challenging, he was ordered to pay the costs (in fact only his own, since it was a staff case—see para. 17–19 below). Where there is more than one unsuccessful party, the usual practice of the Court is to make them jointly and severally liable for the costs, as in Joined Cases 209 to 215 and 218/78 *Van Landewyck and others* v. *Commission* [1980] E.C.R. 3125, 3280–3281. This may occur even where the status of the unsuccessful parties is different, as in Joined Cases 197 to 200, 243, 245 and 247/80 *Walzmühle Erling* v. *Council and Commission* [1981] E.C.R. 3211 where the unsuccessful interveners were made jointly liable with the unsuccessful applicants for the whole of the costs (including those of other interveners supporting the successful defendants). Such an order is, however, somewhat unusual, it

333

being the more frequent practice to order an unsuccessful intervener to pay only the costs incurred on account of its intervention, the formula used, *e.g.* in Case 113/77 *NTN Toyo* v. *Council* [1979] E.C.R. 1185, 1211 (see para. 11–23 above). The Court does, in fact, have a complete discretion as to how to divide the costs between several unsuccessful parties, and in Cases 32 and 36 to 82/78 *BMW Belguim* v. *Commission* [1979] E.C.R. 2435, 2483, each unsuccessful applicant in a series of actions for the annulment of a Commission competition decision imposing fines upon them was ordered to pay a part of the costs of the Commission "corresponding to the amount of the fine imposed upon it expressed as a percentage of the total fines." Conversely in Joined Cases 241 etc./78 *DGV* v. *Council and Commission* [1981] E.C.R. 1731, it was held that the recoverable costs should be shared by the successful applicants in proportion to the compensation they received.

17–08   Where the identification of a main issue is less clear, then under article 69(3) of the Rules, the Court may order the parties to bear their own costs where each party succeeds on some and fails on other heads, or where the circumstances are "exceptional." An example amongst many of the former situation is Case 27/76 *United Brands* v. *Commission* [1978] E.C.R. 207, 308–309, where one provision of the Commission's decision was annulled, and the fine imposed on the applicant was reduced, but the applicant was otherwise unsuccessful, and each party was ordered to bear its own costs, both in the main acation and on an application for interim measures; a similar example may also be found in Case 85/76 *Hoffman-LaRoche* v. *Commission* [1979] E.C.R. 461, 557–558. Although the principle is expressed to apply where a party has succeeded on some "heads" and failed on others, which appears to imply only one action, it has been extended to linked joined cases: in Joined Cases 275/80 and 24/81 *Krupp Stahl* v. *Commission* [1981] E.C.R. 2489, where the Commission failed in Case 275/80 and the applicant failed in Case 24/81, it was held that as a result of the joinder of the cases it was impossible to tell which costs related to which case, so that each party should simply bear its own costs in both cases rather than meet the other party's costs in one of them.

There are, however, instances where the Court has made more complex awards. In Case 16/81 *Modena* v. *H.A.* [1962] E.C.R. 289, 307, where the applicant failed on three out of the four main points at issue, it was ordered "in view of the size of the amounts in dispute" that the applicant should pay only *three-fifths* (rather than three-quarters) of the defendant's costs. Such fractional awards have indeed taken account not only of the number of heads on which a party has been successful but also of the respective conduct of the parties. In Case 11/63 *Lepape* v. *H.A.* [1964] E.C.R. 61, 78, although the applicant succeeded only in a small part of his claim, the Court stated that "account must be taken . . . of the fact that he has been obliged to make an application in order to obtain recognition of his rights," and the High Authority was ordered to pay half the applicant's costs.

17–09   The alternative ground on which the parties may be ordered to bear their own costs is the existence of "exceptional" circumstances. Insofar as these arise from the parties' conduct, the matter would appear to be closely related to the categorisation of such conduct as vexatious or unreasonable under the second sub-paragraph of article 69(3) (see paras. 17–11, 17–12 below). However, what might be categorised as the legal background to the case may also be relevant. In Joined Cases 46 and 47/59 *Meroni* v. *H.A.* [1962] E.C.R. 411, 427, although the applicants failed in their actions, the High Authority was ordered to pay its own costs, not because of anything it had done, but because, in the Court's view, the applicants had only brought their actions because they were "unaware that the Court would receive claims made after the closing of the accounts of the [steel scrap] equalization scheme, without holding them to be outside the period of limitation" and they could not be blamed for this lack of awareness. A similar approach has been followed where the action can be attributed to the deficiencies of Community legislation. Thus, in Case 26/67 *Danvin* v. *Commission* [1968] E.C.R. 315, 322–323, the unsuccessful applicant was required to pay only one-quarter of his own costs on the grounds that "the silence of the Staff Regulations as to the legal position of a deputy was such as to create uncertainty with regard to the rules of law applicable," the applicant assistant accounting officer having replaced the chief accounting officer of the European Development Fund for a period of 16 months. Indeed in Case 18/70 *X* v. *Council* [1972] E.C.R. 1205, 1209, the unsuccessful applicant was not actually required to pay any of her own costs in the light of the fact that "the action was caused by the legal uncertainty arising from the continuing absence of the implementing rules under art. 73 of the Staff Regulations" relating to the insurance cover provided for officials of the Communities. The same result was reached in relation to the same provision of the Staff Regulations in Case 74/72 *Di Blasi* v. *Commission* [1973] E.C.R. 847, 857, although the First Chamber there regarded the action as having been in any event unreasonably caused by the Commission in that it revoked a decision at issue only after the proceedings had been commenced.

17–10 The Court would also appear to have regard to the public interest, or the interest of Community legality, in the bringing of the action as a relevant factor. In Case 66/76 *C.F.D.T.* v. *Council* [1977] E.C.R. 305, 311, where an action brought by a trade union against the Council under the ECSC Treaty was held to be inadmissible under both Article 33 and article 38 of that Treaty, it was held that the fact that the proceedings were instituted "with the sole aim of ensuring that the Consultative Committee is representative, a requirement expressly laid down by art. 18 of the Treaty" constituted exceptional circumstances justifying an order that each party should bear its own costs. This legal interest may in fact be mixed with a personal interest, as in Case 23/76 *Pellegrini* v. *Commission* [1976] E.C.R. 1807, 1822. This action related to tenders for a contract for the cleaning of the Euratom Research Centre at Ispra, a function carried out for many years by the applicant firm. Although the action was unsuccessful, each party was nonetheless ordered to pay its own costs, on the grounds that "since it had been informed by the Commission that its work in the past had been entirely satisfactory, and had learned that the prices of [the successful tenderer] were markedly higher than its own, the applicant had good reason to consider itself justified in asking the Commission to explain before the Court the grounds for its choice."

17–11   Although in its terms the second sub-paragraph of article 69(3) states that the Court may order a *successful* party to pay costs which it considers that party to have unreasonably or vexatiously caused the other party to have incurred, it is of particular importance in conjunction with article 70 of the Rules relating to staff cases (see para. 17–19 below). In principle, under article 70, an unsuccessful applicant in a staff case will not have to pay the successful institution's costs, but a finding that the action has been brought unreasonably or vexatiously will lead to the *un*successful official being required to meet the institution's costs. To give a few recent examples, in Case 116/78 Rev. *Bellintani* v. *Commission* [1980] E.C.R. 23, 28–29 it was held that the application for revision (see para. 8–32 above) was "obviously unfounded and even reckless" so that the applicants should be ordered to bear the whole of the costs; in Joined Cases 6 and 97/79 *Grassi* v. *Council* [1980] E.C.R. 2141, 2161–2162, where the applicant sought the partial annulment of a periodic report on him, the Second Chamber took the view that "as a result of his complaints and by means of the internal revision procedure within the Council administration he could have had the assessments on him raised and reasons given therefor in a way which ought to have satisfied him" and concluded that "the bringing of the persistence in a legal action must be regarded as vexatious," and the same formula was repeated in Joined Cases 122 and 123/79 *Schiavo* v. *Council* [1981] E.C.R. 473, 492 in relation to similar facts, although there both actions were held in any event to be inadmissible; and in Case 731/79 *B.* v. *Parliament* [1981] E.C.R. 107, 118, which concerned the procedures for the determination whether an official was suffering from an occupational disease and whether he should be retired on grounds of permanent invalidity, it was found that "having regard to the facts of the case," which apparently included the applicant's failure to co-operate, the Parliament had been forced to incur the costs of the action unreasonably, so that they should be borne by the applicant. Earlier random examples can be found in Case 57/70 *Van Eick* v. *Commission* [1971] E.C.R. 613, 619, where a combination of the applicant's conduct during the disciplinary proceedings which led to the decision at issue and the fact that the application was clearly inadmissible led to the action being categorised as an abuse of the process of the Court, and in Case 47/70 *Kschwendt* v. *Commission* [1971] E.C.R. 251, 258 where the simple fact that the action was clearly inadmissible was held to be enough to render the applicant official liable to bear all the costs.

17–12   There are instances of non-staff cases where the conduct of the unsuccessful party has been categorised as unreasonable or vexatious, although this would appear to be of little practical consequence. In Case 243/78 *Simmenthal* v. *Commission* [1980] E.C.R. 593, 607, where it was found that the applicant had no interest in continuing the proceedings after the Court had given judgment in Case 92/78 between the same parties on March 6, 1979 ([1979] E.C.R. 777) or at the latest after the Commission had issued a decision giving effect to the requirements of that judgment on April 19, 1979, it was stated that to continue the action was "an abuse of process." However, this finding could in no way add to the burden of costs normally borne by an unsuccessful litigant.

The most frequently encountered situation in which a successful party has been ordered to pay the costs is where it is found that the litigation has been unnecessarily caused by the unreasonable conduct of the defendant institution. In Joined Cases 15 and 29/59 *Knutange* v. *H.A.* [1960] E.C.R. 1, 10 the successful defendant was ordered to pay the costs in Case 15/59, since that action was prompted by receipt of a letter from a High Authority official which implied that the decision at issue had already been taken, when that was not in fact the case, so that the applicant had to lodge two applications when one alone should have been sufficient. Similarly in Joined Cases 16, 17 and 18/59 *Geitling and others* v. *H.A.* [1960] E.C.R. 17, 26, the Court held that although most of the claims were inadmissible, some of them were caused by the way in which the recitals to a High Authority decision were drafted, so that the High Authority should be ordered to pay some of the costs. More particularly, there are a number of staff cases where the defendant institution has been found to have misled the applicant. Hence, in Case 137/79 *Kohll* v. *Commission* [1980] E.C.R. 2601, 2614, the Commission was ordered to pay the unsuccessful applicant's costs on the grounds that it was incorrect information regarding the interpretation of the provision of the Staff Regulations concerning expatriation allowances given to the applicant by a senior Commission official which had given rise to the application. Similarly, the First Chamber ordered the Commission to pay the cost in Joined Cases 783 and 786/79 *Venus and Obert* v. *Commission* [1981] E.C.R. 2445 where the Commission had given the applicants, when it offered them employment, incorrect information with regard to the exchange rates at which they could transfer some of their salary to their home State, information which led the applicants to bring the actions. The same applies where the institution has raised false hopes, as in Case 218/80 *Kruse* v. *Commission* [1981] E.C.R. 2417 where the Second Chamber found that the Commission had assigned the applicant over a long period to duties in a category other than her own and had thus aroused in the applicant "expectations which are understandable but unjustified" leading her to bring an unsuccessful action relating to the duties to which she should be allocated. These cases can effectively be grouped as showing a failure to observe good administrative practice, and the principle has been applied to make the institution pay the cost where there has been undue delay in indicating the applicant's adminstrative position, as in Case 61/74 *Santopietro* v. *Commission* [1975] E.C.R. 483, 490, or where there has been a failure to observe proper processes of consultation, as in Case 125/80 *Arning* v. *Commission* [1981] E.C.R. 2539.

17–13   More generally, it has consistently been held to be vexatious or unreasonable conduct for a party to continue proceedings when it has no further interest in so doing. In Joined Cases 5, 7 and 8/60 *Meroni* v. *H.A.* [1961] E.C.R. 107, 111–112, the decisions of which the applicants sought the annulment were revoked during the course of the proceedings, and it was held that although the applicants were not *bound* to discontinue their application, the costs incurred after the notification of the revocation of the decisions must be considered to have been unreasonably incurred and must be borne by the applicants. A similar view was taken in Case 15/67 *Bauer* v. *Commission* [1967] E.C.R. 397, 402–403, where the report of which the applicant sought the production was annexed to the defendant's statement of defence, and the subsequent continuation of the proceedingss was therefore held to be unnecessary, with the result that the applicant was treated as having unreasonably caused the defendant to incur costs from the time be lodged a reply.

Even lack of due diligence on the part of the successful party may be regarded as causing costs to be incurred unreasonably. In Case 18/62 *Barge* v. *H.A.* [1963] E.C.R. 259, 282–283, it was found that the applicant owed her success to the fact that the Court had ordered her to produce certain electricity invoices. The Court held that she could have produced that information herself before the decisions at issue were taken, or at any rate before commencing proceedings, so that the litigation could have been avoided; the application was therefore ordered to pay the costs. It appears that it may even be unreasonable to rely on the wrong argument: in Case 88/76 *Société pour l'Exportation des Sucres* v. *Commission* [1977] E.C.R. 709, 726–727, an action for the annulment of a Commission Regulation was held to be inadmissible "in view of the lack of legal interest of the applicant." This lack of legal interest arose from the fact that the Regulation, which purported to enter into force on July 1, 1976 prohibiting the cancellation of certain licences, had in fact only been published on July 2, 1976 because of a strike, and therefore could only enter into force on July 2, 1976, whereas the applicant had sought to cancel its licences on July 1, 1976. However, although the Commission was successful, in the sense that the action was held to be inadmissible, it had in fact argued throughout on the presumption that the Regulation was indeed applicable to the situation of the applicant, a presumption which the Court held to be "without foundation," with the result that the Commission was ordered to pay the whole of the costs of the case.

17–14   It should also be noted that there are cases where a successful party has been ordered to pay some but not all of the other party's costs. This may be because the unreasonable conduct relates only to part of the action, but even then the attribution of costs may not be exactly proportional, as in Joined Cases 16, 17 and 18/59 *Geitling and others* v. *H.A.* [1960] E.C.R. 17, 26–27, where the High Authority's conduct was regarded as having given rise to two of seven unsuccessful claims but it was ordered to pay one-third of the costs of the action. Less mathematically calculable is the situation where the Court has treated the successful party's general conduct as giving rise to a partial liability to pay costs, particularly where the conduct involved appears to be of the same general nature as that which has in other cases given rise to a liability to pay the whole of the unsuccessful party's costs, as in Case 60/80 *Kindermann* v. *Commission* [1981] E.C.R. 1329, 1342–1343. This case involved a failure to observe good administrative practices in that the applicant learnt of a reallocation of his duties from his colleagues, who had been informed at a meeting from which the applicant was absent, before he was officially informed by the Commission; nevertheless the First Chamber only ordered the Commission to pay half the applicant's costs.

17–15   It is finally possible for the conduct of both sides in a particular dispute to be categorised as unreasonable in some particular. A striking example is Joined Cases 35/62 and 16/63 *Leroy* v. *H.A.* [1963] E.C.R. 197, 208–209, a staff case in which the applicant was unsuccessful. It was there held that the conduct of the Commission had induced the applicant to bring two actions, where one would have been sufficient, whilst the applicant should have withdrawn Case 35/62, in which he had no further interest, once the Commission decision at issue in Case 16/63 had been taken. In the result, the Commission was ordered to pay the applicant's costs in Case 35/62 up to the date of its later decision, but the applicant was required to pay his own costs in that case thereafter, and (in effect) his own costs in Case 16/63.

17–16   Articles 69(4) and (5) of the Rules deal specifically with withdrawal and settlement of actions (see para. 9–07 above). Their effect is that a party which withdraws its claim or action is in principle liable to pay the costs, whereas in a settlement the Court has a general discretion—although in practice settlements will deal expressly with the matter of costs. Where one of a number of applicants withdraws from a case, its liability would appear to be limited to the costs arising from its participation: in Case 13/57 *Eisen und Stahlindustrie* v. *H.A.* [1958] E.C.R. 265, where one of the applicants withdrew at the hearing, its liability to costs was fixed at one-half of that of the other applicants who unsuccessfully continued to judgment. On the other hand, the Court has been willing to give effect to agreements under which the applicant has withdrawn the action or a particular claim on terms that the defendant will meet the costs, as in Joined Cases 16, 17 and 18/59 *Geitling and others* v. *H.A.* [1960] E.C.R. 17 at 26–27. It appears from Joined Cases 109 and 114/75 *National Carbonising Co.* v. *Commission* [1975] E.C.R. 381 that the costs will not have to be borne by an applicant which withdraws its application where the other parties state at the time of withdrawal that they do not seek an order as to costs, irrespective of whether they claimed costs in their original conclusions. The question of what amounts to "conduct of the opposite party" justifying discontinuance was considered in Joined Cases 79 and 82/63 *Reynier* v. *Commission* [1964] E.C.R. 259, 268–269. There it is reported that the applicants discontinued other proceedings in Cases 98 and 99/63 after the Commission gave an undertaking at the hearing in Cases 79 and 82/63 that if the applicants were successful in those actions, it would reclassify them in Grade A3 from January 1, 1962. The Second Chamber took the view that if this declaration had been made earlier, it would have made Cases 98 and 99/63 unnecessary, but, made when it was , it did justify their discontinuance; the Commission was ultimately ordered to pay the costs in those discontinued actions.

17–17   Finally, as has been noted, where a party fails to withdraw its application when it no longer has an interest in continuing the proceedings, it may be regarded as acting unreasonably and be ordered to pay the costs incurred thereafter, even if the other party is liable for the costs incurred up to that point. In Joined Cases 5, 7, and 8/60 *Meroni* v. *H.A.* [1961] E.C.R. 107, the High Authority stated in its rejoinder that it had revoked the decisions which were at issue, and offered to pay the costs up to the date of that revocation. However, the applicants did not discontinue the proceedings, and the Court held that although they were not obliged to withdraw, since they no longer had any interest in continuing the proceedings, they were liable to meet the costs incurred after the notification of the revocation of the original decisions.

The part of the judgment dealing with costs is enforceable in exactly the same way as any other element of a judgment of the Court imposing a pecuniary obligation (see para. 8–20 above). By virtue of Articles 187 and 192 of the EEC Treaty, and 159 and 164 of the Euratom Treaty, such an obligation is enforceable against persons "other than States" under the rules of civil procedure of the State in which enforcement is carried out, and under Articles 44 and 92 of the ECSC Treaty it is enforceable in the same way even against Member States (although the practical utility of this may be doubtful—see para. 8–19 above). The only role of the European Court itself under these provisions is that it may suspend its own decision, as it recognised in Case 4/73— Enforcement *Nold* v. *Ruhrkohle A.G.* [1977] E.C.R. 1, 3. Enforcement at the national level is reflected in article 71 of the Rules which provides that the costs of enforcement are recoverable according to the scale in force in the State where enforcement takes place.

17–18   The effect of the enforcement provisions was summarised in the *Nold* case as being that it is for the national authorities to decide any question which enforcement may raise, but without prejudice to the actual enforceability of the decision itself. In that case, the applicant sought a declaration that its liability to pay costs (quantified at [1975] E.C.R. 985) was extinguished by renunciation or waiver, but it was held that "the Court has no jurisdiction to try the application made by the applicant, since the appropriate national authority is alone competent to decide on the admissibility and where appropriate the merits of such claims."

One other factor may perhaps also be regarded as related to enforcement by national procedures within a Member State. Although article 75(2) of the Rules provides that debtors other than the cashier of the Court "shall make payment in the currency of their country of origin," it was held in Case 6/72 *Continental Can* v. *Commission* [1975] E.C.R. 495, 496 that the fixing of recoverable costs must be effected on the basis of the national currencies of the Member States. In that order this requirement was expressed to reflect the fact that by definition the lawyers involved must be entitled to practise before a court of a Member State; nevertheless, it would appear also to be relevant to enforcement.

C. LIABILITY FOR COSTS: STAFF CASES

Rules of Procedure

Article 70

17–19   Without prejudice to the second subparagraph of Article 69(3) of these rules, in proceedings under Article 95(3) of these rules, institutions shall bear their own costs.

17–20   Article 95(3) of the Rules of Procedure, to which article 70 refers, governs "proceedings commenced by an official or other servant of an institution against the institution," more conveniently known as "staff cases." The rule laid down in article 70 is in effect that an institution involved in such proceedings must bear its own costs, irrespective of the outcome, unless those costs have been, in the terms of the second sub-paragraph of article 69(3) "unreasonably or vexatiously caused" by the official, in which case the official may be ordered to pay them; hence staff cases are a fruitful source of discussion of what amounts to unreasonable or vexatious conduct (see para. 17–11 above). It also is of fundamental importance to define what is meant by an "official" and an "institution" in this context. So far as the former term is concerned, it is clear that it goes beyond those actually employed as officials (defined by the Staff Regulations and Conditions of Employment of other servants as including "temporary and auxiliary staff" but not "local staff") to cover those seeking that status. In Case 23/64 *Vandevyvere* v. *Parliament* [1965] E.C.R. 157, 163–164 and 167–168, a candidate in a recruitment competition challenging the recruitment procedure was held to fall within the concept, a view which has been consistently followed since. Similarly, in Case 65/74 *Porrini* v. *EAEC and Comont* [1975] E.C.R. 319, 327–329, where actions were brought by employees of maintenance and cleaning firms which had concluded contracts for services at the Euratom Research Centre at Ispra seeking recognition as staff employed by the Community, it was held that their claim to be treated as "local staff" was a matter of national law, but their claim to the status of officials or servants other than local staff fell within the European Court's jurisdiction to hear "staff cases"

17–21   In the same way, the concept of an "institution" has been taken beyond those listed in the basic Treaties. In Case 110/75 *Mills* v. *European Investment Bank* [1976] E.C.R. 1613, 1626, article 70 of the Rules was applied "by analogy" to the European Investment Bank, and in Case 184/80 *Van Zaanen* v. *Court of Auditors* [1981] E.C.R. 1951 it was applied "by analogy" to the Court of Auditors. On the other hand, there is recent authority to the effect that an institution is only liable to meet its costs in an action brought against it by an official if that action is brought under the special provisions governing staff cases (see para. 2–36 above), rather than the general Treaty provisions: in Case 64/80 *Guiffida* v. *Council* [1981] E.C.R. 693, 703–704, two officials brought an action under Article 173 of the EEC Treaty for the annulment of a

341

Council Regulation amending the Staff Regulations, an action which failed since they were unable to show that the Regulation was of direct and individual concern to them, and they were ordered by the Third Chamber to pay the costs since the action was not brought under Article 179 of the Treaty and the Staff Regulations to which it refers. Nevertheless there are earlier cases where applicants have unsuccessfully invoked generally-available remedies *in addition* to those specifically available to staff without being ordered to pay the institution's costs. Thus, a claim for damages under Article 215 of the EEC Treaty would appear to have been invoked by an official without adverse consequences as to costs in Case 9/75 *Meyer Burckhardt* v. *Commission* [1975] E.C.R. 1171, 1183–1184 and in Case 48/76 *Reinarz* v.*Commission and Council* [1977] E.C.R. 291, 299.

17–22   With regard to the scope of an institution's "own costs," it has been noted in the context of the hearing of witnesses (see para. 6–22 above) that it was held in Joined Cases 19 and 65/63 *Prakash* v. *Commission* [1965] E.C.R. 533 561–562 and repeated in Case 34/65 *Mosthaf* v. *Commission* [1966] E.C.R. 521, 532, that these costs include the expenses of all witnesses who are officials of that institution giving evidence as such officials, even if their evidence was against the interests of the institutions and in favour of the applicant official. The same view had earlier been expressed in Case 84/63 *De Vos Van Steenwijk* v.*Commission* [1964] E.C.R. 321, 335. However, in Case 43/74 *Guillot* v. *Commission* [1977] E.C.R. 1309, 1338, where the Commission was in principle left to bear its own costs, the unsuccessful applicant was ordered to bear the costs of hearing the witnesses, since these witnesses were only called because the applicant's account of the facts conflicted with that put forward by the Commission, and his account was not ultimately accepted by the Court.

So far as the official is concerned, article 70 of the Rules only exempts him from paying the institution's costs, and it does not limit his liability to his own costs. Hence, if a private intervener, usually another official, intervenes to support the successful institution, the applicant official will be ordered to pay the intervener's costs, as in Case 130/75 *Prais* v. *Council* [1976] E.C.R. 1589, 1600, where the First Chamber held that "the intervener had a legitimate right to intervene to protect his appointment . . . and it is, therefore, not appropriate that, having succeeded in his intervention, he should be made to bear his own costs."

17–23   With regard to the official's own costs, although articles 90 and 91 of the Staff Regulations (see para. 2–36 above) generally require a remedy to be sought within the institution before the matter may be brought before the European Court, the expenses incurred in obtaining legal advice whilst seeking an internal remedy will not be regarded as recoverable costs. Indeed, in Case 54/77 *Herpels* v. *Commission* [1978] E.C.R. 585, 601, a claim for compensation for the expenses incurred in the applicant's consulting a lawyer to clarify his legal position in order to lodge an internal complaint was treated as vexatious, expressly to discourage such claims. The First Chamber stated that "although it is not possible to prohibit the seeking of legal advice by those concerned even at this stage, it is their own decision and the institution concerned cannot be held liable for the consequences."

D. ORDERS ON COSTS

Rules of Procedure

Article 74

17–24   1. If there is a dispute concerning the costs to be recovered, the Chamber to which the case has been assigned shall, on application by the party concerned and after hearing the opposite party and the Advocate-General, make an order, from which no appeal shall lie.

2. The parties may, for the purposes of enforcement apply for an authenticated copy of the order.

17–25   The Rules of Procedure do not provide any specific system of taxation of costs; rather, article 74 enables the Chamber to which the case has been assigned to make an order "if there is a dispute concerning the costs." Nevertheless, since the question of liability for costs will be determined in the main judgment, the quantum of the costs is the most usual source of dispute leading to an application for an order. However, such orders are couched in global terms, and the Chambers of the Court have usually been unwilling to subdivide a global award in relation to the specific sources of expenditure by the successful party. This is clearly shown in Case 17/68 *Reinarz* v. *Commission* [1970] E.C.R. 1, where the First Chamber was asked to interpret an order it had made fixing the costs recoverable by the applicant; the applicant asked the Chamber in particular to declare the amount in that sum which was to represent counsel's fees, but the First Chamber stated that the only object of its order was to determine the amount of the costs and fees which were to be recovered from the unsuccessful party, for which purpose its order was sufficiently precise. The implication is that the precise allocation of the sum recovered from the unsuccessful party is no concern either of that party or of the Court. This view is confirmed by the order in Case 75/69 *Hake* v. *Commission* [1970] E.C.R. 901, 903, where the Second Chamber pointed out that Community law contains no provision as to scale fees on which to base a calculation of the amount up to which lawyers' remuneration must always be regarded as recoverable costs. As has been noted in discussing the concept of recoverable costs, it appears from *Hake,* taken with the later order in Case 6/72 *Continental Can* v. *Commission* [1975] E.C.R. 495, 496, and in Case 4/73 *Nold* v. *Commission* [1975] E.C.R. 985, 987, that the factors the Court will consider in assessing costs are the facts of the case, its object and nature, its difficulty, its importance from the point of view of Community law, and the volume of work involved for the lawyer, together with the expenses other than fees incurred by the successful party. Whilst the expenses other than fees may be fairly precisely calculable in money terms, the same could hardly be said of the assessment of the importance of the case from the point of view of Community law, and it could therefore be said that the Chamber enjoys a fair measure of discretion. It may, however, be noted that in its order of July 1, 1981 in Case 238/78 *Ireks–Arkady* v. *Council and Commission* [1981] E.C.R. 1723, 1726 the Second Chamber awarded a lump sum to which postal, telephone, telex and photocopying charges were to be added.

17–26   A precondition for the making of an order for costs is the existence of a dispute concerning the costs, and this was interpreted in Case 25/65 *Simet* v. *H.A.* [1967] E.C.R. 113 as meaning a dispute "regarding either the amount of the costs to be recovered or the payment." There, the High Authority had been ordered to bear the costs, but on being sent a statement of fees and expenses by counsel for the applicants, it suggested that he should apply to the Court for an order under article 74 of the Rules, which he duly did. In its observations on this application, the High Authority did not challenge the quantum, but stated that it was opposed to the costs being paid to counsel personally. Against this background, the Second Chamber held that since there was "no dispute" regarding the amount of the costs or their payment, the application was inadmissible; the implication is that the High Authority's qualms did not constitute a dispute, and indeed that it is no concern of the unsuccessful party what happens to the costs once it has paid them either to the other party or his duly authorised agent.

Article 74 of the Rules contains no provision as to the time limit within which an application for an order on costs must be made. The matter was at issue in the order in Case 126/76—costs *Dietz* v. *Commission* [1979] E.C.R. 2131, 2133. There, the judgment requiring the applicant to pay costs was dated December 15, 1977, the Commission sent its detailed account on March 14, 1978, and it applied for an order under article 74 on December 22, 1978. The First Chamber considered only the delay between the initial judgment and the sending of the account, and stated that the Commission had acted within a reasonable period "which can by no means be taken to imply that it had waived its rights," not mentioning the delay between the sending of the account and applying for an order. Quite what delay would be regarded as constituting a waiver of rights remains an open question, but to take a random example, in the *Continental Can* case ([1975] E.C.R. 495), the original judgment was dated February 21, 1973, and the application to the Court under article 74 of the Rules was made two years later, on February 11, 1975, without occasioning any comment.

PRELIMINARY RULINGS

Rules of Procedure
Article 104

17–27   3. It shall be for the national court or tribunal to decide as to the costs of the reference.

17–28   The present text of the first sub-paragraph of article 104(3) of the Rules was introduced in the 1979 amendments, and was no doubt intended as a legislative statement of the existing practice in relation to references for preliminary rulings. However, it would have been more accurate if it had stated that it was for the national court or tribunal to decide as to the costs of the reference "as between the parties to the main action," since Member States, the Commission and where appropriate the Council may participate in the proceedings before the European Court without being parties to the main action (see paras. 4–117, 4–118 above). The attitude of the European Court to costs in references for preliminary rulings was in fact settled in the very first reference in Case 13/61 *De Geus* v. *Bosch* [1962] E.C.R. 45, 54, where it was held that "with regard to the parties, the proceedings in this case are a step in the action pending before [the national court]. The decision as to costs is therefore a matter for that Court." With regard to the costs incurred by the Commission and the Member States, the Court quite simply stated that these "are not recoverable."

17–29   With regard to the factors which the national court should take into consideration in assessing the costs as between the parties, in Case 62/72 *Bollmann* v. *HZA Hamburg Waltershof* [1973] E.C.R. 269, a German court specifically asked whether, in making an order for costs following the reference in Case 40/69 arising out of the same proceedings ([1970] E.C.R. 69), it should take account of the Rules of Community law (*i.e.* the provisions of the Rules of Procedure relating to costs in direct actions) or of the rules of national law. The answer given by the European Court was that in view of the essential difference between contentious proceedings (*i.e.* direct actions ending in a definitive judgment of the European Court) and references for preliminary rulings, the rules laid down solely for contentious proceedings could not "without express provision" extend to proceedings on a reference, and it was held that the global reference in article 103(1) of the Rules (see para. 5–19 above) to the application of article 43 *et seq.* of the Rules in preliminary rulings proceedings once written observations have been lodged did not constitute such an express provision. The Court therefore concluded that "the recovery of costs and the recoverability of expenses necessarily incurred by the parties to the main action for the purposes of an application for a preliminary ruling . . . are governed by the provisions of national law applicable to the said proceedings" and that "it devolves upon the competent national courts to consider, in the context of their national law, the extent to which matters incidental to an application for a preliminary ruling should be taken into account."

17–30   The European Court does take it upon itself, however, to pronounce upon the costs incurred by Member States, the Council or the Commission in exercising their right to submit observations on a reference, since they participate only in the proceedings before the Court. Its invariable order is to state that these costs are not recoverable. This means that where, *e.g.* the validity of an act of the Council or Commission is at issue, a party to the main action who wishes to contest the validity of that act does not run any risk of having to meet the costs of the institution which is its author. On the other hand, since the institution is not a party to the proceedings before the national court, there would appear to be no way in which the party challenging the act may recover his own costs from the institution as such, which may give rise to problems where the other party to the national proceedings takes the same view of the validity of the Community act or remains neutral, as in Case 84/78 *Tomadini* v. *Amministrazione delle Finanze dello Stato* [1979] E.C.R. 1801, 1812.

It should, however, be borne in mind that there is no obligation on the parties to take part in the proceedings before the European Court on a reference for a preliminary ruling (see paras. 4–112, 7–05 above); nevertheless, a total failure to do so is extremely rare.

BIBLIOGRAPHY

Books

Bebr: *Development of Judicial Control of the*
                             European Communities
                             (Nijhoff, The Hague, 1981)

Brown and Jacobs: *The Court of Justice of the European*
                             Communities
                             (Sweet & Maxwell, London, 1983)

Court of Justice of the   Reports presented at the Judicial and
European Communities: Academic Conference, September 1976
                             (CJEC, Luxembourg, 1976)

Donner: *The Rôle of the Lawyer in the European*
                             Communities
                             (Edinburgh UP, Edinburgh 1968)

Hartley: *The Foundations of European Community*
                             Law
                             Oxford University Press, Oxford, 1981)

Jacobs and Durand: *References to the European Court*
                             (Butterworths, London, 1975)

Mackenzie Stuart: *The European Communities and the rule of*
                             law
                             (Stevens, London, 1977)

Schermers: *Judicial Protection in the European*
                             Communities
                             (Kluwer, Deventer, 1979)

Toth: *Legal Protection of individuals in the*
                             European Communities
                             (North Holland, Amsterdam, 1978)

Articles, Essays and Reports

Barav: "The exception of illegality in Community
                             Law: a critical analysis"
                             [1974] C.M.L. Rev. 366
                             "Direct and individual concern : an almost
                             insurmountable barrier to the admissibility
                             of individual appeal to the EEC Court"
                             [1974] C.M.L. Rev. 191
                             "Preliminary censorship?"
                             [1980] E.L. Rev. 443

347

Bridge:

"Community Law and English courts and tribunals; general principles and preliminary rulings"
[1975–1976] E.L. Rev.13

Collins:

"Art. 177 of the EEC Treaty and English interlocutory proceedings"
[1974] I.C.L.Q. 840

Dashwood:

"The Advocate General in the Court of Justice of the European Communities"
[1982] *Legal Studies* 202

Dinnage:

"*Locus standi* and art. 173 of the EEC Treaty"
[1979] E.L. Rev. 15

Donner:

"The European Court and its Functions"
[1973] *Law Teacher* 139
"The constitutional powers of the Court of Justice of the European Communities"
[1974] C.M.L. Rev. 127

Durand:

"Restitution or damages—national court or European Court?"
[1975–1976] E.L. Rev. 431

Elster:

"Non-contractual liability under two legal orders"
[1975] C.M.L. Rev. 284

Freeman:

"References to the Court of Justice under art. 177"
[1975] C.L.P. 176

Gray:

"Interim measures of protection in the European Court"
[1979] E.L. Rev. 80

Grementieri and Golden:

"The United Kingdom and the European Court of Justice"
[1973] Am. J. Comp. Law 665

Harding:

"Decisions addressed to Member States and art. 173 of the Treaty of Rome"
[1976] I.C.L.Q. 15
"Choice of court problem in cases of non-contractual liability under EEC law"
[1979] C.M.L. Rev. 389
"The private interest in challenging Community action"
[1980] E.L. Rev. 354

Hartley: "Concurrent liability in EEC law—a critical review of the cases" [1977] E.L. Rev. 249

House of Lords Select Committee on the European Communities: Session 1978–1979 17th Report (Staff Administrative Tribunal) Session 1979–1980 23rd Report (European Court of Justice)

Jacobs: "When to refer to the European Court of Justice" [1974] L.Q.R. 494

Jones: "The non-contractual liability of the EEC and the availability of an alternative remedy in the national courts" [1981] L.I.E.I. 1

Mackenzie Stuart: "The 'non-contractual' liability of the EEC" [1975] 61 *Proceedings of the British Academy* 1

Mertens de Wilmars and Verougstraete: "Proceedings against Member States for failure to fulfil their obligations" [1970] C.M.L. Rev. 385

Mitchell: "Sed quis custodiet ipso custodes?" [1974] C.M.L. Rev. 351 "The rationality of the European Court of Justice" [1975] *Three Banks Review* 62

Mortelmans: "Observations in the cases governed by art. 177. Procedure and practice" [1979] C.M.L. Rev. 591

Oliver: "Limitation of actions before the European Court" [1978] E.C. Rev. 3

Pescatore: "Aspects of the Court of justice of the European Communities of interest from the point of view of international law" [1979] *Zeitschrift für ausländisches öffentliches Recht und Völkerrecht* 239

Rasmussen: "Why is art.173 interpreted against private plaintiffs?" [1980] E.L. Rev. 112

Schermers: "The law as it stands on the appeal for
                              damages"
                              [1975] L.I.E.I. 113
                              "The law as it stands against Treaty
                              violations by States"
                              [1974] L.I.E.I. 111

Toth: "The law as it stands on the appeal for
                              failure to act"
                              [1975] L.I.E.I. 65

Usher: "Influence of national concepts on decisions
                              of the European Court"
                              [1975–1976] E.L. Rev. 359
                              "The interpretation of Community Law by
                              the European Court of Justice"
                              [1977] *Law Teacher* 162
                              "Exercise by the European Court of its
                              jurisdiction to annul competition decisions"
                              [1980] E.L. Rev. 287
                              "Language and the European Court of
                              Justice"
                              [1981] *The International Contract—Law and
                              Finance Review* 277

Warner: "Some Aspects of the European Court of
                              Justice"
                              [1976] J.S.P.T.L. 15

INDEX

351